Developments in German Politics

Developments in German Politics

Edited by
Gordon Smith
William E. Paterson
Peter H. Merkl
Stephen Padgett

Duke University Press, Durham 1992

First published 1992.

This book is a direct replacement for *Developments in West German Politics*, edited by Gordon Smith, William E. Paterson and Peter H. Merkl, published in the United States by Duke University Press, 1989.

Published in the USA by
DUKE UNIVERSITY PRESS
Durham, North Carolina
and in Great Britain by
The Macmillan Press Ltd.
Houndmills, Basingstoke, Hampshire
and London

Printed in Great Britain

Library of Congress Cataloging-in-Publication Data
Developments in German politics/Gordon Smith . . . [*et al.*] editors.
p. cm.
Includes bibliographical references and index.
ISBN 0-8223-1260-3:   ISBN 0-8223-1266-2 (pbk.)
1. Germany—Politics and government—1990- 2. Germany—
History–Unification. 1990. I. Smith, Gordon R.
DD290.29.D48   1992   92–12051
943.087'9–dc20   CIP

Contents

List of Maps, Figures and Tables

Maps

Figures

Tables

Preface

Our purpose in *Developments in German Politics* is to give an informed assessment of current trends in the Federal Republic. In drawing on material that is often available only in journal articles and in German-language publications, the book provides an up-to-date account of important issues. The discussion of individual topics is combined with sufficient background information for readers who may not have a detailed knowledge of German politics.

The approach adopted here differs from that of usual textbooks, which by their nature can quickly become dated. Even the predecessor to this volume, *Developments in West German Politics*, was suddenly overtaken by the momentous events of late 1989 which led to German unification. The task now is to understand the 'new' Germany.

We should like to express our thanks to the contributors – German, American and British – for their ready cooperation in pooling their expertise and in helping to make *Developments* a worthwhile venture.

Gordon Smith
William E. Paterson
Peter H. Merkl
Stephen Padgett

May 1992

Notes on the Contributors

Russel J. Dalton is Professor of Political Science at the University of California, Irvine and Director of the UCI Research Program on Democratization. His scholarly interests include comparative political behaviour, political parties and political change in advanced industrial societies. He is author of *Citizen Politics in Western Democracies* (1988) and *Politics in Germany* (1992); co-author of *German Transformed* (1981); editor of *Electoral Change in Advanced Industrial Democracies* (1984), *Challenging the Political Order: New Social and Political Movements in Western Democracies* (1990), and *Germany Votes* (1992). He is now completing a book-length study of the environmental movement in Western Europe.

Josef Esser is Professor of Political Science at the University of Frankfurt. Among his publications are: *Gewerkschaften in der Krise* (1982), *Krisenregulierung*, with W. Fach and W. Väth (1983), *Die politische Ökonomie der Liebe*, with A. Drescher and W. Fach (1986), *Technikentwicklung als sozialer Prozess*, with G. Fleischmann (1989).

Christopher Flockton is Senior Lecturer in the Department of Linguistic and International Studies at the University of Surrey. An economist, he has published widely on the German and French economies, including most recently 'The German Economy and the Single European Market', *Politics and Society in Germany, Austria and Switzerland* (vol.2/no.3,1990) and 'The Federal German Economy', in D. Dyker (ed.), *The European Economy*, vol. 2, (1992).

Adrian Hyde-Price is a Lecturer in Politics and International Relations, University of Southampton, and previously a Research Fellow at the Royal Institute of International Affairs. His most recent publication is *European Security Beyond the Cold War: Five Scenarios for the Year 2010* (1991).

Emil Kirchner is Professor of European Studies and Director of the Centre for European Studies, Essex University. His recent publications are: *Decision Making in the European Community: The Council Presidency and European Integration* (1992); 'The Federal Republic of Germany and the European Community', in E. Kolinsky (ed.), *The Federal Republic – Forty Years On* (1991); and, edited with J. Sperling, *The Federal Republic and NATO: 40 Years After* (1991).

Eva Kolinsky is Professor of Modern German Studies at Keele University. She is the author of *Engagierter Expressionismus* (1970), *Parties, Opposition and Society in West Germany* (1984) and *Women in West Germany – Life, Work and Politics* (1989) and editor of *Opposition in Western Europe* (1987), *The Greens in West Germany* (1989), *The Federal Republic of Germany – End of an Era* (1991), *Recasting Germany* (forthcoming), co-editor of *Political Culture in France and Germany*, (1991), general editor of a book series on German studies and co-editor of the journal *German Politics*.

Hans-Werner Lohneis is a Principal Lecturer in German Studies at the Polytechnic of West London. He wrote on the Federal Republic of Germany in *Political Scandals and Cause Célèbres since 1965* (1990) and *Revolutionary and Dissident Movements of the World* (1991).

Steen Mangen teaches European social policy at the London School of Economics and Political Science. He is currently completing two research projects: 'Inner City Europe: Changing Social Uses and Policy Responses' and 'The Welfare State in Post-Franco Spain'. Recent publications include contributions to H. Glennerster and J. Midgley (eds), *The Radical Right and the Welfare State* (1991), E. Kolinsky (ed.), *The Federal Republic of Germany: The End of an Era* (1991) and T. Wilson and D. Wilson (eds), *The State and Social Welfare* (1992).

Barbara Marshall is a Visiting Teacher Fellow at the Refugee Studies Programme, Queen Elizabeth House, University of Oxford. She has published widely on German history and politics, most recently a local study of Hanover (1945–47), which was published as *The Origins of West German Politics* (1989), and a biography of Willy Brandt (1990).

Peter H. Merkl is Professor of Political Science at the University of

California, Santa Barbara. His extensive publications on German and West European politics include *Political Violence and Terror: Motifs and Motivations* (1986), *When Parties Fail . . . Emerging Alternative Organisations* (1988), with K. Lawson, and *The Federal Republic of Germany at Forty* (editor, 1989). His most recent book is *German Reunification in the European Context* (1992).

Stephen Padgett is Jean Monnet Lecturer in European Politics in the Department of Government, University of Essex. He is co-author of *Political Parties and Elections in West Germany* (1986) and *A History of Social Democracy in Postwar Europe* (1991). He has also written widely on the German social democratic party, and on political economy and policy-making in the Federal Republic. He is co-editor of the journal *German Politics*.

William E. Paterson is Salvesen Professor of European Institutions and Director of the Europa Institute, University of Edinburgh. His most recent co-authored books are *Government and the Chemical Industry in Britain and Germany* (1988), *Governing Germany* (1991) and *A History of Social Democracy in Postwar Europe* (1991). Besides numerous books and articles on German politics, the European Community and comparative European politics, he is co-editor of the journal *German Politics*.

Peter Pulzer is Gladstone Professor of Government and Public Administration and Fellow of All Souls College, Oxford. He is author of *The Rise of Political Anti-Semitism in Germany and Austria*, *Political Representation and Elections in Britain*, and *Jews and the German State: The Political History of a Minority, 1848–1933*. In 1988 he was Eric Voegelin Visiting Professor at the University of Munich.

Eckhard Rehbinder is Professor for Business, Environmental and Comparative Law at the University of Frankfurt. His recent publications include *Das Vorsorgeprinzip im internationalen Vergleich* (1991), co-author of *Umweltgesetzbuch – Allgemeiner Teil* (1991), and editor of *Bremer Pflanzenschutzkolloquium* (1991).

Gordon Smith is Professor of Government, London School of Economics. He is co-editor of two journals, *West European Politics* and *German Politics*. He has written extensively on comparative European themes, especially *Politics in Western Europe* (1989). Among his publications on German politics are *Democracy in*

Western Germany (1986) and, as co-editor, *Developments in West German Politics* (1989).

Roland Sturm is Professor of Political Science at the University of Tübingen. Most of his published work has been concerned with comparative politics, policy studies and British and German *Demokratien* (1989), *Großbritannien – Wirtschaft, Gesellschaft, Politik* (1991), and *Die Industriepolitik der Bundesländer und die europäische Integration* (1991).

Glossary of Party Abbreviations and Political Terms

Party Abbreviations

AL	Alternative Liste (Alternative List)
Bündnis '90	Alliance '90 (B '90)
CDU	Christlich Demokratische Union (Christian Democratic Union)
CSU	Christlich-Soziale Union (Christian-Social Union)
DA	Demokratischer Aufbruch ('Democratic Awakening')
Die Grünen	The Green Party
DKP	Deutsche Kommunistische Partei (German Communist Party)
DSU	German Social Union
DVU	German People's Union
FDP	Freie Demokratische Partei (Free Democratic Party)
KPD	Kommunistische Partei Deutschlands (Communist Party of Germany)
NSDAP	Nationalsozialistische Deutsche Arbeiterpartei (National Socialist Workers' Party)
PDS	Party for Democratic Socialism (former SED)
SED	Sozialistische Einheitspartei Deutschlands (Socialist Unity Party of Germany)
SPD	Sozialdemokratische Partei Deutschlands (Social Democratic Party of Germany)

Other Abbreviations

APO	Ausserparlamentarische Opposition (Extra-parliamentary opposition)

BBU	Bund für Bürgerinitiativen und Umweltschutz (Federal Association of Citizens' Initiatives and Environmental Protection)
BDA	Bundesvereinigung der Deutschen Arbeitsgeberverbände (Federation of German Employers' Associations)
DGB	Deutscher Gewerkschaftsbund (Federation of German trade unions)
FDJ	Free German Youth
FRG	Federal Republic of Germany
GDR	German Democratic Republic
GEMU	German Economic and Monetary Union
MdB	Mitglied des Bundestages (Member of Parliament)

Political Terms

Abgrenzung	Demarcation
Aussiedler	Ethnic Germans
Bund	Federation
Bundesbank	Federal Bank
Bundesland	Federal constituent state
Bundesrat	Upper house of federal Parliament
Bundestag	Lower house of federal Parliament
Bundeswehr	Federal armed forces
Deutschlandpolitik	Inner-German policy
Land (pl. Länder	Federal constituent state
Landtag (pl. Landtage)	Land parliament
Mitteleuropa	Central Europe
Ostpolitik	Policy towards the East
Rechtsstaat	State based on the rule of law
Sicherheitspolitik	Security policy
Sozialstaat	'Socially responsible' State
Stasi	State Security Police
Treuhandanstalt	Public Trustee Office
Volkskammer	People's Assembly (GDR)
Volkspartei	People's Party
Die Wende/Wendepolitik	Fundamental change in direction of policy
Westpolitik	Policy towards the West
Wirtschaftswunder	Economic miracle

MAP 1   *Map of the Federal Republic and the Länder*

Introduction

After 40 years of division, the unification of the two German states was rapid and complete: in just 329 days, from the breaching of the Berlin Wall on 9 November 1989 to the formal act of unity on 3 October 1990, the territory of the German Democratic Republic was incorporated into the constitutional, social and economic order of the Federal Republic. Even before formal unification was achieved, however, the problems involved in securing the integration of the two societies were becoming apparent. The years following have served to clarify the scale and nature of the challenge: economic devastation in the East defied quick and easy solutions, the receptiveness of the East German people to the values of liberal democracy was uncertain, and the fulfilment of national aspirations opened up several questions about the identity of the 'new' nation. These are just some of the central issues examined in this volume which provides a systematic account of the process of unification and its internal and external implications.

The starting-point (Chapter 1) is an account of how German unification came to be realised, from the first rumblings of discontent in the latter half of 1989 until the proclamation of German unity in October 1990. The period 1989/90 requires careful study because – although the impulse towards unification never became deflected and indeed appeared to be unstoppable – the events followed one another with confusing speed. Two parallel processes were involved. First, there was the international dimension: the reactions of other states to the prospect of a unified Germany, how their reservations were overcome, and the formulas adopted in order to accommodate a new Germany within existing treaty relationships and organisations. Second, there were the direct negotiations between the two German states accompanied all along by the insistent pressures from within the GDR to hasten unity. In order not to overburden the discussion in this chapter, details of the various treaties are contained in the Appendix at the end of the book.

In Part One on 'The Political and Governing System', Gordon Smith first reviews the main structural features of the Federal Republic (Chapter 2). In fact, they have been little affected by unification – not at least in a formal sense, even though they may be altered in how, and how effectively, they operate as the consequences of unification become more clearly apparent. This initial examination should prove helpful to readers approaching the study of German politics for the first time. In addition, the discussion of political leadership and of Chancellor Kohl – in office since 1982 – serves as an introduction to the political scene in the Federal Republic.

Russell Dalton in Chapter 3 is concerned with two aspects of electoral behaviour. The first is an examination of the nature and causes of basic changes that became apparent in the 1980s which have led to a weakening of party loyalties and increasing electoral volatility. Dalton takes two explanatory models – realignment and dealignment – both with fundamental implications for the future of the party system, and, although the evidence is not decisive either way, it seems that issue-voting is increasing, whilst the impact of the 'new politics' in bringing about a realignment is as yet unproven. The second aspect concerns the arrival of the new Eastern electorate. The first federal election may not be a good guide to future behaviour, and the indications are that a convergence is to be expected, but even though the East German electorate may remain distinctive in some ways, it is unlikely that it will develop a strong basis of social attachment to the political parties.

Following this analysis of electoral behaviour, Gordon Smith (Chapter 4) traces the development of the party system, first showing its principal features prior to unification – the nature of the *Volkspartei* and the key role of the Free Democrats in coalition formation. A new ingredient was added with the democratic upsurge in the GDR and free formation of political parties. The party system that took shape was strongly influenced by the existing pattern in the Federal Republic, and merging of the two systems was completed with the 1990 all-German election. Subsequent to the election, it became apparent that, although the party system at the federal level had changed very little as a consequence of unification, the situation in the Länder had altered: there is a disjunction between party strengths at the two levels with increasing diversity in the make-up of coalitions. It is also apparent that the outlook and prospects of the individual parties has been considerably affected by unification and by its social and economic effects.

In Chapter 5, Roland Sturm emphasises the absence of major change in the institutional and policy-making apparatus at the 'centre'. In the absence of new institutional arrangements to secure the integration of the new Länder, the role of the chancellor has assumed greater importance. But – after Kohl's display of decisive leadership in the *annus mirabilis* of unification – the chancellor has reverted to the more reactive style of his earlier administration. The economic and social disparities between East and West have led to strains at the centre: the country has to be treated even-handedly even though the circumstances are quite different. Inevitably special policy provisions have had to be made to cushion the harsh effects of unification on the new Länder. But practical constraints have hindered the establishment of a uniform system of public adminis-tration and have thus led to difficulties of policy-implementation. German unification was achieved relatively smoothly, but the integration of the two German peoples is still far from complete.

Roland Sturm, in Chapter 6, then examines how the territorial balance has been affected with the addition of the new Länder. He sets out five factors of relevance for the Länder: the division of interest between the richer Western Länder and the poorer Eastern ones; the siding of the poorer Länder with the federal government in opposition to the richer Länder; the reduced relevance of the federal coalition pattern for party-political cooperation in the Länder; the potential veto power of the four large Länder on consti-tutional change; and the awareness of all Länder that their autonomy may be threatened through the increasing role of the federal govern-ment and because of the shift of decision-making to the EC level. All these considerations can be related to the costs imposed by unification and the allocation of the burden – except for the separate dynamic of EC integration – and, unless the Länder can find a way of restoring their position, German federalism could be decisively weakened.

Part Two of the book deals with the external relationships of the Federal Republic – foreign and security policy and Germany within the European Community. William Paterson (Chapter 7) relates the foreign policy perspective to the underlying German question: since the initial creation of a unified German state in 1871, it has largely been interpreted in terms of the compatibility of the German state with its external environment. Germany was never strong enough to impose a lasting European hegemony, and its efforts to do so united other European states against the threat. The post-1945 settlement – the division of Germany and the tight integration of both German states into their respective alliances – meant that the Federal Repub-lic was more dependent than others on the multilateral frameworks of NATO and the EEC to formulate its external policy. Unification has created a less fettered, more powerful Germany, but German policy-makers find it difficult to meet the increased expectations of other states that Germany should play a greater international role. Paterson argues that, with the ending of the European division, the pressing external challenge for Germany is to deal with the consequences of the collapse of the Soviet Union and with the conflicts and changes in East–Central Europe.

Chapter 8 deals with the related issues of security policy. German unification was inseparably bound up with the end of the Cold War, and its conclusion has led to a reassessment of the fundamental principles of the Federal Republic's security policy. Adrian Hyde-Price analyses the new German security framework in terms of the interplay between the external international environment and domestic politics. It is ironic that, given the bitter controversies of the 1980s, the vigorous debate subsequent to unification has resulted in a consensus on the essentials of security policy. The commitment to NATO remains firm with mainstream opinion favouring a strengthening of its European dimension by means of the Western European Union. The major divisive issue – also a constitutional conflict – concerns the deployment of German forces as a part of any international military action. Thus, despite the collapse of the old strategic certainties, the foundations of Germany's security policy remain stable.

In his discussion of the relationship of the Federal Republic with the European Community (Chapter 9), Emil Kirchner argues that, although Germany has been a stalwart supporter of EC integration, it has at times been ambivalent, notably on the matter of agricultural reforms. German unification has had negative repercussions on the working of the EC in the short term, but it has also accelerated moves and clarified commitment towards further economic and political integration, both in Germany and in other EC countries. As a consequence, whilst a German-led Europe in economic terms is a possibility, there is an equally strong likelihood that in the future there will be – in the political realm – a European-led Germany.

Part Three on 'Economic and Social Policy' deals with three important areas of policy: the economy, social policy and environmental policy – all three radically affected by unification. Ultimately, the touchstone of the success of unification will be whether the new Federal Republic successfully meets the challenge of economic and social integration. The social market economy was introduced into the alien environment of the new Länder, and the imposition of common structures served to expose rather than disguise the gulf between the two parts of Germany.

As can be seen from Chapter 10 by Stephen Padgett, the upheaval in the economy was in sharp contrast to the smooth passage of political unification. Currency union laid bare the weakness of the East German economy and precipitated a collapse far worse than had been anticipated. The drastic decline accentuated the already massive imbalance between East and West, giving rise to the difficult problem of managing a 'dual economy'. Unification gave a boost to the already high-performing economy of the old Federal Republic, but it proved impossible to couple the locomotive of growth in the West to the moribund economy of the new Länder. Furthermore, the costs of unity had a destabilising effect on the economy as a whole, a new situation that undermined the old certainties of econ-omic management. In particular, the discipline of fiscal policy was subject to slippage, bringing the government into conflict with the ultra-cautious Bundesbank. Thus, despite the basic robustness of the economy in the West, both fiscal and monetary policy remained sources of concern, with negative implications for Germany's neigh-bours because of the upwards pressure on interest rates.

Steen Mangen (Chapter 11) discusses the twofold problem of social and welfare provision in united Germany: one aspect is the adoption of the existing of West German social policy arrangements in East Germany, and the other concerns the longer-term question of financing welfare in Germany as a whole. The exposure of the new Länder to the market economy swept away the security culture of the 'niche society' that had become dependent on a state-directed welfare system that provided welfare in a variety of forms (subsidies, occupation-centred provision, health-care facilities). In many ways the structures and principles of welfare ruling in Western Germany – decentralised, selective and limited – were ill-suited to the goal of achieving social integration, since they could not give adequate protection during the early phases of transition when the old struc-tures were dismantled, nor were they designed to cope with chronic poverty on a mass scale. Moreover, the failure of health care and pension reforms in the 1980s meant that the financial basis of welfare provision became precarious and expensive, and the burden of social-transfer payments from West to East has imposed further strains on the financing of welfare. If social instability in the East is to be contained, a long-term restructuring of welfare policy may be neces-sary.

Public opinion in the Federal Republic has for long been highly sensitive to environmental issues, with the result that successive governments have contributed to what is now a strongly developed system of environmental legislation and the establishment of a fed-eral ministry for the environment. Eckard Rehbinder (Chapter 12) shows that during the process of unification environmental questions did not at first figure prominently, but the draft Treaty was sub-sequently extended to include an environmental union – thus includ-ing a range of laws applying in Western Germany. Rehbinder details the nature and scale of environmental damage in the former GDR which qualifies for the description of an environmental disaster area. It is essential to rectify this situation which will prove both costly and problematic, and it involves a sharp policy dilemma. Should the federal government forgo further environmental improvement in the West and instead give absolute priority to the East? An important consideration is the fact that much higher gains in pollution control for the same cost can be made by concentrating resources on the new Länder.

Part Four, 'Current Issues', deals with three contemporary issues of leading significance from the many that could be chosen, and all three have a strong political potential. In Chapter 13, Barbara Marshall first gives an account of the extent of the 'migration problem' and then of the special features of German law and political traditions. The two main categories, asylum seekers and ethnic Germans, have a different status under the Basic Law and thus are treated differently. In recent years the numbers of asylum seekers and ethnic Germans seeking to enter the Federal Republic have risen sharply, with consequent social and economic effects. In the labour market, the consequences have been favourable for the economy, although as a result of unification the opportunities for employment have become less favourable. Pressures on housing have also grown, so that in both respects social tensions have become apparent and the expression of anti-foreigner sentiments especially in East Germany with its high levels of unemployment. The political parties have found it difficult to reach agreement on how the rise in immigration should be checked and increasingly look instead to a European-wide solution, although other countries are not eager to share Germany's burden. Within Germany, right-wing radicalism poses a threat, playing on the fears of a loss of national identity, and make it urgent that there should be a basic reappraisal of inherited policies and concepts.

In 'Women in the New Germany' (Chapter 14) Eva Kolinsky examines the contrasts in the roles and opportunities of women in West and East Germany. In the Federal Republic, women combined roles as workers and homemakers. Although they secured improved qualifications, there was no corresponding breakthrough with regard to their employment opportunities. However, in recent years greater efforts were made to correct the imbalance through such measures as social legislation and women's quotas in political parties. In the GDR, emphasis was put on equality for women, and that was largely realised within the educational system. At the same time there was a very high participation rate of women in the workforce, and yet they were badly under-represented in middle management and top positions. Motherhood had to be combined with full-time working –

hence the generous provision of child-care facilities. After unification, women in Eastern Germany have been especially hit by rising unemployment and loss of state support. They are also more passive and conformist than women in Western Germany. Only in respect of the liberal abortion law do they appear to have a radical advantage, although even here they will have to accept legislation applying to the whole of Germany, and they were more restrictive.

Christopher Flockton (Chapter 15) analyses the consequences of the divided economy for labour market policy. Labour market asymmetry, caused by high levels of productivity in the West and low ones in the East, should 'normally' be reflected by large differences in wage levels. But political and social pressures have led to a wage explosion in the new Länder and rapid convergence towards levels in Western Germany. The imbalance between pay and productivity has weakened the economic viability of East German industry – with disastrous consequences for employment. Structural policy aid and investment, wage subsidisation and job creation measures have been used, but in the long term such methods are incompatible with the principles of the market economy. The economic success of the Federal Republic owes much to the 'social partnership' ethos of the trade unions. Their willingness to participate – formally or informally – in economic management meant that, with 'responsible' unions and efficient labour markets, governments could avoid involvement in wage bargaining and having an active labour market policy. But the German model of 'democratic corporatism' was weakening before unification, and the all-German labour market places it under further strain. In the future governments may have to accept greater responsibility for labour market and wages policy.

The final section of the book, 'Ideology and Identity' (Part Five), opens with an analysis by Peter Pulzer (Chapter 16) of political ideology, especially in relation to the anchoring of liberal democracy in Germany: the meanings that can be attached to 'democracy' and how various movements have sought to exploit the term in the demand for 'democratisation'. The German right, in rejecting the 'excesses' of radical reform, has sought to reinvoke the appeal to traditional national values – and that was reflected in the *Historikerstreit* (historians' debate). But nationalism has not shown to be a potent force in the wake of unification, and Pulzer concludes that an ideological vacuum has resulted. However, there are various possible lines of development, and a cleavage between the two parts of Germany or disappointment with the process of European integration could lead to the return of a self-assertive nationalism.

The rapidly changing circumstances of contemporary Germany make it difficult to pin down the sense of 'national identity'. Peter

Merkl in Chapter 17 approaches the problem by analysing the findings of numerous public opinion polls in order to tap several dimensions of the concept: the reawakening of a national consciousness in
East Germany as the moral credibility of the communist regime
began to collapse; the more muted response in West Germany; the
strength of positive identification with the West German political
system and its institutions; how Germans view their past – and the
changes that have become apparent; the special problems of the
'Third Reich generation'; finally, in contrast, the attitudes of young
people in East and West Germany. By the year 2000, it appears that
most Germans favour a European federation and a Germany that
steers clear of international conflict, but there is still an 'inner wall'
between East and West Germany. What may have vanished is the
attraction of dangerous myths about the past – perhaps Germans
today have learned to live without them.

1

German Unity

WILLIAM E. PATERSON AND GORDON SMITH

The Shock of Unification

The 'peaceful revolution' in East Germany – epitomised by the opening of the Berlin Wall on 9 November 1989 – set in train the process of merging the two German states: on 3 October 1990, less than a year later, the Länder of the German Democratic Republic (GDR) formally acceded to the Federal Republic, as provided by Article 23 of the Basic Law. Compressed into these few months were, first, the supplanting of the communist regime in East Germany and its replacement by a democratically-elected government and, second, the complex task of settling all the constitutional and other arrangements both internationally and internally that were necessary to bring the two states and two societies together (see pp. 30–3 for the chronology of unification).

Looking back at these momentous events, we may find it difficult to recapture the sense of stunned amazement felt by Germans and outsiders alike, not only at the speed with which unification had been effected, but that a united Germany should have come about at all. Ever since the effective break up of the Reich in 1945, and with the creation of two rival German states in 1949, it had seemed increasingly unlikely that the map would ever be changed again.

It is true that the Western allies were committed to the cause of restoring German unity, but they appreciated that it could be achieved only on the basis of the free determination of the German people – and, more to the point, only with the sanction of the Soviet Union. They could see no possibility of the Soviet Union willingly making such a concession, nor were they prepared to risk a dangerous confrontation to enforce one. In effect, the *division* of Germany became the basic postulate on which all other calculations – political and strategic – rested. Yet from late 1989 onwards this assumption was shown to be flawed: the Soviet Union was no longer in a position to dictate the future of Germany. The 'shock' of this realisation meant that they had to start making a fundamental reassessment of their own positions and of the new Germany's likely place in Europe.

The shock for Germans in both states was no less profound. Even though the Federal Republic had all along claimed that the division of the country was unjustifiable and that the Federal Republic was itself only a 'temporary creation' (*ein Provisorium*) pending reunification, the fact was that, with the passage of time, the claim had become steadily less realistic in the view of most West Germans. The Preamble of the Basic Law had stated: 'The entire German people are called upon to achieve in free self-determination the unity and freedom of Germany', and for successive West German governments this 'unification imperative' necessarily constrained them in conducting foreign policy and in dealing with the GDR. Yet for 'the people' the injunction had become no more than an empty formula.

Germans could hardly be blamed for taking this attitude, especially in view of the fact that the GDR had gained international recognition. That was one outcome of the Basic Treaty between the two Germanys concluded in 1972. Although the Federal Republic did not recognise the GDR as a 'foreign state' and still insisted on the ultimate goal of reunification, none the less in normalising the relationships between them, the treaty enabled the GDR to claim full state-legitimacy, and through its policy of *Abgrenzung* (demarcation) it was always able to prevent West Germany from forging ever-closer relationships.

It seemed, too, that the GDR had been successful in winning the support of East Germans, although with hindsight this appears to have been more a passive acquiescence rather than a real loyalty. The regime also managed to give the impression that the GDR was economically viable. No doubt it was the most important industrial producer in the Eastern bloc after the Soviet Union, but like other countries in Eastern Europe the GDR faced growing difficulties in keeping pace with technical innovation and in providing for new investment. In the short term output was maintained, but only at the expense of neglecting the infrastructure and by causing deep environmental damage. The threadbare economy gave the East German people a tolerably secure, if grey, level of subsistence. But they were all too aware of the prosperity of West Germans and knew that the gap was widening year by year. The shortcomings were to an extent concealed from the outside world by systematically massaging the relevant statistics – the full extent of this manipulation becoming apparent only when the Federal Republic, after unification, was faced with the task of rebuilding the East German economy.

The real shock for ordinary East Germans was the sudden discovery of 'people power' – that the repressive regime, for all its vast apparatus of control, '*Stasi*' (state security police) and informers, proved helpless when confronted by mass, popular demonstrations. The communist rulers might just have been able to hold the situation in check if they had been prepared to use extreme force against the demonstrators. But to turn the 'party of the people' against the people was too much for the moderates in the leadership to stomach – the spectacle of the massacre in Tiananmen Square served as a grim warning. Even if they had been prepared to stamp out dissent in this way, another form of 'protest' was fast becoming an equally serious threat: growing numbers of East Germans were fleeing the country, an exodus that threatened to reach unmanageable proportions.

German unification sent shock-waves throughout Germany and Europe. Suddenly, Germans had to get used to the idea of being a single nation again, a concept that seemed to have become anachronistic in the new era of supranationalism. Germany's neighbours, East and West, had to accommodate themselves to this potentially powerful 'new' state. Not only had the German map once more been changed, but the European one had as well.

The Catalysts

Paradoxically the most potent catalysts of German unity were the policies of US Secretary of State, John Foster Dulles, and Chancellor Konrad Adenauer the 'comrades in arms' during the Cold War. Their ideas centred on strengthening NATO and the European Communities as a way of containing the economic and security threat to Europe presented by the Soviet Union. Their policies had been the subject of bitter internal dispute in the founding years of the Federal Republic since the aim of integrating the Federal Republic ever more closely into the Western comity of nations was seen as deepening the post-war division of Europe and making German unification more difficult. They had always claimed that their policies would, in the long run, end the division of Europe since the Soviet Union would be unable to keep up and by attempting to compete in the arms field would eventually self-destruct: 'an Upper Volta with rockets' was simply not sustainable.

These views became unfashionable in the 1970s, since the lesson that had been drawn from the erection of the Berlin Wall in 1961 was that Western attempts to use its economic and security muscle against the Soviet control of Eastern Europe and the GDR were counter-productive and simply led to repression of the indigenous populations; detente leading to a gradual loosening-up was seen as the way ahead. The era of detente was brought to an end by the Soviet decision to invade Afghanistan and the imposition of martial law in Poland. The dominant Western response, identified with Ronald Reagan, Margaret Thatcher and Helmut Kohl, was to abandon the rhetoric of detente and to revert to 'a policy of strength'. There is little doubt that the pressure of competing with the West helped to undermine the economic basis of the Soviet Union, but it would have collapsed anyway. The immediate effect of the increasingly obvious economic weakness of the Soviet Union was to help secure the adoption of Mikhail Gorbachev as leader of the Soviet Union in 1985.

Gorbachev's initial agenda of internal *perestroika* and an external policy of *glasnost* gave priority to beginning to address the tasks of economic reconstruction inside the Soviet Union and reducing the burden of external defence by striving for agreement on reductions in the volume of nuclear missiles. After an icy start in 1985 when Chancellor Kohl compared Gorbachev to Josef Goebbels (the Nazi propaganda chief), relations with the Federal Republic swiftly improved. The underlying weakness of the Soviet position was not widely perceived abroad at that time, and the initiative in relation to Germany appeared to lie with Gorbachev. While he urged a traditional Soviet policy of rejecting German unity, he undermined the domestic West German consensus in support of NATO by presenting a new and much less threatening Soviet face.

This situation of advantage was, however, being steadily undermined by gathering economic weakness, and Gorbachev was unable to preserve the dualism of internal reform alongside the Brezhnev doctrine of domination of Eastern Europe. In a speech to the UN in December 1988 he identified himself with 'freedom of choice'. More specifically, he committed himself to the unilateral withdrawal of 50,000 soldiers from Central and Eastern Europe. This was a clear signal of the Soviet Union's declining capacity to impose its will in that area. The Soviet government also accepted the election of Tadeusz Mazowiecki, the former Solidary activist, as the head of the first democratic government in post-war Poland.

For some time the German question remained as an isolated rock in a sea of change. In October 1988, during Chancellor Kohl's visit to Moscow, Gorbachev had restated the traditional Soviet position on German unity. As the Soviet economy deteriorated the situation changed somewhat, and by the time of Gorbachev's visit to Bonn in June 1989 the final communique stressed the principle of self-determination.

By late Summer 1989, the governments of Central Europe were growing bolder in asserting their freedom of manoeuvre *vis-à-vis* the Soviet Union, with the Hungarian government playing a vanguard role. In the Summer of 1989 the Hungarian government began gradually to dismantle the barbed-wire fence that divided it from Austria. The implications of this step for overcoming German division were not immediately clear, but a trickle of East Germans began to slip across the Hungarian border into Austria from May 1989. As the holiday season drew to a close in August the trickle turned into a flood of over 5,000 East Germans a week with thousands more camping in Hungary awaiting permission to leave. On 10 September, the Hungarian government relaxed its border controls and over 12,000 East Germans left through Austria for the Federal Republic. A similar sequence of events then occurred in Czechoslovakia. This mass exodus was a vivid demonstration of the lack of legitimacy of the GDR. It had often been argued that what East Germans really wanted was the opportunity merely to travel to the West, not to leave the GDR. This wish had partially been conceded in principle by the Honecker regime after his visit to Bonn in 1987, although in practice permission to travel was at the absolute discretion of the authorities. The flight made it clear that rejection of the regime, especially by young people who had been brought up in it, was total.

Gorbachev's belief in the continued viability of the GDR was weakened by the mass exodus through Czechoslovakia and Hungary. He displayed a marked lack of enthusiasm for the Honecker government during his visit to the 40th anniversary celebrations of the GDR's foundation on 7 October 1989. It was during this visit that he uttered his famous aside on history punishing those who came too late. It was said in public and his target was unmistakable. Honecker's problem, however, was that any attempt to catch up with history, to reform in response to the popular mood, would simply have reduced the differences between the two regimes and further robbed the GDR of what legitimacy it still possessed.

If the origins of unity lay with the policies of Mikhail Gorbachev and the slackening grip of Soviet power, it needed the actions by the newly emboldened population of the GDR to bring the regime to an end. The impact of the Summer exodus (the exit option) was reinforced, from late September onwards, beginning in Leipzig, by a series of massive demonstrations (the voice option). These demonstrations, which initially called for internal change and reform, were by November calling for unity, the change symbolised by the move from the slogan 'We are the people' to 'We are one people'.

Steps in the Process – External

The events of September, October and early November had largely proceeded without overt action on the part of the federal German government. They had demonstrated the lack of viability of the East German state, but this was still a long way short of achieving unity, and the international dimension of the post-war German settlement meant, of course, that unity, like the initial division, was not a choice that the Germans could make on their own.

The post-war German settlement created two very individual states, and left the victorious allied powers with continuing, institutionalised influence and legal rights in a central area of German concern. Large numbers of troops continued to be stationed in both German states, and Berlin remained in an anomalous and subordinate position in which the allies continued to possess significant legal rights. The German states that had been created as a result of division were also deeply embedded, in many ways more deeply embedded than their neighbours, in the integrated structures for defence and economic integration that characterised both European systems.

The achievement of German unity was thus not something that could be brought about by the two German states alone, but one which required its acceptance by a number of other states and institutions, of whom by far the most important were the four allied powers and the European Community. The difficulties that the external environment posed have been well expressed by Karl Kaiser:

> First, how could the concerns about the power of a united Germany be assuaged? Second, how could unification be achieved while also assuring Germany's continuing participation in Western structures of integration, notably NATO? Third, how could unification be accomplished without discrimination and legal restrictions on German sovereignty? Finally, how could there be an international settlement resolving all open questions left from World War II, while avoiding a general peace conference with all of Germany's wartime adversaries? (Kaiser, 1991, 186).

The task of framing a response to these concerns and of devising a German strategy was largely left to the federal government. The government of the GDR was so weak in financial and legitimacy terms and initially so ambivalent in its views on unification that its international impact was scarcely measurable. The advent of the freely elected, pro-unity de Maizière government hardly altered the equation: within the government the key decisions and the responsibility for coordination lay both constitutionally and in practice with the Chancellor and the Chancellor's Office.

Reassuring Other States

The traumatic experiences of 1871–1945 rendered it essential that other states be reassured that they would not be threatened by German unity. The strategy of the federal government to address these fears had a number of components. The central thrust involved a re-emphasis of the commitment of the Federal Republic to an integrated Europe. This strategy led Chancellor Kohl to suggest rapid progress towards Economic and Monetary Union and Political Union, and to stress that Political Union was a precondition of Economic and Monetary Union.

Alongside the reinvigorated commitment to the European Community, the federal government suggested a redesign of the security architecture of the new Europe to accommodate a greater role for the CSCE, while maintaining NATO. The increased role for the CSCE in this context would provide a legitimate basis for a continued role in Europe for the Soviet Union after the relinquishment of its Four Power rights, while continued membership of NATO was necessary to reassure the United States.

German policy also envisaged a reduction in the size of future armed forces and the encouragement of a general arms reduction in Europe. Lastly, and importantly, fears about territorial revisionism were to be reassured by a firm recognition of borders. This general policy was very largely adhered to though there were occasional deviations as on the borders issue when Chancellor Kohl, concerned about the electoral appeal of the far-right Republikaner party appeared to call the finality of the borders with Poland into question.

A central procedural goal for the government was to ensure that internal and external negotiations were properly coordinated and synchronised. It was equally important to ensure consistency across all the external negotiating arenas. These goals might have been achieved within a general international settlement of post-World War II questions, but this solution was deeply unattractive to the federal government since it would have opened up the possibility of interminable delays and exposed Germany to incalculable reparation claims. At the Ottawa CSCE 'Open Skies' Conference of February 1990, it was agreed to proceed on the basis of two-plus-four talks, i.e. the two Germanies would negotiate with each other and simultaneously acting together they would negotiate with the Four Powers. This procedure was to prove amazingly effective and was a stark contrast to the position that the two German states had been allotted in the negotiations for the 1971 Berlin Quadrapartite Agreement where they had been excluded from direct participation.

The Positions of the Powers

For the two-plus-four talks to succeed a favourable, or at least an accommodating, attitude on the part of the Four Powers was required. The United States' government was much less concerned about the dangers of a united Germany than the other powers. The United States had gained in confidence as communism visibly collapsed and as an extra-European power with 'can-do', future oriented public values its response was much less conditioned by negative historical memories than that of the European powers:

> For Britain and France, German unity was foremost a question of accommodating a new power. For the United States it represented, above all, the prevalence of American-supported values in Europe and the success of the postwar struggle against Soviet expansionism and its imperial hold over central Europe. Consequently American statesmen could support German unity in terms rarely heard from their counterparts in Europe, including Germans themselves (Kaiser, 1991, 188).

United States' support for unity was immediate and unwavering. It stressed the importance of the new Germany being fully sovereign, including the freedom to choose alliances. In the Washington view, this meant in essence the right for a unified Germany to remain in NATO. While the United States' position remained constant, those of the other Powers evolved during the negotiating process. The French reaction was initially dual track. The first response of Mitterrand was to think in terms of a mild version of an anti-German alliance, and his visit to the GDR and to Kiev in December 1989 reflected this attitude. He very quickly realised that this was an unrealistic policy given American support for German unity and the weakness of the other Powers. Henceforward France stuck very consistently to the alternative track of anchoring Germany by deepening European integration. France remained, however, very sensitive about lack of consultation and on the extension of German power in the East, and French displeasure at the lack of consultation in the wake of the Gorbachev–Kohl meeting in the Caucasus in July 1990 was apparent. French support of further integration was buttressed by an insistence on the definitive settlement of the borders' issue.

The hesitations of the Soviet Union were naturally more profound; even when they have been overcome President Gorbachev had the problem of making them acceptable to key Soviet elites, especially the army. Under the pressure of events Gorbachev had become reconciled to German unity by January 1990. At that time, however, he still clung to the old Soviet formula of neutrality for a unified Germany. By February, the Soviet leadership had realised that NATO membership was probably inevitable, but tried to postpone the day of reckoning by a bewildering series of proposals for German membership in both NATO and the Warsaw Pact (Adomeit, 1991). These ideas carried little conviction since by this time the Warsaw Pact was on the verge of disintegration. The key Soviet interest remained the fate of the Soviet troops stationed in East Germany and the conditions for their withdrawal.

The British government adopted a much more reserved attitude towards German unity than the other Western powers (Padgett, 1990). Its initial reaction was to pour cold water on the likelihood of immediate unity. This position was superseded by the argument that unification should not even be considered until the democratic revolution in Eastern Europe was complete. Any precipitate endorsement of unification would prove unacceptable to the Soviet Union and undermine President Gorbachev. This standpoint became untenable after the Soviet Union accepted unification in principle in January 1990, and Britain moved into line at the Ottawa meeting in February. The British government remained noticeably less enthusiastic than the Americans or the French, and Mrs Thatcher continued to place emphasis on the need to reassure Germany's neighbours. Her deeply felt and long established commitment to the preservation of sovereignty and her visceral reaction to attempts at supranational integration excluded the prospect of containing a unified Germany by deeper integration. Mrs Thatcher's preference was for a wider and looser Europe where the core issues would remain the prerogative of national governments and German dominance would be diluted by these restrictions on the scope of Community policies and the effects of further Community enlargement. Neither of these assumptions looked tenable. The attempt to implement the first left Britain dangerously isolated during the Italian Presidency of Autumn 1990, and the early admittance of East European states would have derailed the Single Market Programme which the Thatcher Government supported and would have placed intolerable pressures on the Community budget. In any case, the fragile economies of these East European countries left them looking for economic support from Germany rather than on containing her.

The Security Equation

The North Atlantic Alliance as a framework for the American nuclear guarantee was a defining element of the Federal Republic (Paterson, 1989). For most of the history of the Federal Republic its citizens were deeply conscious of a Soviet threat and they perceived a core function of the West German state through its adherence to NATO as deterring the Soviet Union. The way in which the Federal Republic joined NATO through the Western European Treaty gave its membership a more encompassing character than in other states: all German forces were assigned to NATO; there was no independent German planning function, nor was the Federal Republic allowed to possess nuclear weapons. This structure was still entirely intact in 1989, though the public support for NATO had come under increasing strain in the late 1980s (Paterson, 1989).

The security issue was an extremely intractable element of the unity negotiations since the Federal government had to secure the agreement of all four Powers. The United States, Britain and the federal government were strongly committed to a continued American presence in Europe which entailed support for NATO. They were also convinced that it was in everybody's interest for a unified Germany to be wholly in NATO for there to be no ambiguities about the German position.

The Soviet Union was initially totally opposed to the continued membership of a united Germany in NATO. The Chancellor's Office and the United States' administration were both convinced that Soviet economic weakness was so great that they would have to concede, and the negotiations were fundamentally concerned with presenting German membership of NATO in a way that Gorbachev could sell it to his domestic public and the army leaders. The basic formula which was finally agreed at the Kohl–Gorbachev meeting in the Caucasus in July 1990 involved a planned reduction of German forces, no non-German NATO presence in the five new Länder until Soviet withdrawal had been completed, and a phased Soviet withdrawal to be completed in 1994 along with massive German financial inducements.

Making the security solution acceptable to the Soviet Union involved two further elements. As the unity negotiations progressed, the United States and Britain continually emphasised that the Soviet Union had an interest in securing a united Germany safely contained in NATO. The German Foreign Minister Hans-Dietrich Genscher also devoted a great deal of work to developing and extending the CSCE, a framework which could plausibly be presented as the security policy analogue of Mikhail Gorbachev's 'common European home'.

The Borders' Issue and Berlin

Until the onset of the German unity negotiations the dominant view inside and outside Germany was that the question of Germany's borders had been resolved by the Ostpolitik of the 1970s which had in effect recognised the permanence of Germany's Eastern borders. This view was always subject to the rather remote caveat that 'only a final peace settlement' as stipulated by the Potsdam Convention 'could bring about the definitive recognition of borders' (Kaiser, 1991, 200). The only border issue about which there was any real controversy was that with Poland; it was generally assumed that the border had been accepted on the basis of the Oder–Neisse line.

Unfortunately the onset of the unity process had been preceded by the electoral rise of the Republican Party. Chancellor Kohl and his advisers feared that the Republicans would play an important role in the election scheduled for December 1990. It is important to remember that the CDU/CSU had been losing support until the start of the unification process. Chancellor Kohl was therefore hesitant about calming Polish fears over the permanence of the German–Polish border settlement and failed to endorse Foreign Minister Genscher's UN Statement of September 1989 that the Polish people, 'shall know that its desire to live in secure borders will not be called into question by we Germans now or in the future through territorial revisionism'. The Chancellor's position was a weak one since it was opposed by all the other Powers, and it became increasingly clear that it had to be dropped if the unity negotiations were not to be imperilled. The final settlement of the two-plus-four talks called on Germany and Poland to confirm their borders by treaty and to drop Article 23 which was removed from the Basic Law in the Unity Treaty, and a Treaty was signed with Poland on 14 November 1990.

Had any of the Four Powers maintained a serious intention of delaying the unification process after early 1990, then the Berlin question, where the allies possessed very considerable rights, would have been the sticking point, since in giving up those responsibilities outside the context of a final settlement Conference on World War II issues they were giving up significant rights. It was vital for the federal government that the allies abrogate all rights in Berlin, or the situation would have arisen that Germany had acquired unity without full sovereignty. In fact all the allies, including the Soviet Union, adopted a constructive view throughout the negotiations and the Four Powers agreed upon a formal declaration, issued jointly in

New York on 1 October 1990, on the suspension of their rights and responsibilities in Berlin. The date of entry into force of the Unification Treaty and the full restoration of Germany's sovereignty thus coincided on 3 October 1990 (Wilms, 1991), although it was not until March 1991 that the settlement was ratified by all four powers.

The European Community

For successive governments of the FRG commitment to the European Community has been a touchstone of policy. This policy coexisted with and had to take account of the federal government's unity aspirations. A singular feature of the post-war political division of Germany was the persistence of relatively close economic relations. The first interzonal trade agreement, providing for free trade between the two parts of Germany, was signed in Frankfurt-am-Main immediately after the creation of the two German states in October 1949. It represented on the West German side a desire to keep the German question open and to soften the edges of the choice that had been imposed. It was also an important interest for the FRG to try to reduce the isolated status of West Berlin (Bulmer and Paterson, 1987).

In the negotiations to establish the European Community the other partners had agreed to a Protocol on Interzonal Trade being added to the Treaty of Rome. In the case of France, this was seen as a *quid pro quo* for the arrangements to accommodate France's ex-colonies. However, all partners recognised that such a protocol was necessary for West German participation. It was the price that had to be paid to ensure the FRG's integration in the West. This becomes clear if we look at Article 1 of the Protocol. Its territorial application was imprecise and implicitly underwrote the position being taken by the federal government at that time of not recognising the Oder–Neisse line; it referred to German territories outside the area of application of the Basic Law.

Once German unity became a realistic possibility in December 1989 the question immediately arose as to the compatibility of German unity and the European Community. No one publicly suggested that Germany should choose, but there was much uncertainty and confusion as to how it should be accomplished and what the long-term effect would be on the Community. Would it, for instance, prove to be so time-consuming and expensive as to derail the Single Market Programme? Should it be accompanied, as Mrs Thatcher suggested, by an extension of the Community eastwards?

The European Community's response to the developing German situation was defined in the first instance by the French and Irish

Presidencies and by the Commission. The French government responded with speed and agility and proceeded to implement its deepening strategy at the Strasbourg Summit of 8–9 December 1989 which secured agreement to the convening of Intergovernmental Conferences (IGCs) on economic and monetary union and on political union at the end of 1990. The Council had been preceded by much talk of a Franco–German rift and an alleged cooling of German enthusiasm for political union, but to the visible disappointment of Mrs Thatcher there was no evidence of either at the Summit. Chancellor Kohl remained enthusiastic about political union and in any case perceived the convening of the IGCs as part of the price of French support. Germany was not yet manifestly centre stage at the Council, and the Commission was instructed to negotiate only a trade and cooperation agreement with the GDR, but the key theme of linking German unity to European integration had been established.

Events moved very quickly in January–February 1990. The inevitability of German unification now became widely accepted, though with differing degrees of enthusiasm among the Member States, a situation which left the initiative with the Commission. German unity was welcomed by EC Commission President Jacques Delors at an early point. Delors, like Mitterrand, quickly became convinced of its inevitability, and his policy reflected three overriding aims:

1. to preserve and strengthen Germany's European vocation;
2. to avoid the derailment of the Single Market Programme;
3. to ensure that the Commission had some influence over events in Germany.

Delors set the tone for the Commission's response, but it should be noted that Vice-President Leon Brittan adopted a more negative tone and continually expressed concern at the dangers to competition policy inherent in German unity.

Whilst the Commission quickly resolved that the European Community would simply expand to encompass the territory of the whole of the new state after unification, the European Parliament initially argued in favour of an accession procedure which would have required assent by national parliaments and would have accorded a major role to the European Parliament (Article 237, EC Treaty). This was rejected by the Commission and the Council, and their favoured procedure was rendered much easier by the decision of the federal government to press for incorporation of the GDR through Article 23 rather than Article 146 of the Basic Law (see p. 25–7 below). Use of Article 146 would have dragged out unification negotiations and strengthened the case of those who argued that what was being contemplated was the accession of a new member.

The Commission issued its formal proposal on 18 April 1990. It envisaged a three-stage process:

1. after German economic and monetary union (GEMU) was achieved, East German law should gradually be adapted to West German and EC law;
2. after completion of German unity EC legislation should apply;
3. the total integration of the new unified German state into the EC.

The Commission proposal stressed German responsibility for, but Community interest in German unity. Accordingly unity should be carried out within a Community framework, and this should be expressed in any GEMU treaty. The Commission wanted to be involved in the negotiations to keep GEMU and EMU moving in step. Reflecting the fears of Leon Brittan, the Commission wished to be informed and consulted on the granting of aid to the GDR. The Commission also argued that incorporation of the GDR would not require a treaty revision with all the ratification complications that would have entailed. The Commission paper also took a notably optimistic view of the economic prospects of the GDR, which it argued would lead to increased resources for the Community. The Commission proposal was adopted at the Dublin Summit (28 April 1990); the EC Commission's definitive proposals were originally scheduled to be taken in two readings in September and November but the bringing forward of the unity date to 3 October 1990 led to the Parliament dealing with the first reading on 11 and 13 September. The common position of the Council was reached on 7 November and it was approved by Parliament on 21 November.

The final agreement was very favourable to Germany, and in difficult areas significant concessions were made, e.g. in the food-processing industry exemptions were granted for almost 80 per cent of food legislation. On state aid, the Commission document talked of a 'sensitive and flexible application', with exemptions immediately granted to shipbuilding and steel. Despite calling in a number of cases, the Commission took a lenient view of mergers and takeovers. An understanding view was also taken of difficulties in meeting environmental legislation, and East Germany was given until 1996 to meet air and water quality standards. At the insistence of a number of Member States, the Commission did attempt to tighten up the rules on what was to count as 'new' and 'old' plant; 'new' plant had to meet current EC levels immediately, but there was an obvious temptation to have all plant classified as 'old'.

Steps in the Process – Internal

In the early stages of the upheaval in East Germany, the federal government played no part: the dynamic came from the catalysts in Eastern Europe and from within the GDR – the twin pressures of 'voice' and 'exit' mounted by East Germans. No doubt West Germans were taken aback by the speed at which events unfolded, but it would anyway have been hard for the federal government to intervene early on: the eventual outcome of the popular revolution was unpredictable, it was uncertain how the Soviet Union might react, and any 'meddling' on the part of the Federal Republic could result in harsh retribution accorded to the population – memories of the abortive 1953 uprising were still present. The Federal Republic was also held back by the terms of the Basic Treaty of 1972, a key element of which was the 'inviolability' of the common border between the two states.

Initially, however, the process of change within the GDR needed no outside reinforcement, as was shown by the tottering collapse of the SED's monopoly of power. First, on 18 October, Honecker was ousted from the leadership of the party, to be briefly succeeded by the more flexible Egon Krenz, a choice favoured by the Soviet Union. But the short-lived Krenz experiment lacked credibility with the people, and the concessions that were made simply increased their appetite for wholesale change. The all-important climb-down was the promise to allow freer travel, which – instead of acting as a safety-valve for popular frustrations, as it might have done had it been kept in the past – led from 9 November onwards to the breaking of the dam.

Krenz in turn was replaced a few days later; this time by Hans Modrow, a Communist with a genuine desire to reform and restructure the GDR, a process which necessarily involved cooperation with opposition groups, many of whom were convinced that the choice was not between old-style communism and West German capitalism, but through the adoption of a 'third way', and that meant that the process of reform should be carried through without outside intervention. These groups, such as New Forum and B'90, were initially of critical value in giving leadership to a popular movement which otherwise lacked a clear focus, but their influence quickly waned once the emphasis shifted in favour of unification.

Modrow took two important initiatives. One was directed towards the FRG, the other introduced a form of all-party, governmental forum, the so-called 'Round Table'. The opening of the dialogue with the FRG was signalled by Modrow's initial government statement of 17 November, in which he floated the idea of a 'contractual union' (*Vertragsgemeinschaft*) between the two states.

Helmut Kohl wasted no time in formulating a detailed response: in a speech to the Bundestag (28 November) he presented a 10-point plan, a series of steps charting the course to a unified German state. Point 5 of this declaration specified the aim of setting up 'confederative structures between the two states with the goal of creating a federation, a federal state order in Germany'. Several of the other points in the statement were instrumental to this end – assistance to the GDR, cooperation in several areas of activity, the formation of a common inter-parliamentary group. But such aid and cooperation was also made conditional upon the continuation of the process of reform and – most critically – upon the holding of free elections in the GDR. Other points in Kohl's declaration sought to reassure the outside world: the process of unification would be set firmly in the context of continuing East–West cooperation and in harmony with the European Community.

There are three noteworthy aspects of this 10-point plan. First, it was significant that Kohl acted without first consulting the Western allies; they were caught off balance, and from then onwards it became clear that the FRG intended to be prominent in shaping the course of events. Second, no time-scale was contained in the proposals but, in allowing for the operation of 'confederative structures' in the interim, it has to be assumed that Kohl at that time was thinking in terms of years rather than months for unification to be completed. Third, in being the first person to show how unification could and should be realised, and not as just a distant aspiration, Kohl gained an impetus which set him apart from other politicians in West Germany and which was later to give his party, the CDU, and the FDP a decisive advantage in the first all-German election. More generally, it should be said that from the time Kohl presented his 10-point plan until German unity was achieved, he was to display an amazing sureness of touch and single-minded purpose.

The other important initiative taken by the Modrow government – although, in truth, forced upon it by the pressure of the people – was the incorporation of opposition parties, along with representatives of the churches, into the 'Round Table' consultations (see also Chapter 4). At first it was decided to hold free elections the following May, but the rapidly worsening economic and political situation, together with the continuing flight to the FRG, made it necessary to advance the election to March. Even though at the beginning of

February the Communists took a minority position in government, but with Modrow continuing as prime minister, the shift in power failed to impart any legitimacy to the tainted system.

By then it was clear that only the how and when of unification had to be settled. Modrow's proposal, with the backing of the Soviet Union, that unification should be on the basis of German neutrality, was rejected by the federal government, although it responded positively towards the proposal for a first stage of economic and monetary union. None the less, it was clear that no West German help would be forthcoming until the election had been held, in the expectation that the result would almost certainly lead to the formation of an entirely non-Communist government. The outcome of the March election was a massive vote for the pro-unification parties (see Chapter 4), and it meant that there were no longer any fundamental obstacles to a speedy settlement being reached, all the more so because through the election the East German CDU had become the dominant force, as it was in West Germany.

Lothar de Maizière (CDU) headed a 'grand coalition' of CDU, Liberals and SPD. The principal and almost sole task of the new government was to get the best terms it could for East Germany in being absorbed into a market economy and in embracing the West German legal and constitutional order. Within both the GDR and the FRG there were divided views as to how the constitutional problem should be handled. The Basic Law provided two quite different mechanisms: Article 23 left the door open for 'other parts of Germany' to accede to the FRG and thus simply to accept the existing constitutional order as it stood – the precedent was the accession of the Saarland through the passing of a federal law in 1956. Article 146, however, spelt out a much more radical approach: 'This Basic Law shall cease to be in force on the day on which a constitution adopted by a free decision of the German people comes into force'.

During the first flush of enthusiasm for unification, Article 146 seemed the obvious option, and it cannot be denied that it was included in the Basic Law expressly to provide for the eventuality of German unification one day becoming reality. Especially in the GDR it appeared that Article 146 would give the opportunity to secure a number of social rights in the form of a 'social charter', a view widely favoured in the West German SPD. But it soon became clear that the Kohl government was not prepared to wait for the lengthy process of devising and ratifying a new constitution. It also had little inclination to treat the GDR and the FRG as equal partners. Why, anyway, should the Basic Law which had served the West German people so well, now be subject to change, especially at a time when so many pressing economic and social problems had to be tackled?

The course of this debate made it quite evident that the GDR was to be treated as the supplicant. For the most part that was true in relation to the First State Treaty outlining the terms of Currency, Economic and Social Union which came into force on 1 July 1990 as a prelude to full unification (the terms of the latter were contained in the Second State Treaty concluded late in August). The first treaty was the more urgent, since the East German economy was in a state of near collapse, and confidence could be restored only if the Deutschemark was immediately introduced as the common currency, and the same applied to adopting the welfare and social provisions obtaining in the FRG. The restoration of confidence could not be of much immediate benefit to the collapsing East German economy, but it would at least stem the tide of East Germans (*Übersiedler*) still leaving for the Federal Republic.

The provisions of this treaty, concluded in May and coming into force on 1 July, were complex (see Appendix, pp. 353–4). Significantly, the final version closely followed the terms of the draft version which had been prepared exclusively by the West German side – the new GDR government was given little scope to bargain – showing that there was no question of treating East Germans as equal partners. Moreover, the preamble to the treaty already established that Article 23 was to be the method of effecting unification.

Besides institutionalising the social market economy, making the Deutschemark the sole legal currency, giving the Bundesbank the exclusive powers of the central bank, the treaty regulated the principles of social insurance – pensions, unemployment, and health insurance. It was a complete package, designed to harmonise the two social and economic systems without delay. This 'shock treatment' for the GDR people was made slightly more palatable by the 1:1 ratio adopted for the conversion of wages, pensions and savings (for the exact amounts and specifications, see Appendix, p. 353). The final decision for this very favourable rate of exchange was a political one and taken by Helmut Kohl in the face of the great reluctance of the Bundesbank. For a short while at least, East Germans were able to enjoy a buying spree, before the harsher aspects of economic union began to become apparent.

From then onwards, the chief concern was to settle the form, the details and timing of complete political unification, which anyway had to wait upon the outcome of the two-plus-four negotiations, settling Germany's borders and international position, and concluded in September. What appeared to threaten the smooth passage of the second treaty, the Unification Treaty, were the divisions within the

GDR governing coalition, especially over the timing respectively of an election and the date of unification, and this dispute led to the break-up of the coalition. Finally, however, agreement was reached that the elections would be held *after* unification, and using the West German electoral system. Once this procedure was agreed, the way was clear for ratification of the Unification Treaty by the Volkskammer and by the West German Bundestag and Bundesrat. The treaty itself, contained in over 1000 pages of text (see Appendix, p. 356 for the main provisions) was overwhelmingly based on the draft version worked out by the federal government; it regulated the ways in which the laws and administration of the FRG should be applied to the five newly-reconstituted Länder in the GDR: Saxony, Thuringia, Saxony-Anhalt, Brandenburg and Mecklenburg–West Pomerania. With their accession on 3 October 1990, the GDR ceased to exist. In retrospect, we can see that, from late 1989 onwards, the GDR was destined to become what Stefan Heym called 'nothing but a footnote in world history', but its legacy could prove to be rather more important for the future of Germany.

From early 1990 onwards it became clear that the GDR was doomed and that unification was the inevitable outcome. Yet some questions will perhaps never be finally answered. Admittedly, the idea that there could be a workable alternative – expressed in the call for a 'third way' – was simply unrealistic. The unresolvable questions concern the speed with which unification was effected and the means used to achieve it. With the knowledge now of the social and economic consequences of unification – large-scale unemployment, economic bankruptcy, social dislocation – it is natural to ask whether they could have been avoided or at least ameliorated if a different course had been adopted. Should not Article 146 have been employed rather than Article 23, on the argument that the people of the GDR should have felt themselves to be equal partners? Would it not have been preferable for an all-party government of 'national unity' to have been formed in the Federal Republic to handle all the tricky and often contentious issues relating to unification? One criticism that can be made is that party interests were too much in evidence, especially with the forthcoming federal election looming. An all-party approach might also have avoided the unseemly scramble of the West German parties 'taking over' in East Germany. It can also be questioned whether the terms of monetary union were appropriate: the rate(s) of exchange chosen amounted to a sharp upwards revaluation of the East German currency and at one stroke made whole industries hopelessly uncompetitive. This debate will no doubt continue, and yet, well founded as some criticisms are, it has to be admitted that any other course might well have led to delay, confusion and possibly to a more divided German nation.

East Germany: Overcoming a Double Legacy

What is even more difficult perhaps is tackling what was left by 40 years of communist dictatorship in people's minds and in the cultural life of the country and in human relations. For four decades Germans in the east and in the west of the country led lives based on totally different premises. Bringing them together again, bridging the gulf that separates those minds will be one of the great tasks of the nineties (H. Kohl, Edinburgh, 1991).

The GDR, like other states with totalitarian pretensions, recognised no barrier between the public and private spheres and was held together by the myriad activities of the Staatssicherheitsdienst (Stasi) who in turn relied on countless numbers of part-time informers. These arrangements have left behind a very dangerous legacy for the new state. The scale of Stasi operations meant that it was nearly impossible to have any sort of public function in the GDR without some contact with it. This, combined with the decision to open the Stasi files, has meant that almost every politician who had lived in the GDR is potentially vulnerable. Thus, Manfred Stolpe, SPD minister-president of Brandenburg, came under intense pressure because of alleged links with the Stasi, and a large number of the most prominent, including Lothar de Maizière (CDU) and Ibrahiim Böhme (SPD) have already been forced to resign. The effect of this insecurity is to leave the political leadership in the five new Länder largely in the hands of 'Wessis' (West Germans). Early in 1992 the CDU minister-president of Thuringia, Josef Duckac, was ousted. No suitable replacement could be found locally, with the result that Bernhard Vogel (formerly CDU minister-president in the Rhineland-Palatinate) was asked to take over.

It has also raised major public policy issues in relation to whether or not officials, including judges and professors, should be replaced. In general there has been a much more marked readiness to replace compromised officials than after 1945 since, unlike 1945, alternative uncompromised candidates can be found from West Germany to carry out the essential tasks. Such a policy naturally carries with it the danger of deepening divisions (at least temporarily) between the West and the East.

These divisions persist in myriad ways, of which one of the most fundamental is that the West and the East share a different past and this divergence begins not in 1945 but in 1933. An essential element in the experience of post-war West Germans was coming to terms with and accepting responsibility for the events of 1933–45 as part of the general acceptance of Western liberal values. The Marxist ideology of the GDR played down any notion of responsibility and precluded many questions about the Nazi regime. The uncomfortable result for the former citizens of the GDR is that they are now faced with coming to terms with a view of that period which places more emphasis on individual and collective responsibility. The tendency of many in the East to regard themselves as passive victims of succeeding dictatorships is to some extent called into question by this development. The failure to come to terms with the Nazi period is also reflected in the support given by some younger people to neo-Nazi parties.

It is, however, the behaviour of the former citizens of the GDR between 1949 and 1989 that raises the sharpest and most divergent responses. Many in the West point to the lack of resistance and to the readiness of those who remained in the GDR to cooperate with the regime, including the Stasi. They in turn respond angrily that only those who have lived through a dictatorship are in any position to judge the infinitely nuanced positions that were taken. These disputes have been especially intense between writers and intellectuals who fled or were expelled and those who remained like Christa Wolf and in relation to the trials of border guards accused of shooting people attempting to flee the GDR.

At the moment these controversies are, if anything, gaining in intensity fuelled by the disclosures of the Stasi documents and by West German impatience with those who live in the East. There is little readiness to emphasise the part that the East Germans themselves played in bringing the GDR to an end, a major theme in the immediate aftermath of unification. The differences will persist for some time, but they will lose much of their edge with time and provided that the economy of the five new Länder can be successfully integrated.

Appendix: The Chronology of German Unification

	1989	
May	7	Local elections in GDR. Falsified results lead to widespread protests.
July/Aug./ Sept.		East German refugees enter West German embassies in East Berlin and Eastern Europe.
Sept.	10	Manifesto of 'New Forum' published.
	11	Hungary opens its borders to Austria (allowing East Germans through). Thousands flee to West Germany.
Oct.	7	40th anniversary of the GDR.
	9	Mass demonstrations for democratic reforms in Leipzig.
	18	Erich Honecker resigns. Egon Krenz becomes new general secretary of the SED.
Nov.	4	Huge mass demonstration (1 million) in East Berlin for democratic reforms and free travel.
	7	Government of the GDR under Willi Stoph resigns.
	8	Politbureau, except Krenz, resigns *en bloc*.
	9	Opening of the borders and the Berlin Wall.
	28	Helmut Kohl's 10-point plan for eventual unification. No timetable.
Dec.	1	The Volkskammer abolishes the constitutional provision for the 'leading role' of the SED.
	6	Egon Krenz resigns. Hans Modrow appointed.
	7	'Round Table' (new democratic movements and the old 'bloc' parties and mass organisations) meet for the first time.
	8–9	European Council (Strasbourg): heads of state and government affirm their commitment to

German unity in the 'perspective of European integration'.

19   Kohl visits Dresden. Demonstrators demand German unification.

22   Opening of Brandenburg Gate.

1990

Jan.   9   Modrow promises to abolish the 'Ministry for State Security' and any successor.

15   Demonstrators occupy the 'Stasi' headquarters in Berlin's Norrmannenstrasse.

28   The Modrow government and the 'Round Table' agree to bring the free elections forward to 18 March 1990.

Feb.   1   'Germany united Fatherland', a plan by Modrow for the unification of Germany.

7   Chancellor Kohl presents proposals on German Economic and Monetary Union (GEMU) to Cabinet.

12   The so-called two-plus-four negotiations (between the two German states and the four victorious allies) are agreed upon at Ottawa 'Open Skies' Conference. FRG offers GDR economic and monetary union.

12–13   Modrow visit to Bonn. Kohl refuses loans before election.

Mar.   8   Bundestag Resolution on Polish border.

14   First two-plus-four talks at official level, Bonn.

18   Free elections in the GDR. The 'Alliance for Germany' (CDU, DSU, Democratic Awakening) gain 48.1 per cent of the vote on a fast unity ticket; SPD 21.8 per cent; PDS 16.3 per cent. A grand coalition under de Maizière (CDU) is formed.

Apr.   28   European Council (Dublin) adopts Commission proposal to integrate the GDR territory into the Community without treaty modification, but subject to transitional measures, by staged approach (interim, transitional, final).

May   5   First two-plus-four talks at ministerial level.

	18	State Treaty (*Staatsvertrag*) negotiations completed. Finance Ministers Waigel (FRG) and Romberg (GDR) sign GEMU treaty.
Jun.	**21**	The parliaments of FRG and GDR unanimously endorse Poland's existing western borders (Oder–Neisse line).
Jul.	**1**	German–German monetary union takes effect.
	14–16	Gorbachev–Kohl meeting in Caucasus – agreement reached on German membership of NATO and Soviet troop withdrawal by 1994. Allows two-plus-four negotiations to proceed.
Aug.	**2**	'Election treaty' between East and West Germany but the GDR will join the FRG before the elections.
	19	President von Weizsäcker announces all-German elections for 2 Dec.
	21	EC Commission adopts package of transitional measures and proposed interim measures in case negotiations on transitional arrangements not complete before unification.
	30	Second state treaty. The GDR accedes to the FRG. West German law, with a few exceptions, will become all-German law.
	31	Signature of Treaty of Union (*Einigungsvertrag*) by Interior Ministers Schäuble (FRG) and Krause (GDR).
Sept.	**12**	Treaty on the Final Settlement with Respect to Germany signed in Moscow by two-plus-four Foreign Ministers.
	20	Bundestag and Volkskammer approve Unity Treaty.
	25	Signature in Bonn of Exchanges of Notes on: presence and stationing of foreign forces in Germany; presence of allied forces in Berlin; and agreement on Berlin matters.
Oct.	**1**	Signature of Declaration suspending Four Powers Rights and Responsibilities.
	3	Unification Day. The five new Länder and Berlin join the FRG. The GDR ceases to exist.

8   Bundesrat approves Unity Treaty.

Dec.   **2**   First all-German and all-Berlin elections take place.

PART ONE

The Political and Governing System

2

The Nature of the Unified State

GORDON SMITH

The 'State without a Centre' Revisited

With total defeat in the Second World War, the German state, the Reich, was entirely shattered. First there was the loss of the Eastern territories to Poland and the Soviet Union (see Map 2.1). Second, there was the division of the much smaller Germany into two rival states – the FRG and the GDR. Weak as the Federal Republic was initially, it soon won a reputation for political stability. Integral to its success has been the nature of the constitutional order as established by the Basic Law of 1949. Shorn from East Germany and divorced from Berlin its historic centre, the Federal Republic grew up as a 'state without a centre' (Smith, 1989). Bonn, chosen as the capital of West Germany, was no more than a provincial city, and none of the others – such as Hamburg, Frankfurt or Munich – emerged as a metropolitan nexus on a par with, say, Paris or London. Yet this provincialism was to prove a source of strength: if there was no dominant centre, there was no underprivileged periphery either. In this respect the federal arrangements set out in the Basic Law played a key part in ensuring a balanced development of the Länder. West Germany emerged as a stable political system precisely because decision-making powers were dispersed.

There were anxieties that this prized stability could be put in jeopardy as a consequence of unification. The decision to reinstate Berlin as the capital (von Beyme, 1991b), and later to move the federal government and the Bundestag there as well, was regarded by many in West Germany with misgiving, for would it not lead to

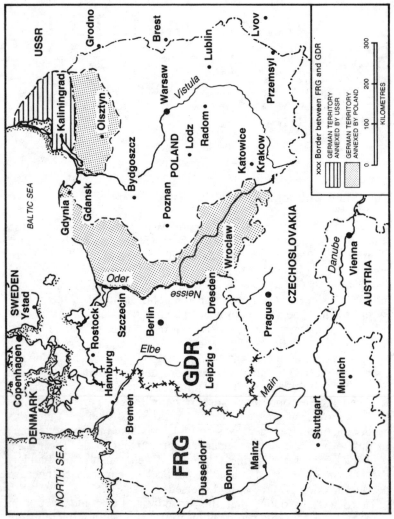

MAP 2   *Germany after 1949*

an undesirable centralisation of political power and reawaken the negative associations of Prussian dominance and the Nazi era? Yet it is doubtful whether this one change could have such a drastic effect. After all, the experience West Germans have had with their political institutions has been so favourable that a mere shift of the seat of government is unlikely to threaten established patterns of decision-making. In addition, constitutional changes consequent upon unification have thus far been minimal – in this sense the new Germany is the old FRG 'writ large' – and it is in the provisions of the Basic Law that we can appreciate how the constitution has contributed to political stability and continuity.

A 'Cooperative' Constitution

Under the terms of the Unification Treaty, a commission to consider changes in the constitution was established. In principle, the recommendations of the commission could be far-reaching, but its proposals have to be adopted by a two-thirds majority. Since the composition of the commission reflects party strength in the Bundesrat and Bundestag (32 representatives from each body) a large measure of inter-party agreement is required. For this reason only those changes that attract broad agreement – such as the protection of the environment and a possible reorganisation of the Länder (for instance, the merging of Berlin and Brandenburg) – are likely to be incorporated into the Basic Law.

None of the fundamental features of the Basic Law is questioned by the major parties, since it represents the original party consensus at the founding of the FRG: the Christian Democratic belief in the social responsibility of the state, as well as the Social Democratic emphasis on social justice, is expressed by the concept of the *Sozialstaat* in the Basic Law. Liberal principles, the protection of individual liberties and civil rights, are enshrined by the normative force of the *Rechtsstaat*, a state bound by the rule of law (Kommers, 1989).

What characterises the Basic Law more than any other feature is the expression given to the doctrine of 'constitutionalism' – that is, limited government, checks and balances, and a dispersion of decision-making authority. The total effect is complex because the power and competences of various institutions meet at several levels, and different sets of actors become involved in policy-making and policy implementation. The result is that policies can be agreed and carried out only if at *some* stage an integrative solution is forthcoming. A consensus need not be present at the outset – party positions may be sharply opposed and the interests of the Länder quite divergent – but it is in the way the structures are designed and operate that agreed solutions are found. The institutional structures provided in the Basic Law amount to a set of consensus-*inducing* mechanisms: it is the process that helps fashion the consensus, rather than the latter being present beforehand.

Nevertheless, constitutional devices by themselves would not have proved efficacious if the political and party system had developed in a different way: a fragmented and polarised party system – reminiscent of the Weimar Republic – might have led to the checks and balances of the Basic Law becoming a recipe for deadlock and immobility. The concentration of political power in the three moderate parties, CDU–CSU, SPD and FDP, was thus essential to the successful operation of the Basic Law. Following unification, their hold remains undisputed, and for this reason it has to be concluded that the Basic Law will continue to function in much the same way as it did for West Germany.

Principles of German Federalism

The leading features of federalism – possibly the most significant of all the balancing mechanisms in the Basic Law – can be summarised as follows under five headings:

Subsidiarity

This principle, as applied to the federal system, requires that, 'State functions should be allocated to the lowest level of government in the first instance. Only if the task proves to be beyond that level's capacity, should it be passed up the hierarchy. In the Basic Law subsidiarity is expressed through the Länder being responsible for legislative powers other than those explicitly assigned to the federation' (Bulmer, 1989, 41). The concept of *Selbstverwaltung* (local self-administration) is an expression of the principle of subsidiarity.

Division of Legislative Competences

The distribution of legislative authority is naturally more complex than the principle of subsidiarity implies. Besides those powers which are the exclusive concern of the federation and those that are the preserve of the Länder, there are two further categories where the powers are shared, the so-called 'framework' laws and areas in which the powers of federation and Länder are concurrent (see Table 2.1).

With framework laws, the federation lays down the basic conditions, leaving the Länder to legislate the particular requirements and detail for their own needs. For areas covered by concurrent legislation, the Länder may pass laws to the extent that the federation has not done so.

TABLE 2.1 *Legislative competences of the Federation and Länder*

Federation	Länder
Exclusive powers	Exclusive powers
Foreign affairs	Cultural affairs (including broadcasting)
Defence	
Citizenship	Education
Passports, immigration, etc	Health Service
Currency matters	Police
Customs and free movement of goods	
Post and telecommunications	
Framework conditions	
Principles of higher education Hunting and conservation The press and the film industry Land distribution and regional planning	
Concurrent powers	
Civil and criminal law and sentencing Registration of births, deaths and marriages The law of association and assembly Residence and establishment of aliens Production and use of nuclear energy	

Source:
Bulmer (1989).

Division of Administrative Responsibility

The principle of subsidiarity applies in particular to policy implementation. The Länder have the prime responsibility for administration, not the federal ministries (with obvious exceptions such as defence and foreign affairs). For this reason, the bulk of public officials are employed in the Länder, and the federal ministries are relatively small.

Interdependence of Federation and Länder

As a consequence of the 'mixing' of legislative and administrative competences, there is a need for strong coordination between federal and Land authorities. A close network of intergovernmental relationships, permanent committees numbering several hundred, helps to ensure that the two sets of authority work properly together. Of leading importance are certain federal-wide policy-making bodies: the Science and Education Councils, the Financial Planning Council and the Economic Planning Council. The 'intertwining' of policy formation and implementation, a *Politikverflechtung*, promotes a form of intergovernmentalism and a bargaining relationship which is quite different from traditional models of federalism.

Apportionment of Revenues

The Basic Law sets out the responsibilities of federation, Länder and local government for particular heads of expenditure as well as establishing the sources of revenue for each. By itself, such a distribution would take no account of the disparity between the richer and poorer Länder, nor of the fact that Land revenues are not sufficient to meet all the commitments that new federal legislation imposes on Länder budgets. The remedy is found through a system of 'financial equalisation' (*Finanzausgleich*) which works in two ways. One is by means of a horizontal redistribution, from the richer Länder to the less affluent ones, the other is a vertical compensation coming to all Länder from the federation. Some idea of how significant the Länder are in the field of public finance is shown by the high proportion (some two-thirds) of public expenditure made by the Länder and local authorities.

German unification changed none of the essential features of the federal system (except for dropping Article 23), since all that was altered was the number of constituent Länder. The problems involved in the changing territorial balance are discussed in Chapter 6 of this volume (pp. 119–34). Here it is relevant to point to three factors. One works to the benefit of the new Länder: Article 30 of the Basic Law gives the federation the responsibility to legislate for the 'maintenance of . . . economic unity, especially the maintenance of uniformity of living conditions'. Although this wording does not amount to an injunction, nonetheless the normative intent is clear. A second consequence of unification is that a previous trend towards federal centralisation (Bulmer, 1989) may have been accentuated, since the new Länder, given their economic plight, are far more dependent on the federal government than any of the West German

Länder ever were. A third factor is the question of 'administrative competence': the high level of expertise of qualified administrators has yet to be built up in East Germany; this deficiency is exacerbated by the sudden introduction of an entirely new system of public administration and administrative law.

Parliamentary Institutions: Bundestag and Bundesrat

The German Parliament in its two houses combines two disparate functions: the Bundestag represents the principle of parliamentary government – the chancellor and his ministers are responsible to the Bundestag; the Bundesrat upholds the federal principle in representing the interests of the Länder. Yet both are concerned with all aspects of federal legislation. Neither chamber was radically affected by unification, although the size of both was increased. The Bundestag, elected by proportional representation, has become a very large assembly, 664 members, as a consequence of unification. In contrast, the Bundesrat has remained a relatively small body with the Länder governments sharing its 68 votes. Whilst the outcome of the first all-German election made little difference to the hold exercised by the three established parties in the Bundestag, the situation in the Bundesrat has become more complex (see Chapters 4 and 6).

The Bundestag

The actual election of the chancellor by the Bundestag at the beginning of its four-year term, and its authority to dismiss a serving chancellor, both emphasise the principle of parliamentary government: the chancellor is solely responsible to the Bundestag. The work of the Bundestag is primarily concerned with legislative matters, and for this reason is described as an *Arbeitsparlament*, a 'working parliament' rather than a debating or *Redeparlament*. In being geared to the government's legislative programme, the Bundestag has developed as a body of experts, and the focus of its activity is in the specialised committees corresponding to the federal ministries. In other ways, the Bundestag is relatively divorced from the government and its ministers. Thus, parliamentary groups of the parties (*Fraktionen*) preserve their own identity: government ministers sit separately from their party *Fraktion*, and party speakers have one allocation in debate and ministers another. The sense of distance is increased by the fact that recruitment to ministerial office is usually from prominent ministers of the Länder rather than from the Bundestag. However, the chancellor – and through him the federal ministers – have to maintain the support of the coalition parties. An all-important link is the leader of a party's *Fraktion*, and the chancellor will be concerned to have his own choice of the *Fraktion* leader. Restiveness within a governing party is most likely to result from agreements the chancellor has made with the coalition partner. Compromises are necessary but they have to be 'sold' to the parliamentary party. The greatest threat to a government is the risk that a coalition will break up, and for this reason it is the relationship between the coalition parties that is of overriding importance rather than the Bundestag itself expressing a lack of confidence in the chancellor.

The Bundesrat

Quite different considerations affect the federal government in its dealings with the Bundesrat. The composition of the Bundesrat, delegates sent by Länder governments and acting on instructions of a Land government, reflects party fortunes in the Länder: the party majority in the Bundesrat need not correspond to that in the Bundestag, and coalitions in the Länder need not be the same as the federal coalition. The various delegations are there to serve their Länder interests, and the federal government has no direct way of ensuring that its legislation will meet approval even by those Länder governments consisting of the same party or parties as the federal government. One consequence of unification has been greatly to magnify the disparity between the political composition of government at federal and Land levels (see Chapters 4 and 6).

The problem would not be so great if the powers of the Bundesrat were less formidable. Besides the requirement to secure a two-thirds majority in both houses for constitutional amendments, the Bundesrat has a wide legislative competence, including approval of the federal budget. In particular, the Bundesrat has a power of absolute veto over all legislation directly affecting the Länder. Since the Länder are required to implement the bulk of federal legislation – and therefore legislative measures inevitably have to deal with this aspect – there is a high premium set on securing the cooperation of a majority in the Bundesrat.

It is important to note that the Bundesrat is not solely a legislative organ. Thus the Basic Law stipulates that the Länder shall participate *through* the Bundesrat in the legislation *and* the administration of the federation (Article 50). The idea that the Bundesrat is a 'meeting-place of governments' is reinforced through the participation of the federal government in the work of the Bundesrat, both in consultation and by its representation on Bundesrat committees.

More than any other institution, the Bundesrat exemplifies the 'cooperative' character of the German constitutional system. The checks and balances, the admixture of federal and Land competences, and the blurring of the administrative and legislative spheres – these all show the complex relationships involved in fashioning a consensus.

Constitutional Jurisdiction

The ideal of the *Rechtsstaat* had long been a prominent feature of the German legal tradition, as it was in popular thinking, and yet it was not until the framing of the Basic Law that the *Rechtsstaat* was given a firm constitutional anchor. In describing the FRG as a *Rechtsstaat* the Basic Law established a norm to condition the behaviour and expectations of all participants.

The claim to be a *Rechtsstaat*, and thus to make the Basic Law itself the superior force in the state, could not have been sustained without the means to ensure its authoritative interpretation. This power is given to the Federal Constitutional Court. The Court, the guardian of the constitution, is the final arbiter in ruling between competing claims. Its stature is enhanced by the complete independence it has from political and other pressures. Although the judges of the court are appointed in a quasi-political manner (by the Bundesrat and the Bundestag), there is no evidence that they have been beholden either to the government or to the political parties.

What makes the Court so powerful in enforcing constitutional norms is the wide competence it has. Besides upholding the personal freedoms set out in Articles 1–19 of the Basic Law, it arbitrates on disputes between the major organs of states, protects the federal–Land balance, rules on the constitutionality of political parties, and exercises a controlling function on federal legislation. The Court's power with regard to federal legislation is impressive: not only can it rule on the constitutionality of laws directly they have been enacted, its role has developed so far that it can almost be described as a third legislative body. The Court has a *de facto* power of amending legislation. Thus, in giving its reasons why a particular law does not properly conform to a relevant provision of the Basic Law (which provision *is* taken to be applicable the Court decides) it can indicate how the law should be changed in order to be acceptable to the Court. The lesson for a government is that in framing legislation it is just as important to gauge the Court's likely reaction as to pay attention to objections from the Bundestag or Bundesrat.

The wide sweep of constitutional jurisdiction may have led to an undesirable 'judicialisation of politics', but the Constitutional Court has become an integral part of the political system and has developed into a formidable check on government. Precisely this security against the exercise of arbitrary authority – bearing in mind the excesses of the Communist regime in the GDR – is what East Germans are likely to welcome.

The Chancellor: Powers and Constraints

The leading part played by Chancellor Kohl in securing German unification draws attention to the key place a chancellor holds in the political system. Yet the powers given to a chancellor in the Basic Law are not that much different from other heads of parliamentary governments, and in some respects he is in a weaker constitutional position.

His major supports in the Basic Law are those that strengthen his position *vis-à-vis* the Bundestag: his election for a four-year term gives the chancellor a measure of security, since he can be dismissed only by the Bundestag, by a majority of its members electing a successor, the vote of 'constructive no-confidence' (Article 67), a device that prevents governments being overturned by purely negative majorities. Within government, the chancellor has the sole power to appoint and dismiss ministers – they are responsible to him and not to the Bundestag. He has as well, according to the Basic Law, the right to decide general lines of government policy, the *Richtlinienkompetenz* (Article 65). The present situation of the chancellor owes much to the deliberate downgrading of the federal presidency in the Basic Law. In the Weimar Republic, the president emerged as a rival source of authority to the chancellor and as a means of undermining the parliamentary system. Now parliamentary government cannot be subverted by constitutional means, and – weak though a chancellor may prove to be in practice – no one can challenge his legitimate authority.

A chancellor, however, is ringed about with constraints. First, there are those factors that affect the federal government as a whole. Thus, not only does the existence of the Länder and, more generally, the federal system limit the scope of the federal government, the Bundesrat also acts as a formidable hurdle to be negotiated if the federal government is to implement its legislative programme. In financial matters, too, both the Länder and the Bundesrat can impose checks. The Länder, with a large proportion of public spending under their control, make it difficult for the federal government to insist on its own views with regard to budgetary policy. The Bundesrat, with a direct say in the passing of the federal budget, naturally gives full expression to the interests and priorities of the individual Land governments.

Other constraints affect the chancellor more directly. Even though he alone is responsible for overall government policy and can appoint and dismiss ministers, he is restricted by the principle of the autonomy of departmental ministers (*Ressortprinzip*), specified in the Basic Law (Article 65), and is unable to interfere directly in their work. Even more confining is the specifically political constraint: the need to rely on a coalition partner in government. This requirement, since no party in recent times has been able to secure an overall majority, gives the junior partner the power of effective veto over government policies.

In order to appreciate the limitations facing a German chancellor, the contrast should be made with other parliamentary systems – for instance, with a British prime minister. The latter does not have to deal with the states in a federal system, nor with a powerful second chamber. There is no powerful Constitutional Court available to put a check on government legislation, and there is no principle of departmental autonomy to keep a prime minister at arm's length. Nor does the governing party in Britain usually have to rely on a coalition partner which would severely limit its freedom of action. To these differences can be added the fact that other parliamentary governments do not have to contend with the independent authority of a central bank. German governments have to accept the autonomy of the Bundesbank, with its independent responsibility for monetary policy.

Political Leadership

It may appear that, with so many restrictions, a German chancellor is handicapped in exercising political leadership and prevented from giving firm direction to his government. Yet that conclusion is at odds with the record. Chancellors in the post-1949 era, such as Adenauer, Brandt, Schmidt and, latterly, Kohl have all been significant political leaders and have made important contributions to the development of the Federal Republic. Moreover, for the most part they have stayed in office far longer than has been the case for other West European heads of government (see Table 2.2).

A chancellor has several political resources at his disposal (Smith, 1991), although their significance has changed over time and successive chancellors have shown strength in different ways. The *electoral* dimension is one such 'resource'. Federal elections have the character of a contest between two rival leaders or 'chancellor candidates'.

This personalisation of electoral campaigns gives the victorious leader considerable prestige. At one time, the popularity of a serving chancellor gave a 'chancellor bonus' to his party through winning the election. This chancellor effect, however, has waned since the early 1980s, and the 'bonus' is quite easily transferred to the junior coalition party rather than the chancellor's party, at least in part thanks to the electoral system which gives voters the opportunity to 'split' their votes between two parties (see Chapter 3). The disappearance of the chancellor bonus does not necessarily weaken the status of the chancellor, since a 'vote for the coalition' can be interpreted as a sign of confidence in the record of his government. However, the outcome – a stagnant or declining vote for the party – may lead to restiveness and dissatisfaction with the chancellor.

TABLE 2.2   *Chancellors and coalitions, 1949–92*

Chancellor	Period	Years	Coalitions	Departure
Adenauer	1949–63	14	CDU/CSU, FDP (and smaller parties)[1]	Resignation
Erhard	1963–6	3	CDU/CSU, FDP	Resignation
Kiesinger	1966–9	3	CDU/CSU, SPD	Election defeat
Brandt	1969–74	5	SPD, FDP	Resignation
Schmidt	1974–82	8	SPD, FDP	Bundestag defeat
Kohl	1982–	(11)	CDU/CSU, FDP	

Note:
1 CDU/CSU had an absolute majority from 1957 to 1961.

Much therefore depends on the standing a chancellor has with his own party – his second major resource – and the extent to which he is able to exercise control over it. Three factors have to be taken into account. The first is the federal system which inevitably determines the structure of party organisation. In one way, the Land basis of party organisation, and the independent status that a Land minister-president and the ruling party enjoy, restricts the chancellor even though he controls the federal party organisation. But in another way he enjoys the benefit of greater autonomy for himself, since the parties in the Länder find it difficult to unite themselves sufficiently to challenge the chancellor. A second factor relevant to the relationship of the chancellor with his party is the comparative weakness of the party *Fraktion* in the Bundestag. Unlike many other parliamentary systems, the Bundestag has never become the effective locus of party sovereignty. Even though the parliamentary party may be uneasy about particular government measures and not be convinced about a general line of policy, large-scale revolts against the leadership have been entirely absent whichever party has been in office. The third factor to be taken into account is whether the chancellor is also the chairman, effectively the leader, of the federal party. The two posts are usually taken by the same person. If they are, then the chancellor, mainly through the party's general secretary, has control over party organisation and can maintain close links with all leading officials. If the chancellor is solely in control of the federal government, then he faces the danger of becoming isolated and thus weakened – as was the case with Erhard and Schmidt.

Undoubtedly, the basis of the chancellor's authority lies in the control over government that he exercises. To an extent he is inhibited by the constraints already outlined, but in practice the test of his leadership lies in his ability to coordinate the work of government, to impart a clear direction to policy, and to operate harmoniously with the junior party in the coalition. The chancellor has at his disposal the chancellor's office, the *Kanzleramt*, which has effectively become a ministry in its own right, not one with administrative responsibilities but, with its various sections, acting both as an instrument for coordination and as a resource for policy development. Moreover, the *Kanzleramt* has two other functions: first, to ensure that the chancellor's policies are effectively disseminated to the wider public, through the press office; second, to perform a similar task *vis-à-vis* his own party.

Significantly none of the chancellor's organisational resources can ensure a trouble-free relationship with a coalition party, and the more effective a chancellor is in determinedly pushing his own policy options, the less pleased the coalition partner may be, and at times he may have to choose between ensuring backing from his own party and risking the break-up of the coalition. To keep both parties satisfied requires considerable skills – a gift that few chancellors have had.

The basic resource of the chancellor is his sole responsibility to establish general policy and establish priorities. It has proved difficult to initiate radical new policies in purely domestic affairs, since the web of constraints and the necessity to work through the existing consensus makes innovation a slow process. But in the broad portmanteau of external relations (to include foreign affairs, the European Community, security, and hitherto inner-German relations) a chancellor had far greater freedom of action. The reputation of most chancellors – Adenauer, Brandt, Schmidt, Kohl – has been won in an arena outside that of domestic politics.

Helmut Kohl as Chancellor

A summary of the resources available to a chancellor provides a set of criteria to assess the performance of individual chancellors. The chancellorship of Helmut Kohl, in particular, presents problems of evaluation and surprising contrasts. From taking office in 1982, when the FDP defected from the SPD coalition headed by Helmut Schmidt to side with the CDU, Kohl's tenure of office can be divided into two distinct periods: from 1982–9, and then from 1989 onwards. For the first seven years Kohl's performance was quite unremarkable; indeed, it might be said that he survived almost 'by default'. Yet, beginning in 1989, Kohl's leadership underwent a transformation: He became not only the architect of German unification but a statesman of European calibre. How is this transformation to be explained?

Kohl's hold on office after 1982 was largely a result of the weakness of the SPD: the party was in disarray after Schmidt's downfall, and neither in the 1983 or 1987 elections could it offer a credible alternative to the CDU–FDP coalition. For its part, the FDP – once having made the switch to the CDU – felt no temptation to change sides again. Kohl's performance in these years evoked no popular enthusiasm or respect – he was described as a 'bumbling dilettante' notable for making diplomatic gaffes. Moreover, even though Kohl had become chancellor promising a fundamental change in the course of German politics, *'die Wende'*, there was remarkably little alteration of direction during the 1980s. The elections showed that Kohl himself was far less popular than his party or the coalition.

What, then, of the resources he had available? The electoral resource became more of a 'chancellor deficit' than a 'chancellor bonus', and he made no positive mark in foreign policy, an area dominated by the foreign minister, Hans-Dietrich Genscher (FDP). Yet he had two strong attributes: he proved to be adept both in party management as well as in the coordination of the government and the coalition. These two strengths were sufficient to keep him in office despite the generally negative judgement of his abilities. Kohl is *par excellence* a professional politician. He made his early career in the youth wing of the party (*Jung-Demokraten*). Later he became minister-president of the Rhineland–Palatinate, and success at the Land level is almost a *sine qua non* in German politics for advancement at the federal level, rather than straight entry into the Bundestag. Kohl could also draw on his long experience in the CDU (he had first been chancellor candidate in 1976), and in dealing with the 'troublesome' Bavarian CSU which under the leadership of Franz-Josef Strauss had waged a hostile campaign against him since the mid-1970s.

These qualities did not help early in 1989, when there were open moves in the CDU to oust him following serious election defeats in the Länder. In fighting for his political life, Kohl undertook a string of measures to restore his popularity with the party and to regain public credibility. Perhaps the most significant change came in his dealings with the Western allies, in particular holding out against the modernisation of short-range nuclear weapons. In this respect he was reflecting the tide of public opinion within the FRG. But what it showed Kohl was that standing up for German interests gave him a chance to rally the CDU.

The discovery that he could successfully play on national sentiments was to prove the key in Kohl's transformation later in 1989 when, from early Autumn onwards, he took all the initiatives in bringing about national unification. He was prepared to force the pace, not only *vis-à-vis* the GDR, but in relation to the Western Powers as well. Kohl's handling of the negotiations that took place during 1990 – on an inner-German level as well as externally – secured his lasting reputation. Having succeeded in promoting German national interests, and with unified Germany a major force in Europe, the way was open for Chancellor Kohl to use the new position to exploit foreign policy resources in Eastern Europe and within the EC to strengthen further his domestic standing.

Yet the onset of two domestic issues that led to a questioning of the adequacy of Kohl's leadership. First, there was the political impasse reached in efforts to curtail the influx of asylum-seekers. Although the Chancellor was able to blame the SPD and the FDP for their failure to agree on effective measures, the growth in support for extreme right parties took support away from the CDU. Second, in the early part of 1992 the outbreak of labour unrest damaged the government's standing. Many argued that Kohl was responsible for the deterioration because he had misled the people about the high cost of rebuilding East Germany, and the trade unions based demands on the grounds that ordinary wage-earners had been forced to bear too much of the burden. A trial of strength with the public sector unions in May 1992 led to wage increases being conceded above the rate of inflation, thus adding to Germany's economic problems. Kohl's prestige suffered in consequence, and his position was not helped by the disarray in the CDU's coalition partner, the FDP, following the resignation of Hams-Dietrich Genscher, who, as the long-serving foreign minister, had added stability to Kohl's government. Germany's internal difficulties had wider international implications, Helmut Kohl suddenly appeared to be a far less convincing European leader than he was just after German unification.

3

Two German Electorates?

RUSSELL J. DALTON

The democratic revolution in East Germany illustrates the importance of the citizenry in shaping the course of politics. Even if the
public's influence is normally less dramatic and decisive, citizen
beliefs have always been an important factor in the political development of the Federal Republic. Early analyses focused on the need
to reshape the political beliefs inherited from the Third Reich and
to integrate citizens into the pluralist and democratic forms of the
new system. There is extensive evidence on the transformation of
the Western political culture over the past generation, creating
democratic and participatory political norms, support for the welfare
state, an endorsement of Germany's Western-oriented international
policies, and a robust system of party competition (Baker et al.,
1981; Conradt, 1980; Dalton, 1992).

German unification now raises many new questions about the
citizenry in the unified Germany, and their political beliefs. Scientific
evidence was lacking on the state of public opinion in the East,
but the government clearly intended to create a distinct 'socialist
personality' among the public. This personality would stress socialist
economics, communist political principles, and international solidarity with the Soviet Union. The GDR ostensibly had a multiparty
system and national elections, but this presented only the illusion of
democracy – political power was firmly held by the Communists.
Residents in the five new Länder are now learning about democracy
and partisan competition for the first time, even if some of the formal
structures of politics may seem familiar.

The FRG's second democratic transition raises questions about
the distribution of political values in the unified electorate and the
ability of the party system to integrate 10 million new voters from

the East. Having merged, in at least formal terms, to what extent are the beliefs of Western and Eastern Germans politically compatible? Or, are there now two German electorates?

The goal of this chapter is twofold. First, we want to continue monitoring the long-term electoral trends that shape the nature of partisan politics in the FRG (Dalton, 1989). The FRG experienced a gradual decline in the importance of social cleavages that had traditionally structured partisan competition, primarily class and religious divisions. In their place, new political controversies and new bases of political competition were developing. Reflecting these changes, the party system displayed increasing partisan volatility and fragmentation. The Bundestag election of 1990 provides a new opportunity to consider whether German union has hastened or retarded these trends.

Our second goal is to compare the electorates of the West and East. To what extent have forty years of life under different economic and political systems created two distinct German electorates? A comparison of political beliefs can tell us a great deal about the cultural impact of the GDR on its citizens. In addition, the political attitudes and behaviours of the two publics define the political environment in which the process of German unification will occur. Germany's 'peaceful revolution' of 1989 underscored the importance of people power, and we can now study how the people view politics in the new Germany.

From Stability to Electoral Change

For the first three decades of its existence, the party system of the Federal Republic was noted for its growing stability and cohesion. Fourteen parties competed in the first national elections in 1949, and eleven won seats in the Bundestag. In just a few short years, however, voters rejected the appeals of narrow special interest parties and radical parties on the extreme left and right. Most citizens concentrated their support behind one of the two largest parties. On the right, the CDU/CSU consolidated the support of several smaller parties and became the major conservative force in electoral politics. The Social Democratic party (SPD) similarly dominated the left end of the political spectrum. The small Free Democratic party (FDP) continued the liberal tradition from the pre-war party system. After the 1961 election only these three parties were present in Parliament, and the structure of a stable 'two-and-a-half' party system was established. Other political measures displayed the public's integration into the party system over this period (Baker *et al.*, 1981; Loewenberg, 1979).

This pattern of electoral stabilisation and ideological convergence reversed for the party system of the 1980s. For example, David Conradt (1989, p. 129) has presented evidence of a long term increase in individual vote shifts between elections (though for contradictory evidence see Klingemann, 1985; Zelle, 1990). Between the 1957 and 1961 elections, for instance, barely 10 per cent of the active electorate changed their voting preferences between elections. This percentage nearly doubled during the 1980s.

Split-ticket voting provides another sign of the weakening of party commitments. When West Germans go to the polls in federal elections they cast two votes. The first vote (*Erststimme*) is for a candidate to represent the electoral district. The second vote (*Zweitstimme*) is for a party list that provides the basis for a proportional allocation of parliamentary seats. A voter may, therefore, split his or her ballot by selecting a district constituency candidate of one party and another party with the party list vote. The amount of split-ticket voting has inched upward in recent elections. Up until the late 1960s, less than 10 per cent of all voters split their ballots. The number of ticket-splitters then increased in the 1980s. About 14 per cent of the electorate split their ballot in 1987, and this grew to 16 per cent in 1990.

Another sign of the erosion of traditional party alignments is the growing fragmentation of the FRG's party system. Until recently, the party system appeared to be evolving toward large 'catch-all' parties that would unify the voters in two competing party blocs: CDU/CSU and SPD. The two major parties still dominate the partisan landscape, but their share of the party list votes decreased during the 1980s. In 1976 the two major parties accounted for 91.2 per cent of the vote; their share eroded to 81.3 per cent in 1987, which further dropped to 80 per cent in 1990.

The increase in party fragmentation is, of course, closely linked to the emergence of the Green party (Die Grünen) in the 1980s. In 1983 the Greens first won Bundestag representation and acted as a public spokesperson for New Left causes, such as environmental protection, sexual equality, and a restructuring of Germany's international relationships. The party system further fragmented with the emergence of a neo-conservative party, the Republicans, in the 1989 Berlin and European parliament elections. The Republicans represent a reaction to the social and political changes that were transforming German society and politics. They call for a return to 'traditional' social values, harsher treatment of guest workers, and a more nationalistic foreign policy.

Even before the process of German unification had started, therefore, the FRG party system was experiencing increasing volatility and fragmentation. Unification then injected new uncertainty into this already fluid environment. The events of unification were themselves sufficient to produce a new wave of partisan change. Unification tapped a variety of political emotions among the German public, and restructured the political agenda. Because of the dominance of the unification issue, 1990 was not a 'normal' election. Moreover, the electorate itself had undergone a profound change. Although most East Germans were familiar with the party system of the FRG, they had observed Western-style democratic politics only from afar. Now, more than ten million new voters would enter the electorate – voters with very different political experiences and possibly different political values. The integration of these new voters into the Western party system presented a real challenge for the FRG.

Models of Electoral Change

While the evidence of increasing fluidity in voting patterns is clear cut, there is more uncertainty concerning the cause of these patterns. Most analysts resort to either a *realignment* or *dealignment* model to explain these processes of partisan change (Dalton *et al.*, 1984, chap. 15). The two models provide different explanations of the causes underlying the long-term partisan trends in the West. They also provide different reference points for judging electoral developments in the East.

The realignment approach analyses electoral history in terms of the social group bases of party support. Most political parties represent a distinct social clientele and institutionalise this support through a variety of formal and informal mechanisms. With the passage of time, however, group alignments are often strained by the failures of a party to deliver on its promises or by a changing political agenda that obviates the issues that initially defined political conflict. When this occurs, the electoral system may experience a *partisan realignment*. A 'realignment' is defined as a significant shift in the group bases of party coalitions, and usually in the distribution of popular support among the parties as a result. The patterns of group support may shift abruptly (a critical realignment) or may follow a slower evolutionary change (a secular realignment). Realignments have been a regular feature of American electoral politics for well over a century and probably since the emergence of the first mass party coalitions around 1800. Similar realignments have occurred in European party systems, such as the rise of the British Labour party in the early 1900s or the Gaullist realignment in the French party system of the late 1950s.

Partial evidence in support of the realignment model comes from changes in the structure of German society over the past few decades. The strength and stability of party alignments in the FRG during the 1950s and 1960s were partially drawn from the underlying structure that class, religion, and other social cleavages gave to the party system. Many voters closely identified with their social class, religious group, community, or region. Social networks within these groups were tightly drawn and individuals listened to the advice of the unions or church leaders in making decisions.

The social transformation of the post-war FRG has, however, gradually eroded these group cleavages and thus created the potential for partisan change (Baker *et al.*, 1981; Dalton, 1988). Increasing social and geographic mobility weakened the bonds that linked individuals to group and community networks. Government policies and social forces developed an advanced industrial society in the Federal Republic, which altered the social composition of the electorate. Other developments increased the social and political diversity of society, eroding the closed structure of traditional social networks and attenuating the impact of social cues on partisan behaviour.

The realignment model explains the heightened partisan volatility of the 1980s as an indicator of the realigning forces existing within the FRG's party system. As old political cleavages weaken and new cleavages gain force, partisan volatility and fragmentation often accompany this transition. Indeed, discussions of contemporary partisan politics often claim that the traditional economic and religious cleavages of the Federal Republic are being superseded by the new political conflicts of an advanced industrial society (Inglehart, 1990). After voters eventually realign themselves to represent the new constellation of political forces, the realignment model predicts that voting patterns should restabilise around the new base of political cleavage.

The dealignment model presents a contrasting view of the processes of partisan change. While the realignment model focuses on the group-based patterns of partisan support, the dealignment model emphasises the electorate's psychological attachment to parties. A dealignment period exists when many voters lack firm affiliations with any political party.

From the dealignment perspective, the growing volatility of the FRG party system during the 1980s was not the result of a realignment in partisan loyalties, but reflected a general erosion in the strength of partisan attachments. Analysts explain contemporary dealignment as due either to the public's growing political sophistication, which decreases the need for habitual party loyalties (Dalton, 1988, chap. 9), or to the electorate's growing alienation from partisan politics (Raschke, 1982). In either case, with many voters lacking firm ties to a preferred party, voting behaviour becomes more fluid and unpredictable.

These two models provide contrasting explanations of the sources of the partisan change we have observed, and their ultimate resolution. The applicability of these models to electoral politics in the West can help us to understand how and why the party system has been changing. The fit of either model to the Eastern electorate is obviously a more open question. Both models do, however, provide a reference standard for judging the patterns of electoral support in the East. A comparison of these frameworks also can highlight the similarities and differences within the unified German electorate.

The Evidence of Realignment

The realignment model suggests that the present fluidity in FRG voting results is due to shifts in the group bases of party support. As social forces disrupt long-standing partisan loyalties and stimulate the formation of new party allegiances, the party system experiences heightened volatility and fragmentation during the transition period. If a realignment is occurring, we should see social groups shifting their traditional patterns of party support to endorse a new party.

Social Class and Party Support

One potential locus for a realignment in voting patterns is the class cleavage. The FRG's party system is partially built upon the traditional class conflict between the bourgeoisie and proletariat, and more broadly the problems of providing economic well-being and security to all members of society. These economic conflicts initially helped structure the party system. The CDU is the party of business and the middle class, just as the SPD has remained the advocate of the working class interests and the political ally of the labour unions. This class division produced a clear partisan alignment in the FRG. Each party bloc was embedded in its own network of support groups and offered voters a distinct political programme catering to these group interests.

Despite the historical importance of the class cleavage, four decades of electoral results point to an unmistakable decline in class voting differences within the West German party system (Figure

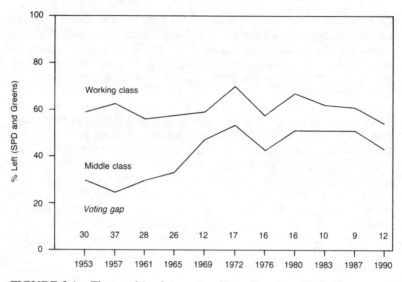

FIGURE 3.1   *The trend in class voting, West Germany, 1953–90*

Source: West German Election Studies.

3.1). At the height of class-based voting in 1957, the SPD received a majority of working class votes (61 per cent) but only a small share (24 per cent) of middle class votes. In overall terms, this represented a 37 percentage point gap in the class bases of party support, rivalling the level of class voting found in Britain and other class-polarised party systems. Over the next decade, the success of the *Wirtschafts-wunder* and moderating party differences (such as the SPD's embrace of centrist policies in the 1959 Godesberg Programme) decreased the level of class voting. The conciliatory climate of the Grand Coalition (1966–9), during which the CDU/CSU and SPD shared control of the federal government, pushed class voting levels even lower in the 1969 election. By the 1980s, class voting differences were nearly non-existent, averaging less than 10 per cent in the federal elections of 1983 and 1987. Voting differences based on other class characteristics, such as income or education, displayed a similar downward trend in their influence.

In one sense, this shift in class voting patterns fulfils the basic definition of a realignment: increasing SPD support among middle class voters improved the party's electoral showing and enabled it to control the federal government from 1969 until 1982. And yet, if we probe the data more deeply, the evidence becomes more complex. There are two separate components of the middle class: the *old middle class* of business owners and professionals and the *new middle class* of salaried white collar workers and government employees. These two strata display two distinct voting patterns (Pappi and Terwey, 1982). First, voting differences between the two traditional class antagonists – the working class and the *old* middle class – have held fairly constant over time. Franz-Urban Pappi and Michael Terwey cite this evidence to argue that the fundamental basis of the class cleavage has not changed. And yet this interpretation overlooks the fact that the declining number of voters who belong to these two class strata is undermining the importance of the traditional class cleavage. In the early 1950s nearly three-quarters of the electorate belonged either to the old middle class or to the working class; today these strata represent barely half the electorate.

The overall decline of class differences in Figure 3.1 is therefore due primarily to the growth in the size of the *new* middle class and changes in the voting patterns of this stratum. The growing number of new middle class voters has increased the partisan significance of this social group. From barely a fifth of the labour force in 1950, the new middle class now accounts for about half of all employees. This change in the composition of the middle class is electorally significant because the new middle class holds political values which have led them to deviate from the voting tendencies of the traditional middle class.

In an indirect way, the declining relevance of the class cleavage is documented by data that track voter perceptions of the partisan leanings of social class groups (business and labour) over time (Table 3.1). Perceptions of the partisan leanings of big business and labour have become *more distinct* while class-based voting has *narrowed*! In 1965, barely a quarter of the public thought that big business leaned toward the CDU; by 1990 nearly three-quarters of the public felt that business leaned toward the CDU/CSU. Public images of the SPD leanings of the labour unions also became more clear cut over this period. Thus, the general narrowing of class voting differences is not due to a blurring of the class images of the major parties, but to voters who no longer follow these cues in making their voting decisions.

German unification creates a new context in which to view patterns of class-based voting. In the West, the issues of unification dominated the 1990 election and temporarily eclipsed other political concerns. Ongoing public interests in the structure of social welfare pro-grammes, social benefits, issues of environmental quality, and many other topics were overshadowed by debates on the course of unifi-cation. Kaase and Schrott (1991) show that over three-quarters of the political news during the 1990 campaign was in some way tied

TABLE 3.1   *Political leanings of social institutions, 1965–90*

	1965	1969	1972	1976	1980	1983	1990
Bib business leans towards							
CDU/CSU	28	36	62	41	54	72	70
Neither party	19	37	21	41	22	6	18
SPD	5	12	8	5	9	2	11
Difference	23	24	53	36	45	70	59
Labour unions lean toward							
CDU/CSU	5	2	2	1	1	2	11
Neither party	13	20	19	21	12	6	19
SPD	46	69	74	71	78	79	74
Difference	−41	−67	−72	−70	−77	−77	−63
Catholic Church leans toward							
CDU/CSU	53	66	73	63	81	78	72
Neither party	12	23	20	31	13	12	23
SPD	3	2	1	0	1	0	3
Difference	50	64	72	63	80	78	69

Source:
1965–83 data from INFAS, *Politogramm: Bundestagswahl 1983*, 129; 1990 data are
from the Comparative National Election Project – German National Elections
1990, conducted by Max Kaase, Hans-Dieter Klingemann, Manfred Kuechler, and
Franz-Urban Pappi. The question wording in 1990 differed somewhat from the earlier
years, but the general question was comparable.

to unification. At the same time, many aspects of the unification
issue had distinct economic consequences that might reinvigorate
class differences. Even by late 1990, unemployment was rapidly
growing in the East; many Westerners were also beginning to worry
that unification would mean tax increases and mounting inflation for
the West.

The top panel of Table 3.2 presents class voting differences for
the Western electorate in 1990. German unification left-class voting
patterns relatively unchanged. Although the SPD lost considerable
overall support in the election, the party still polled a plurality of
working class voters (46 per cent). Conversely, most middle class
voters gave their support to the CDU/CSU, especially among members of the old middle class. If we simply calculate the difference in

the percentage leftist (SPD and Greens) between working class and middle class voters, the 12 per cent gap in party support barely differs from the two prior elections (Figure 3.1).

TABLE 3.2 *Class voting patterns, 1990*

Party	Working class	Old middle class	New middle class	Combined middle class
Western Germany				
CDU/CSU	43.3	62.9	46.2	49.5
FDP	5.7	14.5	14.5	14.5
SPD	45.8	17.7	33.1	30.2
Greens	5.2	4.8	6.2	5.9
Total (%)	100	100	100	100
(*N*)	(212)	(124)	(519)	(643)
Eastern Germany				
CDU/CSU	51.2	63.6	41.5	42.7
FDP	14.2	15.2	18.2	18.0
SPD	24.6	15.2	22.0	21.5
Greens/Bündnis '90	5.3	3.0	10.0	9.5
PDS	4.7	3.0	6.7	7.9
Total (%)	100	100	100	100
(*N*)	(338)	(460)	(33)	(494)

Source:
December 1990 Election Study. Conducted by Forschungsgruppe Wahlen for the Zweites Deutsches Fernsehen (ZDF).

While class voting patterns have a long evolutionary history in the West, their status in the East is less certain. It is difficult to apply Western notions of social class to the occupational structure inherited from the Communist GDR. The economy was overwhelmingly comprised of state-owned enterprises; the GDR was ostensibly a state of and for the working class. Similarly, in place of the new middle class in the West, the East had party functionaries, governmental appointees, and managers of state enterprises. The traditional contrast between the bourgeoisie and proletariat in a capitalist system was thus largely irrelevant to Easterners. Market-based class distinctions are starting to develop in the GDR, but at the beginning of the 1990s they were still weakly defined. In addition, the intermediary institutions that could link the parties to class groups, such as the unions and business associations, were themselves still developing. Finally, there were programmatic differences between the Eastern and Western parties (see Chapter 4 in this volume). The Eastern CDU, for instance, advocated policies that were more liberal than its Western counterpart; the Eastern SPD initially seemed to be a party of intellectuals with only weak ties to the working class. These factors should have attenuated class voting differences among the Eastern electorate.

The lower panel of Table 3.2 presents class differences in voting behaviour for citizens in the five new Länder. The most striking finding is the *reversal* of the basic class alignment of the Western party system. The Eastern CDU was able to win a majority of the working class vote (51.2), but fared less well among the middle class (42.7). Conversely, the leftist parties – SPD, Greens/Bündnis '90, and PDS – garnered more votes among the middle class than among their 'normal' constituency in the working class. While the few self-employed professionals in the survey (only 25 voters out of 832) strongly supported the CDU, white collar salaried employees disproportionately endorsed leftist parties. Translating these statistics into the class voting measures of Figure 3.1, there is a negative class voting index of −8 among the Eastern electorate in 1990.

The realignment model's focus on class voting patterns thus yields two different results for the Western and Eastern electorates. In the West, the changing voting behaviour of the new middle class produced a secular realignment over the years 1960–90. As the new middle class gradually changed its voting patterns after the 1950s, overall levels of class voting decreased. This secular realignment also contained elements of a dealignment, however. The shift in voting patterns was located among a social group – the new middle class – that held an ambiguous position in the political structure of the Federal Republic (Kerr, 1990). Furthermore, new middle class voters changed their party support from heavily favouring one party to dividing their votes about equally between left and right. The overall result was not an exchange of the traditional bourgeoisie–proletariat cleavage for another clear social alignment, but the erosion of the traditional class cleavage without a new class cleavage (as yet) emerging in its place. This ambiguity undoubtedly contributed to the heightened partisan volatility of the 1980s.

Class voting patterns yield very different lessons for the Eastern electorate. The elections of 1990 represented the beginning of real democratic politics in the East. All else being equal, partisan behaviour and electoral politics should gradually develop greater stability and coherence in the years ahead – much as in the Federal Republic during the early post-war elections. At the same time, class voting patterns in Eastern Germany began with a reversal of the class alignment found in virtually all Western democracies (Lijphart,

1984). The crucial question, therefore, is whether the 1990 election was a short-term deviation due to the unique political context of unification, or whether it reflected an enduring feature of electoral politics in the five new Länder.

There are many reasons to suspect that Eastern voting patterns will move toward the Western model. Even after only a brief period, the unique factors of the 1990 elections are beginning to change. Kohl's promises that no one would be worse off because of unification look less sincere in the face of 30 per cent unemployment, rising taxes and inflation in the East. The economic costs of unification severely hurt the CDU's fortunes in subsequent Land elections in West Germany, and may stimulate traditional class reactions to these economic hardships. Moreover, economic interest groups are rapidly developing in the East, providing a formal means of intermediation between social groups and the parties. The parties, too, are changing. The Eastern SPD initially was a party of middle class activists and middle class goals; it is now reaching out to workers in the East. As the market economy spreads East, the ties between business and the CDU also are likely to strengthen. In short, as the political and social integration of Germany progresses, electoral alignments in the East should converge with the 'normal' class voting patterns in the West.

There is, however, no reason why Eastern voters must follow Western patterns. The dramatic events of German union are the type of historical experience that can have an enduring impact on party alignments. For instance, the Civil War in the United States created a Southern party system that fundamentally differed from the North in its structure and patterns of voter support, and which endured in this anomalous position for over a century. Although public opinion surveys after 1991 show a convergence of class differences in partisanship among Easterners, the basic reversal of class lines remains. A continuation of such differences would generate the same type of intraparty conflict observed in the American case; the Eastern and Western wings of the major parties would represent different clienteles, and this should ultimately be reflected in different policy goals. This would heighten intraparty conflict within the major parties, and further weaken the political parties.

Future elections will begin to indicate which path Eastern voters will follow, and this evidence also will address the question of how distinctive the two electorates will remain. But the inevitable result of either path seems to be a continued weakening of the social class basis of electoral politics in the Federal Republic.

Religion and Party Support

Historically, the religious cleavage provided a second basis for partisan division in the party system. The CDU/CSU was founded as a religious alliance between Catholics and Protestants, and its 'Christian' label openly proclaimed its religious orientation. Conversely, the SPD had normalised its relations with the Catholic church in the 1960s, but it still was more responsive to secular interests within society.

The historical conflict between the Catholic church and liberal/socialist parties still clearly appears in voting alignments in the West (Figure 3.2). The gap in SPD voting support between Catholics and Protestants remains, within a 20–25 point range for most of the years 1960–90; Catholics disproportionately support the Union parties, while a majority of Protestants vote for the SPD. Religious voting patterns have narrowed somewhat in recent elections, though they still average close to 20 per cent. In 1990, a 17 per cent gap continued to separate Protestants and Catholics in their support for Leftist parties. The voting gap between religious and non-religious individuals displays the same marked persistence over time (Dalton, 1988, chap. 8). Furthermore, perceptions of the partisan leanings of the Catholic church suggest that religious cues also remain distinct (See Table 3.1 above).

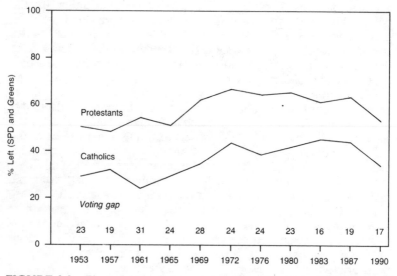

FIGURE 3.2   *The trend in religious voting, West Germany, 1953–90*

Source: *Euro-Barometer* surveys of the European Communities; 1990 West German Media Study.

The impact of the religious cleavage on Eastern voters was uncertain because of the GDR's political history. The churches were one of the few social institutions that could act independent of the SED state, but the state limited their political involvement. Unification also upset the religious balance of politics in the Federal Republic; Catholics and Protestants are roughly at parity in the West, but the East is heavily Protestant. In addition, the GDR government had successfully promoted the secularisation of society during its forty-year rule. For instance, a 1991 opinion poll found that 59 per cent of Westerners never doubted the existence of God, compared with only 27 per cent of Easterners.

Given these differences, religious voting patterns in the five new Länder parallel those found in the West to a surprising degree. The leftist parties did poorly among most social groups in the East. But the voting gap between Catholics and Protestants in leftist party support was 17 per cent – exactly the same as for the Western electorate. Thus Eastern voters have quickly replicated the religious voting patterns found in earlier West German elections.

Despite the apparent endurance of the religious cleavage in the West and the emergence of similar patterns in the East, the importance of religion as a basis of voting behaviour is declining – albeit in a different way than the class cleavage. Voting differences between denominations (and between religious and non-religious voters) still exist, but the secularisation of society on both sides of the former border has substantially increased the absolute number of non-religious individuals. These trends were already well developed for the Western electorate, and have been accelerated by the inclusion of Easterners. People who attend church regularly are still well integrated into a religious network and maintain distinct voting patterns; but their numbers have decreased. Over the past generation, the proportion of regular church attenders has decreased by nearly half in the West, and church attendance is even lower in the East. By definition, secular voters are not basing their party preferences on religious cues. Thus, we again find that the changing composition of the electorate is lessening the partisan significance of traditional social cues by decreasing the number of individuals to whom these cues are relevant.

The New Politics and Party Support

As old social cleavages faded in Western Germany, the realignment approach led scholars to search for potential new sources of group competition that could replace the weakening ties of class, religion and other social cleavages. Earlier research has suggested several other social cleavages as a potential source of partisan division: for example, education or life style variables (Gluchowski, 1987; Feist and Krieger, 1987). The impact of these characteristics is still weak, however. Regional differences may increase as a result of unification, but past regional differences in the Federal Republic have been fairly modest.

One potential new basis for political conflict among the Western electorate has been the growing interest in issues of life style norms, cultural values, and the quality of life. Ronald Inglehart has described these new political issues as evolving from the transformation of citizen values in advanced industrial societies (Inglehart, 1984; 1990). Inglehart maintains that as a society makes progress in addressing traditional economic and security needs, a growing share of the public shifts its attention to *postmaterial* goals that are still in short supply, such as the quality of life, self-expression, and personal freedom. These changing value priorities add issues such as environmental protection, nuclear energy, expanding citizen participation, sexual equality, consumer advocacy, disarmament, and human rights to the political agenda. These postmaterial or 'New Politics' issues may provide the necessary catalyst for a new basis of political cleavage.

To a much more modest extent, a similar counter-culture also developed among young people in the East. Environmental activism provided one of the early bases of opposition to the state, and Eastern youth were broadly familiar with the alternative movement and youth culture in the West. For instance, when Michael Jackson performed at an outdoor concert in West Berlin in 1988, East Berlin youth listened to the concert from behind the Wall. When members of the Western Greens travelled to the East, they met with autonomous peace groups and environmental groups. On the whole, however, the New Politics is a predominately Western phenomenon. Most Easterners want first to share in the affluence and consumer society of the West, before they begin to strive for postmaterial goals.

Partisan polarisation along the New Politics cleavage has grown over the past two decades among Western voters (Figure 3.3). During the 1970s, voters interested in New Politics' goals gave disproportionate support to the SPD, although the party was only partially responsive to these new issue demands. The formation of the Green party prior to the 1980 election created a focal point for the postmaterial agenda and brought value politics into the electoral arena. About a third of postmaterialists voted for the Greens in the 1983 and 1987 elections, far beyond the party's total electoral returns.

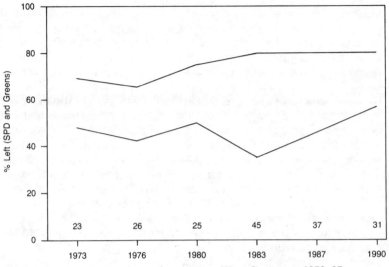

FIGURE 3.3 *The trend in values voting, West Germany, 1973–87*

Source: IPOS survey (May–June 1990); data provided by Dieter Roth, Forschungsgruppe Wahlen

The overall relationship between postmaterial values and voting choice has decreased slightly in the last two elections, though it remains larger than for the class or religious cleavage. In 1990, the events of unification and party actions complicated the vote choice for prospective Green voters. The Western Green party was deeply divided over unification issues and broader questions of the party's political philosophy. In addition, the SPD chancellor candidate was a strong advocate of Green and New Left policies that appealed to many potential voters for Die Grünen. The overall impact of postmaterial values in 1990 thus reflects continued support for the Green party among postmaterialists, as well as new support for the SPD.

A comparable question on value priorities was not asked in Eastern electoral surveys – which is itself an indication that these concerns are presently less important in the East. However, the small core of Green voters in the East did make their presence felt in the election. The alliance of the Eastern Greens and Bündis '90 actually fared better than their Western counterparts and gained entry into the parliament.

Despite the strong relationship between value priorities and voting behaviour for the Western electorate, several factors still limit the realignment potential of the New Politics' cleavage. Partisan realignment is normally based on clearly defined and highly cohesive social groups that develop institutional ties to the parties and provide clear voting cues to their members. A realignment normally yields a new, stable party alignment, formalised by the group's institutional representatives who mobilise the votes of their members for the chosen party. Postmaterialists, however, generally oppose disciplined organisational structures, such as unions and churches. Postmaterialists are thus unlikely to unite into exclusive associational groups that can be easily and predictably mobilised for a specific party. The continuing internal battles and disarray within the Green party attest to the anti-organisational tendencies of the movement (Kitschelt, 1988). The New Politics represent an issue cleavage that identifies only a community of like-minded individuals. Without a firm social base, an issue-based cleavage is likely to be more fluid and unpredictable than social group cleavages such as class and religion.

The action of the major established parties also has restricted the realignment potential of the New Politics. In the past, the three established parties have taken ambivalent positions on the overall New Politics agenda: supporting some specific issues, opposing some, and ignoring others. This lack of clear representation initially led to the creation of the Greens as an advocate for the New Politics' agenda. The success of the Greens caused the established parties to give more attention to New Politics causes, but the older parties still hesitated to turn away from their historical support networks when old and new issue interests might come into conflict. The SPD's attempt to attract both Old Left (union) and New Left (Green) voters in 1990 represented a break from this pattern, but the SPD's poor showing at the polls lessened its enthusiasm for this strategy. Because the Greens have been unable to translate the New Politics' agenda into policy outcomes, the realigning potential of the New Politics cleavage remains limited. And now, reunification further confounds the impact of the New Politics' cleavage. The massive economic problems of the East overshadow the concerns of a New Politics agenda. Some Easterners even worry that the pro-environment and non-materialist goals of New Politics' groups from the West could undermine the economic development of the East. The massive environmental problems in the new Länder will keep these issues on the political agenda, but possibly with less force than in the affluent West.

In summary, the social cleavages that have traditionally structured voting patterns in the Federal Republic are eroding in electoral importance, and the inclusion of new voters from the East will further attenuate these cleavages. The declining impact of class and religious cleavages arises from compositional changes that decrease the number of voters integrated into traditional social groups, and presumably from a declining reliance on such group cues as criteria for electoral decisions. These social group networks are even more weakly formed in the East. Social and partisan networks may strengthen in the new Länder as the democratic political system takes root, but the overall contribution of unification is to weaken the impact of traditional social cleavages still further.

The New Politics issues that were motivating voters in the 1980s may provide the first step in a gradual realignment process. However, this process so far has been incomplete. The erosion of traditional party alignments did not produce a New Politics alignment to restabilise the party system. Furthermore, the new economic, social and cultural issues raised by unification are likely further to complicate electoral politics and postpone any clear restructuring of party positions. New political challenges are also being mounted on the right, such as by the German Republican party and the right-wing German People's Party (DVU). The realignment approach thus underscores the conclusion that the Federal Republic is a system in flux.

The Evidence of Dealignment

The dealignment model provides another framework for viewing German electoral politics. This model analyses politics in terms of the electorate's psychological *identification* with a preferred political party. Such internalised party attachments are generally socialised early in life, often as part of a family political inheritance. These developing party ties can structure a voter's view of the political world, provide a source of cues for judging political phenomena, and promote stability in individual voting behaviour.

An emphasis on the public's psychological attachments to political parties suggests that Western and Eastern electorates are following two different courses. Among the Western public, the stabilisation and consolidation of the party system during the 1950s and 1960s created an environment in which popular attachments to the political parties strengthened (Baker *et al.*, 1981; Norpoth, 1983). During the 1980s, however, this trend toward partisanship among Western voters slowed, or even reversed (Dalton, 1989; Schultz, 1987).

Two broad sets of factors seem to account for this decline in partisanship. First, the recent performance of the parties casts them in a negative light for many voters. As we noted above, the established political parties were generally unresponsive to the new political issues that emerged on the centre of the political stage in the

1980s. Other political institutions – such as citizen action groups or public interest lobbies – appeared to represent these new political interests. The stature of the established parties was further eroded by the renewal of economic difficulties in the late 1970s and early 1980s. In addition, a series of political scandals at the national level (such as the Flick affair) and a flood of minor party scandals at the state and local levels (such as the election dirty tricks' affair in Schleswig–Holstein) tarnished party images. The parties appeared to be self-interested and self-centred organisations, which created feelings of partisan antipathy on the part of the public. A 1983 national poll of better-educated West Germans found that the party system evoked the least faith of any of the dozen social and political institutions included in the survey (USIA, 1984). In short, these developments were creating an environment in which citizens were turning away from partisan politics in general, creating a partisan dealignment.

Second, the growing sophistication of the German electorate also worked to weaken individual party ties. Similar to the decline of partisanship in the United States (Shively, 1979), German dealignment is concentrated among politically sophisticated and better-educated voters (Dalton and Rohrschneider, 1990). With growing interest and knowledge about politics, voters are better able to make their own political decisions without depending on party attachments. Furthermore, issue-oriented voters are more likely to defect from their normal party predispositions, which then erodes these predispositions and makes further defections even more likely. The concentration of these new independents among the ranks of the politically involved creates a potential for further political change (see Dalton, 1984).

The patterns of party identification should be very different for voters in the five new Länder. Because the party system is new to the East, few voters should (or could) display the types of deep affective partisan loyalties that are meant by a sense of 'party identification'. Although some early research suggests that many Easterners had latent affinities for specific parties in the Federal Republic, these were not long-term attachments born of early life experiences that we normally equate with the concept of party identification.

Table 3.3 describes the trend in party identification among Western voters (1972–91) and Eastern levels of partisanship for 1991. The Western data indicate a slight erosion in the strength of party attachments during the 1980s, which continued into the 1990 election. In the 1972 election, for instance, 55 per cent of the electorate felt 'strong' or 'very strong' party ties; by 1990, this group of strong partisans had declined to 40 per cent of the public. In other terms, approximately three-quarters of the public expressed some degree of partisan attachment in 1972, only 20 per cent were complete independents. The percentage of non-partisans increases to reach a high point of 27 per cent in 1990. Not only does the overall percentage of those expressing partisan attachments decrease over time, but the strength of partisanship within the various parties also decreases (Dalton and Rohrschneider, 1990). The heightened partisan volatility and uncertainty of the 1980s thus coincides with a weakening of the public's partisan ties (cf. Zelle, 1990).

TABLE 3.3   *The strength of partisanship, 1972–90*

	Western public							East
	1972	1976	1980	1983	1987	1990	1991	1991
Very strong	17	12	13	10	10	11	12	4
Strong	38	35	33	29	31	29	23	22
Weak	20	35	29	35	31	31	37	35
No party, don't know	20	16	19	22	25	27	27	37
Refused, no answer	5	3	6	4	3	2	2	3
Total	100	100	100	100	100	100	100	100

Source:
Data from German Election Studies. Each election time-point combined the results of multiple pre-election and post-election surveys; the 1991 point is based on an April 1991 survey conducted by the Forschungsgruppe Wahlen.

Regular measurement of the strength of partisan ties did not begin in Eastern surveys until early 1991. By then, most voters had already had significant electoral experience with the FRG parties. They had participated in two national elections (the March 1990 Volkskammer elections and the December Bundestag elections) as well as regional and local contests. Survey results still show that Eastern voters were significantly more hesitant in their expression of party attachments. Only 4 per cent of Easterners claimed to hold strong party ties, and over a third of the public (37 per cent) were explicitly non-partisan. As might have been expected, party ties were still in the process of formation for many Eastern voters.

Both the Western and Eastern publics display evidence of weak psychological ties binding the electorate to the political parties, but we interpret these findings differently for each. The continuing dealignment in the West is significant because the strength of these ties is related to the stability of voting preferences, split-ticket voting and the other indicators of electoral volatility that we have studied (Baker *et al.*, 1981, 204–21). Moreover, the overall level of decline is similar to the widely heralded partisan dealignments in Britain and the United States (Sarlvik and Crewe, 1983; Beck, 1984). In Britain, the proportion of the electorate that identified with a major party fell only 6 per cent between 1964 and 1979; the number of partisan identifiers in the United States decreased by approximately 10 per cent between 1964 and 1980. Yet in both nations these incremental shifts strongly affected the nature of electoral politics. Thus even the modest decrease in partisanship among Western Germans deserves our continued attention and provides some support for the dealignment model.

In contrast, the initially weak partisan attachments among Easterners will probably follow a different course in the years ahead. Past research indicates that party attachments normally strengthen through repeated electoral experiences, especially in newly-formed party systems (Converse, 1969). Thus, the current situation in the East might be closer to the post-war experience of the Federal Republic, where party ties strengthened as the party system took root, than to the contemporary Western electorate. The rapidity with which Easterners develop these attachments will be an important measure of their development of stable political orientations and their integration into the FRG's party system.

Comparing Political Beliefs

Both the realignment and dealignment models discuss the patterns of electoral change as flowing from different processes and leading to different consequences, but both agree on the immediate description of German electoral politics. The long-term determinants of partisanship, such as group cues as party attachments, have decreased in impact among the Western electorate, and remain underdeveloped among the Eastern public. Consequently, as these long-term factors play a diminished role in electoral decisions, the political values and issue beliefs of individual voters become more important as a basis of political decision-making.

This development gains added force from the events of German unification. As we noted in the introduction, until 1989 both the FRG and GDR had tried to create a distinct set of political values among their respective publics. To the extent that these efforts were successful, German unification represents the merger of two quite different electorates, with different political norms and different expectations of society and the political system. Thus, the last and most direct test of the similarities between East and West is to compare the political values of both electorates.

We can, of course, compare citizens in the East and West on a virtually unlimited set of political attitudes (Dalton, 1992; Weidenfeld and Krote, 1991; *Der Spiegel*, 1990). The two publics display sharp differences in their perceptions of the process and prospects of German unification (Kuechler, 1992). Religious values and perceptions of the economic situation also vary sharply across the two electorates. Other research, however, finds remarkably similar profiles in social values, political norms, and even images of the superpowers. On questions of democratic norms, for example, the two publics express almost identical commitments to the pluralist values underlying the political system of the Federal Republic.

Any comparison of East–West political beliefs will inevitably present some evidence of similarity and dissimilarity. The most basic comparisons, however, involve the political values derived from the socioeconomic systems and past socialisation patterns of the Federal Republic and GDR.

Figure 3.4 presents results from a 1990 survey that was designed to tap these basic political values. The first impression that one draws from these data is the broad similarity in political values between the two electorates. East–West differences on most questions are modest, suggesting that forty years of separation has not created two separate electorates.

When one looks more closely at the pattern of East–West differences, even more surprising results emerge. Several items in Figure 3.4 tap the contrast between the GDR's socialist economic principles and the market-oriented system of the Federal Republic. Despite the East German government's efforts to create a socialist personality, Easterners appear even more capitalistic than their relatives in the West. For instance, residents in the new Länder express greater support for a society that relies on a free market economy, reject income equality in favour of performance criteria, and link living standards to an individual's economic contributions. Even more ironically, Easterners are more likely to endorse 'a society that has people participate in political decisions even if it leads to delays'; Westerners lean toward 'a society that leaves important political decisions up to those who are responsible for them and who can decide quickly'. Forty years of socialism (and the collapse of this system) apparently taught Easterners *not* to be good socialists.

Certainly there are many differences in the beliefs and behaviours of the two publics; forty years apart have left unmistakable traces in political and social life. At the same time, the political legacy of the separation appear less dramatic than one might have expected. The results of Figure 3.4 and other opinion polls must surely be dis-

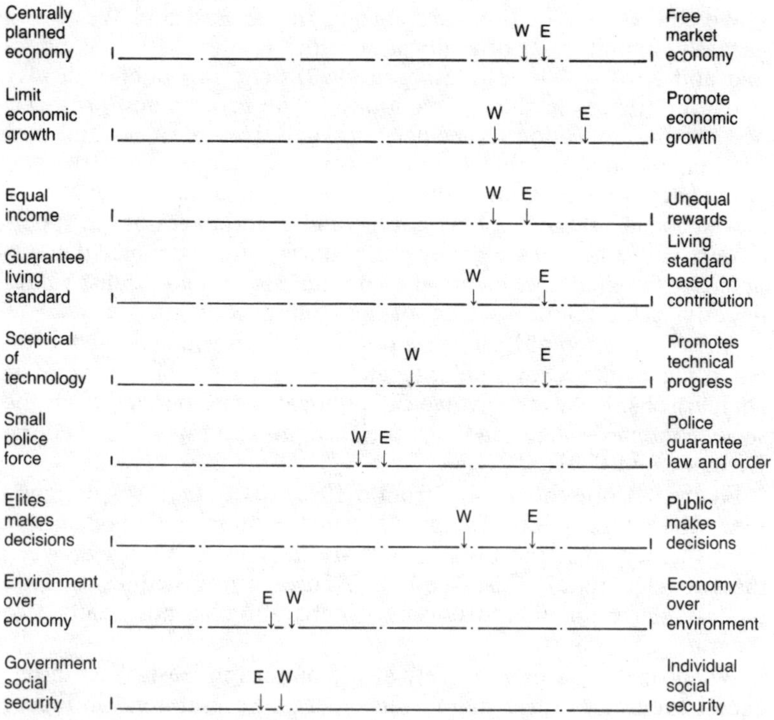

Centrally planned economy				W E	Free market economy
Limit economic growth				W · · E	Promote economic growth
Equal income				W E	Unequal rewards
Guarantee living standard				W · · E	Living standard based on contribution
Sceptical of technology			W · · E		Promotes technical progress
Small police force			W E		Police guarantee law and order
Elites makes decisions				W · E	Public makes decisions
Environment over economy		E W			Economy over environment
Government social security		E W			Individual social security

FIGURE 3.4 *Social values of the German electorates, 1990*

heartening for the SED officials who had attempted to create a socialist personality in the East.

The German Electorate(s)

This chapter has highlighted two broad characteristics of electoral politics that may affect the future course of the political system. First, our findings underscore the considerable potential for electoral change that now exists in the Federal Republic. For the past two decades, there has been a gradual decrease in the importance of long-term influences on voting choice. The influence of social class on voting preferences has weakened, as has the impact of religion, residence, and other social characteristics. Similarly, the recent dealignment trend signals a decrease in the impact of enduring partisan loyalties on voting decisions. Fewer Western voters now approach elections with fixed party predispositions based either on social characteristics or early-learned partisan ties. It is not that voters lack partisan predispositions, but the nature of these predispositions is shifting from *strong ties* (group and party attachments) to *weak ties* (issues and perceptions of party performance). Much like the findings of American or British electorate research, German political developments have weakened the traditional bases of partisan support without producing new, enduring bases of support that might revitalise the party system (see, e.g., Wattenberg, 1990; Rose and McAllister, 1986). Indeed, it is the lack of a new stable alignment that appears to be the most distinctive feature of contemporary party systems (Dalton *et al.*, 1984; Franklin *et al.*, 1992).

Citizens in the five new Länder, of course, have a very different electoral history. Rather than an erosion of previous social and partisan ties, the Eastern electorate is still learning about democratic politics and the rough-and-tumble life of partisan campaigns. Easterners understandably begin this experience with weaker party ties and less certainty about the general structure of political competition. One factor to watch is how quickly they adapt to the political structures of the West, or whether they remain only weakly tied to the party system.

The modest impact of long-term determinants of party choice for both Western and Eastern voters is likely to strengthen the role that the public's policy preferences play within the German electoral process. Although most voters will still habitually support a preferred party, the tentativeness of these bonds will increase the potential that a particular issue or election campaign may sway their voting choice, at least temporarily. More and more, party issue positions and political images will influence voter choices, as a substantial group of floating voters reacts to the immediate political stimuli of the election campaign. There is even some evidence that candidate images are playing a growing role in voters' decision-making. This shift toward issue-based voting behaviour is likely to make policy considerations a more important aspect of elections while injecting considerable fluidity into electoral politics – at least until (if ever) a new stable group basis of party support forms.

A second implication of our findings concerns the pattern of similarity between Western and Eastern Germans. The East German government spent forty years attempting to create a new socialist personality in the East, using the tools of political education with great force. If this was the GDR's goal, it apparently failed. The basic opinion profile of the two electorates displays more similarity than we would have expected given the divergent courses of the two German nations since 1945. Although there are sharp differences in East–West opinions toward the unification process and other specific policy beliefs, there is a broad overlap in their basic social and political values. Willy Brandt may have been correct when he suggested as soon as the Wall fell that the two Germanies shared a common bond and could grow together. At the least, the new Germany begins with a basis of commonality among its citizens, rather than sharply different political norms.

In summary, the patterns discussed here do not lend themselves to a simple prediction of the future of the German party system. An already complex situation in the 1980s has become even more complex in the early 1990s. It appears that electoral politics will be characterised by continued diversity in voting patterns. A system of frozen social cleavages and stable party alignments is less likely to develop in a society where voters are sophisticated, political interests are diverse, and individual choice is given greater latitude. Even the new political conflicts that are competing for the public's attention seem destined to create additional sources of partisan change rather than recreating the stable electoral structure of the past. This diversity and fluidity may, in fact, constitute the major new development for German electoral politics and the contemporary electoral politics of other advanced industrial societies.

Note

This research was partially supported by a grant from the Center for German and European Studies, University of California, Berkeley. The survey data utilised in this chapter were made available by the Inter-university Consortium for Political and Social Research (ICPSR) in Ann Arbor, the Zentralarchiv für empirische Sozialforschung in Cologne, and the Forschungsgruppe Wahlen in Mannheim. Neither the archives nor the original collectors of the data bear any responsibility for the analyses presented here.

4

The 'New' Party System

GORDON SMITH

Stability versus Change

One of the puzzling features of the German party system is its apparent resistance to change despite indications – and frequent forecasts – that change is imminent. The static character of the party system is evident in two respects. One is the composition of the party system and the relative strength of the component parties within it. Thus, prior to unification, the only new party to win federal representation since the early 1950s had been the Greens in 1983, and until then there had been a three-party system (CDU/CSU, SPD and FDP) since 1961. Although the fortunes of the three parties fluctuated over the years, there was no decisive trend: in 1987 the CDU/CSU share of the vote was 44.3 per cent, as compared with 45.3 per cent in 1961, and for the same years the SPD's share was 37.0 and 36.2 per cent respectively.

The static quality of the party system is evident in a second respect, namely the way in which it functions (that is, how governing coalitions are formed) – which is a good guide both to the nature of party interaction and to the degree of policy distance (that is, the compatibility of the parties). In fact, the pattern of coalition formation since 1969 has been unchanging: the alternation in office of the SPD and the CDU/CSU was brought about by the switch of the FDP from the SPD to the CDU/CSU in 1982, and this coalition of the Free Democrats and Christian Democrats remained in power after the all-German election of December 1990.

Yet in spite of this record of stability, there have been good reasons for believing that however 'frozen' the German party system had been in the past, it was becoming more vulnerable to change than at first sight appears. During the 1980s there were several unsettling factors. One was the rise of the Greens. In electoral terms their impact proved to be relatively modest, but their influence went much further: they were seen as the harbinger of the 'New Politics' which, in promoting postmaterialist values and new forms of political action, posed a potent threat to the established parties, especially in their attraction for younger voters. There was also more general evidence of electoral change in the sense that voters were no longer prepared to identify themselves so strongly with individual parties, so that the potential for electoral volatility was increasing. In the 1980s, too, the major parties experienced declining party member- ship and a loss of standing with the public. Both the CDU and the SPD were beset by financial and other scandals, and they contributed to a widespread *Parteiverdrossenheit*, a 'disenchantment' with party politics.

None of these factors, however, was to prove decisive in upsetting the party system. But even more remarkable was the resilience of the existing system in both structure and format in face of the chal- lenge of German unification. Far from the party system being thrown into the melting-pot, superficially there was little change at all. In the 1987 federal election the three main parties (CDU/CSU, SPD and FDP) totalled 90.4 per cent of the vote; in the 1990 federal election their aggregate share was 88.3 per cent. This was a minimal decline considering that in 1990 several 'indigenous' East German parties were also in contention, and it is all the more striking bearing in mind the addition of a large, new and relatively 'untried' electorate (about a fifth of the whole) which had suddenly been grafted onto a competitive party system.

Despite the impression that unification has left the party system largely unaffected, it would be mistaken to conclude that it is immu- table. Thus – as will be discussed later – if the gradual electoral trend against the two major parties continues, the way will be open for substantial change, not just in the number of parties, but an alteration of the whole balance of the party system. Such a develop- ment need not be destabilising, and a future pattern could be one of 'diffused multipartism'. Moreover, a form of diffusion may already be affecting the cohesion of individual parties, a development that arises from the territorial dimension of the party system. The enlargement of the Federal Republic, and with it the greater diffi- culty of reconciling the interests of the Länder, puts added strains on the federal parties. However, before examining these possibilities, we should first look at the development of the party system up to and including the December 1990 election.

The Party System before Unification

Throughout the life of the Federal Republic, the dominance of a particular *kind* of party – *Volkspartei* or people's party – has been a defining feature of the party system. The central characteristics of such parties and the consequences for the party system can be summarised as follows:

1. The principal parties (CDU and SPD) have a moderate, pragmatic outlook and minimise their ideological differences.
2. The *Volkspartei* has a broad electoral appeal, and its strongly integrative nature makes it difficult for parties with an ideological or sectional basis to compete.
3. Political strategies and electoral competition lead to a centripetal party system, rather than a polarising one.
4. The dominant position of the CDU and SPD gives rise to periodic alternation in government. In German circumstances, however, this alternation has been imperfect, and – because of the continuing presence of the small FDP – it could be described as a 'frustrated' two-party system.

The evolution towards a *Volkspartei*-dominated system took place rapidly in the 1950s largely because of the success of Christian democracy being able to make a broad interdenominational and interclass appeal, relying on an ethos of social responsibility coupled with a commitment to the market economy – the 'social market economy'. With the adoption of its Godesberg Programme in 1959, the SPD abandoned its socialist doctrine and adopted the *Volkspartei* label. In subsequent years, the SPD was able to exploit its new competitive position, closing the gap with the CDU and overhauling the latter in the 1972 election.

One inevitable consequence of the rise to dominance of the CDU and SPD was the squeezing-out of smaller parties, a process helped by the requirement of the electoral law stipulating that only parties with 5 per cent of the federal vote can win parliamentary representation. Yet, this apparently inexorable march towards a straight two-party system was never completed. What resulted was a stable three-party system from 1961 onwards – or, better, a 'two-and-a-half'-party one – until the addition of the Greens in 1983. The reasons for and the consequences of this 'third-party' element in German politics are essential to an understanding of contemporary developments and the working of the party system.

The survival of the Free Democrats (and by the same token its

TABLE 4.1 *Elections to the Bundestag, 1949–1990*

	1949	1953	1957	1961	1965	1969	1972	1976	1980	1983	1987	1990
Electorate (millions)	31.2	33.1	35.4	37.4	38.5	38.7	41.4	42.0	43.2	44.0	44.9	60.4
Turnout (%)	78.5	86.0	87.8	87.7	86.8	86.7	91.1	90.7	88.7	89.1	84.4	74.7
					% Zweitstimmen/list vote							
CDU/CSU	31.0	45.2	50.2	45.3	47.6	46.1	44.9	48.6	44.5	48.8	44.3	43.8
SPD	29.2	28.8	31.8	36.2	39.3	42.7	45.8	42.6	42.9	38.2	37.0	33.5
FDP	11.9	9.5	7.7	12.8	9.5	5.8	8.4	7.9	10.6	6.9	9.1	11.0
Greens	–	–	–	–	–	–	–	–	–	–	8.3	4.1
Others	27.8	16.5	10.3	5.7	3.5	5.5	0.9	0.9	0.5	0.5	1.2	5.0

Note:
For 1990, the vote for the West German Greens and the East German Greens/Bündnis '90 has been combined. See also Table 4.3, p 88, for the 1990 election.

inability to increase its vote much beyond 10 per cent at best) can be explained on several grounds:

- Like other Liberal parties in Western Europe, the FDP combines elements of traditional 'left' and 'right' orientation: the 'economic right' and the 'political left' (Smith, 1989). This combination may prevent the FDP building up large support, but it makes the party acceptable to the CDU on a range of market–economic issues, and to the SPD on the basis of common ground over social issues and civil rights.
- The FDP's broad coalition acceptability has enabled the party to serve for long periods in government, continuously since 1969 and in total longer than either the CDU or SPD. This governing presence gives the party a strong national profile and compensates for the FDP's usually weaker standing in the Länder and low party membership. For example, the fact that Hans-Dietrich Genscher was foreign minister from 1974 until 1992 was one of the FDP's greatest assets.
- The electoral system, which gives voters the opportunity for 'ticket-splitting' (giving the first/constituency vote to one party and the second/party list vote to another), benefits the FDP for two reasons. One is that voters may give their 'first' vote to the party of their first choice and the 'second' vote to the FDP – and be ignorant of the fact that the 'second' vote is actually decisive in determining the parties' allocation of Bundestag seats. The other reason is the tendency of many voters to vote for the *existing coalition* rather than for the majority party in it, possibly as a way of checking the larger party or even 'punishing' it – without going to the extreme of voting for the opposing major party; it is a qualified form of 'opposition from within'. In other words, the FDP depends to an important degree on 'loaned' votes (*Leihstimmen*). But they are 'on loan' and not a core of reliable support. This phenomenon also helps to account for the longevity of coalitions: the FDP risks losing heavily if the party defaults on its coalition partner.

The effect of the FDP on the functioning of the party system has been profound. Its positioning 'between' the CDU and SPD has given it a pivotal role in determining coalition composition, and, because of its indispensability to the major party, gives the FDP an influence on government.policy and share of ministerial posts out of all proportion to the party's size. Inevitably, in addition to the centre-leaving inclination of a *Volkspartei*, the FDP has been able to impose a 'centripetal bind' on the party system. The combined effect of the two elements helps explain the cautious, compromise–consensual style of German policy-making.

These characteristics of the FDP and the party system have been well in evidence during the whole period since 1969. The initial SPD-FDP coalition formed in 1969 reflected a move within the FDP against its previously dominant economic–conservative wing and towards social and political reform. The two parties were united in support of Brandt's Ostpolitik and for the FDP it signified a switch from the nationalist tendencies of right-wing liberals. Nonetheless, the FDP's belief in market liberalism and fiscal prudence (against increasing government spending, the public debt and taxation) ran counter to the more collective and interventionist orientation of the SPD. What cemented the coalition for so long was the presence of Chancellor Helmut Schmidt, who succeeded Brandt in 1974. Schmidt's undoubted managerial ability was well suited to cope with the economic shocks of the oil prices crises, and to a large extent his outlook on economic affairs corresponded with that of the FDP. But the break eventually came in 1982, when the chancellor and the SPD refused to meet demands for retrenchment demanded by the FDP, from its 'economic' wing, then in the ascendant.

Nevertheless, the FDP paid a price for its defection to the CDU: the party was internally divided and its vote slumped in the 1983 election to 6.9 per cent compared with 10.6 per cent in 1980; that the FDP cleared the 5 per cent hurdle at all was certainly due to 'rescue' votes coming from the CDU side. Yet, having made the break, the FDP had no problem in adjusting to the new coalition, especially under Chancellor Kohl, with his promise of taking a new direction or 'turnabout' (*die Wende*) in a range of economic and social policies. On this level the coalition proved to be highly durable and, with the CDU's acceptance of the outcome of the previous coalition's Ostpolitik together with the fact that Genscher was given a largely free hand as foreign minister, there was no profound disagreement. The only cause for coalition tension was the intense rivalry and hostility between the FDP and the quasi-independent, sister party of the CDU – the Christian-Social Union (CSU) in Bavaria. The CSU, with roots in clerical conservatism, strong on 'law and order', and hostile to the libertarian and secular traditions of liberalism, would dearly have liked to have seen the FDP disappear under the 5 per cent barrier, for the CSU would then have had greater influence on government policy – and a greater share of ministerial positions. For its part, the FDP rather benefited from the dissension, since it allowed the party a safe way of practising 'opposition from within' without coming into direct conflict with the CDU.

The neat, triangular pattern of coalition politics in the three-party system (Pappi, 1984) was threatened – but not broken – by the arrival of the Greens on the federal stage in 1983. Their modest share of the vote (5.6 per cent) gives little indication of their impact on the established parties and their potential completely to reshape the structure and functioning of the party system. The Greens, in combining the 'New Politics' (postmaterialist values, anti-establishment, unconventional political action) with a left-radicalism that gave a haven for the 'homeless' radical left, estranged from the moderate SPD, posed a difficult problem for SPD strategists. On the one hand, they saw the possibility of a new alignment on the left, for such a formation would enable the party to promote policies it could not implement if it continued to be beholden to the FDP. On the other hand, the Greens were a threat to the SPD: any increase in Green support would come predominantly from the SPD and primarily from younger voters whom the SPD could ill-afford to lose. Moreover, Green policies on the economy (anti-growth) were quite at odds with the 'old politics' of the traditional, unionist wing of the SPD. Added to these doubts was the unpredictability of the Greens: they were a disruptive force in politics, and could they be relied upon to stick to coalition agreements? The doubts were later to be confirmed by experience in the Länder: early experiments in 'red–green' government failed (in Hesse, 1987; in Berlin, 1989).

For the FDP, the prospect of a federal line-up of the SPD and Greens on one side and the CDU and FDP on the other, a two-bloc party system, was not at all to its liking. The FDP would lose its pivotal power and could even become a virtual client party of the CDU. However, even though the Greens improved their showing in 1987 (to 8.3 per cent) the actual working of the party system was unaffected. More searching tests of its resilience were to come in a unified Germany.

Transition to a Democratic System in the GDR

If one were to judge solely by the number of parties represented in the people's assembly (Volkskammer) of the former GDR, there had been a flourishing multiparty system in existence ever since the republic was set up in 1949. Appearances were, however, deceptive: only those parties that were prepared to accept the undisputed leadership of the Communist regime were allowed to function, and the decisions of the ruling Socialist Unity Party (SED) were not open to question. The Volkskammer served merely as a democratic figleaf, and was used as a convenient platform to demonstrate the unity of the people. Elections to the Volkskammer were non-competitive; instead, voters were presented with a single list of all the parties as a single 'block' which they were encouraged to endorse. The actual distribution of seats among these parties was already fixed beforehand, and the SED and its close allies were allocated the lion's share.

This 'block' party system was a peculiar amalgam. The SED itself was a product of a forced merger in 1946 of the old SPD with the much weaker KPD and was pushed through as a means of ensuring Communist dominance – from the outset the SED proved to be a hardline Marxist–Leninist party. Other parties in the block, at least to begin with, had better democratic credentials – the CDU and the Liberals (LDPD) – but they were soon turned into compliant partners, and their office holders enjoyed the benefits of quasi-official status. Other parties, such as the National Democratic Party (NDPD) and the Farmers' Party (DBP) were simply set up as a way of channelling particular sections of the population into the common fold.

Discontent with the obvious 'fixing' of the results for the local elections in May 1989 – the block parties won 'only' 98.85 per cent of the vote, their lowest share in the history of the GDR – was an early prelude to the events later in the year and the 'peaceful revolution' beginning in October. Suddenly, democratic opposition to the crumbling power of the Communists was legalised, and the immediate response was the appearance of a multiplicity of new parties and citizens' groups. The mushroom growth of political organisations spanned the whole party spectrum, and were in addition to the existing block parties which were now eager to show their democratic aspirations. From this welter of political activity, a nascent party system began to take shape. Its basis was the 'Round Table', an ad hoc device which gave a structure for dialogue and the negotiation between the SED and other block parties sitting as one group and the various opposition parties. What could not be too long delayed – in view of the ever-growing numbers leaving the GDR for West Germany, a flow which threatened to become unstoppable – was a free election, to be held in March 1990. It was in the course of the campaign and the result that the real pattern of political forces properly crystallised.

The fact that no fewer than 24 parties, organisations and alliances contested the March election gives some idea of the variety involved. Given the difficulty of finding an adequate way of classifying them, little is gained by displaying them on a conventional left–right axis. A convenient way of grouping into three categories, roughly according to the origins of their formation, gives an indication of party attitudes towards unification.

Parallel and 'Imported' Parties

This label refers to parties that had close historical ties with those in West Germany or were set up in the GDR based on a West German counterpart. The list includes the CDU, a former block party, and the DSU (German Social Union) modelled on the Bavarian CSU. The 'resurrected' SPD, and the FDP (initially three liberal parties, one of which was the former block member) were the others.

Indigenous/New Parties

This group has numerous representatives. Most important were the citizens' movements which sprang up in the early phases of the revolutionary period and favoured a 'third way' – neither the West German model nor that of the old GDR. The prominent movements taking this line were Neues Forum and Demokratie Jetzt which in alliance contested the March election as Bündnis '90. The Greens/Womens' List had obvious affinities with the West German Greens, but since those in East Germany strenuously insisted on their independence, reciprocated from the West German side, they are best treated as distinctive. Of the remainder – which all proved to be quite ephemeral – only the conservative Demokratischer Aufbruch (DA) requires mention, but the DA was soon to join the 'Alliance for Germany' (with the CSU and DSU) and later merged with the CDU).

Indigenous/Old Parties

These had no true West German counterparts and were the former block parties. The only important one was the old SED which changed its name to the Party of Democratic Socialism (PDS). Also in this category are the NDPD and the Democratic Farmers' Party (DBP).

The outcome of the March election was hailed as a 'vote for unification', since the three parties in the 'Alliance for Germany', principally the CDU, took almost 48 per cent of the vote. If the vote for the SPD is added, together with that for the Liberals, around 75 per cent of those voting could be regarded as identifying themselves with the Federal Republic (see Table 4.2). This analysis needs some qualification, especially in respect of the 'when' and 'how' of unification. Thus, the SPD called for a slower process and wanted a new

constitution for the whole of Germany rather than simple absorption
into the Federal Republic – that is, by means of Article 146 of the
Basic Law and not Article 23.

TABLE 4.2   *Elections to the Volkskammer, March 1990*

	%
1. Christian Democratic Union (CDU)	40.8
German Social Union (DSU)	6.3
Demokratischer Aufbruch	0.9
(Total 'Alliance for Germany')	(48.0)
Social Democratic Party (SPD)	21.9
Free Democratic Union	5.3
2. Greens/Women's List	2.0
Bündis '90 (New Forum)	2.9
3. PDS (Party for Democratic Socialism)	16.4
DBP (Farmers)	2.2
NDPD (National Democratic Party)	0.4
Others	0.8

Electorate 12.4 million; turnout 93.2 per cent

What prevented a virtual clean sweep on the part of the West
German-related parties was the surprising resilience shown by the
PDS with 16 per cent support. Partly this survival was thanks to the
arrival of a new cadre of leaders and the new image the former SED
was projecting, but it was also an indication of the large number of
beneficiaries under the old regime, party functionaries and others,
who feared for their future in a united Germany. Apart from the
PDS, ony the Greens and Bündis '90 looked likely to have any kind
of future.

In retrospect, it may be thought that – if the West German parties
had been less concerned (or less able) – to intervene so directly and
so massively in the run-up to the election, then the party landscape
might have taken a radically different appearance. That may well
not have benefited the PDS, but could have worked more to the
advantage of the citizens' movements and parties in our third group.
But they laboured under the handicap of shortage of time, few
resources and little political experience. Yet, even so, it is doubtful
whether the trend would have been much different: the popular call
for 'Unity Now!' was an irresistible invitation for a takeover by the
West German parties. Subsequent to the election, the SED/PDS-led
government was replaced by a coalition of the 'parallel' parties of
the first group, and it was naturally dominated by the CDU, with

Lothar de Maizière as prime minister. It proved to be an unhappy combination, both the FDP and SPD eventually withdrawing from the government because of disagreement on the terms being negotiated with the Federal Republic, although in fact there was very little basis for the East German government to have a serious negotiating position, and the East German CDU still retained its popularity, winning control in four of the five newly-constituted Länder in elections held just after the unification (see 'The Parties in the Länder' below).

The All-German Election of December 1990

In principle the sudden acquisition of several million new voters could have been expected to have a destabilising effect on any party system, or at least to signal a fundamental restructuring. Yet in the German case the overall impression is that unification made remarkably little difference to the pattern of party representation: the CDU–FDP coalition was comfortably confirmed in office, the SPD continued to trail in opposition, and the smaller parties made little impact. Although the dominant issue of German unification has to be considered as the decisive factor in apparently reinforcing the static nature of the party system, it is important to appreciate the various ways in which the influence of the issue was transmitted through the individual parties.

Above all else, the contrast between the attitudes of the SPD and the CDU towards the prospect of German unity is central to any explanation. The contrast had its origins in the different perspectives the two parties had developed during the course of the 1970s and 1980s. For its part, the SPD had not only largely abandoned unification as a practical goal, but more importantly perhaps even its desirability, since it came increasingly to regard the permanent existence of two German states as itself a valuable contribution to European stability. The CDU, however, followed a different course. On one level it came to accept the outcome of Brandt's Ostpolitik and was prepared to work for a normalisation of relationships between the two states, but on another level the CDU made efforts to keep the 'national idea' alive and refused to abandon unification as the ultimate aim. In effect, the CDU pursued a 'double strategy' (Clemens, 1989a), with the result that, once the collapse of the GDR looked like coming about, Kohl and the CDU were ideally placed to exploit the cause of unification.

The SPD was wrong-footed on the issue, and it was additionally handicapped by the choice it made in nominating Oskar Lafontaine as the party's chancellor candidate. Lafontaine would have been an attractive person for the party if unification had not come onto the agenda, since on other issues – the environment, defence and the economy – he was in a position to give the SPD a more radical image, essential if the expected challenge from the Greens was to be countered. Yet it soon became evident that Lafontaine had little personal sympathy with the cause of unification, and since the issue could not be dodged, he concentrated his attack on the costs to be met in bringing the two economic and social systems together, and attacked the government for trying to minimise the huge burden that West Germany would have to shoulder. In taking this negative position, Lafontaine became a guaranteed vote-loser in East Germany, and at that stage the West German electorate was still inclined to take the CDU's line on trust– that nobody would be worse off as a consequence of unification. The outcome for the SPD was disastrous: with only 33.5 per cent of the vote in December 1990, it was the party's worst showing since the 1950s (see Table 4.3).

What additionally told against the SPD was the timing of the election, since if it had been held later, during 1991, some of the negative consequences would have become apparent – precisely that development the CDU wished to avoid by having the election out of the way as soon as possibe. That the SPD performed so poorly in East Germany (24.3 per cent) is scarcely surprising, especially when two other factors are taken into account. One is the competition offered by the PDS, which took some support that might otherwise have gone to the SPD. The second is that the SPD in East

TABLE 4.3   *Elections to the Bundestag, December 1990*

	West (%)		East (%)	Germany (%)		Seats
Turnout	78.6		74.7	77.8		
CDU	35.5	} 44.3	41.8	36.7	} 43.8	268
CSU	8.8		–	7.1		51
SPD	35.7		24.3	33.5		239
FDP	10.6		12.9	11.0		79
Greens (West)	4.8		0.1	3.9		0
Bündnis '90/Greens (East)	–		6.0	1.2		8
PDS	0.3		11.1	2.4		17
Republicans	2.3		1.3	2.1		0
NPD	0.3		0.0	0.3		0
DSU	–		1.0	0.2		0

Germany had to be built up from scratch, unlike the CDU which quickly took advantage of the ready-made organisational framework and large membership of its block forerunner.

The CDU's good fortunes were the obverse of the SPD's misfortunes: the wholehearted welcome to unification coupled with a strategy to delay answering the question 'Who pays, and how much?' until the (early) election had been held. Yet despite Kohl's high profile and the weakness of the SPD, the result of the election – measured by voting support – was hardly a sweeping victory for the CDU or an acclamation in favour of Helmut Kohl. The CDU/CSU's share, at 43.8 per cent, was marginally the party's worst showing since 1949, and there was no marked difference in performance in the two parts of Germany (44.3 per cent in West Germany; 42.8 per cent in East Germany, including the DSU).

Three reasons can be advanced for this relatively disappointing outcome. One is that by the time of the December election the downside effects of the unification were becoming clear: in East Germany, the costs to be paid in terms of unemployment and higher prices were already becoming apparent; in West Germany, it was commonly accepted that the tax burden would rise – although the SPD did not win any credit for its warnings. A second reason was the sharp decline in voter turnout, especially in East Germany, which may have adversely affected the CDU. Thus, in the March 1990 election participation reached the dizzy height of 93.2 per cent, but fell to 74.7 per cent in December. In March, the CDU-related parties in the 'Alliance for Germany' won almost an absolute majority, so that the fall in December can partly be ascribed to abstentions – the voters regarding a CDU victory as a foregone conclusion or else because of simple 'election weariness' – the federal election followed both the March election in East Germany and the subsequent October Land elections. The third reason – a constant factor in German politics – was the role played by the FDP.

There is no doubt that the FDP was the clear winner of the election in both parts of Germany. The performance of the Liberals in the East German March election was modest, with only just over 5 per cent, but rose to 12.9 per cent in December. The gains made can be partly attributed to the 'coalition effect', already noted, which benefited the FDP as the junior partner. But the FDP also managed to gain a head start on other parties in opting for an early fusion of the Liberal parties in East and West Germany, bringing with it the huge membership of the old block party – quite dwarfing the modest West German figure. But of decisive importance was the person of Hans-Dietrich Genscher, since he originally came from East Germany, and that fact, together with his high standing in East Germany, contributed to the FDP's success.

The FDP, because of its coalition linkages, is in a qualitatively different position from the other small parties. Very little now remains of the plethora of new parties that contested the March election in East Germany. For that election, the method of proportional representation used had been extraordinarily generous: a party needed to win only 0.27 per cent of the vote to be awarded a seat. For the all-German election, it was originally intended to make the 5 per cent clause apply over the whole country (that is, a party would have to win 5 per cent of the total national vote to gain representation). However, following a ruling by the Federal Constitutional Court (on an action brought by the PDS) the barrier was made less formidable in stipulating that a party need obtain only 5 per cent in either East or West Germany. The PDS was 'saved' by the change, since although it managed to win a modest 11.1 per cent in East Germany, over the Federal Republic as a whole it recorded only 2.4 per cent. This change also rescued the East German 'Alliance '90/Greens' which scored 6.0 per cent in East Germany. Ironically, the West German Greens – lukewarm to unification and hostile to a takeover by the Federal Republic – decided against forming a united party before the election, with the result that their vote of just 4.8 per cent in West Germany led to their exclusion from the Bundestag.

There is little likelihood that the modified 5 per cent clause will be retained for future federal elections. If that is the case, then the PDS must have an uncertain future, at least at federal level. For the Greens, however, the 1990 election gives a less reliable guide, since the party's fall in support (from 8.3 per cent in 1987) is attributable to the perceived irrelevance of the particular Green concerns in the context of the overriding unification issue; but it does not necessarily indicate a long-term decline in the party's attractions.

The Party System in the Länder

One notable effect of the German unification has been to increase the number of constituent Länder from the previous 10 to 16, with the addition of the five East German Länder and the formation of the whole of Berlin as a new city-state. An immediate consequence has been to complicate considerably the relationships between the federal government and the Länder. Partly this change is due to the greater variation in regional interests which are now given expression, but partly, too, it results from the wide disjunction that has become apparent between the political complexion of the federal government on the one side and the predominant colouring of the individual Land governments on the other. Both elements of this complexity and imbalance are reflected in the Bundesrat, and for this reason the party system in the Länder has to be treated as a second dimension of the party system in addition to the federal level (see also Chapter 6).

Although there is no necessary correspondence between the predominance of one party or coalition in federal government and party control in the individual Länder, in fact periods of sharp divergence have been few – the major exception was during the time of the SPD–FDP coalition, 1969–82, when the CDU came to have control of a majority of the Länder and thus also of the Bundesrat. The result was a kind of 'split' party system which disappeared when the CDU regained control of the federal government in 1982. What, however, occurred from 1990 onwards was a re-emergence of the 'split', taking shape over three stages: (1) prior to unification; (2) enlargement through unification; (3) post-unification. Taking these stages in turn, we can observe how party fortunes have fluctuated, and with what effect.

Changes Prior to Unification

For most of the life of the Federal Republic, the CDU, whether or not in control of federal government, had been able to control a voting majority in the Bundesrat. But by the mid-1980s this superiority was lost, especially when in 1985 the SPD wrested control of the Saarland from the CDU which the latter had governed since the early 1960s. However, the period was also marked by unstable coalitions in some Länder (Hesse and Hamburg) where the presence of the Greens made it difficult for the SPD to fashion stable alliances. A temporary consolidation of the SPD's position came early in 1990 when the party ousted the CDU–FDP coalition in Lower Saxony, besides securing absolute majorities in North Rhine–Westphalia and the Saarland. For a while, until unification, the SPD had a slight majority in the Bundesrat.

Enlargement Through Unification

Elections in the five new East German Länder were held in October 1990 shortly after unification. In four (Saxony–Anhalt, Thuringia, Mecklenburg–West Pomerania and Saxony) the CDU won control, with the SPD succeeding only in Brandenburg and forming a coalition with the FDP and B'90. The result of the first all-Berlin election, held along with the federal election in December, further strengthened the position of the CDU, although there it was necessary to form a coalition with the SPD. Through enlargement, it seemed that the CDU was well positioned to control a majority in the Bundesrat.

Post-unification Developments

Two elections held in the first half of 1991 reinforced what was apparently an underlying trend in favour of the SPD, in marked contrast to the party's weak federal showing. In January 1991 the CDU lost Hesse to the SPD (in coalition with the Greens), and in April the SPD won control of the Rhineland–Palatinate which the CDU had ruled for the previous 45 years. In addition, the June 1991 election in Hamburg gave the SPD an overall majority. These victories meant that for a short while the SPD had a clear majority in the Bundesrat. Although far short of a two-thirds majority which would enable it to exercise an effective veto over all the federal government's legislation, it was sufficient to give the SPD a strong bargaining position, especially in the conciliation committee (*Vermittlungsausschuss*) in which compromises between the Bundestag and Bundesrat have to be found. Yet, the September 1991 election in Bremen showed that the SPD, too, was vulnerable: the immigration issue dominated the election, causing the SPD heavy losses and forcing the party into a so-called 'traffic-light' coalition with the FDP and Greens.

The size of the Bundesrat and the apportionment of votes among the Länder changed considerably as a result of unification, with the largest Länder being given a greater share. Table 4.4 shows the composition of the Länder governments (as in January 1992) and also indicates whether their voting power is controlled by the parties in federal coalition or by opposition parties. In some cases coalitions are 'mixed', so that these Bundesrat votes – especially on issues of federal significance – cannot be counted as under the control of either side. Thus, the coalition pact may specify that in cases of disagreement between the parties over a particular issue, the Bundesrat delegation will be required to abstain from voting.

The present pattern of party control and the party system in the Länder is substantially different from that existing in former years. The salient features can be summarised as follows:

1. The CDU/CSU now (April 1992) have outright control only in one western Land, namely Bavaria (CSU). The main strength of the CDU is thus in the new Länder. Yet, the CDU's success in

TABLE 4.4 *Government and opposition in Bundesrat and Länder*

Land	Government	Opposition	'Mixed'	Governing parties
Saxony–Anhalt	4			CDU/FDP
Thuringia	4			CDU/FDP
Mecklenburg-West Pomerania	3			CDU/FDP
Brandenburg			4	SPD/FDP/B'90
Saxony	4			CDU
Berlin			4	CDU/SPD
Schleswig-Holstein		4		SPD
Hamburg		3		SPD
Bremen			3	SPD/FDP/Gr.
Lower Saxony		6		SPD/Gr.
North Rhine–Westphalia		6		SPD
Hesse		4		SPD/Gr.
Rhineland–Palatinate			4	SPD/FDP
Saarland		3		SPD
Baden–Württemberg			6	CDU/SPD
Bavaria	6			CSU
	21	26	21	

Note: The composition of Land governments as in May 1992.

Total = 68 Votes
Allocation of votes:
  million/votes
Less than 2 = 3
Over   2 = 4
Over   6 = 5
Over   7 = 6

the east was largely due to the 'unification bonus'. If that proves to be of transitory value, the CDU would be in danger of being relegated to a minority status, irrespective of its federal position.

2. Historically, the shifting nature of coalitions in some Länder, where these no longer corresponded to the federal line-up, has been interpreted as foreshadowing a change in coalition at the federal level. Thus, there are now three coalitions linking the SPD and FDP (Brandenburg, Bremen, Rhineland–Palatinate) which is an indication of this kind, and three (Saxony–Anhalt, Thuringia and Mecklenburg) that link the CDU with the FDP.

3. Although in the past coalitions between the SPD and the Greens have proved to be unstable, the ones presently in place appear to be more durable (Bremen, Lower Saxony and Hesse), because the Greens as a result of their defeat in the 1990 federal election have the incentive to behave more 'responsibly' in the Länder. This development has implications for a possible federal alignment of the two parties.

4. The party system has become far more complex. Not only is there the basic division between government and opposition parties, the extent of 'mixed' coalitions makes the process of decision-making in the Bundesrat less predictable and subject to heavy compromise. Two other divisions have to be taken into account: the interests of the new versus the old Länder, and the richer versus the poorer ones. To a large extent, this amounts to a single division. But the differences between the more and less affluent Western Länder are also of significance (see Chapter 6).

Party Perspectives and Prospects

With a fresh federal election not due until some date in 1994, there is ample time for the party system to 'settle down' and for the impact of unification to be absorbed by the parties. The balance of the parties following the all-German election and developments of the party system in the Länder do, however, set the parameters within which the individual parties have to fashion their strategies. The ensuing period will determine whether the smaller parties have a chance of survival and whether the established ones can satisfactorily resolve no fewer than four *interlinked* questions: party leadership and succession; electoral strategies; policy platform and ideological direction; coalition possibilities.

The CDU/CSU

For the CDU the interconnection of the various questions is secured, even dominated by, the nature of the party's leadership: Helmut Kohl, chancellor since 1982 and party chairman since 1973, rivals Adenauer's record for political longevity (chancellor from 1949 to 1963). Yet the parallel could be taken further: Adenauer's legacy to the CDU was to leave it bereft of a self-confident leadership cadre and with no clear sense of direction. Kohl's leadership, and especially his tight control over party organisation, has made the question of leadership succession a difficult one for the party to resolve. In the event, with a string of election victories (1983, 1987 and 1990), Kohl now appears quite capable of leading the party successfully into the next federal election. However, it should not be forgotten just how low his reputation had fallen prior to the boost to his fortunes through German unification, and his popularity may prove to have been a temporary respite.

As a *Volkspartei*, the CDU has consistently followed an electoral strategy designed to secure the electoral middle ground. Franz-Josef Strauss (CSU), as chancellor candidate in 1980, exceptionally, took the CDU/CSU on a right-wing course, and the experiment failed. Nonetheless, a section of the party's electorate does have right-wing sympathies, and the occasional threat from small right-wing parties is a warning against moving too near a liberal–centrist position. That was the case in the early part of 1989 when the right-wing Republicans suddenly began to rob the CDU of support. Kohl's reaction in removing the party's liberal-minded secretary-general, Heiner Geissler, followed by the opportune playing of the 'national card', temporarily staved off the Republican challenge. But the potential of right-wing or even extremist forces remains, as has become evident in reactions to the immigration issue – for instance, the upsurge in support for the extremist DVU (German People's Union) in the 1991 Bremen election, and in 1992 the Republicans in Baden-Württemberg.

In order to reconcile the two 'pulls' on the CDU – the moderation of the *Volkspartei* in one direction and the less compromising element of conservative nationalism in the other – the party requires an adept pragmatist, such as Kohl, to hold the party together and maintain its paramount position. What complicates the problem is the factor of 'coalition dependency', since the CDU (reliant as it is on the FDP) risks coalition tensions or even break-up unless the FDP is itself prepared to follow the same line. There are few difficulties in the area of economic and monetary policy, but acute ones when it comes to matters affecting civil rights – the question of controlling the influx of migrants and asylum-seekers is a case in point.

The CSU has always represented the mainstay of the conservative wing of Christian Democracy, but its influence on the party's direction is declining. This decline can be attributed in part to the demise of Strauss who over several decades used 'his' CSU to harry liberal tendencies in the CDU and to attack Kohl's 'incompetent' leadership. But even more serious for the CSU is its weakening position as a result of unification, restricted as the party is to its Bavarian stronghold. Its attempt to establish a partner party in East Germany proved a failure, since the DSU (German Social Union) secured just 1 per cent in the 1990 election (0.2 per cent overall). In the past, the CSU could count on up to 10 per cent of the West German vote. In 1990 its West German vote was 8.8 per cent, but only 7.1 per cent in Germany as a whole. This relative decline may appear to be marginal, but what really tells is the comparison with the FDP: the rivalry and antagonism between the two is shown within the coalition and for the share of ministerial posts. The CSU used to have the edge on the FDP, but the latter, through its success in East Germany and 11 per cent overall, has relegated the CSU to a minority position. One consequence could be that the German right, hitherto partially satisfied by the conservative brake supplied by the CSU, will look outside of the CDU/CSU.

The SPD

The problems of the CDU are those of success, but for the SPD they are ones of failure across the whole range of interlinked questions: weak and inappropriate leadership, absence of clear electoral strategy, a misdirected policy platform, and an indecisive attitude towards possible coalitions. These weaknesses were not all of the SPD's own making, and that is especially true in respect of coalition formation. On the one side, the FDP's coalition with the CDU since 1982 proved to be too securely based for the SPD to prise apart, and – on the other side – an attempt to build a federal alliance with the Greens would have made the SPD a hostage to fortune, not only because of the 'unreliability' of the Greens, but because the prospect of such a link-up would have cost the SPD some of its traditional support. Moreover, the arithmetic of forming a coalition did not add up to a majority in either direction. The SPD's rather pathetic and unrealistic aim of winning an absolute majority in 1987 (in fact, it won just 37 per cent) only underlined its hopeless governing aspirations, and its weakness was further emphasised in 1990 (33.5 per cent). Its basic orientation as a *Volkspartei* is directed to exercising or sharing governing power, but if this aim becomes unrealisable, then the *Volkspartei* has little to fall back upon, since it is difficult to make the fundamental switch to follow a strategy of 'opposition in principle'. That would entail a fundamental reappraisal of the party's basic programme which was certainly not evident in the SPD's *Grundsatzprogramm* formally adopted in December 1989, even though its gestation had preoccupied the party for several years.

Two streams of thinking run through the party; one, identified with the 'old left', has its roots in the traditions of working class social democracy, the trade unions and blue collar workers. The other, the 'new left', is associated with the changing social composition of the SPD – higher-educated, middle class, and white collar employees. This stream has absorbed some of the ideas associated with the 'New Politics' – that is, broadly, the priority given to postmaterial values such as the quality of life rather than an emphasis on economic growth. By the same token, the SPD appeals to two distinct electorates, and reconciling their differing interests presents the party with thorny problems in devising an effective electoral strategy. The kind of tension that can arise became evident over the vexed issue of asylum-seekers, with disastrous results for the SPD in the 1991 Bremen election: grass-roots support for the party slumped, largely because the leadership was unwilling to move away from its open-door policy and concern for minority rights, apparently regardless of the social tensions that resulted from the influx of asylum-seekers into cities such as Bremen ahd Hamburg.

These internal difficulties of the party have been given full expression by those who have occupied leadership positions, especially in the years following the toppling of Chancellor Schmidt in 1982. Indeed, the decline of Schmidt's authority within the SPD was largely caused by the rise of the 'New Politics' forces, exemplified by the peace movement, and Schmidt was a representative figure of the 'old left'. Johannes Rau, the failed chancellor candidate in 1987 and minister-president of North Rhine–Westphalia, is similarly to be counted in this category. But for the 1990 election the SPD chose to run Oskar Lafontaine, minister-president of the Saarland, as chancellor candidate; although a maverick personality in some respects, Lafontaine epitomises the younger, new-left generation in the party. Ironically, Lafontaine might have been more successful in 1987 and Rau in 1990 – in 1987 the new left would have given the SPD a more distinctive profile, but in 1990, with the issue of German unification crowding out all other issues from the campaign, a traditional candidate, such as Rau, would have been better able to show the SPD's 'national credentials' in a more positive light.

In the aftermath of the 1990 election defeat, the SPD faced the task of redefining its position in the new German society. The choice of Björn Engholm, minister-president of Schleswig–Holstein (both as the likely chancellor candidate and as party chairman), can be regarded as effecting a compromise between the party's two streams, since Engholm combines the attractions of representing the younger generation in the party, without at the same time having the polarising character of Lafontaine. It could be the case, too, that the SPD will recover lost ground, not so much through is own efforts in finding a workable electoral strategy, but rather in benefiting from problems encountered by the CDU, as already shown by Land elections in 1991/2. Yet, any success the party may enjoy 'by default' will not be a firm basis for a restoration of the SPD to a leading place in a future government.

The FDP

The FDP's role in securing unification in partnership with the CDU has resulted in the party gaining greater electoral security than possibly at any time in its previous history. Its strong representation in the Länder, together with the fact that it is now represented in the governments of 6 of the 16 Länder, means that the FDP no longer has to rely almost exclusively on its federal presence to bolster its hitherto shaky electoral hold.

One feature of the party's altered circumstances is the relative strength of the FDP in East Germany (12.9 per cent). For the future, much depends on what happens to CDU support in the new Länder as a consequence of the economic problems of unification; it is the FDP rather than the SPD that is likely to emerge as the principal beneficiary if voters there turn away from the CDU. As often proved to be the case in the past, and as previously noted, it has been the FDP as the junior party in coalition that benefits from a 'vote for the coalition' rather than the major party. Moreover, it is clear that – at least in popular perceptions – it is the CDU/CSU ministers who are regarded as bearing the prime responsibility for taking difficult or unpopular economic decisions.

Against these positive factors, there are negative ones to be taken into account. For many years, the Free Democrats have relied heavily on the presence of Hans-Dietrich Genscher as the party's most important federal asset. His significant role in the Ostpolitik, and especially in fostering good relations with the Soviet Union, gave the FDP a prominence it would not otherwise have had. Thus, Genscher's departure in May 1992, together with the fact that the path-breaking era in relationships with Eastern Europe has now come to an end, may both rob the FDP of its special claim for attention.

It may be the case that the FDP is not only able to hold on to its present electoral following but even improve its position. Yet, whilst this gives the party an assured place in the party system, it does not of itself guarantee that the FDP will be able to exercise greater power within the party system: failing a majority combination of the SPD with the Free Democrats, the latter have little alternative but to continue in coalition with the CDU, since the prospect of going into opposition is unwelcome – whenever the party has been out of government it has lost votes at the succeeding election. Thus, although the FDP may gain greater weight within a CDU-led coalition, it will be unable to use its ultimate weapon of defection from it. One possibility, not entirely to be dismissed as unrealistic, is a three-party alternative to a CDU government, namely, the SPD with both the FDP and the Greens. Yet this kind of combination (as in Brandenburg and Bremen) is unlikely to appeal to FDP voters on the federal level, since the implications of such a coalition would run directly counter to the economic liberalism strongly favoured by the party.

The Smaller Parties

Of the smaller parties, only the Greens appear able to retain a place in federal politics, despite being marginalised as a result of the 1990 election. The point about the Greens is that, unlike the FDP which in the past was almost totally dependent on having a federal presence in order to compensate for its weak support and organisation in the Länder, for the Greens the reverse is true: the party grew up from its bases in the Länder, contesting local issues.

It is also the case that it is precisely this Land basis of the Greens that has contributed to federal weakness, in the sense that the Länder parties have practised considerable autonomy – itself a principle on which the Greens were founded. To this feature has to be added the factionalism within the party at all levels, especially the division between the fundamentalist and realist wings of the party. The shock effect of the 1990 election made it an existential question for the party to show itself capable of working within the Land party system, with the result that the Greens have become 'coalitionable' as far as the SPD is concerned. That now applies in several of the Länder, but federally the SPD is unlikely to consider any alignment until the Greens clear the electoral threshold – and it is not in the SPD's electoral interests that they should.

In the past, the Greens were able to make headway because of their ability to put new issues onto the political agenda. Yet many of the issues – such as the environment and women's rights – have been taken up by the other parties. Much depends on the ability of the Greens to promote this agenda-setting function, but – following the ascendancy of the realists who wish to behave responsibly especially when in coalition – they may have forfeited one of their most effective mobilising strategies: to use direct and unconventional forms of political activity, often flouting the law in order to put their case across. These tactics proved attractive to younger voters, the claim to be an 'anti-party' party, but – in becoming increasingly conventional – the Greens will have to rely more on organisational skills to compete with other parties. Unfortunately, however, spontaneity rather than organisation has characterised the Greens: they would have to become a quite different kind of party.

The former East German Communists (PDS) have very little chance of survival federally, except in the unlikely event of the electoral law used in 1990 being retained in the future. Its federal-wide vote (2.4 per cent) as opposed to its share in East Germany alone (11.1 per cent) means that the PDS must either make significant advances in West Germany or somehow recover a following in East Germany. Neither eventuality is realistic. In the old Federal Republic, the German Communist Party (DKP) soldiered on for decades, but with minuscule support. Of course, that is not quite comparing like with like, and the new PDS with its attractive leader, Gregor Gysi may have some radical appeal, but to an extent the party will be in contention with the Greens and B'90: they are all in competition for the favours of a restricted pool of voters with radical sympathies. Only if economic conditions become worse in East Germany, and stay that way, will the new-look socialism attract disgruntled voters. A more realistic scenario is for the PDS to survive in a few eastern Länder; the more interesting question is whether or not its support will float off to the SPD.

One recurring problem is that of assessing the potential of right-wing extremism in Germany, which may be far larger than the numerous extremist parties that have come and gone since 1949 have been able to tap. The only one that looked at all likely to become a significant force was the NPD (National Democratic Party of Germany) when in 1969 it narrowly failed to enter the Bundestag with 4.3 per cent of the vote.   The extreme right has again become a significant force – and with effective leaders: Franz Schönhuber for the Republicans and Gerhard Frey for the German People's Union (DVU). The Republicans had early successes in Bavaria (1986), West Berlin (1989) and for the European Parliament election (1989). In the wave of enthusiasm for German unification, both were temporarily eclipsed at the 1990 federal election. But the upsurge in right-wing support became more pronounced in 1991 and 1992. In Bremen (September 1991) the DVU scored 6.2 per cent, and 6.3 per cent in Schleswig-Holstein (April 1992). The Republicans in Baden-Württemberg (April 1992) even became the third largest party, ahead of the FDP and the Greens, with 10.9 per cent. Both parties play on popular resentment against 'economic migrants' and the lack of decisive action by the established parties. The extreme right could extend its influence more widely in Germany. In particular, the new Länder may prove susceptible to right-wing propaganda, since the combination of economic hardship, social dislocation and pronounced anti-immigrant sentiments provides fertile ground for extremist parties to cultivate.

How New is the Party System?

Nothing in the foregoing account of the individual parties indicates a fundamental restructuring of the party system, certainly not in any way that would match the restructuring of Germany after 1990. What, however, has gradually become evident is that neither the CDU nor the SPD is likely to enjoy the high and secure levels of support that they did in the past. A long-term trend is evident in taking the development of their combined vote over the span of all the federal elections (see Table 4.5).

TABLE 4.5   *The decline in aggregate vote of CDU/CSU and SPD*

Election year	(%)
1972	90.7
1976	91.2 (peak vote)
1980	87.4
1983	87.0
1987	81.3
1990	77.3

If the process of electoral dealignment continues (see Chapter 3 in this volume), even if only to a moderate degree, then the resulting electoral volatility will add to the insecurity of the two major parties.

Even so, if there is a gradual erosion of the dominance of the *Volksparteien* – the most characteristic feature of the German party system – there is absolutely no indication of just how the party system is evolving. It is true that the Free Democrats now have a more secure anchorage, largely thanks to the increase in support from East Germany, but it has been far from a dramatic upturn. Nor is it evident that the FDP will be able to enhance its pivotal role in the party system by adding a few percentage points to its vote.

In the past, there have been signs that small/new/extremist parties could have an impact on the party system. Yet the record shows that they have made little difference: it is too early to speculate on how right-wing extremism could gain a foothold at a federal level in the new Germany, although the potential is present. At one time, the Greens represented an unknown quantity, but – since the shock of the 1990 election – they have become just one more orthodox party, certainly surviving, but scarcely representing a basic threat to the existing party system. It is something of a paradox that, on the one hand, the *Volkspartei* is held to be under increasing threat, yet on the other no convincing picture has emerged of what an alternative might be.

5

Government at the Centre

ROLAND STURM

The Absorption of the GDR

For East Germany unification meant the complete disappearance of its democratically elected Parliament, the Volkskammer. It also meant the step by step dismantling of its administrative and constitutional framework which had been built up over decades. The introduction of a federal system with the creation of democratically elected Länder parliaments was intended to fill the gap left by the demise of central government institutions in the eastern Länder. Government in this way moved geographically closer to the people, but at the same time moved further away, from Berlin to Bonn. More important, however, the special channels of interest representation of the East at the level of central government, which had given the East a voice as long as the possibility of bilateral negotiations between the governments of the old FRG and the GDR still existed, dried up. Unification thus meant that at the level of central government the political personnel of the East had to work as minorities in separate parliamentary parties, and in the constitutional framework of the old FRG. Immediately after unification in October 1990 144 MPs from the former GDR joined the Bundestag, delegated to the federal Parliament by the East German Volkskammer. In December 1990, 123 MPs out of a total of 662 were elected to represent what used to be East Germany.

On the one hand this situation is the logical consequence of national integration. On the other, it caused certain tensions. The formal incorporation of the political discourse in East Germany into a political and institutional framework with a successful record in West Germany was achieved within months. Partisan conflict was restructured along the lines drawn in Bonn, election campaigns were fought by West German professionals, and parliamentary parties organised East German MPs into the Bonn government–opposition rituals. So party political integration at the national level was well ahead of the actual degree of social and political unity achieved. With the exception of two smallish parties of GDR origin, the new MPs from Eastern Germany had difficulties in defining a role in Parliament for themselves and for their voters at home. Parliament itself did not institutionalise a committee or working group on East Germany, similar in nature, for example, to the Scottish committees at Westminster, which would have provided a forum for them.

The decision whether or not to adapt the structures of government at the centre to the challenges stemming from unification was left to the Bonn parliamentary parties and the political elite of the old FRG. Their perception of the process of governing was that in the West, parliamentary government had proved its superior qualities. In addition, immediately after unification there was a conviction in government circles that what remained to be solved in the process of unification were only temporary economic problems, restricted to the former GDR. This led to an underestimation of the political and administrative dimensions of unification and reduced the reactions of the government at the centre to incrementalism in the fields of both policies and of institutional reform. Central government remained on the defensive, reluctant to admit that the incremental changes unification had forced upon it added up to something more fundamental, namely a shaking up of old certainties not only in the East, but also – and this is of central importance – in the West.

Restructuring Government at the Centre?

Given the historic importance of German unification it might have been expected that the federal government would have been confronted with the question of how to reorganise and adjust to the new environment of a greater Germany. From the beginning it was uncontroversial that the Ministry for Inner-German Relations, which had mainly concentrated its work on the publication of state of the nation reports and on providing money for buying the freedom of political prisoners held in custody in the GDR, had become obsolete. Its civil servants were given new jobs in the Interior Ministry, whilst its internal administration was delegated to the new Health Ministry. It might have been assumed that the government would see a need for a new ministry (or new ministries) to cope with the problems of unification, and above all economic reconstruction in the East. The first Adenauer government had a Marhall Plan ministry (1949–53) and the second Adenauer government one on European Economic Cooperation (1953–7). Chencellor Kohl was, however, convinced that the traditional organisational framework of government sufficed.

This was underlined by the amount of energy and ingenuity he invested in restructuring his cabinet in a way which almost exclusively reflected the political dynamics of the old FRG. To satisfy all interests in his party, the CDU, and of his coalition partners the Bavarian CSU and the Liberals (FDP) he inflated the number of junior ministers to 34 (from the record number of 27). To raise the number of women in his cabinet (now in charge of four of the nineteen ministries) he subdivided the former Ministry for the Young, the Family, Women and Health into three. The new ministries for the Family and Pensioners, for Women and the Young, and for Health are each headed by a woman. The additional jobs at the junior ministerial level also helped the Chancellor to fine-tune the influence of his coalition partners, who got five (FDP) and four (CSU) cabinet seats. Ministerial appointments for East German politicians were made available for only three relatively minor positions. The two CDU politicians of East German origin who were regarded as having ministerial calibre were Günther Krause, who had managed the GDR's negotiations on the unity treaty, and Angela Merkel, who played the part of 'the woman from the East'. She was appointed Minister for Women and the Young, whereas Günther Krause was put in charge of the Transport department, the most important ministry of the three going to Easterners. The former chairman of the Liberals in East Germany inherited the relatively uninfluential Education and Science Ministry from his liberal predecessor Möllemann, who was promoted to the Economics Ministry.

The two highest representatives of the former GDR, both members of the Chancellor's party, were allowed to play only a minor role in the now united Germany. Efforts to elect the last Prime Minister of the GDR, Lothar de Maizière, into the office of Speaker of the Bundestag were given up, when severe doubts about his relationship with the GDR's secret police (Stasi) were raised. It would have been difficult to find enough support for him in parliament in any event, because the popular Speaker Rita Süssmuth declared her intention to stay on, and had already found strong cross-party support both because of her personality and because of the feeling that a woman should remain in this high and respected office. Lothar de Maizière was given party functions in the CDU as member of the party's leadership and as head of its programme commiteee. This was little more than a face-saving arrangement, and in September 1991 de Maizière resigned from this position, giving up both his seat in Parliament and the chairmanship of the Brandenburg CDU in the course of a quarrel with the Chancellor. On the surface this conflict was about strategy to prevent the erosion of the CDU's support in East Germany, but the fact that de Maizière's Stasi connection remained a grey issue, even used against him by members of his own party, played a major role.

The last head of state of the GDR and Speaker of the East German parliament, Sabine Bergmann-Pohl, lacked in the Chancellor's eyes ministerial calibre, but it seemed well-nigh impossible to send her into the political wilderness. The compromise found was a junior minister's post in the newly founded Health Ministry. What East German politicians began to feel about their role in cabinet surfaced when in mid-1991 Günther Krause had to defend himself against charges of corruption. He then expressed his suspicion that there was a conspiracy to get rid of East Germans in top positions, because of a more general assumption that to govern the East efficiently one needs West German personnel.

Central to all these cabinet arrangements remained Chancellor Kohl. He was elected into office by Parliament with 58.7 per cent of the votes cast, his best-ever result. In his cabinet there are only three ministers capable of mounting a serious challenge to his policy decisions. One was Hans-Dietrich Genscher, the Liberal Foreign Minister and *éminence grise* of the larger coalition partner, the FDP. Helmut Kohl had a good working relationship with Genscher based on the fact that he avoided trespassing on Genscher's preserves, much to the dislike of the CSU. The second cabinet heavyweight is Theo Waigel, party chairman of the coalition partner CSU and Finance Minister. Waigel is in the uncomfortable position of having to defend the financial consequences of all costly cabinet decisions on German unity without having enough influence to control the decision-making process. In contrast to his still much admired predecessor as party chairman, Franz-Josef Strauss, he is a cabinet minister under cabinet discipline, and finds it much harder than Strauss to play the double role of publicity-seeking internal critic and loyal supporter of Helmut Kohl, a role which so well suits the Bavarian preference for autonomy from central government. The third cabinet minister with special standing is Wolfgang Schäuble of the CDU, an efficient cabinet manager and now in charge of the Interior Ministry. He is ultra-loyal to Helmut Kohl, and Kohl himself has repeatedly stressed that he sees in Schäuble his most likely successor. Schäuble, however, suffered an assassination attempt which left him partially paralysed and confined to a wheelchair. A critical test for him will be how he masters the job of leader of the CDU/CSU parliamentary party, for which he is a candidate after the next cabinet reshuffle.

The 1990 Kohl cabinet has been described as one of the weakest in the history of the Federal Republic, easily dominated by Helmut Kohl as long as he sticks to certain rules, which basically requires him to respect his coalition partners and their party political self-interests.

Much depends on Helmut Kohl when decisions are to be made; indecisiveness on his part quickly leads to governmental inertia. The Chancellor's decisive role in bringing about German unification with such speed and without major foreign policy conflicts created the impression that Kohl had given up the wait-and-see attitude characteristic of his administration in the past in favour of a more assertive interpretation of his role. After unification, however, he returned to his old style of non-decision and reactive incrementalism. He trusted those economists and advisers who told him that social and economic integration of Germany did not require an increase in the role of the state in the economy. What would happen in Eastern Germany was a second 'Economic Miracle' after the model of West Germany's economic upswing after the Second World War.

Federal government thus took over only those tasks for which there was no administrative and/or financial infrastructure in the East. In the field of culture, for example, Article 35(6) of the Unification Treaty gave the central government the responsibility for the former GDR cultural fund until 31 December 1994, and Article 35(7) in paragraph 7 allowed federal government to finance other cultural projects where necessary. Provisions of this kind, which touch on policy fields which are under the jurisdiction of the Länder, had the potential to bring federal government into conflict with the Länder, which fear the erosion of their autonomy.

Towards a New Consensus?

This kind of minimalist interventionism, designed to ease the transition period for East Germany, proved to be insufficient when the expected economic revival of the East did not materialise. As it became increasingly difficult for the government to remain passive, the first minister to break ranks was the Liberal Economics Minister Möllemann who advocated a more planned and long-term approach to decision-making. In February 1991 he initiated a strategic plan for an economic revival of East Germany (*Strategie Aufschwung Ost*). This plan is intended to be given intellectual support by two new working groups under the guidance of the Economics Ministry. One is the so-called '*Strategiedialog*', in which representatives of both sides of industry are to meet regularly and in secrecy to defuse potential social conflicts. The second is the '*Strategieforum*', which has the task of giving advice to the Minister. In it, experts (journalists, representatives of industry, unions, politicians of a certain standing) debate. It is too early for a judgement on the merits or demerits of this model, but soon after it had been presented to the public, it became obvious that central government had to move faster and to do more than merely promote discussion.

In the atmosphere of growing discontent and anti-government demonstrations in the east in the Spring of 1991, the opposition party, the Social Democrats, suggested the setting up of a Round Table with the government and all relevant social and political forces of the country. The Chancellor reacted cautiously, denying rumours of an imminent Grand Coalition, but approaching the opposition and inviting its then leader, Hans-Jochen Vogel, to meet to discuss the current situation and the problems of unification. The result of this meeting was not a 'Grand Coalition', but what the press began to call a 'Grand Consensus'.

The leadership of both government and opposition announced that they would set up joint committees with the task of working out a conceptual framework for getting to grips with the East's social and economic problems. One committee was to concentrate on administrative reform, property rights and land ownership, the other on the job market and unemployment. Ideas raised in these committees were to be debated in a plenary session, in which the chairpersons of all parties and the leaders of their parliamentary parties were to take part. After an initiative by the Social Democrats and with the agreement of the government, the Greens were also invited to the talks. The PDS, the successor organisation of the East German Communist Party (SED), was excluded from this forum.

Immediately after this agreement between the leaders of the government and the opposition had been made public, disagreement arose between the elites of both parties over how the agreement should be interpreted. To reassure the worried critics in his party, Vogel stressed that this arrangement with the government would not, as the SPD's then chairman-elect Björn Engholm feared, be allowed to give the government a chance to share the blame for its political failures. A short-lived debate followed, over whether or not an early election was necessary. The government had raised taxes, and was thus in breach of its electoral campaign which had promised not to do so. The Chancellor was quick to point out that the new arrangement with the opposition was not meant to give the Social Democrats access to government by the back door: the committees would be able only to make suggestions, and it would remain the government's privilege to decide which of these suggestions to accept, to modify or to ignore.

This statement greatly satisfied the CDU's coalition partners, above all the Liberals, who had begun to fear the prospects of an informal or formal Grand Coalition. But Helmut Kohl's remarks also seemed to confirm the suspicions of the critics in the SPD, who were not ready to participate in a government think-tank. The party leadership stressed that it would not hesitate to end the cooperation with the government if the government was not ready to change some of its policies. In late April 1991 the first meetings of the joint committees took place with the results feared by the SPD. The government side listened, the opposition argued and nothing happened. The pressure for consensus government mounted, however. With the loss of the Land election in Rhineland–Palatinate, the CDU had also lost its majority in the federal chamber, the Bundesrat. For all laws affecting the jurisdiction of the Länder, (and this includes the implementation of laws by Länder public administrations), the government needs the support of the opposition. Still, the cycle of interparty committee meetings was brought to an end with the proviso that it could be reconvened if required. As is the rule when Bundestag and Bundesrat have different majorities, the Bundesrat and the conciliation committee (*Vermittlungsausschuss*) are now the central institutions for the management of consensus politics in Germany. The return to the old mechanisms of conflict resolution showed that speculation even on a broad consensus between the two major parties was premature. The government has a comfortable majority in the Bundestag, and as long as the Chancellor believes in an economic success in East Germany before the next general election, he has no incentive to play down policy differences. For the SPD it would be strategically ill-advised to support the policies of a government which in 1991 commanded less popularity than any previous government in the Federal Republic.

The fact that the CDU had by mid-1991 considerably lost ground in the West German Länder, and remained in power there only in Baden-Württemberg, temporarily upset the balance in the Bonn coalition. Helmut Kohl did not have to fear a leadership challenge in his own party, which lacked qualified personnel. But the Bavarian CSU demanded a response to the electoral decline of the Christian Democrats in the Länder. For the CSU this meant taking a less liberal position towards moral questions (especially abortion) and placing restrictions on the political activities of the FDP's Foreign Minister Genscher. Threats were heard that the CSU might leave the government coalition and might start to compete with the CDU in elections outside Bavaria. A meeting between the CDU and CSU at the Bavarian monastery of Irsee, planned by the CSU as an occasion to force policy changes on Helmut Kohl, resulted in a triumph for the Chancellor. Without seriously questioning his own policy preferences he succeeded in making the CSU state officially that a territorial expansion of its party organisation was out of the question.

Nevertheless, fears remained in the coalition over negative trends in government popularity, attributed by many to the Chancellor's inability to exercise leadership. New poll data in May 1991 showed for the first time a strongly diminished support for the Chancellor and his party in the new Länder, a trend which became more pronounced during the year. The CDU had lost almost a third of its former support there, and the Social Democrats had doubled their own, leading the CDU by over 10 per cent. This nourished rumours of an imminent coalition realignment, especially of the prospect of a coalition between the FDP and the Social Democrats should Kohl be unable to regain the political initiative. Continuing attacks by the CSU on the Liberals added to this speculation.

In Summer 1991 the CSU even suggested the setting up of a CSU-led European ministry to limit Foreign Minister Genscher's competences, and it attacked Genscher for not doing enough for the recognition of the independence of Slovenia and Croatia and the Baltic states.

Policy-making for a Divided Polity

Speculation of this kind did not contribute to solving the problems of policy-making in the new political environment. The treaties of 1990 on monetary, economic and social union and on German unity contained detailed provisions for a common policy framework. However, this did not completely solve the problem of formulating policy at the centre for what remained as distinct political 'regions' in east and west. Divided policy-making stems from the economic division of Germany. The transformation from state-ownership to capitalism in the new eastern Länder required special provisions, and even a separate institution. Article 25(1) of the Unification Treaty created the Treuhandanstalt, with the task of 'restructuring formerly state-owned companies to make them competitive and to privatise them'. In the meantime the Treuhandanstalt is also responsible for organising the 'fading out' of firms from the market and for providing alternative employment.

Another reason for the syndrome of divided policy-making is that there are problems in East Germany, which do not exist in the West, such as the legal consequences of government crimes in the former GDR (corruption, the shooting of people who tried to flee to the

West); the forced adoption of children in the former GDR by 'politically reliable' parents; or the problem of finding the parents (or mother, or father) of children left behind in the GDR when the adults fled. Divided policy-making also arises from differences in moral and cultural attitudes in East and West which stem from forty years of separate development. This is shown in such diverse and unrelated phenomena as the exaggerated responsiveness in the East to right-wing radicalism, the explosion of the number of people killed in traffic accidents after unification, or more liberal attitudes in the East towards abortion.

In a united Germany the syndrome of dual policy-making is anachronistic and may become increasingly problematical. Different policies in the two parts of Germany serve to cement the divide between East and West. Moreover, the majority principle in politics cannot forever be suspended to give 15 million East Germans a veto power or a permanent special status. Privileged treatment of East Germany would certainly increase the tendency in the West to see unification as a burden. It would also create a cycle of decision-making in which decisions conferring temporary privileges in the east provoke demands in the west for equal treatment, with unintended and negative consequences.

A good example of such a spill-over effect is the planning for the construction of new motorways, railway lines and waterways between West and East. Because of the central economic importance of such infrastructure investments, the Transport Ministry, headed by the East German, Günther Krause, suggested the introduction of a streamlined planning procedure in the East which would reduce the opportunities for citizen participation and circumvent lengthy arguments over environmental impact. West German industry was quick to point out that such 'simplifications' of the planning procedures would also be useful for West Germany and could help to remove obstacles to investment there. The next logical step would therefore be to deregulate infrastructure planning in the whole of Germany. This would on the one hand avoid the usual planning periods for public works in Germany of ten to twenty years. It might also mean in certain circumstances an end to the right for individual citizens to go to the courts (*Verwaltungsgericht*) to challenge the decisions of the public administration.

Another instance of divided policy-making is the different legal provision for abortion in East and West Germany. (According to Article 31(4) of the unification treaty, this will cease to apply by 1993 at the latest.) Whereas the GDR allowed abortions in the first three months after conception, in the Federal Republic a legal abortion was possible only in the case of emergency situations, which included 'social emergencies', and after a procedure of consultation. After unification there was a controversy on whether the different regulations should apply with regard to the geographical place a woman had an abortion (*Tatortprinzip*), or with regard to where she lived (*Wohnortprinzip*). The latter would have meant that a West German woman who had an abortion in East Germany would have been prosecuted, whereas an East German woman under exactly the same circumstances would have had a legal right to abortion. The final decision to restrict this right to the territory of the former GDR has, however, not made the legislative framework more coherent. West German women who want an abortion, can now go to a hospital in one of the East German Länder (or for that matter by tube from West Berlin to East Berlin) to exercise a right which is outlawed in the West.

Rebuilding Public Administration in the East

Policy-making in Germany is not only still partially divided; in East Germany it is also beset with an unresolved problem of implementation. German unification confronted the system of public administration in the East with three major challenges. First a reorganisation of its structure, because of the introduction of Länder in East Germany and the redefinition of the tasks of local government. This has meant a much greater autonomy for subnational and local governments, and increased responsibilities for the now democratically elected decision-makers in the East.

Secondly, the Communist legacy was of special importance in the field of public administration. Not only had the top positions in the ex-GDR been held by loyal regime supporters, but public administration was also under the permanent surveillance of the secret police, the Stasi. In practice it has been enormously difficult to get rid of this legacy. One reason was certainly the staying power of old functionaries,and the support provided by the remains of the Stasi network. Moreover, with the old GDR society in the grip of Communist dictatorship, almost everybody with ability and an interest in holding a public office was in one way or the other involved with the regime. Additionally, the view among the population of the former GDR that politics is a dirty business of which one has enough, and the prevalence of individualist values over public service, contributes to the shortage of personnel with democratic credentials in public administration.

Thirdly, the completely new legal framework surrounding public administration has led to severe dislocation. Though GDR law was not completely substituted overnight by the legal system of the old FRG, little provision was made for adaptation. The time period for temporary arrangements was limited and these arrangements themselves had to be learned. In addition public administration was confronted with an increased demand for services, because of the sheer number of people needing help with social problems resulting from the breakdown of the East German economy. Public administration in the East found itself facing practical problems of adapting to new and unfamiliar procedures, and severe communication problems. With a badly functioning telephone system and the total absence of other modern means of communication, public services depended initially on good fortune, personal initiative and proximity to communication resources.

Inevitably, low quality public administration served to inhibit much-needed investment, provoking calls for intervention by federal government. The latter responded by sending civil servants by way of a Bonn-Berlin shuttle. This civil service emergency help was, however, slow to produce the results hoped for. One reason is that the German civil service is mainly under the jurisdiction of the Länder. The federal government could reorganise only the army, the customs, and the postal and telecom services. For the unification of the two railway administrations, Deutsche Reichsbahn (East) and Deutsche Bundesbahn (West), a transition period has been agreed upon to enable the Reichsbahn to become more efficient and to modernise its tracks and cars. Help was given by the federal government also for the reorganisation of the internal revenue service and the training of civil servants. In addition to the shuttle there were in April 1991, 4,239 West German civil servants on placement in the new Länder, and their number has increased. About two-thirds of these civil servants had worked before in the Länder public service. 750 civil servants were sent from SPD-governed North Rhine–Westphalia to SPD-governed Brandenburg; 400 came from Baden–Württemberg to Saxony; 500 from Bavaria to Thuringia; 500 from Lower Saxony to Saxony–Anhalt; and 116 from Bremen and Hamburg to Mecklenburg–West Pomerania.

The Länder themselves did not hesitate to send personnel, but they did this according to their own preferences and criteria. The result was uncoordinated intervention, lacking balance and direction, especially in the field of the public administration of daily needs and rule-making. Without a dramatic change in the quality of public administration it was calculated that it would, for example, take 22 years to deal with the 1.3 million applications of people claiming property rights in the former GDR. To coordinate the efforts made for the support of East Germany's public administration a Task

Force (*Arbeitsstab neue Länder*) was set up by the federal government, chaired by Walter Priesnitz, the former chief administrator of the now dissolved Ministry for Inner-German Relations.

Not only the coordination of support measures, but also the quantity and quality of civil servants going East had to be improved. With regard to quantities, the West German Länder felt that they had come to the limit of what they could do without seriously endangering the functioning of their own administration. The quality of civil servants ready to move to the East is a factor the Länder cannot influence. Civil servants can, of course, be sent to different parts of the Länder who employ them, but they cannot against their will be transferred to other parts of Germany. Working in East Germany was so unattractive (as one civil servant was quoted as saying: 'prices like in New York, living conditions Moscow style') that even generous inducements and incentives did not yield the results hoped for. To overcome the strict rules of the civil service law, a more 'generous' legal framework is planned. The German public, especially in the East, has reacted with little understanding to the government's efforts to make 'privileged' civil servants do what the public regards as their national duty. In the East expertise by itself is no guarantee of success. It may have the counterproductive effect that Westerners are regarded as arrogant (*Besserwessis*), undermining the public cooperation essential to public administration.

What Future for the Bundesbank?

Unification also produced an organisational problem for the Bundesbank as a central government institution. With five new Länder, some believed that the formula of one representative on the Bundesbank board for each Land would mean that the board would be too big for informal decision-making. Former Bundesbank President Karl Otto Pöhl produced a plan for the organisational integration of the new Eastern Länder into the Bundesbank structure which would have radically restructured the old board. The treaty on German unity stipulated that the Bundesbank Act had to be reformed in the first twelve months after unification, i.e. by October 1991. It did not say anything about the principles for such a reform. Immediately after unification the Bundesbank established a temporary branch organisation in East Berlin responsible for the former GDR as a whole. This centralist solution was incompatible with the bank's traditionally federal structure. Bank President Pöhl argued in favour of a middle way between centralism and decentralisation. Instead of having 16 Länder central banks with their respective representatives on the bank's board, he suggested an eight-region solution. Bavaria (in Munich), Baden–Württemberg (in Stuttgart) and North Rhine–Westphalia (in Düsseldorf) were to keep their Länder central banks. Five more central banks would have been set up in Frankfurt (for the Saarland, Rhineland-Palatinate and Hesse), in Hanover (for Lower Saxony, Bremen, and Saxony-Anhalt), in Hamburg (for Hamburg, Mecklenburg-West Pomerania, and Schleswig-Holstein), in Berlin (for Berlin and Brandenburg), and in Dresden (for Saxony and Thuringia).

Pöhl's argument was twofold. On the one hand he wanted to avoid diminishing the role of the ten-person directorate on the bank's board in relation to the regional bankers (16 according to the old rules). On the other hand he thought that enlarging the directorate would undermine its efficiency, flexibility, and capacity for quick decisions. The major conflict was not between Pöhl and the federal government, which argued that the Land level of central banking would anyhow be reduced to a third-rate status within the framework of European Monetary Union, but with the Länder governments, especially with those who may have lost their Bundesbank branch. They saw the Pöhl plan as an attack on federalism, which had to be rejected not only because the Bundesbank has its roots in the Länder (its predecessor was a Länder bank), but above all because the Länder were determined to resist any centralisation of political and economic responsibilities. In late April 1991 Rhineland–Palatinate took the initiative in the Bundesrat for a revision of the Bundesbank Act, which would give each of the existing 16 Länder its own representative on the bank's board. The only Land which did not agree to this initiative was Hamburg, which put forward the example of the US Federal Reserve, which only has 12 district banks in a country of 50 states which are much larger than the German Länder. The federal government at first did not take sides in this debate, but stressed that in its opinion the Bundesbank Act could be amended without the consent of the Länder. In June 1991, however, Theo Waigel, the Finance Minister presented a government bill to the public, which in substance was similar to Pöhl's draft. The bill reduced the number of Länder branches of the Bundesbank to nine. It guaranteed only Bavaria, Baden–Württemberg, North Rhine–Westphalia and Saxony a branch of its own. The pairs of Länder Hesse/Thuringia, Rhineland–Palatinate/Saarland and Berlin/Brandenburg were to be given one branch each and two more branches were to be set up for the two groups of Länder: Schleswig-Holstein/Hamburg/Mecklenburg–West Pomerania and Lower Saxony/Bremen/Saxony–Anhalt.

When in Spring 1991 Chancellor Kohl failed to back Pöhl's scheme for a Bundesbank reform, and when the Bundesrat against the advice of the Bundesbank board filled the vacant seat of the Saarland (one of the Länder not represented in Pöhl's blueprint for a new board), the Bundesbank President announced his resignation. His decision highlighted a more profound and longer-term development. Unification has provoked a steady decline of the relationship between the federal government and the Bundesbank, with the erosion of the Bank's statutory autonomy.

In this atmosphere Pöhl's successor, the former vice-president of the Bundesbank, Helmut Schlesinger, has had no choice but to concentrate on the defence of the bank's institutional autonomy. Whether this autonomy will be safeguarded in the national context and in what form will probably be seen more clearly in 1993. Then Schlesinger will have to leave office for political reasons (there is no formal age limit for the membership on the Bundesbank board) and will be substituted by Hans Tietmeyer (CDU), who is close to the Kohl government and played a crucial role as its adviser in the decision-making process on German monetary union.

A New Constitution and a New Centre?

Government at the centre tended to regard problems of policy-making and policy implementation as of secondary importance, merely temporary hiccups on the road to national integration. It concentrated its energies on what it thought to be the decisions crucial to the framework of the future German polity. What is striking in this context is the Kohl government's unwillingness to involve the German people through referenda in central decisions on unification, the question of the capital of Germany, or a new constitution. German unification started with a constitutional non-event. The GDR merely accepted West Germany's 'Basic Law' and by doing so it joined the FRG in a procedure under Article 23 of the Basic Law. However Article 5 of the unification treaty opened up a perspective for constitutional reform. It stipulated that during the first two years of German unity, decisions should be made on amendments to the Basic Law. The article mentions four possible areas of reform. The first relates to the balance between central government and the Länder in the German federal system, where the Länder want more guarantees of their political and financial autonomy. Secondly, the decision on whether Berlin and Brandenburg should remain two separate Länder, or be merged into one. Thirdly the introduction of general aims for the German polity, which all governments would have to take into account (here the safeguarding of a healthy environment is of central importance). Finally, the application of Article 146 of the Basic Law, which would give the Germans for the first time in the history of the FRG the opportunity to vote in a referendum on their constitution.

For constitutional reform a two-thirds majority in both the Bundestag and the Bundesrat is needed. A consensus is evolving on some symbolic amendments to the constitution, which could give greater weight to efforts to improve the situation of women in society and for safeguarding the environment. What remains controversial is the future role of the army, especially with regard to possible missions out of the NATO area (see Chapter 8).

Preparations for the constitutional body responsible for the formulation of amendments to the Basic Law were marked by conflict over its membership and agenda. Whilst the government wanted a commission with equal representation of Bundestag and Bundesrat, the SPD preferred an election of the 120 member-strong commission (with 50 per cent female and 50 per cent male members) by the Bundesversammlung. The latter is composed of all members of the Bundestag and an equal number of persons elected by the parliaments of all the Länder. Länder representatives would not necessarily have to be politicians, a principle the SPD wanted to see embodied in the composition of the constitutional commission. Both the SPD and the Liberals favour a referendum on the new constitution.

Although the question of a new German capital had already been settled by Article 2 of the unification treaty, the decision on the future seat of government had been postponed. A short time after unification, the Federal President, Richard von Weizsäcker, had already publicly announced his preference for Berlin over Bonn. He not only repeatedly publicly stressed his point of view, he also wrote a memorandum, in which he threatened not to go to Berlin if government and Parliament decided to stay in Bonn. In April 1991 the Chancellor took the public by surprise stating (officially merely as one of the MPs) that he too wanted Berlin to become the seat of government. On 20 June 1991, the federal parliament with a majority of 18 votes decided in favour of Berlin. This decision triggered off a planning process in which the details of a move to Berlin were worked out by the end of 1991. But the transfer of government functions to Berlin will take at least ten to twelve years. Bonn was promised compensations (regional aid, alternative use of government buildings) and is to remain the administrative centre of German government. The Bundestag also advised the Bundesrat to stay in Bonn. The latter decided in July 1991 with a majority of eight votes to do so, but announced that at a later stage that in the light of new experiences it might rethink its decision.

Unification – An Interruption of Normality?

Unification has been treated by the government at the centre as a temporary aberration from normalcy. Arguably this is the source of some of the political problems which arose after unification. Government formation, political discourse, policy-making and implementation have all remained largely within the framework of the old FRG. Little attention has been given to the creation of a new framework for a united Germany. Critical voices, e.g. the Bundesbank, have been attacked instead of being given a creative role. The government has felt comfortable in its role as constitution-maker, but here too, by disregarding the possibility of involving the people in referenda, it will have to pay the price of reduced legitimacy of its decisions. Unification has transformed and will continue to change the lives of many Germans. The government at the centre reacted to the revolutionary changes in the German polity with political routine, incrementalism, and institutional conservatism. The economic situation of East Germany continues to encourage the syndrome of divided policy-making. In regional policy the new German Länder are granted a special status. It is widely recognised that divided policy-making is not a solution, but merely an expression of a lack of national integration. This is exemplified by the failure of the police in the east to cope with attacks on asylum-seekers, and the public appearance of right-wing radicals. The shortcomings of the public administration is shown by the failure of tax offices in the East to collect revenues legally due to them. In public debate, particularly concerning the GDR's past, a kind of new all-German responsibility is discussed, but largely in terms of individual involvement: e.g. the role of the late Franz-Josef Strauss in questionable business transfers with representatives of the former GDR. In such a climate it is small wonder that the east German MPs demand that all MPs (in east and west) should undergo a procedure to disclose any relationship with the Stasi.

In a sense it could be concluded that the central government's incrementalism will ultimately win. To be sure it heightens the sense of frustration in both East and West with government at the centre. However, it also provides a framework for routine political business, in which conflict remains below the level at which it challenges the institutional framework of central government.

6

The Changing Territorial Balance

ROLAND STURM

The Changed Federal Situation

German unification has become something of a litmus test for one of the country's most successful and most celebrated constitutional features, a deeply entrenched federalism. German federalism, far from being divisive either in the relationship between the Länder or in their dealings with central government, has in practice been based on bargaining processes facilitated by an informal consensus orientation. The increase in the number of Länder on unification from 11 to 16 (see Table 6.1) has heightened the tensions (the potential, but also the real ones) between the federal and Länder levels and among the Länder themselves. It has also added to the strain under which the Länder already have to operate, because of the threats to their autonomy through political and economic integration on the European level. Not only have fundamental questions about the distribution of competences and financial resources in the federal state re-emerged, the traditional logic of decision-making on controversial issues is in turmoil, and even the existence of the Länder in their present boundaries is being seriously questioned. The changed and changing territorial balance as a result of unification has also made political outcomes much less predictable, because competing lines of conflict overlap in the Länder's collective decision-making process in the Bundesrat and in other institutions of cooperative federalism.

TABLE 6.1 *The German Länder, 1992*

Land	Capital	Member of the FRG since	Population (million) 1990	Area in 1000 Km²	Seats in the Bundesrat (before unification)
Baden-Württemberg	Stuttgart	1949(1952[1])	9.4	35.7	6 (5)
Bavaria (Free State)	Munich	1949	11.0	70.5	6 (5)
Berlin	(City State)[2]	1990[3]	3.2	0.8	4 (3)
Brandenburg	Potsdam	1990	2.6	29.0	4 (0)
Bremen	(City State)[2]	1949	0.6	0.4	3 (3)
Hamburg	(City State)[2]	1949	1.6	0.7	3 (3)
Hesse	Wiesbaden	1949	5.5	21.1	4 (4)
Lower Saxony	Hanover	1949	7.1	47.3	6 (5)
Mecklenburg-West Pomerania	Schwerin	1990	1.9	23.8	3 (0)
North Rhine-Westphalia	Düsseldorf	1949	16.8	34.0	6 (5)
Rhineland-Palatinate	Mainz	1949	3.6	19.8	4 (4)
Saarland	Saarbrücken	1957	1.0	2.5	3 (3)
Saxony (Free State)	Dresden	1990	4.9	18.3	4 (0)
Saxony-Anhalt	Magdeburg	1990	2.9	20.4	4 (0)
Schleswig-Holstein	Kiel	1949	2.5	15.7	4 (4)
Thuringia	Erfurt	1990	2.6	16.3	4 (0)

Notes:
[1] Amalgamation of the Länder Württemberg-Hohenzollern, Baden and Württemberg-Baden, all three members of the FRG since 1949.
[2] Functions as both a Land and local government.
[3] End of Four-Power status and unification of Berlin.

The New Logic of Political Decision-making

There are at least five dimensions which after unification affect the process of collective decision-making at the Land level:

- differences of interests between the German Länder in the West and the Länder in the East;
- differences of interests between a coalition of the poorer Länder and the federal government on the one hand and the richer Länder on the other;
- the reduced relevance of the coalition pattern at the federal level for party political cooperation in the Länder;
- an increased importance of the veto power of the four large Länder with regard to constitutional changes; and
- an increased awareness of all Länder of the dangers to their relative autonomy through intervention both at the national and at the EC level.

All these dimensions in their present form are new for post-war federalism and have changed the traditional logic of interest intermediation based on one or both of two patterns. They have either modified the principle of defining conflicts between the Länder by reference to party political loyalties of Land governments, or have substituted the lobbyism of groups of Länder in favour of a multi-dimensional definition of Länder interests.

The first two new challenges listed above focus on the divide between rich and poor Länder. In itself this divide is not a new phenomenon, but in the old FRG the gap between the poorest and the richest Land was much narrower. In addition, the traditional framework of interest intermediation produced, at least until the early 1980s, results by consensus. When in the first half of the 1980s the Constitutional Court was asked to decide on the degree to which Lower Saxony's oil proceeds should be taken into account in the system of fiscal equalisation between the Länder, this was the first sign of a decreasing efficiency of the Länder's bargaining for consensus.

In the late 1980s and early 1990s the Constitutional Court was even more pushed into the role of an arbitrator on conflicts between the Länder. Hardly had it prescribed changes in the fiscal equalisation arrangements to settle the question of how to deal with Lower Saxony's oil income in 1986 when a new round of court cases was started by different groups of Länder. The city-states Hamburg and Bremen (now joined by the new city-state Berlin) demanded a greater share of financial resources than they had received hitherto on the basis of a population-plus-x formula. They argued that their case was a special one, because they had not only to finance Land needs, but also finance their other function, namely local government. For this reason and because they wanted a compensation for their role as major German ports, Hamburg and Bremen asked the Constutitonal Court to rule in their favour. The Saarland tried to make a similar case at the Court for a greater share of revenues in compensation for its declining coal and steel industries. Hamburg also wanted more from the fiscal equalisation process to pay for the expenses of 'political leadership', which are said to be relatively higher in smaller Länder, an argument which has already been accepted for Bremen and the Saarland. Both the Saarland and Schleswig–Holstein wanted the Constitutional Court to redefine fiscal equalisation in such a way that it would give them additional resources for financing their local government. Hesse and Baden–Württemberg, as the paymasters in the fiscal equalisation process, had a quite different perspective. They sought a Constitutional Court ruling against their exclusion from federal financial aid for the Länder, made available by the Structural Aid Act (*Strukturhilfegesetz*) of 1988. This Act aimed to help the Länder shoulder the growing burden of social aid expenses at the local level.

The Poor Against the Rich

The existing division between the richer Länder in the West, mainly Baden–Württemberg, Hesse, Bavaria and North Rhine–Westphalia, and the poorer ones, mainly the Saarland, Bremen, Lower Saxony, and Schleswig–Holstein, is complicated by the addition of a new poverty line between Germany's western and eastern Länder. What, under these circumstances, are the strategic options for groups of Länder when they try to accommodate their interests in the process of political decision-making?

One possibility is for the eastern Länder to form a block to press their common interests. At a very early stage Hennis (1990) had advised the East German Länder to do just that, and there are signs of such cooperation becoming institutionalised. Thus there is Berlin's bid to become a sixth 'new Land', an extension of the formula, 'the five new Länder', used for the former GDR, and Berlin sees itself as possibly taking the lead in an East–West confrontation. What also threatens the consensus between East and West is a neglect of traditional bargaining processes by the new Länder. This led to conflicts between the Länder when in April 1991 the four CDU-governed Eastern Länder ignored joint decisions of the Länder education ministers' conference, and even missed a meeting of a Länder committee on the future school system in Germany. The Eastern Länder have in the meantime initiated a degree of inter-Land coordination. The governments of the six Länder (including Berlin) meet at regional conferences, where they formulate their demands for financial aid from Bonn and from the other Länder. They have also agreed on the establishment of an office to coordinate their strategies following the breakdown of their trade with Eastern Europe. In May 1991 they succeeded in securing additional financial support for their universities. For the next five years they will raise DM 1.76 billion, 75 per cent of which will have to come from federal government and the rest from the eastern Länder themselves. This decision is of special interest for three reasons: first, it shows the readiness of the federal government to step in to assume responsibilities which traditionally (and for constitutional reasons) have been Länder concerns. Secondly, this development was quite separate from the joint Länder planning decisions on the future of the universities and their financing. Thirdly, it is significant that the other Länder refused to co-finance this special programme for the new Länder to avoid paying twice over.

For economic and political reasons (reinforced by the fact that the Land elections in the East will next be held in the same year) and because of common traditions of political culture, in a way the separate identity of the former GDR lives on. The East–West dimension of the conflict between the poor and the rich Länder hinders integration.

The second line of division between the richer and the poorer Länder described by Scharpf (1990) and Boldt (1991), is the confrontation between all the poorer Länder, East and West, plus the federal government against the richer ones. For that scenario, too, one can find signs in current political debate. All the poorer Länder have asked the federal government to bail them out of their financial difficulties. The Saarland has taken the lead in forming a new alliance between the eastern Länder, itself and Bremen to put pressure on the federal government for increased aid. Although they describe themselves as 'poor', they differ in their view of their relationship with the federal government. In West Germany relative Land autonomy is seen as the basis of federalism and democracy, but in East Germany priority is given to the need for federal financing of policies rather than to quarrels about competences between the Land and federal government. The poorer Länder in the West in this respect react more like the rich Länder. They are sensitive to what they see as efforts of the federal government to use financial inducements to extend its jurisdiction.

With regard to the divide between poor and rich Länder the minister-president of Schleswig–Holstein, Björn Engholm (Herz 1991), envisaged a German federalism with three classes of Länder. In the 'first world' there will be the financially and economically healthy ones, namely Hesse, Bavaria, and Baden–Württemberg; in the 'second' those who just manage to make ends meet, but have no financial room for manoeuvre, and therefore lack the ability to do more than administer existing policies. The 'third world' of German federalism will consist of a number of bankrupt Länder that depend on the federal government for their survival. If in the near future up to ten Länder, as Engholm estimates, are forced to beg help from the federal government whenever they want to initiate new policies this dependent relationship, he argues, will lead to an irreversible decay of German federalism.

A Disappearing Land–Federal Coalition Nexus

There is a growing readiness of parties at Land level – enhanced by unification – to cooperate with other parties irrespective of the line-up at the federal level. Thus the 1987 Hamburg SPD–FDP coalition was the first to break the pattern of CDU–FDP coalitions which are to be found only in the new Länder (see Table 6.2). The Hamburg example was followed by an SPD–FDP coalition in Rhineland–Palatinate in 1991.

On the Land level the Greens are, to some extent (in contrast to the PDS) no longer seen as an anti-system party unfit to govern. In two Länder, Hesse and Lower Saxony, they are junior partners of the SPD in government. In Brandenburg the partnership of the human rights movement 'Bündnis '90' with the FDP and SPD created a so-called red-yellow-green 'traffic-light coalition, as was the case in Bremen when the SPD lost its overall majority in the 1991 Land election. In Berlin a grand coalition between the CDU and the Social Democrats is in power.

What political consequences do the varied landscape of Länder coalitions have? The most important one is certainly that it has become more difficult than at any earlier point in time of the FRG's history to divide the Länder strictly according to party political criteria, and to judge by these the relative strength of the parties in the Länder. If one counts the party affiliations of only the heads of government, one can find that one of the Land heads is a member of the CSU, six are from the CDU and nine are from the SPD. This does nto mean, however, that the Social Democrats have a guaranteed nine to seven majority in their favour among the Länder,

TABLE 6.2 *The political landscape of the Länder, 1992*

Land	Since	Governing Party/ coalition	Head of government (party)
Baden-Württemberg	1992	CDU/SPD	Erwin Teufel (CDU)
Bavaria	1966	CSU	Max Streibl (CSU)
Berlin	1990	CDU/SPD	Eberhard Diepgen (CDU)
Brandenburg	1990	SPD/FDP/Bündnis	Manfred Stolpe (SPD)
Bremen	1991	SPD/FDP/Greens	Klaus Wedemeier (SPD)
Hamburg	1991	SPD	Henning Voscherau (SPD)
Hesse	1991	SPD/Greens	Hans Bichel (SPD)
Lower Saxony	1990	SPD/Greens	Gerhard Schröder (SPD)
Mecklenburg/West Pomerania	1990	CDU/FDP	Berndt Seite (CDU)
North Rhine-Westphalia	1980	SPD	Johannes Rau (SPD)
Rhineland-Palatinate	1991	SPD/FDP	Rudolf Scharping (SPD)
Saarland	1985	SPD	Oskar Lafontaine (SPD)
Saxony	1990	CDU	Kurt Biedenkopf (CDU)
Saxony-Anhalt	1990	CDU/FDP	Werner Münch (CDU)
Schleswig-Holstein	1988	SPD	Björn Engholm (SPD)
Thuringia	1990	CDU/FDP	Bernhard Vogel (CDU)

and even less so in the Bundesrat. Coalition treaties between the SPD and the Liberals in Hamburg (from 1987 to 1991) and Rhineland–Palatinate force the respective Land delegates to abstain from a vote in the Bundesrat when there is a major conflict of interests with the federal government. The Greens are not necessarily a more reliable partner for the SPD, since they find it difficult to agree to compromises when under pressure from the new social movements, their special clientèle.

There is a secure base of support for the Bonn coalition only in five Länder, four of which are in the former GDR. In 1992 the CDU lost overall control of Baden-Württemberg, leaving only the CSU in Bavaria. The SPD governs alone in four Länder, and is in a coalition only with the Greens in two more. The remaining four Länder governments straddle the federal divide between government and opposition.

More important for the outcome of the political decision-making process in the Bundesrat than the mere number of Länder governed by the party or the other is the relative weight expressed in seats these Länder have (see Table 6.1). Of a total of 68 Bundesrat seats the parties forming the federal government control 21 against the opposition parties' 26. Of the remaining 21 seats in the hands of 'mixed' coalitions, 11 are Länder in which the Social Democrats are the major coalition party. One could conclude that it should be easier for the opposition parties to control the Bundesrat than for the federal government to do so. (See Table, p. 93).

The new dynamics of the decision-making process make such a predictable outcome unlikely. First, the weaker the party-political divide becomes for structuring political conflict, the more important are the economic questions for defining a Land government's stance on a particular issue: issue coalitions may be able to realign loyalties. Second, there is the redefinition of the role of the CSU in German politics. Formerly, the CSU was able to occupy a pivotal position in the Bundesrat, switching between its federal responsibilities in government and its representation of Bavarian interests, the latter not necessarily identical with the wishes of the federal government. Now, the CSU is permanently marginalised in the Bundesrat. Instead of controlling 5 out of 44 seats in the old Bundesrat, the CSU's share has fallen to 6 out of 68 and, more importantly, the new pattern of Länder coalitions has made clear-cut confrontations between government and opposition in the Bundesrat far less likely.

Safeguarding Länder Constitutional Rights

The fourth and fifth new aspects of political decision-making on the Land level have to do with the constitutional balance between the Länder, and between the Länder and the federal government. The relative influence on Bundesrat decisions the individual Länder have was debated in 1990 when a compromise had to be found in the unification treaty on the provision for the future number of Länder seats. The first draft of the treaty proved to be unacceptable both to the larger and the smaller Länder, though for different reasons. Eventually a compromise was reached on the initiative of Oscar Lafontaine, minister-president of the Saarland. The new provisions of the unification treaty changed the number of seats for each Land in the Bundesrat only slightly by giving the big four Länder each one more seat. The revised formula for Länder representation in the

Bundesrat is: (1) at least three seats for every Land, (2) Länder with a population of more than 2 million have four seats, (3) Länder with a population of more than 6 million have five seats (at the moment there is no such Land); (4) Länder with more than 7 million inhabitants have six seats.

The bargaining process, which led to this compromise provides interesting insights into the power structure of pre-unification German federalism, especially on the delicate balance between party-political and Länder interests, a power structure which was already confronted with the cross-pressures stemming from German unification. Whereas Lafontaine's success can be explained by the traditional consensus-building mechanisms, they do not sufficiently explain why the two governments agreed on the eventual compromise. Both sought a financial price for their consent. The Länder granted to the federal government as compensation control over 15 per cent of the resources of the German Unity Fund for infrastructure expenditure affecting the former GDR as a whole. The East German government won for its Länder a greater share of the national VAT income.

Though the Lafontaine initiative reduced the share of the Bundesrat seats for the big four Länder to 35 per cent of the total, the latter were successful in defending their minimum demand, namely to control a number of seats large enough to block a two-thirds majority in the Bundesrat, necessary for changes in the federal constitution. The big four Länder see themselves as the true defenders of federalism, because of their economic potential and the fact that they represent 57 per cent of the German people in the new Germany. Who else but they would be able to resist when the federal government made attractive offers to trade Länder autonomy against further financial aid? The efforts to secure for themselves a veto power to block changes in the constitution showed, however, more than altruism. The big four Länder now also have a fallback position in the case of a broad constitutional reform coaliton of the other Länder and the federal government.

When it comes to the defence of federalism in its present form, there is also a line of conflict which unites all the Länder, because they are in a similar situation of being threatened by marginalisation in the political decision-making process. They oppose the trend to uniformity in the whole of Germany – a tendency reinforced by the federal government's interpretation of the preconditions for a welfare state. After unification, the federal government, because of financial weakness in the East took over new tasks, which are in the West under Länder jurisdiction, thus nourishing the suspicion that the federal government may be making permanent inroads into the

competences of the Länder. The aim of creating the financial preconditions for a withdrawal of the federal government seems a distant
prospect. An initiative by the federal education minister of East
German origin, Rainer Ortlep (FDP) in May 1991 would have meant
an extended jurisdiction for the federal government in the areas of
education and science. The Länder successfully fought off this attack
on their autonomy in these areas which they regard as being essential
for German federalism. Uniformity combined with a loss of Länder
competences has also been forced on the Länder by European
integration, a process which no doubt will be difficult to reverse.

Fiscal Federalism: Who Pays for Unification?

When the debate on the sharing out of the financial burden brought
about by unification started between the Länder and the federal
government in the Spring of 1990, the conservative–liberal Bonn
government had a secure majority in the Bundesrat. It scarcely
informed those Länder governed by Social Democrats about the
problems of unification, but still stressed the Länder's financial
responsibility for helping East Germany. Both the federal government and the Bundesbank saw sufficient reserves in the Länder
budgets for a major cost-sharing effort. From the Länder point of
view this was a one-sided misinterpretation of financial realities
which, for example, did not take into account the severe cutbacks
in services and investments which had been necessary on the Länder
level to achieve relative financial stability, and were now taken as a
pretext by the federal government for making the Länder pay. In
addition they argued that the federal government should make use
of the 'peace dividend' it would receive as a result of the end of the
East–West conflict; further, that Bonn should redirect the money for
expenditure which had become obsolete after unification, such as
regional aid for the territory in the border zone to the GDR, or the
subsidies to West Berlin.

In April 1990 the federal Finance Minister, Theo Waigel (CSU),
tried in vain to win Länder approval for a transfer of an increased
share of the national VAT income into the federal government at
the cost of the Länder. Waigel proposed a change of the federal–
Länder VAT ratio from 65 per cent: 35 per cent to 71 per cent:29
per cent. The Länder were not willing to give away large amounts
of present and future income without any control over the use made
of it. Lower Saxony, then governed by a CDU–FDP coalition, took
the initiative for an alternative model, proposing the institutionalis-

ation of a 'Germany Fund' to which the Länder, local government and the federal government would contribute.

This idea was modified by the federal government and became the model for the special 'German Unity' fund, to the establishment of which the federal government and the Länder agreed in mid-1990. For a period of four years DM 115 billion were made available. The western Länder and the federal government jointly finance 95 billion, with 40 per cent of the Länder share contributed by local government. Another 20 billion is to come from a reduction of the federal government's expenditure resulting from savings made because of unification. Relative to their size the Länder contribute different shares. North Rhine–Westphalia pays 27.4 per cent of the Länder contribution, Bavaria 17.5 per cent, Baden–Württemberg 15.7 per cent, Lower Saxony 10.9 per cent, Hesse 9.3 per cent, Rhineland–Palatinate 5.8 per cent, Schleswig–Holstein 3.8 per cent, Berlin 3.3 per cent, Hamburg 3.2 per cent, Saarland 1.7 per cent and Bremen 1.4 per cent. At first it seemed that the Länder had been made to pay more than they could really afford. After all, they had in addition also costly partnership arrangements with East German regions on a Land–region basis. Until 1994 these will add up to a transfer of human and technical resources of about DM 70 billion. It soon turned out, however, that the arrangement had a great advantage for the Länder. All additional needs for financial resources to help East Germany, not covered by the German Unity Fund, would in theory be the federal government's responsibility, because the fund arrangement precisely defined the contribution of each Land.

Against the wishes of the federal and the GDR governments the West German Länder also successfully fought off an immediate integration of the East German Länder into the fiscal equalisation arrangements between the Länder, with the help of which the poorer Länder receive transfer payments from the richer ones to guarantee them an average Länder income. The unity treaty in Article 7 foresaw an integration of the East German Länder into the fiscal equalisation mechanism for 1995. The fate of this provision remains, however, uncertain. One unsolved problem is the sheer size of financial transfers to the East which seem to be necessary if the economic downturn in the East is not soon reversed. No West German Land can afford to lose the billions a mathematical equalisation formula would demand and still survive economically. Another problem is that those West German Länder now desperately needing help themselves would become net payers. Even on the basis of mid-1991 figures, all Länder, except the two virtually bankrupt ones, Bremen and Saarland, would have to find additional resources for the East German Länder. The latter would receive between 3.8 billion (Mecklenburg–West Pomerania) and 9.3 billion DM (Saxony) annually. As a consequence there seems to be unanimity among the Länder that not only can the fiscal equalisation arrangement *not* be employed in the present situation, but also that the logic of these arrangements leads to nonsensical results, if – as is the case today – the disparities in the financial strength of the Länder exceed a certain limit. What is needed from the point of view of at least the better-off Länder is a new system which does at least three things:

(1) It regroups competences between the Länder and the federal government, thereby granting the Länder a greater degree of autonomy.
(2) It creates an effective mechanism for combining special tax income with well-defined expenditure programmes, so that Länder expenditures for the purpose of fulfilling federal tasks become clearly identifiable and, ideally, sooner or later cease to exist.
(3) It creates taxes which are under the sole jurisdiction of the Länder.

The poorer Länder are hesitant to claim for themselves the same degree of fiscal autonomy. So far they have been the ones who profited most from joint policy-making with the federal government, and they are the ones most likely to be the losers when different Länder tax structures become weapons in a competition for attracting investment.

After the dispute between the federal government and the Länder on the two financial questions mentioned had been settled, a new dispute broke out over VAT. The federal Finance Minister had planned to distribute the Länder's VAT share of 35 per cent to all German Länder, West and East, by the traditional yardstick of the size of the respective Land population. The West German Länder feared that this would mean an income reduction of four to five billion DM for them. The compromise found for the Unity Treaty (Article 7.3) was gradually to increase the VAT share per person in East Germany, starting with a share of 55 per cent in 1992, to 65 per cent in 1993, and 70 per cent in 1994, with special provisions for Berlin. This compromise did not, however, survive the economic breakdown in East Germany in early 1991. The Unity Treaty had provided for such a situation by a revision clause (Article 7.6) which allowed for a change in the financial arrangements if this was required by new circumstances. The federal government, itself in an awkward position, because it now had to raise taxes to finance German unity, put pressure on the West German Länder to accept a greater financial burden. The Länder agreed to give the East German Länder from 1991 a full (100 per cent per head) share of VAT income, which means that until 1994 they will transfer to them an additional amount of 17 billion DM.

In mid-1991, when no end for the malaise of the East German economy was still in sight, the Structural Aid Act of 1988 (*Strukturhilfegesetz*) became a new target for the attack by the federal government of the West German Länder's unwillingness to contribute an ever-increasing fund for the support of the East. As mentioned above, this Act was originally meant to help the poorer West German Länder to cope with the increasing costs of long-term unemployment and other social and infrastructural problems. Hesse and Baden–Württemberg who were excluded from the fund created by this Act (as was West Berlin which had all through been kept alive by federal transfer payments) for obvious reasons had already argued in May 1990 for an end of this fund, and had advocated its use for financing East German reconstruction. The other Länder had already anticipated the receipt of fund money in making their long-term financial plans. Bavaria was to receive 158 million DM annually, Bremen 63, Hamburg 113, Lower Saxony 652, North Rhine–Westphalia 756, Rhineland–Palatinate 272, the Saarland 112 and Schleswig–Holstein 252 million DM. In November 1991 the federal government introduced a bill to phase out the Structural Aid Act by 1992. The federal funds thus saved are to be channelled to East Germany.

The financial framework of German federalism, originally planned as an instrument for fine-tuning the economic convergence of the West German Länder to guarantee comparable standards of living throughout West Germany, has now been reduced to a gigantic aid programme for the East German Länder. What was left of financial autonomy on the Länder level after almost ten years of a neo-conservative strategy at the federal level, eager to hand down the social costs caused by economic problems to the Länder, is now severely threatened by the challenge of German unification.

Restructuring German Federalism

During the debate on the future of German federalism after unification an old argument was revived, namely that a number of the economic problems of the Länder could be solved if their boundaries were redrawn. A smaller number of Länder with a comparable financial strength could thus be created. This restructuring would reduce conflict between richer and poorer Länder and would make all Länder (but especially the poorer ones) less dependent on federal aid. It would also facilitate fiscal equalisation processes, if they were still necessary, because the income differences between the Länder would be much smaller. Länder of this size would also be more respected partners in Europe.

All this not only sounds very logical, it is also the kind of thinking that is favoured by Article 29 of the Basic Law. There is certainly no lack of blueprints for a redrawing of Länder boundaries. In the old FRG party-political interests in preserving post-war Länder boundaries, together with the inertia of existing administrative structures, prevented a reform in the early 1970s. Unification, with the need to extend federalism to East Germany, gave arguments for boundary revisions new plausibility. For a brief period in April 1990 there seemed to be a chance for an all-party consensus on a large-scale reform. The most influential model suggested by Hamburg's federal representative, Horst Gobrecht (SPD), favoured a seven-Länder solution. It would have left Bavaria, Baden–Württemberg, and North Rhine–Westphalia intact in their present boundaries, and would have added four new Länder, a Northern Land, a Southwest Land and two Länder created by the division of the former GDR. All these Länder would have had a similar size of population, between 9 million people in the southern part of the former GDR and 12.2 million in the second largest Land to be created, the Northern Land. The only Land with a population total outside this range would have been North Rhine–Westphalia with more than 17 million inhabitants. It is not by chance that this suggestion came from Hamburg, because before unification the redrawing of Länder boundaries had been a topic debated above all in the north of Germany. It was then seen as vehicle for helping the north to catch up in the competition with the more prosperous South.

Judged by the experience with similar earlier efforts the lack of enduring support for the Gobrecht plan in West Germany was not surprising. In East Germany, efficiency arguments, although debated during the de Maizière government, were not influential for the shape of the new East German Länder. The most important yardstick for the final decisions made seems to have been the *status quo ante*, namely the Länder structure which had existed in East Germany for the short period of time between 1947 and 1952, and which was, contrary to popular misconception, itself an artificial product. In 1947 a military order by the Soviet military administration had revived (and extended by parts of former Prussian provinces) the Länder of Mecklenburg, Saxony, and Thuringia, and had created the new Länder Brandenburg and Saxony–Anhalt out of the Western parts of Prussian provinces and the Land Anhalt. The Law re-introducing Länder in the GDR in July 1990 only marginally changed the

1947 Länder boundaries. Boundary changes were made to honour the now democratically-elected local government structures, which with 1278 communities were incompatible with the 1947 Länder boundaries. The 1990 Länder Act allowed for referenda in those communities affected by these changes as to which Land they preferred to belong to. One option, held open by the Unity Treaty, is a possible agreement of Berlin and Brandenburg to merge. After the decision of mid-1991 to move the centre of government to Berlin the likelihood of a merger of both Länder has increased. Berlin needs the room Brandenburg can provide for its fast-growing population, whereas Brandenburg will be able to influence decisions in this large agglomeration at its heart only when it has access at the political level.

After the first new elections in the East German Länder in October 1990 and the all-Berlin election of December 1990, the debate on a redrawing of Länder boundaries died down, paradoxically at a time when the economic arguments for a reduction of the number of Länder had become more convincing than ever. Now that the new governments and bureaucracies have been installed, the same forces of inertia that have so far made impossible a restructuring of federalism in the West have started to dominate politics in the East.

German federalism seems to have lost the ability to take its own functional prerequisites seriously. None the less, every Land would vehemently deny the view that its status tends to resemble an inefficient administrative unit. It can, however, hardly be denied that unification has severely weakened the financial, and to some extent even the political, impetus for safeguarding the relative autonomy of the Länder. Complaints about the increasingly unitary nature of German federalism were common in the old FRG, and even more so after the reforms of the Basic Law in the late 1960s which centralised taxation and opened the door for a role for federal government in policy fields that used to be the sole prerogative of the Länder.

After unification and facing the 1992 Single Market, the situation in which the Länder find themselves, is one characterised by political inconsistency. Economically unification has further undermined their status. The Länder hope that they are just going through a transitory phase and will finally win back more economic independence, including more powers to tax. Ideally this should give the Länder a greater ability to finance their expenditures without any federal help. This is the rationale of Bavaria's demand (October 1991) that the Länder should be given control of social security funds by way of a regionalisation of the social security administration. A more pessimistic view sees the financial problems of East Germany as long-term ones not letting the Länder off the hook.

Tensions in the Federal System

Politically, demands for more autonomy are heard louder than ever. The Länder want a reduction of the competences of the federal government, and a veto whenever the federal government intends to transfer policy fields now under their jurisdiction to international organisations, above all to the Community. In the political debate within the two major parties the Länder minister-presidents to claim an independent role for themselves. In the 1980s the CDU parliamentary party in the Bundestag had to live with the very vocal 'partnership' of the CDU Länder heads, and in the 1990s the same kind of tension is developing for the SPD. When the 16 heads of the Länder met the first time in November 1990 they solemnly declared that they wanted a reform of the constitution to strengthen the role of the Länder. This consensus is, however, relatively weak when Länder interests are in conflict with each other. For the champions of federalism, the difficult task ahead is threefold: to survive the financial pressures of unification, to defend the political dimension of the Länder's relative autonomy both against the federal government and against EC intervention. This above all means securing general acceptance for the principle of subsidiarity, and convincing the Länder in East Germany that whatever the financial costs, the relative autonomy of each Land remains essential for federalism and for German democracy. Both the Single Market with its corollary of European regions in economic competition and the 'postmodern' view of the political process will eventually affect East Germany. Individualism, a plurality of life-styles, democratic control and decentralised flexibility (for example by way of a strengthened role of the forgotten Länder parliaments) will have priority over social equality. Outside influences such as these in combination with limits to financial largesse will in the 1990s confront each Land with the decisive question of its *raison d'être*.

PART TWO

Germany and the World

7

Gulliver Unbound: The Changing Context of Foreign Policy

WILLIAM E. PATERSON

> When the workmen found it was impossible for me to break loose, they cut all the strings that bound me; whereupon I rose up, with as melancholy a disposition as ever I had in my life. But the noise and astonishment of the people, at seeing me rise and walk, are not to be expressed (Swift, *Gulliver's Travels*).

Willy Brandt's lapidary aphorism 'an economic giant, but a political dwarf,' alerts us to the disparity between the power resources available to the West German state and its relative lack of autonomy and influence. The roots of this disparity were multifarious and complex. They included geographical position, the legacy of history, the security dependence on the United States, the vulnerability of Berlin, the nature of the foreign policy goals pursued by the federal government and the difficulties inherent at both a conceptual and operational level in its status as part of a divided nation. A central, but not exclusive, concern of this chapter will be to examine these grounds and to establish whether they have been transcended by unity. It will then consider some major foreign policy dilemmas facing the new Germany.

Geographical Position

Germany's geographical position in the heart of Europe was traditionally associated with a very highly developed sense of vulnerability, which led to a preoccupation with national frontiers and a marked emphasis on military power. This sense of vulnerability remained in the Federal Republic. The Federal Republic was physically at the point where the two global competitive systems met and shared a thousand-mile border with its adversary, the GDR. Its 'waist', the distance between its eastern and western borders, was only 225 km at its narrowest, 480 km at its widest point. This configuration left very little room for retreat since a few initial defeats could have led to the whole territory being overrun. Moreover, two-thirds of the population lived less than 200 km from the eastern border. The pervasive fear of the Soviet Union in the early years of the Federal Republic led to a reversal of Germany's traditional position. Germany's geographical position had conditioned it to think of itself as a central European power. In the post-war period bipolarity excluded Mitteleuropa (Central Europe) and successive federal governments dominated by the imperatives of security and access to markets made the Federal Republic the first German regime to be exclusively and unequivocally a Western power. This position was slightly modified by the normalisation of relations with Eastern Europe through Ostpolitik but, despite fears to the contrary, the Federal Republic remained very firmly anchored in the West, and in this sense geographical categories were superseded.

Historical Constraints

West German foreign policy was perhaps more pervasively affected in both its aims and style by the historical experience of the nineteenth century than any other modern state. From its inception in 1871 the unified German nation state, despite the fact that it never at any point included all Germans, proved impossible to integrate into the international system. German policy-makers were obsessed with the idea of *Einkreisung* (encirclement) by their powerful Western and Eastern neighbours while other powers felt threatened by what they saw as the dynamic and expansionary character of the unified Germany. This tension between Germany and its European neighbours was to dominate European history between 1871 and 1945. The criminal nature of the Hitler regime, its total defeat and the occupation and division of Germany by foreign powers continued to inform both the style and goals of the foreign policy of the Federal

Republic. The actions of the Hitler regime had a very profound impact; a major motive in the European policy of the Federal Republic in the 1950s was to win acceptance and moral credibility. It also played an important role in both the goals and style of Ostpolitik. Despite opposition arguments that German crimes in Eastern Europe had been matched by those of the post-war communist regimes and that a sort of moral equivalence had been created, the West German government in its policy of Ostpolitik acted on the assumption that the federal government had a special responsibility to try and do something to recompense the states of Eastern Europe for the acts carried out by the Third Reich. The moral dimension was also very apparent in the style of negotiation, symbolised most vividly by Willy Brandt's gesture of dropping to his knees at the site of the Warsaw Ghetto.

The further recognition that the criminality of the Third Reich had been accompanied by – and was to some extent a product of – hysterical nationalism, along with the scale of German defeat in 1945, meant that policy-makers were not able to mobilise strong nationalist sentiments in support of foreign policy goals as was the case in Britain or France. Nowhere was the apparent British popular enthusiasm for the Falklands episode less understood than in the Federal Republic; Italians and Spaniards may have been more critical, but West Germans were simply baffled and the roots of their bafflement lay in recent German history and their experience of living in Europe's first post-national state.

The total defeat of the Third Reich was a traumatic experience common to all the policy-makers of the Federal Republic after 1949 though the present generation of policy-makers now remember it, if at all, as teenagers rather than as adult participants. The key lesson that they drew was the necessity for Germany not to exploit its full power potential, which would only unite other powers against it, but to associate the exercise of the power of the nascent state with the emerging alliance and institutional structures. In this sense the Federal Republic's lack of 'giant' status represented a deliberate choice.

One of the central orientations of West German foreign policy was a product of defeat and occupation. The developing tension between the Western allies and the Soviet Union led to the breakdown of Four Power Control in Germany and a commitment by the United States' government to stabilise the Western occupied zones and create a West German state. In origin, then, the West German state was a foreign policy in search of a state rather than a state in search of a foreign policy. The creation of the new state on the basis of the division of the unified state that had existed since 1871 carried with it the inevitable corollary that the foreign policy of the new state would have a central commitment to the reunification of Germany. This commitment was given para-constitutional status by its incorporation into the Basic Law.

The Ambiguity of Interest

The division of Germany and the truncated identity of the Federal Republic rendered the already inchoate concepts of interest and national interest even more ambiguous than in relation to the foreign policy of other states. The disjunction between the West German state and the German nation immediately raised obstacles in talking of 'national interest'. There could be a German national interest, but it remained for a long time unthinkable to conceive of a West German national interest. To be sure West German governments argued from 1949 that the Federal Republic in a real sense did represent the whole German nation, or at least that part of it within the 1937 boundaries. This '*Alleinvertretungsanspruch*' (sole right of representation) was based on the argument that only those Germans living in the Federal Republic had been able to vote for a freely elected government. The federal government was thus the only legitimate German government and its primary duty, constitutionally anchored in the Basic Law, was to work for German reunification. The Federal Republic thus continually proclaimed a national interest of the Germans in self-determination, an aspiration which it alone could legitimately represent.

This concept was buttressed after 1955 by the Hallstein doctrine, which argued that recognition of the GDR would be considered an unfriendly act by the Federal Republic. Only the USSR was permitted, because of its centrality to any possible reunification negotiations, to maintain dual diplomatic relations. In the bipolar international system of the 1950s and early 1960s the Hallstein doctrine, with the support of the United States, prevailed, and no non-communist state recognised the GDR.

This whole complex in which for some foreign policy purposes at least the Federal Republic proclaimed itself as the spokesman for a German national interest, came under extreme pressure from the late 1960s. In following the move to detente by the superpowers in the early 1960s, the West Germans had to give up their insistence that German reunification should precede detente and to accommodate themselves to a less bipolar international system. In this new system the Hallstein doctrine became more and more expensive to uphold and, from the late 1960s onwards, it began to be breached. The erection of the Berlin Wall in 1961 did not immediately herald the long-awaited collapse of the GDR but, if anything, the regime appeared to consolidate itself after 1961.

In differing degrees these developments led to the Ostpolitik of the Social-Liberal Coalition, which first took office in 1969. A central thrust of Ostpolitik and of the 'normalisation' of relations with the states of Eastern Europe was a new relationship with the GDR. From the perspective of the Bonn government, the new relationship was based on the concept of '*Wandel durch Annäherung*' (change through rapprochement) first articulated by Egon Bahr and Willy Brandt in 1963 as a response to the challenge posed by the Berlin Wall. Brandt and Bahr argued that a continually hostile attitude to the GDR and a denial of all state attributes to it (the policy of all federal governments hitherto) had not led to the collapse of the GDR but had simply strengthened the repressive character of the regime. In their view some accommodation with the regime in East Germany would encourage its rulers to behave less repressively to their own population. Equally importantly, the regime would feel free to make the borders more porous, to allow renewed contact between the citizens of the two German states. The new policy towards East Germany was therefore squarely based on the doctrine of 'two states of one German nation' (Brandt). This mirrored a decline in the popular belief of the likelihood of reunification. Public belief in, and concern with, reunification and the related question of the Oder–Neisse Line dropped sharply throughout the 1960s. However, the federal government took care in the Basic Treaty of 1972, which established relations with the GDR, not to accord it full international recognition, never to speak of it as 'Ausland' (foreign territory) and to attempt to uphold the openness of the German question.

The full international recognition of the GDR would have run up against constitutional objections and would almost certainly have been found unconstitutional by the Federal Constitutional Court. Moreover, an unambiguous assertion of totally separate identities for the two German states would have left the position of West Berlin hopelessly exposed. However, the degree of recognition accorded by the Basic Treaty to the GDR certainly upgraded the legitimacy of the GDR and blunted the force of the Federal Republic's claim to speak for an all-German interest. Moreover the conclusion of the Treaty also in a paradoxical way both reduced and increased the role of the Federal Republic. Its ability to speak for an all-German national interest was reduced but its self-proclaimed provisional status, as a state which would in the foreseeable future be transcended by an all-German state, was rendered much less plausible (see Chapter 1 in this volume) and its appearance of permanency increased. This appearance of permanency was further strengthened by attitudinal changes and a growth in specific loyalties to the institutions and existence of the Federal Republic. By the early 1970s more West Germans (41 as against 38 per cent) understood the expression 'our national interests' to mean those of the Federal Republic rather than the collective interest of Germans living in the two states (Niethammer, 1972, 45).

'The German Question must remain open while the Brandenburg Gate remains closed' (Richard von Weizsäcker). The special position of Berlin, restraints associated with the Basic Law and the continued illiberality of the GDR regime alluded to in Weizsäcker's comment prevented the Federal Republic from according the GDR full international recognition. In default of this, confusion persisted, at least at the declaratory level, as to the nature of the general interest that the Federal Republic claimed to be pursuing. The Kohl government did not resolve, but deepened, the confusion. It stressed 'the openness' of the German question much more than its predecessor, while at the same time, through the Honecker visit in 1987, further upgrading the GDR regime. Moreover, it began to use the term *Staatsraison* (*Raison d'état*) of the Federal Republic very frequently. This term, of course, lacked the deep emotional resource of an appeal to national interest, but it did assume some permanent and enduring interests of the Federal Republic.

Whilst appeals to a German national interest in self-determination were for a long period a central element of West German foreign policy at the declaratory level, the intractability of the problem and the lack of interest of the superpowers meant that in normal times it received relatively little attention by West German policy-makers except for the reflexive need to stress the openness of the German Question (*On y parle toujours, on y pense jamais.*).

The key feature of West German foreign policy was the manner in which its policy towards the West, the core area, was not made in terms of some historically conditioned perception of national interests. It was formulated rather within the context of transnational institutional structures, a situation which reflected the rather conditional sovereignty of the Federal Republic. This was clearest in relation to defence and security and the need for Western support on the Berlin question. The Federal Republic had no independent planning capacity, and all its strategic planning was NATO based. It had no regular forces which were not assigned to NATO and could not operate out of area; its defence and security policies were formulated in terms of alliance needs rather than of specific West German interests. The structures assumed that the Federal Republic's security interests, in contrast to the arrangements for Britain and France were, and always would be, identical to and coextensive with alliance interests. All alliance members had to accommodate their policies to alliance policy if they wished to remain in the alliance, but the Federal Republic was unique in NATO in the degree to which it lacked autonomy in strategic planning.

The situation was much less stark, but was arguably analogous, in the area of 'low politics' in relation to the European Community. The Federal Republic, under Adenauer, was committed to the creation of federalist institutions in Western Europe. Its set of policy-making instruments, unlike its French equivalent, was very loose since it was not framed to identify a coherent tightly drawn national interest. It was also notably porous since it was not designed to defend the West German state against a supranational Commission. Adenauer's closest foreign policy confidant, Walter Hallstein, became the first president of the Commission and continued to work for a much more integrated Europe in close cooperation with the federal government. The situation gradually changed, and the federal government over the years, especially during the Schmidt chancellorship, moved away from its commitment to supranational institutions, but it has not yet developed a set of tightly organised policy instruments to identify and assert an overall set of West German interests in the Community. Under Kohl the West German government reversed Schmidt's reserved policy towards the Commission.

Power Resources and Constraints

The Federal Republic had considerable power resources. Its armed forces of around half a million men were approximately equal in size to those of France. It had the strongest land and air forces in Western Europe and was second only to the United States in its contribution to NATO. It was also by far the predominant economy in Western Europe, with a GNP nearly twice as large as its nearest competitor. Moreover, it was preeminently an export oriented manufacturing economy and was the third most important trading nation in the world.

By these traditional indices the Federal Republic was a very powerful state, and yet the constraints on its exercise of these power resources appeared as impressive as the resources themselves. This was most apparent in relation to military resources. Under the Western European Union Treaty of May 1955 the Federal Republic was barred from possessing biological, chemical or nuclear weapons of its own. This gave it a markedly inferior status to Britain and France. All West German forces were assigned to NATO, it had no independent planning function and the forces could not operate out of area. The use of West German military force could be conceived of only in allied terms, a constraint reinforced by the presence of the troops of six allied states on the territory of the Federal Republic. The constraints on the exercise of the economic power of the Federal Republic were of a quite different order. The functional equivalents of alliance control of West Germany's military power certainly existed in the very early years of the Federal Republic, most notably the International Ruhr Authority (IAR). The desire to impose external control on the potential of German heavy industry may also have been a motive in the genesis of the European Coal and Steel Community. It has, however, played little or no part in its practice. The constraints derived rather from internal pressure. The federal government was constrained in relation to the exercise of its economic power in the European Community by resistance among West German public opinion to any pronounced paymaster role for the Federal Republic. This severely restricted the degree to which the federal government could use its great economic resources to exert influence in the European Community. No such resistance was present in public opinion to the use of the economic resources of the federal government for the furthering of German–German relations and economic inducements were a central element of the bargaining strategy of successive federal governments after the early 1970s in their dealings with the GDR. Economic and technological benefits were also part of the Warsaw and Moscow Treaties, and central to the policy of Ostpolitik.

Foreign and Security Policy after Unity

German unity removed nearly all the dependent features which defined the role of the Federal Republic in the international arena. By the time unity was achieved on 3 October 1990, Germany had regained its full sovereignty though it accepted a continued constraint on the possession of biological, chemical and nuclear weapons (see Chapter 1 in this volume). The resolution of the Berlin issue was particularly important since it had been a major source of leverage on successive governments of the Federal Republic by the Soviet adversary and the Western allies. Indeed the transformation of Berlin's status from Four Power occupation to future German capital is perhaps the most potent symbol of the changes wrought by unity. Germany's status had in any case been upgraded by President Bush's offer of 'partners in leadership' in Spring 1989 before the achievement of unity.

Prior to and immediately after unity, attention focused on the increase in German economic power resources brought about by unity. This argument was then clouded by the difficulties experienced in transforming the economies of the five new Länder. Over the longer term Germany will be more powerful economically once it has sorted out these problems.

The Limits of Independence

The new Germany may be less encumbered, but this does not necessarily mean that it will be more successful in the area of external policy than in the past. Throughout the post-war era the Federal Republic had access to a set of very effective ready made institutional tool kits to deal with problems in the external environment. The security threat from the East was addressed by NATO, an organisation in which by far the largest military, intellectual, financial and manpower contribution was made by the United States. Access to external markets provided by the European Community allowed the Federal Republic to build up large and persisting trade balances with all its neighbours.

The external environment in which the Federal Republic now has to operate is a much more complex one. German unity did not take place in a vacuum but as a consequence of the decline in the power of the Soviet Union, and unity was accompanied by the ending of the European division generally and the collapse of the communist regimes of Eastern Europe in particular. In confronting its radically altered environment the Federal Republic has to respond to greatly increased external expectations of the role it might play. At first sight, the chances of the Federal Republic fulfilling these expectations are high. The Federal Republic has grown in power resources relative to other states and the unity process swept away the remnants of the post-war settlement designed to contain Germany. Governmental change takes place slowly in Germany and it possesses a particularly experienced Chancellor and Europe's longest serving Foreign Minister.

The barriers that remain to inhibit Germany playing an enhanced role are, however, formidable. German public opinion on security matters developed in relation to a perceived Soviet threat, and the passing of that threat has left a public opinion which seeks a quiescent Swiss-like role for Germany. This is especially true of opinion in the five new Länder. German political elites whose whole post-war experience was that of making decisions from within supranational and alliance structures will find it very difficult to articulate and formulate a specific German interest; the more especially since post-war policy was so successful.

The political elites are also unnerved and unsettled by a radical agenda shift. While they can cope with the changing agenda of the European Community three particular areas pose especially pressing problems for Germany which are not susceptible to any of the presently available tools in the existing NATO/EC institutional tool kit. Problems, of course, also exist in relation to the Community and to NATO, but they are less novel and are analysed in Chapters 8 and 9.

Collapse and Change in the Soviet Union

For much of the post-war period the Federal Republic had no need to develop a separate policy towards the Soviet Union. It was unwilling to contemplate unity on the terms offered by the Soviet Union, and the Soviet Union was perceived primarily in terms of the threat it posed to German security. Responsibility for addressing that threat was a matter for NATO rather than for the Federal Republic.

This situation was dramatically altered by the unity process. The German government, and Chancellor Kohl in particular, were very conscious of the role played by Mikhail Gorbachev in bringing about the change. This sense of indebtedness to Gorbachev was a feature of all Kohl's major speeches after 1989 and his sense of shock during the attempted coup against Gorbachev in August 1991 was palpable.

The grounds for supporting Gorbachev were of course deeper than mere gratitude. Germany has a vital interest in the smooth completion of the Soviet military withdrawal by 1994, a withdrawal that could have been endangered by Gorbachev's replacement by hardliners. The Federal Republic also has a vital interest in the avoidance of total breakdown and mass migration.

Taken together, these factors influenced the federal government in backing Mikhail Gorbachev very strongly. Conscious that the difficulties of the Soviet economy were too profound to be dealt with by Germany alone, Chancellor Kohl lobbied incessantly for the other Western powers, especially Japan and the United States, to share the burden of economic transformation of the Soviet Union. The condition of the US budget made a positive US response extremely unlikely and Japan still had territorial arguments with the Soviet Union. It was Kohl who insisted that Gorbachev make his ill-fated plea to the G7 Conference in July 1991. Germany itself has by 1991 provided over DM 60m in economic aid to the Soviet Union, approximately 56 per cent of all Western aid to date.

However, in this decisive phase of developments, in this process of the opening of this huge country, we must not sit back as pure spectators saying that what is happening there is something on which we shall keep a watching brief and that later on when decisions have been made we will come in and help them. We must help them help themselves sensibly and feasibly. I am absolutely persuaded that this is vital at this point in time. This will help the Soviet Union to develop in a way that will ensure peace for us all. This is a point I have also made in Washington time and time again, because there are western voices suggesting something different. But I think any policy aimed at bringing about the dissolution of the Soviet Union as a whole is political folly (Kohl, 1991).

Kohl's support for Gorbachev led to a major policy incoherence. Whereas German policy generally stressed self-determination, the federal government was very muted in its support for the Baltic Republics and little pressure was exerted on the Soviet leadership to move quickly on that issue. 'The Soviet leadership will realise that in the end the right to self-determination will prevail' (Helmut Kohl, 1991).

The failed coup in August 1991 and the gradual break up of the Soviet Union occasioned some adjustments in German policy. Support for Gorbachev was reduced and support for Yeltsin increased, a change symbolised by his visit to Germany in November 1991. Hans-Dietrich Genscher announced the recognition of the Baltic States on 28 August and called on the Community to move quickly to conclude association agreements with them.

The German strategy of pouring aid into the Soviet Union now looks even less promising. In the absence of settled institutional structures, administrative competence and plausible programmes for economic reform, aid will simply disappear into a black hole. In this connection German experience with the rather less daunting terrain of the five new Länder has been a salutary lesson for the federal government. Unfortunately the consequences of a breakdown in that area are so serious that the federal government is condemned to seeking solutions to the crisis. So far, no solution appears to be in sight.

If there are no immediately apparent solutions to the problem of the break up of the Soviet Union, the federal government is convinced that the loosening of the structures allows it to do something to staunch the flow of ethnic Germans to Germany (see Chapter 13 in this volume). In the first half of 1991, 77,000 Germans left the Soviet Union for Germany. German policy is now pointed towards encouraging the refounding of the Volga Republic as a homeland for ethnic Germans. In future a proportion of German aid will be channelled towards the new autonomous republic to encourage Germans to settle there instead of migrating to Germany.

Eastern Europe and the Rediscovery of 'Mitteleuropa'

The erosion of Soviet power was quickly reflected in the downfall of communist regimes throughout Eastern Europe. This transition was entirely welcome to the Federal Republic and it presented it with a number of new opportunities.

The opening up of Eastern Europe created a huge potential market of 118 million people, excluding the Soviet Union, 118 million people with a hunger for an individualistic Western consumer life style. The geographical position of Germany, its contacts in the area and the strength of its export oriented economy guarantee that Germany will be the major beneficiary of a growth in East European demand. East Europe is also a promising alternative to southern Europe for the siting of the more labour intensive sections of German industrial production. Unlike southern Europe, which is at some distance from the golden triangle, Poland, Czechoslovakia and Hungary are neighbours of Germany. German investments in Eastern Europe have accordingly dwarfed those of its European neighbours. The successful transformation of the economies of Eastern Europe will of course also dramatically improve the prospects of the five new Länder.

The competition for ascendancy between Anglo–American deregulatory agendas and the German social market model played out in Western Europe in the 1980s is now being repeated in Eastern Europe. In both cases, it is the German model which is proving by far the most attractive.

> Economically, East Europeans wanted to emulate the West German Wirt-schaftswunder as the best agent of transition to democratic order and once established as its most reliable guarantor . . . With most aspects of the postwar German order enjoying great respect in Eastern Europe, it comes as no surprise that some countries have actively sought to emulate West German institutions in the establishment of their new polities. This ranges from the Hungarians' adoption of the West German electoral system to the Czechoslovaks' more than fleeting interest in the Federal Republic's constitution, the Basic Law (Markovits and Reich, 1991, 16).

The benefits to Germany of a peaceful and successful transformation in Czechoslovakia, Hungary and Poland are very high. If their economies could be brought up to a sufficient level they could be brought into the Community quickly and a zone of stability could be created around Germany from Poland, down through Czechoslovakia and Hungary to Austria and Slovenia.

German policy has accordingly given a high priority to these areas. In effect this represents the rediscovery of *Mitteleuropa*: a typical Kohl speech always expresses the view that Prague and Warsaw are at the heart of Europe. The first stage of the policy has involved the conclusion of 'good-neighbourly' agreements, a logical extension of Ostpolitik of the 1970s.

Agreements have been signed with Poland (17 June 1991), Czechoslovakia (7 October 1991) and an agreement with Hungary is due to be concluded. These treaties are designed to recognise the finality of post-war frontiers in default of a final Peace Treaty and to secure some rights for the German minorities and to provide aid for these countries. Both issues proved difficult to resolve in the case of Poland, given the strength of Silesian Refugee associations and Germany's history in the area, but after a pronounced wobble during the unity negotiations Kohl came down heavily in favour of giving priority to good relations with neighbours rather than domestic political imperatives. He compared these treaties rather optimistically to the tradition of Adenauer's Franco–German project.

> As a young man after the war, in my own part of Germany on the border between France and Germany, I was able to see how an age-old enmity between two nations was overcome. Friendly links were established between governments; more importantly, the people themselves, and the young people especially, became friends. We would now dearly like to see the same thing happening with our Polish neighbours. We now have a border of hundreds of kilometres between our two countries and we do not want to see prosperity barriers arising in Europe between the rich and the poor, the haves and the have nots. It is not only a question of matching prosperity levels. It is important to ensure that people can get together again. This is why we have opened our borders to our neighbours – Czechoslovakia and Poland – and we should be delighted to see all other EC countries following suit as soon as possible. (Kohl, 1991).

A major problem for this policy is that the Poles' immediate neighbours are not the post-national West Germans but the less tolerant former East Germans. Nevertheless there is no doubting the German government's desire not only to recognise these borders but also to transform their meaning.

East Europe presents significant opportunities for the New Germany, and it will undoubtedly assume a much more dominant position *vis-à-vis* its eastern than its western neighbours. In the short term, however, it is a problem area. The scale of the investment required would put almost intolerable strain on a German budget weighed down by the cost of supporting unity, the former Soviet Union and the structural funds of the European Community. Successive attempts at burden-sharing have received very little support from the United States and Japan. Yet Germany cannot afford to fail. The new capital of Berlin is less than 100 km from the Polish border. This dilemma is a powerful incentive for Germany to support a single currency which would unlock European savings as a whole for potential investment in the East.

It is, however, beyond the potential zone of stability that German policy runs into its most severe difficulties. In the rest of Eastern Europe the ethnic and communal tensions which while certainly present in Hungary and Czechoslovakia seem soluble without recourse to violence, threaten to spin out of control.

The Balkans Imbroglio

Undoubtedly the most difficult problem for Germany is the situation in Yugoslavia. German inhibitions in the security area rule out active support for military intervention (Chapter 8 in this volume). It is also much more difficult than in the Polish or Czech cases to jump over the shadow of Germany's history. In these two cases, the federal government was able to take a generous attitude and to discount the voice or votes of the refugee element. In an intra-ethnic struggle, it is a question of choosing sides, and the Federal Republic has decisively sided with the former German allies of Slovenia and Croatia. This policy has been justified in terms of support for the principle of self-determination that was played down in the morally much more clear cut case of the Baltics. Perhaps even more crucially, it has led to extreme strain on a common European position with the German government announcing its intention to recognise Slovenia and Croatia some time before its European partners. The reasons that have been adduced for this step include the presence of 700,000 Yugoslav workers, mainly Croats and Slovenes, in Germany and heavy lobbying by the Catholic Church. Whatever the grounds, Germany's contribution to a Common European foreign policy in Yugoslavia has been regarded as less than helpful by all its Community partners. Its insistence on persisting with its recognition policy also indicates a departure from Germany's normally automatic support for EC foreign policy positions.

Germany and Global Political Challenges

The political horizon of the Federal Republic was largely restricted to the European area. Its views on areas outside Europe have rarely been advanced or sought, and when they have been articulated, as on South Africa and the Middle East, it has been from within the protective lager of the European Political Cooperation mechanism. The ending of the Cold War, the virtual demise of the Soviet Union and the weakening economic readiness of the United States to underwrite international public goods like security has coincided with a greatly increased expectation of what Germany can contribute to the maintenance of international order. The United States in particular was keen to offer Germany a 'partners in leadership' role. Unfortunately for the United States this is a role, as the Gulf Crisis demonstrated, which neither German public opinion nor German elite opinion is equipped to respond to. The German response to the Gulf Crisis was hesitant, unsure and put some considerable strain on the German–American relationship.

In a damage limitation exercise the German government made very considerable financial contributions to the allies, but this brought it no increase in influence. The government intends to remove the constitutional inhibition to participating in out of area conflict (Article 87A), but this will not take the issue much further. For real change to occur what Germany needs is a sustained public discourse on the specific geopolitical strategic interests of Germany, and under what circumstances force might be employed. There is little sign of such a debate as yet.

The hesitations Germany displays about essaying a more ambitious security role are largely absent in terms of contributing to global economic stability. Germany is bearing the lion's share of the burden in Eastern Europe and the Soviet Union without much help from either the United States or Japan. It has also played a key role in the GATT negotiations though it has not yet unequivocally decided to throw its weight in the direction of concluding the Uruguay Round at the expense of domestic interests, especially agriculture.

The German government has also made sustained efforts to use its economic power to bring about global environmental improvements by attempting to push for a linkage between debt cancellation and environmental improvements.

The traumatic political history of twentieth-century Germany will ensure that Germany remains a 'civilian power'; it will continue to resist efforts by the United States to tie it into some more ambitious security role. Germany will also persist in giving priority to multilateral frameworks. A gradual reduction of the American presence in

Europe is assumed, and the Federal Republic will continue to push for the development of a strengthened European defence identity, but it will go to great lengths to avoid a breach with the United States. It will, of course, also bring the incoherence of its own security discussion and its reluctance to make choices into the debates taking place within multilateral frameworks.

The central external problems for Germany, as for the European Community as a whole, involve how to respond to the collapse of the Soviet Union and bring about change in Eastern Europe. The federal government has no patent answer to the collapse of the Soviet Union or the problems of ethnic conflict in Eastern Europe. Its central policy thrust will be to aid the transformation of Poland, Czechoslovakia and Hungary and to create a zone of stability around Germany. If this succeeds, these states will then be able to join the European Community. They will, however, continue to be very dependent on Germany. This is likely to engender some tension in intra-Community dynamics, and the French in particular may feel aggrieved. This, of course, explains why the French government has given such priority to 'deepening' before 'widening'. Such a change in central Europe will impose enormous demands on German public and private funds, and the key question for the internal stability of Germany as well as the success of future external policy of the new Germany must relate to the future prospects of the German economy. Will it be able to bear the combined weight of internal and external demands that have been placed on it? At present (See Chapter 10 in this volume) the answer still looks likely to be positive. By itself, it is not enough to guarantee success, but failure in this area would surely prejudice everything else.

8

Uncertainties of Security Policy

ADRIAN HYDE-PRICE

Germany is the nerve centre of security policy decisions on Europe. This is due to the fact that this country has the geostrategically important central location. Everything which happens here always affects the fate of the rest of Europe (Wettig, 1991, 14)

Germany's New Role

German unification has been but one – albeit one of the most significant – of the dramatic and largely unexpected changes which have fundamentally transformed the security environment in Europe in recent years. For over forty years, Europe was divided by an Iron Curtain which ran through the heart of Germany and Berlin. The Cold War produced the largest concentration of conventional and nuclear forces in Central Europe the world had ever seen. The FRG and the GDR became integral parts of the two military–political alliance systems that confronted each other across a palisade of tanks, missiles and barbed wire. In this manichaean world, the security policy of the Federal Republic was relatively straightforward: full integration into the NATO alliance, along with a close strategic and political relationship with both Washington and Paris. From the late 1960s onwards, this *Westintegration* was accompanied by a search for a *Europäische Friedensordnung* (a 'European Peace order') in which, it was hoped, Germany would be able to achieve its national self-determination in freedom and peace.

Today, the situation is radically different. Germany is no longer

153

a divided nation on the front line of a bipolar Europe, but is a reunited country at the heart of a reuniting continent. Not only has the end of the Cold War dramatically improved the security environment for Germany, but unification has increased the political weight and importance of the FRG in Europe and the wider international community. As one senior naval officer at the Federal Defence Ministry has written, 'Germany therefore has the opportunity to become a decisive factor and a driving force for peace and progress in Europe and beyond . . . Whether we like to admit it or not, Germany represents for Europe and the world a major power; not only economically, but also politically. It is a power that, in concert with the industrial powers and in the global geopolitical system, will play an even greater role than it so far has' (Weisser, 1991, 39).

By any criteria, post-war West German security policy has proved remarkably successful. It not only helped fashion the international climate which made unification possible, but unification itself was achieved without cost to the Federal Republic's integration into the security structures of the Western community. However, its very success has generated new problems and challenges. Not only have a number of new issues come onto the security agenda in Europe, but some of the basic assumptions of German security policy are now being questioned. With the end of the Cold War and the perceived decline in the 'Soviet threat', the domestic debate on the goals and instruments of German security policy has become even more wide-ranging. It is not merely isolated details of the FRG's security policy that are being questioned, but the basic assumptions and fundamental principles of its *Sicherheitspolitik*. This in turn touches upon the very self-identity of the Germans, along with their conception of their place in Europe and the wider world.

German security policy has therefore entered a period of profound uncertainty. As the Federal Republic struggles to integrate 16 million former GDR citizens, it is also having to restructure its external relations with its neighbours, allies and former enemies. Germany is being forced to redefine its future regional and global role, and this cannot but affect its security policy. The Federal Republic will have to try and balance the commitments arising from its continuing *Westintegration* with its aspirations for a pan-European cooperative security system. It has also to decide how to respond to calls for it to make an ever greater contribution to maintenance of international security in an increasingly turbulent and polycentric globe. In the words of Karl Kaiser, 'A united Germany free of the East–West confrontation on its soil and now one of the world's wealthiest democracies, must face a novel and difficult task: to reconcile its foreign policy traditions with the new responsibilities that inevitably accompany its enhanced position and require the – sometimes unpopular – use of its political, economic and military resources in partnership with others to preserve peace on an unstable globe' (Kaiser, 1991, 205).

The Determinants of Security Policy

German security policy – like that of other countries – is the product of a complex interplay between the external international environment on the one hand, and subjective domestic factors on the other. In terms of the external determinants of security policy, four are decisive in the case of Germany.

Geography

Germany's central location is an inescapable geopolitical reality which has given it a pivotal role in European affairs. Today, Germany's strategic position at the crossroads of Europe means that it has the potential to act as a bridge between East and West, and as a central element in a new pan-European security system.

The Structure of the International System

Bismarck's Second Reich was born into a Europe characterised by a shifting balance of power between competing nation-states; the Federal Republic was created in the context of a bipolar Europe divided into two hostile alliance systems. Today, a united Germany finds itself in a Europe transformed by more complex networks of interdependence and supranational forms of integration. Furthermore, a 'pluralist security community' has emerged in Western Europe which has made military conflict between one-time enemies in this part of the continent inconceivable.

The Pattern of its Alliance Commitments

Since the establishment of the FRG in 1949, its security policy has been formed in a multilateral context, primarily within the NATO alliance. The Federal Republic's clear and unambiguous commitment to close strategic, political and economic integration with the Western powers has been the decisive factor in determining its security policy.

The Policy of Other States Towards Germany

At various times over the past centuries, Germany has perceived a security threat to its vital national interests from either its neighbours or other European great powers – from Austria and France, to Russia and the United Kingdom. Today, however, Germany finds itself in the uniquely favourable situation of enjoying friendly relations with all other major European powers, and not having to face any significant military threat to its political and territorial integrity.

These four structural factors have produced an external security environment which presents both opportunities and challenges to German policy-makers. The nature of the security policy pursued by Germany in response to this external environment will depend to a large extent on the assumptions and perceptions of the key domestic actors involved in the making of security and defence policy. The policy-making elites are in turn influenced by a series of historically-determined domestic forces, stemming from Germany's economic interests, the character of its political system, its social structure and cultural values.

Together, these domestic factors shape what has been called the '*strategic culture*' of a country. In the case of Germany, its strategic culture has been heavily coloured by the country's tragic historical experiences in the first half of this century. The legacy of Nazism and ignominious defeat in war – combined with the 'civilising' impact of a rising standard of living and a social market economy – has led to widespread rejection of militarist values and substantial support for neutralist and even pacificist sentiments. Although German public opinion remains firmly committed to the FRG's *Westintegration*, including membership of NATO (Veen, 1991, 37; Bergsdorf, 1991, 88), there is much less support for a robust nuclear deterrence, and still less support for an 'out-of-area' role for German troops. These views are more strongly marked in the five new eastern Länder (Möller, 1991). Nevertheless, public opinion in Germany (as in most other countries) has only a limited and indirect impact on security policy, which is determined primarily by the political leadership (Payne and Rühle, 1991, 40). In the Federal Republic, it is the Chancellor's office which plays a key role in the formulation of the country's security policy, in consort with the Foreign Minister, Hans-Dietrich Genscher (given his exceptional political longevity and popularity), and the Defence Ministry.

Germany's security policy is formulated by a political leadership deeply influenced by the country's distinctive 'strategic culture'. This has been described by Peter Stratmann as follows:

Since the 1950s nearly all aspects of defence, i.e., objective, conditions and requirements of military operations in case of war, have been fundamentally eradicated from the security consciousness of the West German population. This eradication was an understandable political reflex in view of the fact that the Federal Republic can expect to be secure only if war is entirely prevented. Confronted with the conventional and nuclear offensive and destructive potential of the Soviet Union, it would be meaningless for this tiny, densely-populated and highly-industrialised country, which might be the potential battlefield, to seek security in the capability for a successful defence . . .

Under these circumstances there was a gradual development of a studied amilitary, i.e., purely political, understanding of security policy. The interpretation of NATO strategy as a political means to avoid war by the threat of nuclear retaliation was portrayed positively in contrast to 'warfighting strategies', which were declared to be out-of-date in the nuclear age . . . In the popular version of this argument, the mission of the Bundeswehr would be seen to have failed as soon as the first shot was fired (Kaiser and Roper, 1988, 97–8).

This largely amilitary strategic culture exerts a profound influence on contemporary German security thinking, and colours the political leadership's approach to the new security agenda which is emerging in Europe.

A Changing Security Agenda

A united Germany today faces a radically different security agenda to that which faced the Federal Republic in the first four decades of its existence. Until the late 1980s, the predominant security concern of the FRG was the perceived threat from the concentration of offensively equipped and trained Soviet armoured forces forward-deployed in Eastern Europe. It was this 'Soviet threat' which provided the rationale for the Bundeswehr, for the FRG's comprehensive integration into NATO and for Franco–German defence and security cooperation. In the early 1990s, however, very few Germans continue to believe in the existence of a military threat from the Soviet Union. Indeed, German security policy today is being developed in a uniquely benign international constellation, with no obvious enemy, and no clear and specific security 'threat'. As President Richard von Weizsäcker noted, 'For the first time [in history] we Germans are not a point of contention on the European agenda. Our uniting has not been inflicted on anybody; it is the result of peaceful agreement' (Joffe, 1991, 84). Germany achieved its unification democratically and peacefully on the basis of international agreement, and enjoys good relations with all major states in Europe and the wider international community. This means that the post-war security dilemma facing the Germans has been largely resolved, and the FRG is now in the fortunate situation of having no enemies on or near its borders.

Nevertheless, although the security environment of the Federal Republic has markedly improved over recent years, this does not mean that Germany can exist as an isolated island of peaceful prosperity in an otherwise turbulent world. Violent confrontation remains endemic in the wider international system, whilst within Europe itself there are a number of new sources of both armed conflict and political instability. What is new for the Germans, however, is that the security problems they face are now increasingly diffuse, multifaceted and intangible. There are no clear and specific security 'threats', but rather a number of potential 'risks' and 'challenges'. Moreover, many of the security concerns now facing the FRG are not military, and are not amenable to simple military solutions: rather, they are economic, political, social and environmental in character (Hyde-Price, 1991, 55–9).

The first of these potential security 'challenges' comes from the residual military strength of the former Soviet Union. Despite the collapse of the Warsaw Pact and the drastic reduction in the offensive capability of the Commonwealth of Independent States even the Russian Federation on its own remains a military superpower with awesome conventional and nuclear forces. This, coupled with continuing instability of the former Soviet Union and the concomitant fear of nuclear proliferation, will be a major concern for the FRG's *Sicherheitspolitik* until well into the twenty-first century.

Secondly, there are the security problems generated by the transition from communist authoritarianism to democratic market orientated societies in Eastern Europe. This is closely bound up with the resurgence of ethnic, national and religious conflict throughout the former communist world and the Balkans. As the tragic civil war in Yugoslavia has shown, ethno-national conflicts will be one of Europe's major security worries in the 1990s and beyond. The security problems this poses for Germany stem not just from the fear that inter-communal conflict could spread across the often arbitrarily delineated borders in the Balkans and Eastern Europe: a much more pressing concern for Germany is the fear that social turmoil and economic collapse in the East will generate waves of refugees drawn towards the prosperous stability of the FRG.

Thirdly, there are the so-called 'out-of-area' problems. These include threats to supplies of vital raw materials, markets and maritime trade routes; the spread of ballistic missile technology coupled with the proliferation of chemical and nuclear weapons; terrorism; economically motivated immigration from North Africa, the Eastern Mediterranean and Asia; and the instability generated by the appalling levels of poverty and underdevelopment in the Third World. With the passing of the Cold War, the axis of potential conflict is shifting from East–West to North–South. Indeed, as the Gulf War and the Yugoslav crisis has shown, a southern 'arc of crisis' seems to be emerging, stretching from the Balkans and the Eastern Mediterranean, through the Middle East and the Persian Gulf, to North Africa.

Germany therefore faces a changing security agenda, to which it will have to respond as it comes to terms with the new responsibilities placed upon it following its national unification. The Federal Republic faces a less polarised and antagonistic security environment in Europe and the wider world, but one which at the same time is becoming more uncertain, ambiguous and fragile. In this situation, a number of new themes are beginning to emerge in German security policy.

German Security Policy beyond the Cold War

The first theme of post-unification German *Sicherheitspolitik* is the concern to see multilateral security structures in Europe strengthened. As we have seen, from the very inception of the FRG in 1949, the security policy of the new Republic was firmly embedded in an Atlanticist and West European framework. Unification has been accompanied by repeated calls from the German government to preserve and strengthen these multilateral structures, along with assurances that it does not wish to pursue a more independent national security policy. Thus Chancellor Kohl joined President Mitterrand in calling for the development of a common foreign and security policy – including defence – by the European Community, whilst Defence Minister Gerhard Stoltenberg warned against a 'renationalisation' of defence policies within NATO.

A second theme of German security policy in the 1990s is its emphasis on the need to construct a more cooperative security regime as the basis for a durable *europäische Friedensordnung*. Hans-Dietrich Genscher has often spoken of the need to create a 'new cooperative structure' resting on a number of pillars – a restructured Atlantic alliance, the European Community and the CSCE. Similarly, President Weizsäcker amongst others has declared that 'Our experiences have definitely given us a special responsibility for the concept of peace' (Weizsäcker, 1991, 8), whilst the opposition Social

Democrats have long advocated a system of 'common security'. The Germans have been prominent advocates of bringing the East Europeans into a closer relationship with the Community; of giving NATO a greater responsibility for institutionalised diplomatic liaison and political consultation with former Warsaw Pact countries; and of strengthening the CSCE as a framework for pan-European cooperation. A crucial political element of this new cooperative security structure is integrating the Soviet Union's successor states into a network of European organisations and multilateral structures, in order to prevent the emergence of a new division of Europe and to strengthen the reform process in the former Soviet Union.

These pan-European security concerns of the Germans have led some to fear that Germany may succumb to 'the oldest German temptation', namely, 'to look both East and West, without completely committing itself to either. Tomorrow that instinct might be reawakened by the image of a USSR which is both benign and dependent' (Joffe, 1991, 90). The fear is that Germany's search for a more cooperative pan-European security system might lead it to weaken the military–political ties that bind it strategically to the West. Some critics of the post-unification Soviet–German entente speak darkly of a 'new Rapallo', whilst others fear a new *Sonderweg* ('Special path'), leading Germany to wander between East and West. In fact, fears that Germany's pursuit of a cooperative security system will be at the expense of its long-standing political, economic, cultural and strategic integration into the West – which is now widely accepted in the Federal Republic – are greatly overblown. 'On the contrary', as Robert Blackwill has warned, 'the most salient danger in the next decade is that Germany, and indeed the West, will lose interest in the land across the Bug, and will be insufficiently engaged in the future of the Soviet Union' (Blackwill, 1991, 93). Nevertheless, the fall of the Iron Curtain does open up new opportunities for Germany to pursue its long-standing economic, political and strategic interests in the lands to its East, and this cannot but have an impact on German security policy. Consequently:

> Though the days of Bismarck's *Schaukelpolitik* may be over, Germany's status as *das Land in der Mitte* is not. More than at any other time since the end of World War Two, the opportunities and problems associated with this pivotal position in Europe will stimulate vigorous discussion within Germany over the country's future course and, indeed, its very identity (Sodaro, 1990, 408).

The third theme in German security policy is the need to achieve a parallel strengthening and transformation of the Atlantic alliance, the European Community, the WEU and the CSCE, in order to create a security system based on a multiplicity of overlapping institutions. Of course, different political forces place a different emphasis on different institutions: Christian Democrats, for example, place considerable emphasis on NATO; the FDP on the Western European Union; and the Social Democrats and the Greens on the CSCE. But all the mainstream parties accept the need for an institutionally diverse security system. German security analysts recognise the risk of duplication and competition inherent in this approach, but argue that it reflects the diversity of Europe and its different national traditions, along with the changing security agenda (Weidenfeld, 1990; Nötzold and Rummel, 1990; Krell, 1991). No one body alone, it is argued, can tackle the multiplicity of security issues facing Europe. Security can only be provided by creating a network of overlapping and interlocking bodies in Europe, which together can provide a framework for conflict prevention and crisis management. For example, whilst NATO might be able to address security issues directly affecting its sixteen members in the North Atlantic area, the Community or the CSCE might be more appropriate for tackling economic instability or nationalist conflict in the East. Therefore, it is argued, the relationship between organisations like NATO, the Community and the CSCE should not be seen in zero-sum terms: all these bodies have a distinctive security role to play, and none on their own are sufficient to tackle the range of potential security challenges facing the Federal Republic in the 1990s.

NATO: The Bedrock of German Security

From its very first hours, the fledgling Federal Republic was dependent on the Atlantic alliance for its security and territorial integrity. The FRG formally joined NATO in 1955, and since then West Germany has been a key member of the alliance. Occasionally, some of Germany's Western partners have feared that the FRG might be tempted to accept neutrality in return for unification – as proposed by Stalin in 1952 – but this option was never seriously considered by Bonn. The deeply ingrained commitment of the West German political elite to NATO was evident from the very beginning of the unification process in late 1989, when the right of a united Germany to belong to the alliance was made a central objective of the West German foreign policy. Even following the end of the Cold War, NATO continues to be the lynchpin of German security policy. But whilst Germany remains fully committed to the alliance, a united Germany will inevitably tend to use its strengthened influence in the organisation to achieve a number of changes in NATO's structure and role. For this reason, therefore, it is no exaggeration to suggest that 'The future of NATO will be determined by Germany and the role that a united Germany chooses for itself in the Alliance' (Payne and Rühle, 1991, 38).

There are four main reasons why Germany remains so resolutely committed to NATO. First, the substantial conventional and nuclear forces of the former Soviet Union and its successor states continues to cast a long geostrategic shadow over Central Europe. Second, German engagement in NATO is seen as an important demonstration of its continuing *Westintegration*. This multilateral approach to German security provides assurance both to the Germans and to their neighbours;

> Integration in NATO is also beneficial for the Germans themselves, since they avoid the risk of coming into conflict with the other European countries and incurring the hostility of their neighbours. Within the integration community of NATO, a consensus is established on the basis of the mutual fulfillment of interests. This overcomes the former dilemma that either the European need for security had to be met at the expense of the Germans or the Germans' need for security at the expense of other Europeans (Wettig, 1991, 15).

Third, the governing coalition continues to believe most strongly that a US military commitment to Europe is essential for the peace and security of the continent, and that this must be retained within a transatlantic security structure centred on NATO (Rotfeld and Stützle, 1991, 79). NATO is widely seen in Germany as embodying the commitment of the United States to the security of Western Europe, and as a key institutional expression of a transatlantic community built upon common values and enduring principles. The unification process (specifically the 'two plus four' negotiations) cemented the close Bonn–Washington alliance, and confirmed the importance that both sides attach to their bilateral relationship as 'partners in leadership' (Blackwill, 1991). Although many Germans have criticised the special rights and privileges of American forces stationed in Germany, as well as the inconvenience caused by low-flying and large-scale military exercises, there is a consensus that an American military presence in Europe maintains the regional balance of power, and adds to the overall stability of the continent. In the future, American military forces in Europe may well fall below the figure of 225,000 stipulated in the CFE Treaty – perhaps to less than 100,000. But the German government is likely to welcome a continuing US military presence in Germany within the NATO framework (although not necessarily on the basis of the old allied occupation statutes which gave allied stationed forces special rights and privileges). This will involve the retention of a substantial American military infrastructure in Germany, including stationed forces, major airbases and POMCUS (pre-positioned material) facilities.

Finally, NATO is seen by the majority in Germany as making an important contribution to the general security and stability of the continent. It includes Norway and Turkey, both of which are countries of vital strategic importance on Europe's peripheries, but which belong neither to the European Community nor to the Western European Union WEU; it provides non-nuclear powers like Germany with a shield against nuclear blackmail; and, above all, it is tried and tested collective defensive organisation based on democratic Western values. Marshalling public support for any new security arrangement in Europe will take time. Meanwhile, in the view of many Germans, prudence dictates retaining a strong NATO alliance. NATO's significance as a bulwark of security in an otherwise turbulent Europe is further evidenced in German eyes by the interest expressed throughout Eastern Europe in developing closer relations with the alliance.

But whilst NATO remains the bedrock of German security policy, most Germans argue that the alliance must significantly reform its structure and functions if it is to remain relevant to the changed environment of post-Cold War Europe. To begin with, there is broad consensus that NATO must become a more *European* organisation. The balance of power and resources between the United States and Western Europe has changed dramatically since the early years of NATO, and there is general agreement on both sides of the Atlantic that the Europeans need to assume a greater responsibility for their own defence (Stoltenberg, 1990, 15). The German government is keen to see a 'European pillar' constructed within the alliance, and looks to the WEU and NATO's Eurogroup to provide the institutional expression of this.

The second set of changes to NATO championed by the Germans concern the organisation's relationship with the countries to its East. The Bonn government was a prime mover behind NATO's 'London Declaration' of July 1990 which, amongst other important changes, offered to extend 'the hand of friendship' to its former enemies in the Warsaw Pact. Since then, the Germans have actively encouraged the development of a more complex network of bilateral diplomatic and political links between NATO on the one hand, and the Soviet Union and individual East European countries on the other. For example, in October 1991, Hans-Dietrich Genscher, in a joint initiative with his American counterpart, James Baker, proposed the creation of an institutionalised forum for regular high-level consultation and discussion between the NATO sixteen, the Soviet Union, the three Baltic states and the countries of Eastern Europe. This US–German initiative was formally endorsed by the Rome NATO summit in November 1991, which agreed to establish a 'North Atlantic Consultative Council' along the lines of the Baker–Genscher plan. By strengthening political dialogue across the former East–West divide, the German government hopes that greater mutual understanding and tolerance can be fostered. This is something very much in the interests of Germany, given its geographical proximity to potentially unstable countries in the former communist bloc. Nonetheless, whilst most Germans favour the development of diplomatic and political links with the East Europeans, very few advocate offering firm security guarantees or the promise of future membership of the alliance to individual East European countries. Such a development, most Germans recognise, would be politically divisive within NATO itself, and could exacerbate the security dilemmas of other states in the region excluded from NATO's protective umbrella.

The third set of changes sought by Germany within NATO are to the organisation's military strategy and force structure. The withdrawal of Soviet troops from Central and Eastern Europe and the disbandment of the Warsaw Pact have made the traditional twin pillars of NATO's strategy – forward defence and flexible response – increasingly anachronistic and politically indefensible (Lübkemeier, 1991, 16). As the result of a far-reaching NATO 'Strategy Review' (completed in late 1991), which Germany played a key role in shaping, a new strategic concept was developed for the alliance, based on a greater reliance on reinforcements in the event of war, and smaller, more mobile stationed forces configured in multinational corps. The creation of a NATO Rapid Reaction Corps was welcomed in principle by the German government, although the leading role assigned to British forces within it was the source of some contention. However, the area of greatest difficulty for Germany was the domestically sensitive question of nuclear strategy.

Issues inherent to the strategy of extended nuclear deterrence have for many years now been the source of substantial disagreement between the Bonn government and its major NATO allies in Washington, London and Paris. Following the 1987 Washington INF (Intermediate Nuclear Forces) Treaty, opposition within Germany to NATO's strategy of flexible response focused on SNF (Short-range Nuclear Forces). Opposition to SNF was initially voiced by the SPD, but by 1989 even Alfred Dregger (the Chairman of the CDU/CSU party in the Bundestag) had expressed his unease with these particular short-range weapon systems, which were capable of striking territory only in Germany or East Central Europe. Consequently, in its historic 'London Declaration', NATO – under considerable pressure from the Bonn government – called for the negotiated elimination of ground-launched nuclear forces of the shortest range, and referred to nuclear weapons as 'weapons of last resort' (Wegener, 1990, 5). NATO's new strategic concept no longer demands a robust ladder of nuclear escalation, even though it continues to affirm the war-prevention role of a minimum nuclear deterrence. Thus, as Ulrich Weisser has argued, 'It is becoming clear that future nuclear weapons will serve only the purely political purpose of stabilizing European security structures. In future the Alliance will therefore make do with a minimum of air-based and sea-based nuclear weapons – a minimum that should be defined in cooperation with the Soviet Union and later become a yardstick for further nuclear disarmament' (Weisser, 1991, 42).

Nuclear weapons are therefore no longer a source of acute domestic controversy in Germany in the way they were in the early 1980s. This is due to a number of factors: the improved strategic environment in Central and Eastern Europe; the steady reduction in the number of nuclear systems in Europe following the INF treaty and, more recently, President Bush's unilateral unclear disarmament initiative of September 1991; the willingness of NATO to give up most of its SNF systems, especially nuclear artillery and battlefield nuclear weapons; and the Soviet Union's acceptance of the principle of a minimum nuclear deterrent. This last point means that, as two young German security analysts have argued, 'A system of nuclear deterrence which is contractually agreed or at least tacitly tolerated by all sides – including the Soviet Union – is not an obstacle to comprehensive detente and cooperative efforts' (May and Rühle, 1991, 29). If this is indeed the case, it may remove some of the wind from the sails of the anti-nuclear lobby in Germany, and reduce the political controversies associated with nuclear strategy in Central Europe. Indeed, the issue of most concern to German public opinion today is not NATO's nuclear strategy, but rather the risks of nuclear proliferation arising from the disintegration of the Soviet Union.

A European Defence Identity?

Whilst NATO remains the bedrock of German security policy, the German government is also a firm proponent of a more pronounced European defence identity. The notion of a 'European defence identity' is frequently employed in the security debate in the transatlantic security community, but its precise meaning remains institutionally ambiguous and politically contentious. For 'Atlanticists', it means the 'Europeanisation' of NATO and the development of a European 'pillar' within the Atlantic alliance. This is the interpretation favoured by most policy-makers in London, Washington and the Hague. For 'Europeanists', on the other hand, it implies the creation of an autonomous West European defence organisation, politically linked to the European Community. This interpretation finds its strongest adherents in Paris, Rome and Madrid. In this debate between 'Atlanticists' and 'Europeanists', a pivotal role has been assigned to the WEU – either as NATO's European pillar, or as institutional embodiment of an automonous West European defence organisation.

The Kohl government's position in this debate is somewhat ambivalent, in that Bonn seem to endorse both interpretations simultaneously. On the one hand, Germany enjoys a privileged position as a 'partner in leadership' with the United States, and is committed to preserving a durable and robust NATO. Yet on the other, Chancellor Kohl has also joined with President Mitterrand (in their joint initiatives of 18 April and 6 December 1990) to advocate an accelerated transition to European Political Union within the Community, and has repeatedly called for the development of a common EC foreign and security policy, including defence. Chancellor Kohl hopes that these two seemingly rival approaches to European security – Atlanticist and Europeanist – can be finessed through the medium of the WEU, which he envisages as the bridge between NATO and the EC (Kohl, 1991, 40).

In Chancellor Kohl's view, therefore, there is no contradiction between its commitment to NATO and its desire to see a common EC foreign, security and defence policy. But this position is not sustainable in the medium to long term. As the Americans have pointed out, the decisive issue is where the decisions are taken: in the Atlantic alliance, between the sixteen (which would leave the United States as *primus inter pares*), or in the Community/WEU (which would exclude the United States, along with peripheral European countries like Norway and Turkey). At some stage in its development, therefore, a robust security and defence dimension within the Community would inevitably undermine the current centrality of NATO to German and West European security.

For some in Germany, however, this is very much to be welcomed. Although the dominant school of thought within the German security community has been Atlanticist, there has been a significant minority of German 'Gaullists' who have advocated an unambiguously 'Europeanist' approach. In other words, they have wished to see NATO replaced by an autonomous West European security organisation, analogous to the failed European Defence Community (EDC) of the early 1950s. This school of thought finds adherents on both sides of the political spectrum, from anti-Americans in the SPD, to leading politicians in the CDU. For example, Willy Wimmer (the CDU Parliamentary State Secretary in the Defence Ministry) has advocated the development of a security and defence role for the Community, with NATO as a more limited 'management organisation' facilitating the process of change in Europe (Payne and Rühle, 1991, 40). Similarly, Hans-Gert Poettering (the CDU Chairman of the Security and Disarmament Subcommittee of the European Parliament) has advocated the development of an institutionalised common security and defence policy within the ambit of the Community, through the creation of a 'Community Security Council' (consisting of EC foreign and defence ministers, who would take decisions on the basis of a two-thirds majority rule principle); a multinational European military force (based on the precedent of the Franco–German brigade); and a common arms procurement and defence industry policy (Poettering, 1991, 149). More recently, Volker Rühe, the CDU Secretary-General, has called for the creation of an armed European peace-keeping force under WEU auspices to separate the warring factions in Yugoslavia (*Financial Times*, 1 August 1991).

Although the proposals for a common EC foreign and security policy being discussed by the Intergovernmental Conference in the course of 1991 do not amount to a serious challenge to the preeminence of NATO in West European security structures, the future emergence of an autonomous West European defence organisation could provoke a major crisis in transatlantic relations. In this debate between Atlanticists (found primarily in America, Britain and Holland) and Europeanists (concentrated in France, Italy and Spain), Germany will play a decisive role. At the moment, it is hard to imagine Germany sacrificing the tried and tested security provided by the NATO alliance in favour of an unproven vision of a West European defence community. However, if there is a major crisis in transatlantic relations – arising from, for example, substantial differences over trade issues in GATT, NATO military strategy or 'out-of-area' conflicts – then Germany might seek to develop a qualitatively deeper strategic and military relationship with its allies in the Community, leading to the creation of an independent West European defence organisation.

The CSCE and Cooperative Security in Europe

The Germans have been staunch supporters of the Helsinki process since its inception in 1975. With the end of the Cold War in Europe, the CSCE has acquired a new lease of life, and has now emerged as one of the key institutional supports of Europe's security architecture (along with NATO and the European Community). The Paris Summit of CSCE Heads of State and Government in November 1990 gave the Helsinki process a permanent institutional structure, and also codified a series of principles for the conduct of inter-state relations and human rights (known as the 'Paris Charter for a New Europe'). This was seen as a major achievement for Hans-Dietrich Genscher, who has been amongst the most forceful advocates of a more institutionalised and influential CSCE, which he has described as 'a framework for stability for the dynamic, dramatic and some-times revolutionary developments in Eastern Europe and the Soviet Union' (Atlantic Council, 1990, 19). Nevertheless, there has been considerable debate in Germany as to the precise competencies and potentialities of the CSCE in the new Europe.

The majority view (which includes most of the CDU, FDP and SPD) sees the CSCE as a supplement to the Atlantic alliance and the European Community/WEU, within a pluralist and multidimensional security system in Europe. This majority believes that the CSCE has many positive features: it involves all European states, including the United States and Canada; it has already played an important role in 'standard-setting', especially in the field of human rights; it provides a useful framework for pan-European political dialogue and cooperation; and it provides a proven forum for negotiations on arms control and confidence-building measures. But because the CSCE operates on the basis of unanimous decision-making, most Germans believe that it cannot provide a viable and robust system for collective security in Europe, and therefore cannot replace existing military alliances and collective defence arrangements (Teltschik, 1991a, 24–5).

There is a minority school of thought, however, which finds its adherents amongst radicals on the political left, which envisages a much more ambitious future for the CSCE. Its adherents believe that the Helsinki process has the potential to become the institutional basis for a pan-European system of collective security, replacing the Atlantic alliance and making a West European defence body superfluous. Egon Bahr, for example, has called for the transformation of the CSCE into a regional equivalent of the United Nations, with a European 'security council' (capable of taking decisions on the basis of qualified majority voting) and European peace-keeping forces to intervene when necessary (Rotfeld and Stützle, 1991, 79).

Such a far-reaching transformatioin of the CSCE is unlikely in the foreseeable future, because of the vested national interests involved. Nonetheless, the notion of a stronger security role for the CSCE has received a sympathetic hearing from the Foreign Minister, Hans-Dietrich Genscher. He too has called for the creation of a European Security Council and European 'Green Berets' (modelled on the UN's 'Blue Berets'), along with the construction of a series of 'common spaces' and cooperative projects between East and West in the areas of science, technology, the environment and communications. In some of his speeches over the last few years, he has also come close to suggesting that the CSCE might be able to replace crucial aspects of NATO's current security role ('Genscher für ein neues Sicherheitssystem in Europa', *Süddeutsche Zeitung*, 27 September 1990, 1).

Despite Genscher's obvious and oft-stated sympathy for the CSCE, however, the majority view in Germany is that it cannot provide an effective and credible system of pan-European collective security. Rather, it serves as a framework for political dialogue and negotiation between all its 35 participating countries, and as the 'comprehensive reference framework for sectoral and regional co-operation relating to security and economic policy problems as well as to questions of politico–cultural development' (Nötzold and Rummel, 1990, 219).

An 'Out-of-area' Role for the Bundeswehr?

The most politically controversial and emotionally charged issue on the German security agenda today is the question of how best the FRG should discharge its international responsibilities for world peace. The Gulf War presented the newly united Germany with its first major international test – and in the eyes of many both inside Germany and without, it was a test which found the FRG sorely wanting (Thies, 1991). Germany was called upon by its allies, particularly America, to support the UN-sponsored military operation. But Germany was prevented by the *Grundgesetz* from deploying Bundeswehr forces outside of the NATO area (Bardehle, 1989). Bonn was therefore left in the secondary role of paymaster and diplomatic cheerleader for the Allies in the Gulf.

This unsatisfactory situation led to pledges by Chancellor Kohl and Hans-Dietrich Genscher to revise the constitution to allow German troops to participate in future UN-sponsored out-of-area operations.

However, this has sparked off a heated debate in Germany on the desirability of such a constitutional change. At the moment, the main options being discussed are as follows:

1. *Bundeswehr participation in UN peace-keeping operations.* President Weizsäscker has declared that he has 'been arguing for some time that Germans should create the constitutional preconditions needed for our participation in UN peace-keeping missions – with the 'blue-helmets' (Weizsäcker, 1991, 8). Moreover, at their Bremen Congress in May 1991, the opposition SPD voted in favour of such a change. The position of the SPD is vital because their support is necessary to get the two-thirds majority in the Bundestag required for a constitutional amendment of this sort.
2. *Bundeswehr participation in UN-sanctioned military operations (such as the Gulf War).* Chancellor Kohl has spoken in favour of this, but it is not acceptable to the SPD (*Süddeutsche Zeitung*, 1/2 June 1991).
3. *Bundeswehr participation in WEU 'out-of-area' missions.* Again, Helmut Kohl has advocated this, along with Volker Rühe, but it has been rejected by the SPD chairman Björn Engholm as 'out of the question'.
4. *Bundeswehr participation in NATO 'out-of-area' operations.* This would require a change not only in the *Grundgesetz*, but also in the provisions of the 1949 Treaty of Washington, which limits NATO's military competence to the North Atlantic area. Such a change has not been proposed by the Kohl government, and has been specifically ruled out by Foreign Minister Genscher.
5. *Bundeswehr participation in CSCE 'Green Beret' peace-keeping and interventionary operations.* This has been proposed by both Genscher and proponents of a pan-European collective security system, but is not a realistic possibility in the foreseeable future.

There is a broad recognition in the Federal Republic that the country must assume greater international responsibilities commensurate with its increased weight and importance following unification. As Chancellor Kohl has acknowledged, 'There is no corner in which Germans could shelter from the cold blast of world affairs; neither do we want such a refuge. We want to play our part in constructing a world of peace, freedom and justice' (Kohl, 1991, 17). However, as one might expect from Germany's largely amilitary strategic culture, many Germans would like to see their country concentrate on the economic and political aspects of international security (i.e. reducing the North–South divide and removing the underlying sources of tension and conflict) rather than the military. Amending the constitution to allow the out-of-area deployment of German military forces – except to allow the Bundeswehr to participate in UN peace-keeping operations (as the *Bundesgrenzshutz* (Federal Border Guards) has already been doing in Namibia) – is thus likely to prove highly controversial.

Despite this, the Kohl government has since the Gulf War begun to expand the parameters of legitimate out-of-area deployments of German troops. In March 1991, five minesweepers and two supply ships were dispatched to the Gulf. Then in April 1991, 2000 German troops were sent to Iran to help set up a secure camp for Kudish refugees and to support relief operations. One German defence source claimed this amounted to 'a real operational commitment outside of the NATO area for the first time in Germany's post-war history', although officially it was justified as a 'humanitarian' not 'military' action (*The Guardian*, 24 April 1991, 10).

Towards a New Domestic Consensus?

The unification of Germany was inextricably linked to the end of the Cold War, and led to an historic transformation in the European security system. In this situation of profound change, the past certainties which underpinned West German security policy for four decades have disintegrated. But despite this, a remarkable degree of consensus has crystallised around the main planks of post-unification *Sicherheitspolitik*. The controversies and bitter divisions of the 1980s seem to have been largely forgotten, and a partial convergence has occurred around security policies advocated by the broad centreground of German politics – from the governing coalition to the bulk of the opposition Social Democrats. This includes a continuing commitment to NATO as the bedrock of German security; the parallel development of a European defence identity; strong support for CSCE and a more cooperative security system; and a reduced reliance on extended nuclear deterrence. The single most divisive issue on the German security agenda at present is the controversial question of whether or not the constitution should be revised in order to allow an out-of-area role for German troops. With this exception, security policy in Germany has not been as politically divisive an issue since unification as it was for much of the 1980s. Thus although the old strategic certainties in Europe are well and truly dead, the main lines of post-unification German security policy are unlikely to change significantly in the foreseeable future.

9

The Europe Community: Seeds of Ambivalence

EMIL J. KIRCHNER

Tensions in German–EC Relations

The Federal Republic of Germany is usually described as one of the most committed and supportive members of the European Community. Pro-integrationist proclamations by large parts of the FRG's elites and masses since 1949 and constitutional provisions on the transfer of German sovereignty bear witness to such a description. What this view conceals, however, is a certain amount of ambivalence or tension in Germany's relations with the Community. This ambivalence derived, initially, from the need to promote simultaneously German reunification and European integration. It also originated from the requirements imposed by a federal system, ministerial autonomy, coalition politics, and an independent Bundesbank. German reunification has, to some extent, heightened the prevailing ambivalence in the German position towards EC integration.

German reunification has brought about, for the immediate future, diverging rather than converging policy aims between Germany and the Community in the areas of competition policy, state subsidies, environmental and social policies. It is hampering EC efforts on standardisation. Because Germany draws more heavily now on EC subsidies, primarily from the Common Agricultural Policy (CAP) and structural funds, other EC aid recipients, like the Mediterranean countries, see their shares of EC subsidies being threatened. There is a likelihood that Germany's net contributions to the EC budget will decline, which again has obvious implications for the redistribution and social and economic cohesion of the Community.

On the other hand, German reunification has forced Germany to spell out more explicitly the conditions under which it will concede economic and monetary sovereignty to EC authorities. Equally, it has been an impetus for other EC countries to tie German economic power effectively into an EC framework and/or to share the benefits of German economic and monetary policy. The outcome might thus be greater clarity and certainty on Economic and Monetary Union (EMU) for all the EC countries concerned.

In contrast, the situation concerning a common EC foreign and security policy remained ambiguous, with differing views being held among the French, on the one hand, and the British and Dutch on the other. Whereas the French envisaged more independent EC efforts as a consequence of German reunification and changed circumstances in East–West relations, the British and Dutch sought to maintain existing NATO and American security commitments in Europe. Germany expressed support for each view and thus added yet another layer of ambivalence, if not ambiguity, in its dealings with EC integration.

There can be little doubt that German unification and EC integration are part of the same thing and thus impact on each other. Similarly, German reunification is the culmination of one of the twin aims of the German constitution. The other is to achieve European unification and to transfer German sovereignty to such an entity. For this to happen, German clarity, commitment and leadership will be needed.

How German reunification will affect German–EC relations, whether previous ambivalences in Germany's position towards the Community will give way to new ambivalences, and whether a more integrated and stronger Community will emerge as a consequence of German unification will be examined in the following discussion.

German Unification: Challenges for the Community

Both the speed of German reunification and Chancellor Kohl's role (his 10-point plan and position on the Polish border question) in it caused consternation in EC countries, notably Britain and France. Two views emerged. One view identified German reunification with the arrival of the 'Fourth Reich' and all the 'old' German habits of aggression and dominance. This view was particularly espoused by Nicolas Ridley, the former British minister of Trade and Industry, who accused the Germans of seeking to dominate Europe, through the auspices of the Community and with the connivance of the French. In contrast to this strident and confrontational stance there was also a benign view which was critical of German reunification. According to this view a united Germany would be too big and powerful to make a reliable partner in the Community. Such a Germany, it was feared, would be less committed to the political union of Western Europe generally and to the implementation of the internal market programme in particular. Associated with this view were worries over the negative repercussions a restructuring of the ex-East German economy would have on existing EC structural funds' commitments, CAP payments, competition policy and environmental action programmes. A widely held fear was that German reunification would at best weaken steps towards EMU and at worst make Germany turn its back on the Community. An extension of this view, mostly held in France, was that Germany would forge closer ties with Eastern Europe, especially the Soviet Union, which could push the FRG into neutralism and detract from its commitment to the Community and NATO.

Whilst most EC governments were slow or ambiguous in reacting to the coming down of the Berlin Wall and the GDR regime in November 1989, it was Jacques Delors, the Commission's president, who in a series of moves responded quickly and decisively. His proposal in the Spring of 1990 for a single German state was eventually adopted by the Community as a whole. This proposal was aided by the fact that the EC Treaties allowed for such an eventuality. In other words, accommodating both the enlargement of Germany and the Community could be made without a formal revision of the EC Treaties, which would have required member state parliamentary approval. Accordingly, the territory of the former GDR was to be integrated into the Community's legal framework by 31 December 1992 at the latest, before the scheduled deadline for the completion of a Single Market. For its own part, though growing considerably in population terms, Germany did not press for increased representation on European institutions after unity.

Legally, the five new German Länder were part of the Community from 3 October 1990 and Community legislation is applicable there except for derogations or temporary exemptions. Roughly 80 per cent of the technical regulations were applied straight away, as well as the EC legal instruments on the free movement of capital and of labour, the freedom to supply services, and indirect taxation. In the important field of competition policy, the EC regulations have applied since German EMU was established in July 1990. Derogations are being granted in several areas, in some cases up to 1995. These relate, for example, to fishing policy, environmental policy, the areas of veterinary medicine, agriculture, technical norms, taxes and customs.

The Impact of Unification on the Working of the Community

How will Germany cope with these EC provisions, and how will German unification affect the working of the Community and developments towards EMU? One of the biggest affects of German reunification on the working of the Community is likely to be on social and economic cohesion, a principle explicitly stipulated in the Single European Act (SEA). The share of benefits received by the poorer EC countries will be affected by a higher drawing of EC subsidies by Germany and lower propensity of Germany to be a contributor to EC structural funds (because of large financial transfers to the new Länder, financial aid commitments to the Soviet Union, a drop in *per capita* German income, and an increase in the level of German taxation). This is likely to result in a reconsideration of EC budgetary benefits and deficits for all the countries involved. Nonetheless, it is likely that Germany will remain the largest net contributor to the EC Budget for the foreseeable future.

With regard to CAP, the immediate German reaction appeared to be a hardening of its position in the GATT Uruguay Round, in which it, together with France, opposed a reduction in subsidies by 30 per cent in the Spring of 1991. But Germany has traditionally taken an inflexible and nationalistic line on CAP; it is an area where Germany has been prepared to use its veto (in 1985), the only time the FRG has ever done so.

Although German reunification has repercussions on the internal market proceedings, such as over adjustments in competition policy (involving particularly state subsidies) and in the harmonisation of standards, all in all the impact is likely to be modest and without major disruptions or setbacks. Equally, it may affect the pace of development in the establishment of an EC social and environmental policy, but it will not substantially deflect from the aims expressed in the SEA. Whilst seeking exemptions for the application of environmental and health and safety standards in the five new Länder, Germany can be expected to press for further EC environmental and social policy legislation. The latter will include demands for Community-wide arrangements on worker participation.

However, adverse implications on the German economic and political system from the internal market provisions also deserve consideration. There is within Germany a widespread fear that the creation of the internal market could lead to an undermining of some relatively high standards that German legislation has established over the years in such areas as health, consumer protection, environment or safety standards at work (Leyendecker, 1990, 148). Furthermore, as suggested by Horst Risse (1990), the internal market is a serious challenge to Germany's federal state organisations, and directly affects Länder competences and autonomy, for example, with regard to the EC Broadcasting Directive. As a consequence, the German Länder, either directly or indirectly via the Bundesrat, increasingly advocate that Community action should be taken only if national or local means cannot solve a problem, e.g. the principle of subsidiarity.

Yet the internal market provisions may also present opportunities for the German economic system to improve efficiency in certain sectors. As Hans-Eckart Scharrer (1990, 8) points out, in contrast to the free trade ideology, major sectors of the German economy have been highly regulated and/or shielded from foreign competition. These include coal mining, electric power, road transport, the insurance industry, investment regulations, food and public procurements. According to Scharrer (1990, 9) the challenge of the internal market offers the opportunity to redefine economic and social priorities and revise habits, tenure and regulations which, while once appropriate, have been rendered obsolete in the course of time (Scharrer, 1990, 9).

Thus, whilst German reunification and the development of the internal market impact on each other, the overall effect in either direction appears manageable, requiring minor rather than major adjustments. The same may not be said with regard to plans for EMU.

Unification and European EMU

It might be helpful to separate the short-term from the long-term consequences of German unification on EMU. In the short term, we may expect a weakening of the German economy. Germany has engaged in large-scale borrowing on the credit market both domestically and externally. In 1991 Germany's debt totalled around DM 1600 billion. There was a danger that strong demands for scarce money would lead to high interest rates and expensive loans which could affect the level of German investment. Secondly, if the high debt continues over a number of years, Germany would have to pay considerable sums to its creditors for this interest on the money. Thirdly, Germany's temporary neglect of budget discipline and deflationary policy may make international investors lose confidence in the Deutschemark.

German reunification has sharply lowered Germany's savings rate. It has brought into the country 16 million people who seek to consume goods and services at the same rate as those in the former West Germany, but their level of production is much lower; indeed, a very high proportion are actually unemployed. All this tends to be inflationary, provoking the Bundesbank to raise interest rates twice in 1991 in order to restrict demand. Furthermore, Germany is increasing imports to meet the state-financed demand in the five new Länder. Germany is no longer the big capital exporter it was only a short while ago, reducing significantly its current account surplus. Also, for much of 1991 the value of the Deutschemark against the US dollar had depreciated substantially. Another new phenomenon was that one year after German EMU, *per capita* income in the united Germany was lower than in France. This might affect Germany's ability, or motivation, to provide more money for either EC structural funds or for financial aid to the Soviet Union and Eastern Europe.

Short-term consequences thus affected interest rate synchronisation, the working of the European Monetary System (EMS) and the prospects for EMU. The raising of interest rates in Germany was counter to British interests, which needed British rates to be lowered in 1991, primarily on political grounds. This might lead to a realignment within the EMS, which in turn could again affect the development of EMU.

Another short-term consequence related to the timing of the European Central Bank. In October 1990 Chancellor Kohl had proposed that 1 January 1994 should mark the date for the beginning of phase II of EMU, and Foreign Minister Hans-Dietrich Genscher had stated several times that the European Central Bank should be established as quickly as possible; this was certainly what the French and the Commission had wanted. However, in April 1991 the German government suggested that the new Bank should be set up in 1997, indicating that otherwise it could rival the authority of the Bundesbank within the EMS. They also opposed setting a date for the start of the final phase of EMU until there was a marked convergence of national budgetary deficits, inflation rates and interest rates. Germany seemed, therefore, to be in no hurry to repeat its own experiment on a Community scale, i.e. of imposing monetary union on disparate economies. It is an open question, however, whether Germany, by this action, has significantly delayed EMU. Rather it might have helped the United Kingdom to gain more time and to accept a compromise formula. In the medium term the German action might therefore have made it possible for the whole EMU enterprise to be put on a more comprehensive and secure footing.

In any case, in the medium term there are two reasons why German reunification may have acted as a catalyst for EMU. First, other countries are now more committed to either counteracting German economic strength and the possibility of German economic dominance, or to sharing in the benefits German monetary policies have produced. Secondly, Germany has been forced to spell out more clearly its own conditions for adhering to EMU. The German government and the Bundesbank have established six general conditions for German participation in EMU: the completion of the internal market; price stability as the sole objective of any European Central Bank; a federal structure for the European Central Bank; the political independence of that institution from national and Community institutions; binding restrictions on the monetary financing of national or Community budgets; and parallel progress in the convergence of economic policies and performance. With regard to the European Central Bank, Karl-Otto Pöhl, the former Bundesbank president, remarked in January 1990 that a statutory guarantee of non-interference would not be sufficient. The bank's governing body would need be appointed, as in America and Germany, on long-term contracts that cut across national electoral cycles. And the bank would have to be granted unimpeded use of all instruments of monetary policy – in particular, the monopoly of money creation. In many ways the German conditions appear as attempts to extend the Bundesbank's informal role as the manager of Europe's money, and Germany's preference for fiscal rectitude and price stability (Sperling, 1990).

The strains of German reunification have thus not altered German commitment to EMU. On the contrary, it has reinforced the stringent conditions attached to plans for a move towards a single currency and a central bank. Germany's partners, such as the United Kingdom, have to weigh up whether these conditions are too demanding on sovereignty or whether conceding on these conditions is the price to be paid for Europeanising German economic strength. Though Germany's partners will attempt to tone down some of these conditions, there will also be some interesting alliances which will reinforce German stipulations. On the issue of economic convergence, the FRG is indicating a reluctance to pay for Italy's substantial public debt or for Portugal's uncompetitiveness. Equally, before Germany is willing to accept Spanish requests for and automatic transfer (as in a federal system) from the richer to the poorer nations, it demands that the Mediterranean countries be prepared for some tough medicine to get their economies in shape for the challenge of EMU. This policy concurs very much with British desires. By mid-1991 Britain seemed to be prepared to adopt a single currency and a European Central Bank. But rather than agree to firm dates, like 1997, for this to happen, it proposed 'indicative' and not binding dates for the evolution of EMU. Britain also pressed for economic convergence which would have to be achieved before either a single currency or a central bank could be established.

In contrast, the German suggestion that the establishment of a European Central Bank should be coupled with increased powers and responsibilities of the European Parliament was strongly rejected by Britain as well as by France, Denmark, Ireland and Portugal. For the Germans an increase of the European Parliament's powers was a precondition for them delegating the responsibilities of the Bundes-bank to a European Central Bank. In an effort to meet this precon-dition the Germans sought the support of the Italians, and in April 1991 Hans-Dietrich Genscher and the Italian foreign minister de Michelis presented a joint proposal for a democratic European Par-liament. According to this paper, which was referred to at length in the discussion of the treaty for European Political Union, EC legis-lation can not be passed without a majority vote in the European Parliament. The aim was significantly to expand the powers of the European Parliament and gradually approximate them with those of national parliaments. Whilst Germany contended that this would not weaken national parliaments, Britain, Denmark, Ireland and France feared that as political union progressed it would entail a certain redistribution of powers in favour of the European Parliament and thus were reluctant to see the powers of their national parliaments eroded.

Unification and a Common Foreign and Security Policy

Influenced by the process of German reunification and the Gulf conflict, France campaigned hard in 1990–1, as part of the Inter-governmental Conference on Political Union, for the gradual absorb-tion of the Western European Union (WEU) into the Community as a way of establishing a common foreign and security policy (CFSP). Belgium and Italy supported this drive, but Denmark, Ireland, the Netherlands and the United Kingdom were opposed to such an organic link between the two organisations. Germany, whilst favour-ing this organic link, did not want to affront the Americans or undermine the viability of NATO. This intention was reiterated in Kohl's Edinburgh speech in May 1991 when he remarked that a common foreign and security policy 'must not detract from the Atlan-tic alliance's protective function . . . and when we talk of a common European house, we want the Americans to be tenants in our house'. On the other hand, he also stressed that Europe must be prepared to assume a larger share of the responsibility within the alliance. Hans-Dietrich Genscher, the foreign minister, went a step further when in June 1991 he and James Baker, the American Secretary of State, issued a statement in which they stressed the primacy of NATO over any future European identity (*Independent*, 25 June 1991).

Because of German indecision over the WEU as well as over the Conference on Security and Cooperation in Europe (CSCE), there was a certain amount of tension between the French and the Germans over the continued viability of NATO. There was also disagreement between France and Germany over the handling of the Yugoslav crisis. Whereas France believed that Yugoslavia should be kept as a single state, Germany stressed the principle of self-determination and, with an eye partly on its own experience and partly on a wider European federation, pushed for recognition of Slovenia and Croatia as independent republics. The latter line was adopted by the Community at the end of 1991.

When the defence ministers of the WEU met in Luxembourg on 27 June 1991 they bridged the gap between France and Italy on the one hand, and the United Kingdom and the Netherlands on the other. They confirmed their desire for the WEU to be a full part of the process of European integration, while enhancing its contribution to solidarity with the NATO alliance. Their intention was also to create an independent European rapid reaction force. But the stress was on complementarity rather than duality between WEU and NATO. In addition, there were indications that the Community would obtain some authority over the actions of the WEU in the medium term. However, it should be remembered that the WEU consists of only nine of the EC member states and has no integrated military command structure like NATO.

Germany had the chairmanship of the WEU between July 1991 and June 1992 and thus an opportunity to shape the link between NATO, WEU and the Community. Whether it would be able to use its middle-of-the-road position effectively, clarify its own ambiguities or introduce new elements of ambivalence (as for example, over the role of the CSCE) is too early to tell.

In mid-October 1991 discussions on CFSP were upstaged by a Franco–German announcement that they were ready to commit forces to build a powerful European Army Corps, initially responsible to the WEU. The two governments also proposed that a range of foreign and security policy issues should be decided by the European Community collectively rather than by national governments and that some at least decided by majority vote. Connected to the CFSP are three specific German medium-term objectives: EC enlargement, aid to the Soviet Union, and an EC immigration policy.

In his Edinburgh speech Kohl argued that Europe extends eastwards as well as westwards and that the Community should 'not close the door' on the Eastern European countries. Germany wants Austria and Sweden, to join partly to show the Soviet Union that the Community is not a military alliance. Polish and Czechoslovak membership, they say, would resolve Germany's historical problems with those countries, and together with the membership of Hungary could help to avert possible instability on its Eastern borders.

France was hostile to this prospect, partly shared by southern countries which fear eastern rivals for regional aid. Some French (as well as some Dutch) see Austria as just a German satellite (*The Economist*, 13 July 1991). Delors has taken the French line and discouraged EC enlargement by proposing the European Economic Area (to serve countries like Austria and Sweden), and association agreements with Eastern European countries. Whilst Kohl seemingly gave way to French wishes, events in the Soviet Union in August 1991 reintroduced more urgency to the EC enlargement debate and to the timing and form in which Eastern European countries should be admitted. These developments will most probably also reinforce the German argument about giving more assistance to the Soviet Union, and that a wait-and-see attitude is self-defeating and less than constructive.

Germany alone can neither provide the help needed to shore up the reform policy process in the Soviet Union, nor provide the required framework for trade, cultural and security cooperation. It also needs the Community to forge a common immigration and asylum policy with Eastern Europe to avoid a mass influx of people from there. Germany had lifted visa restrictions on Poles in December 1990; there was already visa-free travel between Germany and Czechoslovakia and Hungary. Kohl launched an attempt at the Luxembourg Summit in June 1991 to introduce a Community-wide policy on immigration, which would have been by majority voting, but Britain resisted such an attempt.

In this respect, it is difficult to see how Germany could be tempted to exchange its role in the Community for an exclusive pact with the Soviet Union. Such a possibility, if it ever existed, has become still less viable after the Soviet upheavals of August 1991. Both its past experience (acknowledging the contribution the Community has made towards West German rehabilitation to the family of nations, towards German reunification, and towards its present economic strength) and its future aims would point rather in the opposite direction.

During 1991 Chancellor Kohl insisted on the synchronising progress between the IGC–EMU and the IGC–Political Union treaties, threatening not to sign the former without sufficient progress on the latter. His aim was to ensure that the Germans would not relinquish control over crucial monetary policy unless its partners forewent political rights and national sovereignty in return. He therefore invited his EC partners to follow his example.

German reunification has thus forced the Community to intensify its integration, but it may also have helped the Community to enhance its economic strength and to elevate its own status as an international actor. This trend has been reinforced by the Gulf conflict, the Yugoslav crisis and the Soviet upheavals in 1991. The Community is moving increasingly into areas where national sovereignty is at stake (witness the move toward the establishment of EMU and the linkage between EMU and Political Union). Through the successful incorporation of German economic prowess into EMU, in which a single European currency and a European Central Bank will be main features, the fears of Germany emerging as a benevolent but oppressive economic hegemon can be overcome. In turn Germany, which since 3 October 1990 speaks more loudly of playing a leading role in the future construction of Europe, could see its short to medium term objectives come to fruition. These objectives concern assisting the Soviet Union economically, establishing a European Union (with a prevailing common security policy), and securing stable relations between Eastern and Western Europe through arms reduction negotiations, association agreements between the Community and Eastern European countries, and a general climate of cooperation.

German Dominance or Interdependence?

Though predictions appear hazardous, it is reasonable to assume that a united Germany will have short term problems in adjusting to the costs relating to environmental, industrial, and welfare policies in the five new Länder. But in the medium term, when economic recovery in these Länder takes shape, the EC single market has come into existence, and trade with Eastern Europe has begun to flourish, economic benefits can be expected both for Germany and other EC member states. The German insistence on economic convergence which is prior to, or parallel with, that of monetary convergence, and on the independent status of the European Central Bank, might delay EMU in the short term but does not deflect from the fundamental commitment Germany holds on this issue. Germany remains committed to the aim of European unification. At the same time, as *The Economist* points out 'Germans talk of a window of opportunity: the rest of the Community cannot count on the Germans remaining such good Europeans for ever' (*The Economist*, 27 July 1991).

However, given its share of GNP and trade share within the Community, Germany has the potential to be a hegemonic power. This view is put forcefully by Andrei Markovits and Simon Reich (1991) who argue that Eastern European countries, by trying to emulate the German economic success and by being 'submissive' to German economic prowess, encourage a German hegemonic development.

Whether such power will materialise depends on the prospects of further EC integration. One of the most important consequences of German reunification, from an EC point of view, has been a need to reappraise the Community and its future direction. Because of fears over German unpredictability, uncertainty or dominance, several EC member states felt it necessary to accelerate the process of European integration via the Intergovernmental Conference on Political Union, and thus complement efforts for the establishment of EMU and a single market. A powerful Germany within the EC framework appeared more attractive to many EC countries than a powerful Germany outside it. Equally, it was felt that making use of a strong German economy could strengthen the Community internally and externally. The German government, having repeatedly declared that it had no ambition to dominate the Community, strongly supported the Intergovernmental Conference on Political Union and particularly pressed for Community policies in the social, health, environmental and immigration field, as well as for greater powers for the European Parliament. Indeed, the European Council at Maastricht, in December 1991, reached agreement on new policies in the field of environment, research, health and transport, increased cooperation on foreign, security and immigration matters, a strengthening of European Parliament powers, and the introduction of a single currency (between 1997 and 1999) (with the United Kingdom having the right to opt in or out at a time of its choosing). However, on social policy Britain forced the other eleven to pursue their aims 'outside' the Treaty confinements.

Of course, it should not be forgotten that at present Germany derives a large share of its trade surplus from commerce with Community and EFTA countries, and thus has implications for its employment, economic growth and welfare system. It is therefore in Germany's interest to support the Community and to avoid member states diverging too much from Germany's own policies. Similarly, it is in the interest of Germany's partners to harness its economic strength, and ensure that it is anchored firmly into the process of political integration. Thus Germany needs the Community and the Community needs Germany. From this we might also deduce that whilst the possibility of a German-led Europe in economic terms is likely, there is an equally strong likelihood that in the future there will be a European-led Germany in the political realm.

A united Germany will become more central than ever to Europe. With the break up of the Soviet Union and the corresponding rise of the Community as a powerful actor, Germany might play a leading role within the Community. However, as German reunification accelerated further EC integration, there is a strong likelihood (which is also an expressed German desire) that German economic power will be tied effectively into the EC framework. Thus, whilst it seems inevitable that a united Germany will speak with a louder voice within the Community, there will also be constraints on Germany. New treaty provisions on Political Union, prevailing decision-making mechanisms with weighted voting within the Council of Ministers, and a German willingness to transfer competences in the economic and monetary sector to EC authorities will increasingly add a European accent to the louder German voice. The more pronounced this accent becomes and the more it is followed by 'European deeds' (on, let's say, a European Central Bank, a single currency and a common foreign and security policy), the more the seeds of ambivalence in the German position toward the Community will diminish and German–EC relations will mature and become more mutually reinforcing.

PART THREE

Economic and Social Policy

10

The New German Economy

STEPHEN PADGETT

Problems of the 'Split Economy'

Building the new German economy involved two inter-related projects: the transformation from state socialism to a liberal order of market capitalism, and the revitalisation of the largely obsolete economy in the Eastern Länder. Unlike other former Soviet bloc countries, which embarked upon a gradual process of change, Germany opted for a rapid transformation. German Economic and Monetary Union (GEMU) preceded the formal act of political unification by three months. At a single stroke, the legal and institutional order of market capitalism was extended to eastern Germany along with the Deutschemark. GEMU was thus an inversion of conventional economic thinking, according to which monetary union represented the final act of a step-by-step process of assimilation and convergence between the constituent economies. The rationale behind GEMU rested on the expectation that the stability of the Deutschemark and the dynamism of the West German economy would create the conditions for rapid take-off in the East German Länder.

This expectation proved to be over-optimistic. Currency union transformed savings in the East into Deutschemark spending power, endowing 17 million consumers with access to Western markets. The resultant surge of demand in the West was coupled with the collapse of demand for consumer goods produced in the former GDR. Exposed to the rigours of market competition, the productive economy in the East experienced an almost immediate crisis, with the collapse of industrial activity and employment. Privatisation, conceived as the motor of reconstruction, proceeded slowly with Western companies hesitant to invest in enterprises of little economic

187

value. The failure of market forces to generate an upturn in economic activity in the first eighteen months after GEMU meant that an enormous financial burden fell upon the state. The belief that reconstruction would be self-financing, covering its costs through privatisation receipts and the fiscal bonus of increased tax revenues generated by growth, was quickly exposed as an illusion. The result was an escalating public sector deficit in the Federal Republic, and a spiral of borrowing to finance it.

Deficit spending sustained vigorous growth in the West in 1990–1, contrasting sharply with a continuing decline in the East. Economic and monetary policy-makers were thus confronted by a syndrome of the 'split economy' which represents the principal problematic of economic management in post-unification Germany. Its resolution depends upon harnessing the economic dynamism of the West to the dead weight of the economy east of the Elbe, an objective which has so far eluded the architects of the new German economy.

This chapter looks at the dynamics of currency union and the shock which it imparted to the economy in the new German Länder. It goes on to examine the instruments of reconstruction in the East and their record of performance in the eighteen months after GEMU. It will analyse the implications of the 'split economy' syndrome for economic and monetary management in the Federal Republic. Finally, it identifies the main policy dilemmas which emerged as the new economic configuration confounded the old orthodoxies and certainties of political economy in the Federal Republic. First, however, it will review the models which have been put forward to explain the process of economic transformation in the east, and to predict the future of the new German economy.

Models of the New German Economy

In the absence of economic theories explaining the transition from a state-socialist command economy to a capitalist market economy, three analogies have been deployed, forming the basis of three scenarios of future development. The most optimistic of these scenarios derives from the 'Economic Miracle' model, which draws on the experience of rapid economic growth in post-war West Germany, and on the more recent examples of take-off in the newly industrialised states of Korea and Taiwan. Superficially, the post-war German miracle grew out of circumstances comparable to those in the new East German Länder – the collapse of a planned economy, a depleted capital stock and a devastated infrastructure. From these inauspicious beginnings, a 'virtuous circle' of strong demand and high investment generated a self-sustaining upswing of economic activity, the starting point for which was the currency reform of 1948. The motor of the post-war miracle was provided by market forces, with the state restricting its intervention to the creation of a favourable environment for investment.

The second model is provided by analogy with the backward *Mezzogiorno* of southern Italy. The permanent under-development of the Italian South coexists with the affluence of the commercial and industrial centres of the North, with little beneficial 'spillover' effect. Southern markets are supplied from outside, with little indigenous industrial production in the south. The northward migration of skilled or adaptable labour leaves a residue of the old and economically weak reliant on state support, and the region is dependent on large-scale government transfer payments. A third model is provided by West Berlin in the 1950s. Geographically isolated from the West by the surrounding GDR, the city displayed many of the economic features of the Italian South. A barrage of regional policy aids and investment incentives, however, were successful in reversing the economic decline of the city, although it continued to require large-scale financial support from the Federal Republic.

Initial government optimism over the post-unification prospects of the East German Länder was based on the assumptions of the Economic Miracle analogy. However, this model overlooks some very significant differences between the economic environment of the post-war Federal Republic and the new East German Länder in the 1990s. After 1945 West Germany was able to compete on equal terms with European neighbours suffering equally from wartime destruction, and rebuilding from a similar level of economic development. The undervaluation of the Deutschemark gave exporters a competitive advantage. There were no competing poles of attraction for domestic investment capital. An influx of refugees from the East flooded the labour market, depressing wage levels. The international economic conjuncture was in the ascendant. Conditions were therefore favourable for rapid economic take-off. In contrast, the structurally weak and backward economy in the Eastern Länder was immediately confronted by competition from the advanced industrial world. Currency union left the East without exchange rate protection. Infrastructure deficiencies meant an unfavourable investment environment, especially since the competitive advantage of low labour costs was dissipated by an immediate upward pressure on wages. A model of economic development relying exclusively on the dynamism of market forces thus appears to be of limited value in the context of the new East German Länder.

On the other hand, the *Mezzogiorno* model is unduly pessimistic.

The strategic location of the new Länder at the gateway to Eastern Europe is in sharp contrast to the geographical marginalisation of the Italian South on the European periphery. Moreover, the Eastern Länder should benefit from the formidable economic resources of the Federal Republic, and from West German growth rates well in excess of those elsewhere in the advanced industrial world. The momentum generated in the West can be expected to provide an impetus for economic growth in the Eastern Länder. However, the Italian example suggests a note of caution in assessing the 'locomotive' effect of growth centres upon under-developed regions.

Economic take-off can be defined as the point at which growth acquires its own momentum and becomes self-sustaining. In the German context this means the point at which the Eastern Länder cease to be economically dependent upon the West. The West Berlin model points to an intermediate state between take-off and permanent under-development. Degeneration is reversed but economic activity continues to be dependent upon external support. In this scenario, the subsidies and investment incentives now regarded as temporary measure would become institutionalised as a permanent condition of economi life in the East. The implications of this scenario are profound: already the burden of supporting the economy in the new German Länder is threatening the economic stability of the Federal Republic.

German EMU

The rapidity with which German Economic and Monetary Union (GEMU) was planned and executed was dictated by the acute problem of migration. Between November 1989 and July 1990 some 400,000 persons crossed permanently from the GDR to the Federal Republic, causing manpower shortages in the East and social problems in the Federal Republic. It was widely recognised that nothing less than immediate currency union would serve to restore a popular belief in the economic future of Eastern Germany and thus to staunch the relentless flow of migrants. This rationale was encapsulated in Chancellor Kohl's much-used formula of 'getting the money to the people rather than the people to the money'. Moreover, GEMU was the central element in the creation of a unified German state, a process which acquired irresistible political momentum once the Western powers, the Soviet Union and the GDR regime itself had come to terms with the principle of unification.

Initially it had been widely assumed that GEMU would be preceded by a gradual process of economic reform, reconstruction and consolidation in the East. This expectation derived from conventional economic thinking, according to which currency union was conceived as the culmination or 'crowning' of a progressive economic assimilation between the constituent units. This process entailed the harmonisation of the institutional and legal frameworks of the respective economic systems, the integration of markets, a convergence of economic performance, and the step-by-step creation of common monetary institutions. The Delors programme for European Monetary Union was conceived upon these gradualist lines. So, too, were the proposals put forward by the Federal Economics Ministry in early February 1990.

The first stage of the Ministry's plan involved the transformation of the state-socialist economy in the East into a market economy through the introduction of private property and entrepreneurial freedoms, the liberalisation of prices, wages, trade and investment, and the creation of a commercial banking system. The second stage involved the control of inflation, the creation of a unified internal market and full currency convertibility at realistic exchange rates. Only then did the plan envisage the final phase – the creation of joint economic and monetary institutions and the adoption of the Deutschemark as a common currency, provisionally scheduled for the end of 1992.

As the drive for unification intensified, however, the gradualist strategy was swiftly superseded by the cabinet decision of 6 February 1990 to embark upon immediate discussions with the GDR government aimed at establishing the terms for the rapid introduction of the Deutschemark into Eastern Germany. Negotiations between the two states began almost immediately and were concluded in May with the State Treaty on Economic Monetary and Social Union. At a single stroke the Treaty made provision for the extension of the legal and institutional framework of the social market economy of the Federal Republic to the GDR.

In short, the State Treaty telescoped the phased integration of the two monetary and economic systems into a single Act. The Treaty came into force simultaneously with the introduction of the Deutschemark into eastern Germany. Whilst it provided the legal foundation for economic integration and assimilation, the practical tasks of renewal and transformation lay ahead. The timing of currency union thus represented an inversion of conventional economic wisdom. It could be seen as a 'shotgun marriage' between two economies organised on diametrically opposite lines and at radically different stages of economic development. On the other hand, one of the prerequisites of economic reconstruction in the East was monetary stability. The quickest and most effective means of achieving this objective was the introduction of the Deutschemark. Moreover, western industrialists and businessmen would not commit themselves to capital investment, another prerequisite of take-off in the East, until the transformation of the old economic order was under way. Currency union was seen as the most effective means of destroying the moribund Leviathan of the GDR economy and of implanting the germs of market capitalism East of the Elbe.

The effectiveness of currency union as a catalyst for economic renewal, however, depended upon the terms on which it was introduced, and in particular upon the rate at which the two currencies were exchanged. Once again politics intervened; during the campaign for the GDR parliamentary election of March 1990, Chancellor Kohl gave a very strong indication that the rate of exchange would be 1:1. Parity exchange was very favourable to East Germans holding their savings in East Marks, and Kohl's commitment was a shrewd political move. In economic terms, however, parity exchange represented a drastic over-valuation of the East Mark, which was currently exchanging against the Deutschemark at an unofficial rate of about seven to one.

Parity exchange carried two principal dangers. First, it was feared that the conversion of savings deposits estimated at 160 billion East Marks would release a surge of demand in the West, with serious inflationary consequences. This fear was greatly exaggerated in view of the relative insignificance of the money stock in the GDR compared with that of the Federal Republic. The second fear concerned the impact of currency union at a parity conversion rate upon the competitiveness of the economy in the East. Exchange rates serve the function of buffers between economies operating at different levels of productivity and efficiency. Low productivity economies can be protected to a certain extent from the full force of international competition by exchange rates which enhance the competitiveness of their exports whilst discouraging imports. Behind this protective barrier, low productivity economies are able to compete in world markets, although at the cost of real wage levels which are low by international standards. Monetary union at a conversion rate which over-valued wages and prices would serve to erode East Germany's comparative advantage as a low wage economy.

In a trade-off between political expediency and economic rationality, and in partial deference to a very sceptical response from West German business and banking interests, the government amended its initial plans. A parity conversion rate was retained for savings up to a ceiling of 4000 East Marks, with a 2:1 rate thereafter. Wages and prices, however, were converted at a rate of 1:1. The full extent of the social gulf between East and West was thus temporarily disguised, only for it to reappear in very sharp relief in the form of a dramatic explosion of unemployment which followed currency union.

Collapse of the Economy in the East

It was widely recognised that GEMU would inevitably precipitate a radical upheaval in the economy of the new German Länder. Indeed part of its purpose was to break up the hard crust of the old economic order, as a precursor to renewal and the transition to a self-sustaining market economy. However, the scale of the disintegration which ensued was far greater than had been anticipated. The OECD reported the 'virtual collapse of production and employment in the five new federal Länder' (OECD, 1991). Industrial output in the second half of 1990 fell by around 50 per cent from the previous year and continued falling during the first half of 1991. A collapse of the labour market saw unemployment or short-time working rise to 3 million or 30 per cent of the labour force in the East. Prior to currency union it had been assumed that between 50 and 70 per cent of GDR industry could survive in a market economy. In the event, only about 25 per cent of industrial plant proved to be economically viable (Deutsche Bank, 1991b).

A number of factors contributed to the scale of the collapse. The GDR economy had been very heavily dependent on trade with the Soviet Union and Eastern Europe. Contrary to widespread belief, the terms of trade under the socialist bloc system had been very favourable to the GDR. It was estimated that some 750,000 jobs were dependent, either directly or indirectly, upon this source. In many industrial sectors, some 50 per cent of output was exported eastwards. With monetary union, trade with Eastern Europe and the Soviet Union was conducted on hard currency terms. Soviet shortages of hard currency meant an immediate collapse of trading relations. In the six months following currency union, exports to Eastern Europe and the Soviet Union fell by over 50 per cent, representing the removal of the mainstay of the economy in the East.

Domestic demand in the Eastern Länder also suffered a drastic decline as currency union gave consumers immediate access to Western markets. Inferior quality standards left East German products at a crippling competitive disadvantage. Furthermore, conditioned by decades of restricted choice, supply shortages and a distorted price system, consumer behaviour in the East did not conform to Western patterns of rational choice. The preference for Western products extended even to those consumer items like foodstuffs where domestic producers were able to compete on equal, or advantageous, price and quality terms.

The demand deficit in Eastern European markets and on the domestic front was not appreciably offset by any compensating increase in exports to the West. The inability to break into Western markets was related in part to the terms of monetary union, which had denied the new German Länder the competitive advantage which Eastern European countries like Poland were able to derive from the devaluation of their currencies. After forty years of isolation from world markets, technological backwardness and poor quality standards in many sectors, the economy was ill-adjusted to Western export requirements. Moreover, under inter-zonal trade agreements with the Federal Republic, GDR products had been packaged and marketed in the West. Exposure to the full rigours of the market revealed the marketing deficiencies of producers in the new Eastern Länder.

At the root of the competitive disadvantage of the economy in the East was the very low level of industrial productivity, reflecting acute deficiencies in the capital stock. Underinvestment and overmanning in the old regime meant that the capital to labour ratio was very low by Western standards. Capital per head of the workforce was estimated at DM 150,000, less than half the West German level (Hoffman, 1991, 17). Even this low estimate of capital intensity was misleading, since a large proportion of plant was technologically backward and incapable of producing to standards acceptable in Western markets. Exposed to the rigours of a market economy, much of the productive capacity in the East was rendered economically obsolete. This effect was exacerbated by an immediate upward pressure on wages, as workers and trade unions sought to narrow the wage gap between East and West. Steep wage increases further undermined the already marginal viability of industrial undertakings.

The key to economic renewal was a rapid infusion of capital from the West, and in particular from the Federal Republic. The commercial opportunities and sense of national purpose generated by unification was expected to encourage the eastward flow of Western capital, giving an immediate 'kick-start' to new economic activity. Infrastructure deficiencies and legal difficulties, however, and the collapse of the economic viability of industrial undertakings in the East, made them unattractive investment propositions, and it proved much harder than expected to attract Western capital. Economic backwardness thus threatened to become a vicious circle, as envisaged by the *Mezzogiorno* scenario, placing a heavy burden upon the public policy instruments which had been created to promote and manage economic transformation and renewal.

Economic Renewal and Transformation

Privatisation was seen as the motor of economic renewal and transformation, and was entrusted to the Treuhandanstalt. This body had been created under the GDR regime as a state holding company to oversee industrial restructuring. With GEMU it became a quasi-public institution, entrusted with the ownership of all the property owned by the state under the GDR regime, and representing a mixture of investment bank, development board and regulatory policy agency. Its chief executive, Detlev Rohwedder, occupied a pivotal position in the political, industrial and commercial life of the Federal Republic. Having been State Secretary in the Economics Ministry in the 1970s, he subsequently spearheaded the reconstruction and recovery of the ailing Hoesch steel group, working in close alliance with the Deutsche Bank. He was thus ideally equipped for the orchestration of reconstruction in the East on the basis of a partnership between politics, industry and finance.

The task of the Treuhandanstalt was twofold. It involved the restructuring of the unwieldy combines which had formed the basis of industrial organisation in the GDR and their disposal into private ownership. Restructuring meant the break up of conglomerates into their constituent parts, the closure of commercially irredeemable plant, and the creation of the potentially viable units for privatisation. In the first year of its operation the Treuhandanstalt gave birth to more new companies than it was able to dispose of, and the number of companies under its control increased to over 10,000. Privatisation entailed protracted negotiations with potential buyers, further complexity often being added by wider considerations of competition issues and balancing the competing claims of German and foreign bidders. However, the major obstacle to privatisation was the uncompetitiveness of many undertakings. The Treuhandanstalt could not hope to dispose of companies unable to cover their operating costs and burdened with a legacy of debt. The slow pace of privatisation and the inevitable closures and job losses which accompanied corporate shakeout led the trustee body into political controversy which was heightened by the terrorist murder of Rohwedder in April 1991.

Receipts from privatisation lagged far behind the costs of restructuring. The financial commitments of the Treuhandanstalt included payments to cover the interest on company debt, support for companies undertaking restructuring operations, payments to cover plant closure and export support. In addition the Treuhandanstalt acted as guarantor for liquidity credits – short-term commercial loans raised privately by companies – which totalled some DM 30 billion by mid-

1991. The cost of guaranteeing liquidity credits was highly unpredictable, depending on the capacity of borrowers for repayment and the scale of defaulting. Treuhandanstalt expenditure in 1990 amounted to DM 4 billion, with projected outgoings for 1991 of around DM 37 billion. Income for 1991 was estimated at around DM 14 billion, with the deficit covered by a facility for borrowing on private capital markets, authorised and limited by the government. Midway through the second year, the expected deficit for 1990–1 was already slightly in excess of government limits, and the risks involved in debt repayments and liquidity credits meant that the overshoot could be considerable. The financial burden on the Treuhandanstalt was a consequence of the risk-shyness of the commercial banks and of the slow pace of private investment flows which were estimated at around DM 5 billion for 1990 and DM 10–15 billion for 1991.

The readiness of Western capital to move into Eastern Germany varied from one sector to another. Initiatives have generally occurred where the exploitation of market opportunities required an *in situ* presence, as in the retail banking and energy sectors. In the bedrock sectors of the West German economy – chemicals, automobile manufacture and machine tools – companies could count on supplying East German markets from existing production plants in the West. In these sectors, antiquated production plant in the East was of limited economic value, and investment initiatives owed more to political considerations of national solidarity than to economic rationality. Volkswagen, with its close links to the state, was one of the first major companies to make commitments to production in the East. Other West German industrial leaders starting up operations in the first eighteen months after GEMU were Daimler–Benz and Opel in motor manufacture, Siemens in electronics, BASF in chemicals, and the heavy industrial conglomerate Metallgesellschaft. A number of foreign concerns also made acquisitions, with the French particularly active.

Apart from the intrinsic commercial weakness of East German companies, a number of factors combined to discourage inward investment. First, entrepreneurial initiatives were stifled by a tangled network of conflicting legal provisions relating to the ownership of commercial property and land. Under the GDR regime, private property and land ownership had been virtually wiped out by expropriation, collectivisation and nationalisation. With the liquidation of the regime, the property claims of former owners, many of whom now resided in the West, became a major political issue. The State Treaty established the principle of restitution – property to which there was a clearly traceable claim was to revert to its original owners, or compensation was to be paid. In the case of commercial property, former owners were empowered to assert part ownership rights where they were dissatisfied with the compensation offered. Although provision was made to override the principle of restitution where it threatened to curtail commercial activity and job creation, legal uncertainties discouraged Treuhandanstalt officials from taking this course. For its part the government was slow and indecisive in its response to calls for the strengthening of the override provision and the imposition of a final deadline for property claims. Legal uncertainty was a powerful disincentive to investment, since new owners faced the threat of expensive third-party claims against their title.

Secondly, the viability of eastern Germany as an investment location depended crucially on infrastructure development, especially in transport, telecommunications and energy, where existing provisions fell far short of meeting the requirements of a modern industrial economy. Moreover, the public authorities in the East (the newly created Länder and the municipalities) on which a large part of the burden of infrastructure development fell, lacked the financial resources to mount an effective response to the challenge. Thirdly, investment was discouraged by the legacy of indebtedness which hung over former GDR state enterprises. In the absence of a general debt amnesty, East German concerns remained potentially liable for interest payments on corporate debts totalling some DM 110 billion. Moreover, the lack of reliable accounting information meant that it was often difficult to ascertain the extent of the liabilities which might arise. Finally the threat of having to assume responsibility for the clean up of environmental pollution was a strong disincentive for investment in some sectors.

The atmosphere of unremitting gloom which prevailed for most of 1991 began to recede slightly in the last quarter of the year with indications that economic collapse might have bottomed out. Increased activity in the construction, mechanical engineering and service sectors, and a shift in consumer demand towards some East German products led to a renewal of optimism in some quarters. Plans for spending in the new Länder announced by some West German concerns were also cited as evidence of an upturn. An acceleration of privatisation activity saw some 3400 disposals in 1991. New privatisations were concentrated in the service sector, which has been identified by some as a lead sector in reconstruction. On the other hand, it is likely that the undertakings remaining in the hands of the Treuhandanstalt will prove rather difficult to dispose of. In general, then, the portents of recovery remain somewhat unclear.

To meet the challenges of reconstruction, an array of policy and financial instruments have been created. Somewhat belatedly in mid-1991, the federal government began drafting legislation to clarify the property question. A Compensation Fund is planned to finance the recompense of former property owners, enabling the principle of restitution to be overridden in favour of new owners, and thus clearing the legal undergrowth in the way of new investment. As a partial solution to the debt problem, a Debt Statute (*Entschuldungs-verordnung*) was enacted, empowering the Treuhandanstalt to write off part or all of company debts upon privatisation. A definitive legal clarification of the debt issue, however, remained unsettled. Infrastructure develoment was addressed through Special Funds placed at the disposal of the Deutsche Bundespost and Deutsche Bundesbahn, the Federal Republic's state run concerns for posts and telecommunications and railways. The German Unity Fund, authoried to raise loans amounting to DM 20 billion in 1990, rising to DM 31 billion for 1991, was established largely to meet the budgetary requirements of the new Länder and muncipalities. To provide inducements for private capital, a battery of investment credits and subsidies was introduced, financed largely through Special Funds attached to the remnants of the post-1945 European Recovery Programme. The impact of these measures on the speed of reconstruction in the East remained uncertain. However, in macroeconomic terms their impact was clear; an immediate increase in the Federal Republic's budget deficit, met by a dramatic increase in the public sector borrowing requirement.

The Performance of the All-German Economy

Optimism over the prospects for economic renewal east of the Elbe rested largely on the dynamism of the West German economy and the self-sustaining impetus which it was hoped that unification would impart. The performance of the economy in the West has gone some distance towards meeting these expectations. A growth rate of 4.6 per cent for 1990 was the highest since 1976, and although it fell back to 2.8 per cent in 1991, this was still very favourable in the context of the international recession. Currency union did not have the severe economic consequences which some had predicted. Demand in the East was initially met by the take-up of surplus capacity in the West, and was subsequently held in check by the tight monetary policies of the Bundesbank. West Germany's formidable trading capacity – the current account surplus had stood at a record high of DM 104 billion in 1989 – enabled it to asborb the explosion of imports into the East without incurring an unmanageable deficit.

These positive indicators bore witness to the resilience of the economy in the West, contrasting sharply with the drastic decline of activity in the new German Länder, where GNP fell by around 20 per cent in 1990 and continued falling in 1991. Divergent growth rates exacerbated the already massive economic imbalance between East and West.

Coupling the locomotive of growth in the West to the backward economy in the East proved extraordinarily difficult. The split economy which resulted meant that the two parts of Germany effectively remained as two separate economic areas, travelling down two very different paths of development. With monetary union, however, it was impossible to treat them as such for the purposes of economic policy. In particular, it was not possible to insulate the West permanently from the inflationary consequences of measures designed to stimulate the economy in the East. Transfer payments to the new Länder – some DM 100bn in 1991, or DM 6000 per head of the population – merely returned westwards, fuelling a demand-led boom which recalled the Keynesian fiscal policies of a previous era.

Fiscal policy in the new Germany was dominated by the repercussions of unification. The overall, long-term implications of government expenditure were impossible to predict with any degree of accuracy. Even annual expenditure requirements were hard to gauge and the Finance Ministry had to make repeated upward reassessments of its budgetary projections. The federal government budget for 1991 contained provision for expenditure of DM 412bn of which DM 93bn was directly attributable to unification. Unemployment payments to the East accounted for a further DM 23bn. Moreover, a high proportion of expenditure in the East fell outside the confines of the federal government budget, taking the form of 'shadow budgets' to support infrastructure development (DM 24bn), the German Unity Fund and other Special Funds (DM 36bn), and the Treuhandanstalt (DM 23bn) and Länder and municipal authorities in the East (DM 25bn) (Deutsche Bank, 1991a).

Unification-related expenditure was not matched by increased revenue. The 'fiscal bonus' of increased tax yields accompanying growth did little to meet the astronomically high expenditure demands of reconstruction. Moreover, the tax yield in the East was relatively low and declined further with the collapse of economic activity in the new Länder. Tax increases were delayed for political reasons – the prospect had been dismissed by the Chancellor in the campaign for the 1990 election – although increased energy prices and telephone charges could be seen as disguised tax increases. An income tax supplement in the form of a *Solidaritätsbeitrag* (solidarity contribution), was not introduced until July 1991. Thus in another triumph for politics over economics, the financial burden of unification was met by public sector borrowing on an unprecedented scale. Government ceilings for public sector borrowing in 1991 had been set at DM 140bn, but by mid-year it was clear that this figure was hopelessly unrealistic. Some estimates predicted that the 1991 borrowing requirement would reach DM 200bn, representing nearly 8 per cent of GNP. Borrowing on this scale represented a dramatic deviation from the cautious fiscal policy customary in the Federal Republic; during the late 1980s the public sector budget fluctuated between slight surplus and a deficit of around 2 per cent of GNP.

The inflationary consequences of deficit budgeting on this scale were controlled for twelve months by the tight monetary policies of the Bundesbank. However, an abrupt increase in the rate of inflation, to 4.5 per cent in Summer 1991, confirmed the view, articulated by the Bank for some time, that current growth rates were unsustainable, and that too great a strain was being placed on monetary policy as an instrument for the control of inflation.

Moreover, the external effects of these monetary policies was the focus of criticism from Germany's neighbours. The maintainance of high German interest rates against international trends led to the steady appreciation of the Deutschemark against other currencies. A widening gulf between the Deutschemark and the US dollar threatened the stability of the international economy. Moreover, tied to the Deutschemark through the ERM of the EMS the European states were forced to maintain their currencies at unrealistically high levels which curtained their capacity to break out of recession. The potential for disruption of the ERM threatened to set back moves within the European Community towards Monetary Union.

Policy Dilemmas

The upheaval of unification has had the effect of changing the parameters of economic policy, defying or rendering obsolete some of the axioms of German political economy. With the break up of economic orthodoxies, policy differences have emerged, eroding the cohesion of the political–economic elite, and disturbing the consensus orientation of policy-making in the Federal Republic.

Fiscal and Monetary Dilemmas

The principal dilemma is whether to finance unification expenditures through *taxation* or *borrowing*. This dilemma sharpened once it became clear that the burden could not be met through the 'fiscal bonus' of a growth-related increase in tax yields. The federal government remains deeply reluctant to countenance large-scale tax increases. In addition to the political unpopularity which it incurs, increased taxation on the scale required would curb the dynamism of the economy in the West, thus reducing the impetus behind renewal in the East. This danger, and the ease with which deficits have so far been met by healthy capital markets, makes borrowing an attractive option. On the other hand it is argued that borrowing merely postpones the pain for the German economy, whilst storing up problems for the future. As the borrowing requirement increases, so too do fears about its inflationary consequences and about the future costs of debt servicing. Moreover, borrowing to finance transfer payments to the East tends to boost consumption without directly addressing the urgent investment requirement.

A third alternative is to restrict expenditure, particularly that associated with costly *subsidies* in the West which appear increasingly anachronistic in view of the relative affluence here. However, state subsidies are often part of quasi-contractual arrangements between the state and industry which enjoy the protection of legal backing. Moreover attempts to cut subsidies in the West to finance spending in the East intensify the already acrimonious debate over the burdens imposed by the clamour of demands emanating from the Eastern Länder. Legal constraints and political sensitivities mean that subsidies are very difficult to dismantle in the short term. Initiatives by FDP Economics Minister Jürgen Möllemann to follow this course have led to coalition conflict without producing significant results. The Bundesbank has been a very strong advocate of reduced spending. Its perception of fiscal indiscipline in government circles has led it to deliver a number of pointed warnings about the scale of the public sector deficit. When its words have failed to produce a response it has twice increased interest rates in order to 'cool down' an overheating economy. Indeed, it has been suggested that the Bundesbank is trying to 'engineer a recession' as a means of controlling inflation.

Attempts by the federal government to tighten the reins on fiscal policy have so far lacked conviction. Indications of a new sense of realism could be detected in Finance Minister Theo Waigel's presentation of the federal budget to the Bundestag in September 1991. Recognising for the first time what the Opposition had been saying for some time, that obligations to the East entailed burdens on the West (*Frankfurter Allgemeine Zeitung*, 2 September 1991), Waigel announced a planned reduction of public sector borrowing for 1992. However, with no immediate plans either for significant expenditure savings or new sources of revenue – increases in Value

Added Tax were not scheduled until 1993 – it was hard to see how this could be realised.

Labour Market Dilemmas

The corollary of the divided or split economy referred to above is an asymmetrical labour market between the two parts of Germany, and the dilemma which it presents is a major issue of public policy in the new German economy. Labour market asymmetry originates in the very low capital to labour ratio in the new German Länder compared to the West, and the correspondingly low level of productivity. Under 'normal' economic circumstances, an alignment of capital to labour ratios could be expected to occur either through the migration of labour to the West, or through investment in the East attracted by the low wage levels which are normally characteristic of low productivity economies. In the new German economy, however, the realignment of the labour market on these lines is inhibited by intervening political factors.

First, the migration of labour to the West is socially and politically unacceptable. Although migration continued after currency union – some 350,000 East Germans resettled in the West in the second half of 1990, and around 100,000 now commute to jobs in the West – public policy is geared to stemming the flow. As we have seen, the express purpose of currency union was to prevent the migration of labour. Secondly, wage levels in the East have been inflated through linkage to the West; linkage results from East German claims, acknowledged as legitimate by politicians in the West, for equality of living standards. The social and political pressure for a narrowing of the wage gap between East and West has created a permissive environment for wage claims which in economic terms can be seen as exaggerated. The framework of collective bargaining also promotes wage linkage. Contrary to expectations, West German unions have been readily accepted in the East, and trade unions are now organised on an all-German basis. The metalworkers' union IG Metall alone has gained around a million members in the five new Länder (Huber, 1991, 41). Partly to protect the labour market and therefore their bargaining power in the West, they have pressed for rapid wage convergence. The metalworkers' and public service workers' unions have now concluded agreements with employers for convergence within three years, and 1991 wage rounds yielded increases of over 50 per cent. Wage convergence despite the differential in productivity means the distortion of the productivity–wage relationship in the East, discouraging the investment required to bring capital–labour ratio into line with the West.

Post-unification wage pressures are not confined to the East. Tight labour markets resulting from the explosion of economic activity in the West place the trade unions in a strong bargaining position. Pay restraint in the late 1980s left wages low in relation to the return on capital. With profits booming the unions are now determined to redress the balance, and the 1991 pay round produced increases averaging 6.6 per cent in the industrial sector. Wage pressures are expected to be equally strong in the 1992 wage round. Moreover, trade unions continue to press their long standing demand for a 35-hour week, which would impart a upward shock to labour costs. Bundesbank moves to increase interest rates can be seen as an attempt to dampen the labour market and reduce wage pressure, but monetary policy is a blunt instrument for this purpose.

One of the main pillars of the economic success of the Federal Republic was the 'social partnership' ethos of the trade unions, and their willingness to participate, formally or informally, in economic management. 'Responsible' unions and efficient labour markets meant that governments have been able to distance themselves from wage bargaining and labour market policy. In the 1980s, however, the German model of 'democratic corporatism' weakened perceptibly (Hancock, 1989, 134–41). Labour market malfunction and a wages spiral in the East, and the erosion of pay discipline in the West, places the model under further strain. The full weight of labour market and wages policy fell increasingly upon government.

This began to occur in Spring 1992, when the government was drawn into a bitter industrial dispute with the public sector workers' union ÖTV. The public sector pay round had been brought forward deliberately with the intention of establishing a benchmark of wage restraint for the private sector to follow. Against the background of coalition instability caused by the resignation of Foreign Minister Genscher, and with the Chancellor's leadership under scrutiny, Kohl embarked on a high risk strategy. An appeal for pay discipline and national solidarity was combined with a deliberate confrontation with ÖTV. The industrial conflict which followed was the most acute and extensive since the early 1970s, paralysing public services and creating a climate of crisis which Kohl hoped would impart a salutory effect upon subsequent pay bargaining. The calculation misfired, however, when after eleven days of strikes the government was forced to back down in a settlement in excess of an agreement it had previously rejected. Coinciding with the political crisis within the coalition, the government's entry into the arena of industrial relations was inopportune and inauspicious. If, as anticipated, the conflict is re-enacted in the private sectors, it will prove very difficult to reconcile pay settlements with government and Bundesbank strategy for controlling inflation, placing additional strains on fiscal and monetary policy.

Dilemmas of Reconstruction in the East

A *state-led* transition to a *market* economy is somewhat anachronistic, and success depends upon finding a judicious mix between public policy instruments and market forces. In principle, policy measures should promote the operation of the market rather than the reverse. However, as we have seen, this is not always possible, due to the intervention of social and political objectives. A case in point is the support through *subsidisation* of uncompetitive enterprises, pending restructuring and privatisation. Indiscriminate aid in the form of liquidity credits and subsidies for short-time working merely serves to support economically unsustainable enterprises, offering no incentive for shake-up. The resultant misallocation of resources maintains uneconomic production, starving potentially viable enterprises of investment capital. Moreover, experience elsewhere suggests that indiscriminate subsidies are self-perpetuating.

Business interests have advocated the replacement of indiscriminate subsidies with more selective investment incentives. One widely advocated instrument is the wage subsidy. Employment bonuses for privatised companies would offset relatively high labour costs, and offer incentives for investment and growth in profitable enterprises, without perpetuating uneconomic production. This form of subsidisation, it is argued, would operate selectively and without undermining the dynamics of a market economy. Its disadvantage is that it could easily become an institutionalised feature of the economy in the East.

Reconstruction raises two further issues. First, *Competition* is seen as an important force for economic regeneration in the East. However, the strict application of competition rules can frustrate otherwise attractive privatisation deals. The dilemma arises when the acquisition of interests in the East by already large West German companies threatens to lead to market dominance on a scale incompatible with federal competition law. The urgently needed takeover of energy supply in the East by a consortium of utilities already dominant in the West was a case in point. The Bundeskartellamt (Federal Cartel Office) has found it very difficult to adjudicate in such cases, and has passed responsibility to the government. Generally, the priority has been placed on privatisation, with gestures to competitive principles being grafted onto the original deal. The second dilemma concerns the very highly developed legal framework of regulation surrounding economic life in the Federal Republic, which has been seen by some as restricting economic potential (Bulmer, 1989, 7). It has been argued that the extension of these regulatory practices to the East will inevitably inhibit take-off.

The Role of the Bundesbank

The sharp differences which have emerged between the federal government and the Bundesbank have tested the relationship between the two, leading to a reappraisal of the constitutional status of the Bank. Bundesbank Statutes charge it with responsibility for 'safeguarding currency stability by means of regulating the money supply and the availability of credit to the economy'. Its independence from government instructions is also guaranteed by statute. On the other hand, the relationship is imbued with a certain amount of ambiguity, since the Bank is also charged with the statutory duty of supporting the general economicy policy of the government, subject to the discharge of its monetary duties. In practice, the relationship becomes even more ambiguous. The Bank's formal claims to independence cannot always be sustained in the highly political environment in which it operates (Kennedy, 1990, 36). Tension between the Bundesbank and the government is not new. The last months of Helmut Schmidt's Social–Liberal coalition were played out against the background of acute conflict, with the Bank dictating monetary policy and using its prestige and authority to encroach deep into economic and fiscal policy arenas.

In the context of unification, however, the roles are reversed with the Kohl government dictating the terms of monetary union and strenuously resisting Bank intervention in fiscal policy. The preference of the Bundesbank for a period of reform in the East, and convergence between the two economies prior to currency union was overridden by the government, and the Bank's subsequent retreat on the issue clearly illustrated the limits to its authority. The lesson was reiterated over the terms of monetary union. Advocating a 2:1 conversion rate with a 1:1 rate restricted to small savers, the Bank was openly critical of government plans for parity conversion. The limited concessions to the Bank's position which were incorporated in the State Treaty could not conceal the fact that the government had once again taken a fundamental issue of monetary policy into its own hands. In fiscal and monetary policy the Bank's statutory right to consultation was flagrantly breached. Plans for financing unification were formulated in the Chancellor's Office and the Finance Ministry. Bundesbank officials are said to have learned of the launch of the German Unity Fund through the press.

The Bundesbank is not without influence in the political economy of post-unification Germany. It has made full use of its powers to set base interest rates, and its independence and prestige are reflected in its ability publicly to disagree with and criticise government policy. However, these resources became diminishing assets by the time of Bundesbank President Karl Otto Pöhl's premature departure from office in July 1991. A variety of reasons were given for Pöhl's resignation, but it was clear that he found his subordination to government unpalatable. Moreover, his role as mediator between the government and the Bank's fractious governing Council had become increasingly untenable. Pöhl's successor, Helmut Schlesinger, is a monetary conservative who shared his predecessor's scepticism over the pace of currency union. The tension between monetary discipline and a relaxed course in fiscal policy, corresponding to conflicting perspectives between the Bundesbank and government, is therefore unlikely to recede. Indeed it is possible that new tensions will surface over the terms of the proposed European Monetary Union.

Take-off or Retrenchment?

Economic take-off and reconstruction in the East is the touchstone of success for German unification. Having been granted political democracy and citizenship in the Federal Republic, the East German people now demand inclusion in the 'economic democracy of consumers' which they perceive in the West. The political imperative for take-off and reconstruction is therefore a pressing one. At the time of writing, however, there was little positive evidence of an upswing of economic activity, despite vast state expenditure in the East. The optimistic assumptions drawn from the experience of the post-war economic miracle have yet to be realised. The first eighteen months after GEMU have severely tested the economic philsophy upon which the miracle was based and which has dominated the political economy of the Federal Republic throughout the post-war years. *Ordnungspolitik* – the creation by the state of favourable conditions for economic activity whilst relying on the market to act as the motive force – has yet to prove itself in the context of the Eastern Länder, and calls for a more interventionist government approach are gaining force.

Other central elements in the political economy of the Federal Republic have also been put under strain. Labour market dilemmas have tested the institutional and attitudinal framework of democratic corporatism. New obligations in the East have reduced the capacity of the state to support subsidy dependent industries in the West.

The Federal Republic has experienced a marked intensification of distributional conflict, the counterpart to which is an erosion of political cohesion. Attempts to restore social and political solidarity in the form of a 'Grand Consensus' have yet to produce tangible results. The fiscal conservatism and monetary stability characteristic of the Federal Republic is another casualty of unification. The resultant tension between Bundesbank and government has imparted additional uncertainty to these policy areas.

Despite the robustness of the economy in the West, fiscal and monetary policy remains delicately balanced. The key question for the future of the new German economy is whether the deficit in the West can be prolonged without incurring runaway inflation and undermining international competitiveness. If the balancing act can be sustained until economic activity in the East gathers self-sustaining momentum, then the prospects are good. The restoration of wage discipline will be central to the resolution of this question. If, on the other hand, the brakes of fiscal and monetary discipline are applied in the interests of restoring stability, the effect is likely to be the retardation of take-off in the East. Failure to regenerate the economy of the Eastern Länder would perpetuate their dependency upon the West. Both alternatives – the dash for take-off and the retreat into retrenchment – are loaded with risks. Success depends upon steering a balanced course between the two, and on resolving the outstanding public policy dilemmas posed by the new German economy.

11

Social Policy: One State, Two-tier Welfare

STEEN MANGEN

The Welfare System: East and West

Prior to 1990 the two Germanies possessed distinct welfare systems, in terms both of organisation and of goals. Operating within the wider framework of the 'middle way' Social Market Economy, the essential feature of the West German model are its pluralism and high degree of decentralisation of functions. According to the subsidiarity principle the central state is the agency of last resort for most welfare functions. The main responsibility for social policy-making is devolved to the federal states and in the provision of many social services the voluntary sector (*freie Träger*) assumes a preeminent role. Subsidiarity also means that social insurance is self-administered by the social partners, with separate schemes indemnifying each major risk. Table 11.1 lists the major features of this welfare system into which the GDR was incorporated. Further discussion is contained in Mangen (1989).

In comparison, social policy-making in the GDR was centralised and service provision state-controlled (Dennis, 1988). For much of its history the emphasis in the GDR was on the primacy of state responsibility (an alien concept in the FRG) since social policy was increasingly perceived as a valuable means of legitimising the SED state (Adams, 1990). Social insurance was in operation, administered by the FDGB or by the state for certain occupations. However, it relied on heavy state subsidisation. Moreover, since the GDR guaranteed wide-ranging rights to work, unemployment insurance did not exist. 'Citizenship' welfare rights in the form of universal

208

TABLE 11.1 *The German welfare system*

OVERARCHING PRINCIPLE: Subsidiarity
The state is provider of last report. Hence priority is attached in social insurance to the principle of self-administration by the social partners and to devolution in welfare services' provision to the voluntary and private sector. For most areas of social policy (except the regulation of social insurance) the federal government largely retains residual powers. Policy-making is devolved to the federal states.

Social insurance

The separate schemes for each risk (sickness, old age, disability, survivors and unemployment) are varyingly organised at local level or according to occupational grouping or 'contracted out' schemes in health care. Unemployment insurance is the only unified federally organised scheme. Except for industrial accidents (which are funded entirely by employers) the system is funded by employers and employees, with varying levels of federal subsidy.

Social assistance

According to the category of need social assistance is provided by the Länder of local authorities.

Health services

The majority of services are provided by the voluntary sector or the private profit-making sector for both inpatient services and outpatient 'office' practice. Local authorities are also active in the hospital sector and in public health.

Social services

These are provided by a large number of voluntary agencies with certain functions being reserved by local authorities. Private profit-making agencies are active, especially in the residential care sector.

flat-rate benefits were a more prominent feature than earnings-related entitlements, although the significance of the latter had been increasing since the 1970s (Bradley Scharf, 1987). In assessing what have generally been regarded as low benefit levels, one has to take into account the wide-scale subsidies of essential items (food, certain clothing, rents, energy costs and public transport) which contributed substantially to the social income of the average East German. Lampert (1990), for example, estimates that subsidised goods accounted for about one-third of average weekly expenditure.

One characteristic of East German welfare that has had serious consequences in the post-unification period was the prominent role of occupational welfare. The state corporations were major suppliers of popularly esteemed social services for their employees: kindergarten, school meals, primary health care facilities such as the polyclinics and job creation and retraining programmes. Given the imperatives to restructure the former GDR economy, these enterprises have been particularly anxious to shed their welfare responsibilities, with deleterious consequences for employees' welfare rights (and especially for female workers) and for increasing the burden elsewhere, notably by the transfer of functions to the local authorities (see below). What the united Germany inherited from the former GDR, then, was a system of social provision characterised more by deficiencies of quality rather than by limited extensiveness.

Social Policy and the Unification Process

During the Round Table discussions prior to the First State Treaty GDR politicians and elements within the Western SPD and Greens urged the preservation of the positive features of the East Germany *'soziale Errungenschaft'* (social achievement). They argued that, otherwise, there was a lot to lose, not least in child care services, heavily subsidised housing and the notion of a 'citizenship' universal basic pension (discussed below). However, several factors combined to limit the force of their argument: the very speed of unification (eleven months separate the fall of the Wall from unification); the rapidly deteriorating economic situation in the GDR; and the almost daily revelations of corruption and crude clientelism in the administration of Eastern public services. Besides, on the Western side there were few incentives to move ground. For one, despite a certain disillusionment with the post-oil crisis social state, there was popular appreciation of the comparatively high quality of West German welfare benefits. The Bonn government was reluctant to reopen a debate on issues that had proved controversial only in the recent past when major policy reforms in health and social security were being legislated. Thus, where concessions were made, they were adopted only as temporary measures.

Significantly, unification negotiations did not give rise to a wider political debate among the *Volksparteien* on the future viability of long-held welfare principles. Although the SPD supported certain reforms – they included a limited minimum pension proposal in their 1990 election manifesto, for example – it was the proclamations of chancellor candidate Lafontaine about the excessive welfare burden on the West caused by the assimilation of the East that provoked media and public discussion. The State Treaties thus specify that in all essential details, West German social legislation was to be applied in the East according to a varying but limited time-scale.

Paradoxically, the unification treaties prescribe a welfare division of Germany of uncertain duration, since what they provided for the new Länder were the structure and service principles of Western welfare without the guarantee of equality of entitlement (Bäcker, 1991). Social equity, it was argued, would be more securely achieved through the rapid implementation of the social market economy which was the only way to stimulate the necessarily high growth rates in the East to pay for welfare gains.

The political aim was to establish very quickly Western plural welfare arrangements in the new Länder (self-administration of social insurance and the subsidiarity of public sector service provision, and so forth). Details of the timetabling of this process are given in Table 11.2. Social benefits were converted at a parity rate between the GDR Mark and the Deutschemark. Critically, future entitlements in the former GDR were to be related to net income trends there rather than to those in Germany as a whole. At the same time Eastern social insurance contributions were significantly increased and Western income tax regulations introduced.

The net effects of all these measures has been tentatively measured by one of the principal economic forecasting institutes, the Deutsches Institut für Wirtschaftsforschung (DIW). It estimates that an Eastern pensioner household's real disposable income in the first year of the Social Union was almost two-thirds that of the Western equivalent. In respect of blue collar households the proportion could reach over three-quarters. However, the DIW stress that these are household data (the income or pension entitlement of the very high percentage of married women in employment boosts household income) rather than income data for individuals and for other household formations East–West ratios are less favourable. Moreover, other things being equal, the increases in wages and benefits levels in future are unlikely fully to compensate for general price increases, nor for insurance contributions or the loss of social entitlements such as the withdrawal of subsidies for essential items. Rents were raised in 1991 by at least 350 per cent, although from an admitttedly very low base (Bank and Kreikebohm, 1991).

The welfare system of the former GDR was poorly understood by Western politicians and the long-run social expenditure implications of unification were seriously underestimated. Contemporary problems were played down as temporary constraints which would be eradicated by a '*Wirtschaftswunder Ost*'. Such a position was in line with Kohl's *Wendepolitik* of the 1980s, with its promise of a return to a stricter subsidiarity of the state, limits on public expenditure and associated tax reductions (Mangen, 1991). After this initial optimistic reliance on economic growth as the generator of additional welfare,

TABLE 11.2   *Welfare provisions and the unification process*

OVERARCHING PRINCIPLE

Benefits converted initially at parity (1 GDR Mark to 1 Deutsche mark). Ratios of western levels vary. Future Eastern benefit increases will reflect income trends in the new Länder.

Care insurance

An all-German scheme to be legislated in 1992. The community care programme enacted in 1987 has applied throughout Germany since 1991.

Child benefit

West German legislation has applied since 1990, Eastern benefits are paid at a higher level because GDR family credits and allied benefits were abolished.

Childbearing benefit and parental leave

West German legislation has applied since 1991.

Disability pensions

Application of the West German legislation since 1990, with certain exceptions.

Drug prices

From 1991 the West German price levels notionally applied, but the pharmaceutical companies, wholesalers and chemists have had to bear a deficit incurred by the Eastern sickness funds to the amount of DM 500 million with a 50 per cent contribution thereafter. Federal subsidies fund the remainder. A sliding scale of deficit funding applies for 1992 and 1993.

Health insurance

From 1991 the plural health insurance system of West Germany has applied in the new states. Locally-based funds are supplemented by 'contracted out' schemes, occupational and private schemes either as new entities or as extensions of West German ones. However, the sickness funds in the two parts of Germany continue to be financed separately.

Industrial accident insurance

West German legislation introduced in 1991.

Maternity leave

Since 1990 West German legislation has applied.

Medical and dental fees

Set at 45 per cent of the West German level. Patient contributions to health care costs delayed until 1992 and thereafter set at 50 per cent of the Western level.

Occupational rehabilitation

Since 1991 West German legislation applies.

TABLE 11.2 *continued*

Retirement pensions

Since 1991 West German legislation applies, and thus a plural system of blue collar, white collar and certain occupational schemes have been introduced. Civil servants enjoy non-contributory pensions. A *social supplement* has been paid to low pension recipients to top up benefits to a predetermined level. It will be payable until 1995.

The former GDR early retirement scheme was replaced in 1991. The early retirement benefit is available from the age of 57, at two-thirds the last average net income.

Social assistance

West German legislation applies after 1991. In general, benefit is payable at 75 per cent of the Western equivalent.

Social courts

The constitutional guarantees by resort to litigation are to be phased in.

Social insurance

Contributions to be jointly funded by employer and employee, except for industrial accidents which is a scheme funded only by employers.

West German criteria apply, but with lower income thresholds.

Social services

The plural system involving voluntary agencies (*freie Träger*) and private sector organisations, supplemented by local authority activities for certain reserved functions, is being phased in.

Special short-time working benefit

Special regulations applied. Unlike in West Germany, the benefit was payable even when guarantees about the long-term security of employment could not be given. The scheme was extended until the end of 1991.

Unemployment insurance

The West German scheme was introduced into the new Länder in 1990.

---

social policies for the East are now being formulated more cautiously. Nevertheless, there is strong resistance to a major redistribution of national income from West to East. In essence, the government's position is to defend long-held, albeit increasingly precarious, welfare principles. The crucial issue is to what degree redistributive welfare would be politically sanctioned and socially tolerated.

The question of 'social solidarity', then, is occupying centre stage in social policy debate, at least among academics and social policy specialists in the major parties. Von Dohnanyi (1990) calculates that, even if GDP growth rate in the former GDR were three times those of the old FRG, it would still be 2007 before *per capita* GDP attained parity. Given the wide-ranging deficits in social security and social services funding in the East, a general rule of thumb estimate is that it will take between ten and fifteen years to fulfil the constitutional guarantee of the *sozialer Rechtsstaat* to offer broadly uniform standards of living throughout the country. The political, not to mention social, risks of such a long transition period must be rated as potentially very serious and worrying for a country where the maintenance of social stability has been a major preoccupation. In this event, pressures for further relaxation of the subsidiarity principle may become irresistible, with a greater and institutionalised federal fiscalisation of the plural welfare system being conceded.

Financing Social Security

Long-term trends in social security expenditure are a function of general economic performance, unemployment rates, wage developments and welfare costs negotiated by suppliers, particularly in the health sector (see Chapter 10 in this volume). Significantly, although ostensibly an all-German insurance system was instigated, apart from the national unemployment scheme Eastern funds continue to be administered separately with independent accounting procedures. To be sure, the new German social insurance system did not inherit much in the way of consolidated funds from GDR schemes since much of social security expenditure there had been raised annually through general taxation. An immediate subsidy of DM 10,500 million was therefore allocated to the new Länder, chiefly to cover deficits arising from pension increases and from the newly-introduced unemployment insurance. In addition, Labour Minister Blüm announced what he canvassed as a one-off, short-term 'seedbed' financial package (*Anschubfinanz*) to assist the effective establishment of the Eastern pension and unemployment schemes. This tactic complemented the government's line adopted in the State Treaty, namely, that Western insurance should not be encumbered by Eastern deficits, thus preserving the sanctity of the equivalence principle (benefits paid out equal income received from contributions). Subsequently, temporary income tax increases and the raising of the national unemployment insurance contribution compromised this position and were highly embarrassing for the government.

The likelihood of long-term and substantial deficits in Eastern social insurance must be rated as high. But, so far, the Labour Minister has refused to speculate and is resorting to ad hoc subsidies as and when they occur, with a hint that reductions in the quality of entitlements may have to be considered.

Beyond the data for 1990, the level of financial need in social security and in the other social services is based on speculative projections. These rely on differing interpretations both about the rate of economic growth which is feasible in the middle run and on broad brush estimates of funding requirements for infrastructural improvements in provisions. It must be stressed that, to date, no comprehensive survey of the state of social services has been undertaken and, therefore, most of the future funding projections presented here are highly speculative.

The five economic forecasting institutes have predicted that the total social expenditure deficit in 1991 will be in excess of DM 30,000 million. Whatever the criteria adopted, most expert commentators concur that the situation is going to get worse before it gets better. This consensus view helped to prompt the government in its 1991 budget proposal to specify the amount of expenditure that would be met by federal funding. Their estimate was that the total deficit in the former GDR would be DM 81,000 million (nine times the volume they predicted in the previous year), of which DM 26,000 million would largely be allocted to spending on child care, pensions and early retirement schemes. Nonetheless, the government remained optimistic, projecting that the deficit would be reduced by more than half by 1994 through new debt raising and increasing the unemployment insurance contribution. This latter move proved highly controversial, since the government was roundly criticised by the SPD and the DGB for a lack of social equity, mainly because privileged non-contributors – civil servants and the self-employed – were excluded from this 'solidarity contribution'.

Financing Social Services

Speculations about future expenditure patterns extend well beyond social security considerations into the area of welfare which is the principal responsibility of local authorities and the voluntary sector. In the reform of institutional arrangements local authorities were identified as key welfare agents. At least temporarily, they have assumed major responsibilities for housing, hospitals, many of the child care facilities previously provided by state enterprises, subsidies for essential items (from 1991), and for the recently installed social assistance scheme.

Apart from the problems associated with combatting the deficiencies in the administrative capacity of their welfare system,

Eastern local authorities are having to devise emergency means of coping with their dire financial state. Their tax-derived income is only about one-tenth of the West German equivalent (the five new Länder have at their disposal one-third the relevant equivalent). DIW has calculated that the combined budgetary deficit of the Eastern states and local authorities in 1991 will amount to DM 1300 per inhabitant. Fiscal pressures are exacerbated by the increasing demand for social services. Even more serious is the housing situation to which local authorities are having to respond. Until 1991 many rents were pegged at 1936 price levels and even the high percentage rent increases in 1991 will not generate an income sufficient to instigate the scale of rehabilitation and new construction which housing experts project will be required. For example, it has been broadly estimated that up to one-fifth of the housing stock could be rated as uninhabitable if West German statutory standards were applied (IdW, 1991). Von Dohnanyi (1990) quotes professional sources as calculating, on their general impressions of the housing stock, that up to DM 200,000 million could be required over the next fifteen years to bring existing units up to standard and an additional DM 100,000 million will be needed for new constructions.

To relieve these fiscal pressures local authorities have been encouraged to sell off housing to sitting tenants and to offer for sale prime site land in their ownership. However, both of these strategies are compromised by the decision of the last GDR government to honour the claims of former owners. For its part, the federal government has reacted to the plight of local authorities with a combination of measures: one-off or short-term earmarked subsidies (for example, for emergency house repairs; to finance kindergartens transferred to them from the public corporations; or to pay for the subsidies for essential items); and low interest credits (for example, for housing improvements). The principal funds available to the new Länder and local authorities, however, derive from the general programme 'Deutsche Einheit' provided by Bonn and the Länder to replace, at least temporarily, the budgetary equalisation mechanism by which rich Länder subsidise poorer ones. In addition, the 1991 budgetary allocation provided for a new scheme, the 'Aufschwung Ost' fund, to stimulate infrastructural investimate and job creation, mainly in the social sector. Further details are given in Table 11.3.

These federal and federal–Länder programmes are intended as short-term interventions, the explicit policy being to phase out such expenditure by the mid-1990s. Subsidies for debt servicing of earlier housing schemes, for example, are to be ended in 1994 and local government will be faced with a debt volume here of up to DM 50,000 million. Furthermore, they are having to assume responsi-

TABLE 11.3 *Unification and welfare funding*

OVERARCHING PRINCIPLE

Federal and federal–Länder subsidies were allocated on a short-term basis. The establishment of the social market economy was identified as the key mechanism for stimulating the economic rejuvenation of the new Länder to provide the means for upgrading welfare provisions.

Housing

Eastern local authorities were temporarily relieved of debt servicing of pre-unification house-building projects.

1990–3: DM 10,000 million modernisation programme specifically for the new federal states (matched federal-Länder funding of low-interest loans).

1991–2: DM 1,000 million federal and Länder funding to promote social housebuilding.

1991: DM 350 million federal allocation for the completion of the pre-unification house-building programme in the East.

1992–4: For each year DM 1,000 million to promote construction of new housing units in areas of special need, e.g. Brandenburg–Pomerania.

Länder and Local authorities

1990: Emergency subsidy of DM 30,000 million for Eastern local authorities.

1990–5: DM 15,000 million low credit funding made available.

1990–4: *'Deutsche Einheit'* Fund temporarily to substitute for the budgetary transfer mechanism between rich and poor Länder. DM 115,000 million allocated.

1991–2: *'Gemeinschaftswerk Aufschwung Ost'*: DM 12,000 million allocated for each year to provide a catalyst for infrastructural investment in the social sector (social and health services, town planning, housing and public transport).

1991: Additional subsidies of DM 5,000 million earmarked to improve the infratructure of the social services.

1991: Projected DM 97,000 million budget allocated for general local authority support.

Social security

1990: DM 10,500 million general subsidy. Also announced was a special 'seedbed' (*Anschubfinanz*) supplement: DM 750 million for pension funds; for unemployment insurance DM 2,000 million in 1990 and DM 3,000 million in 1991. In addition, a one-off federal subsidy of up to DM 35,000 million for the 1991 budgetary deficit.

Unemployment insurance: DM 22,000 million subsidy allocated for 1990, with a maximum federal subsidy of DM 35,000 million announced for 1991.

bility for the remaining subsidies of essential items which Höhnen (1991) estimates currently amount to over DM 30,000 million. The authorities have coped by using whatever means are at their disposal. Principally this has meant job losses or short-time working. The DIW speculate that three-quarters of a million persons will have lost their employment in this sector by the end of 1991. Nor has service provision escaped the consequences of chronic budgetary deficits. Cuts have been implemented in what are generally acknowledged to be seriously overstretched services and, elsewhere, fees for such provisions as kindergarten and old people's homes have been markedly increased. Moreover, local authorities have been sluggish in applying for credits and other subsidies to upgrade welfare institutions, a practice that has recently attracted the criticism of the federal Health Minister.

In addition to these problems Eastern local governments have had to assume responsibility for the new social assistance scheme, expenditure on which will be critically determined, at least in the short run, by the rate of long-term unemployment. In the former FRG in the 1980s the number of social assistance recipients rose by 70 per cent, accounting for 5 per cent of the total population. Apart from the elderly, applying for benefit to top up pensions, the main clientele were the long-term unemployed whose full right to insurance-linked entitlement had expired. With various estimates suggesting that the rate of Eastern unemployment or short-time work could reach 4 million by early 1992, the signs are that social assistance funding, already under intense pressure in the West, could rapidly acquire crisis proportions in the East. Nor will the crisis be confined to the former GDR, since the long-term unemployment there will intensify the continuing propensity of East Germans to move westwards in search of work. Recipient local authorities in the West will therefore be put under renewed pressure, not only in social assistance, but also in providing emergency accommodation and longer-term social housing, at a time when they are complaining of the tremendous task they are facing in coping with the assimilation of ethnic Germans from eastern Europe and in providing for the large increase in asylum seekers.

Integrating Health Care

Health care delivery in West Germany is a plural system with a 'complex' of funders and providers. There are well over 1000 Western sickness funds and no means of cross-subsidisation among them to provide for the effective pooling of risks. Health services in operation maintain a rigid division between the outpatient sector, where there is a neo-monopoly enjoyed by doctors in office practice, and the hospital sector administered by the voluntary and private sector and by municipalities. The system has long been criticised for its perverse incentives to oversupply medical services and, despite severral sustained government efforts to the contrary, health expenditures have proved markedly resistant to cost containment. Critics at the time of the Round Table discussions in 1990 argued that it made no sense to transfer this system to the East in an unchanged form, especially as the GDR health services contained exemplary elements, notably in primary care. Combined lobbying by the West German medical and pharmaceutical organisations, together with pressure from their allies within the FDP, ensured that a more or less total and swift extension of the federal system to the new Länder would be forced through. A major exception, at least temporarily, was made for the polyclinics which were granted a further five years' survival (incidentally one of the longest transitional phases prescribed in the State Treaty).

Labour Ministry calculations specified that the new Eastern sickness funds, which were to be administered separately until economic parity with the West had been achieved, would raise an income equivalent to 45 per cent of that of their Western counterparts. Medical and dental fees in the East were to be levied at the corresponding rate. Recent evidence, however, indicates that there has been a significant demand-led pressure on fees, and many contracts between funders and suppliers have been concluded at amounts up to 60 per cent of the Western equivalent. This has put mounting pressure on the financial capacity of Eastern sickness funds and, in the absence of cross-subsidisation, additional federal funding will be unavoidable, since too frequent an increase in the contribution rate would be an unattractive option for the government.

The reimbursement of pharmaceutical costs has been particularly problematic. Initially Blüm demanded a 55 per cent discount on drug prices in the East. But after a boycott of the Eastern market by West German companies, he settled for a discount of less than half of this amount and agreed a complicated formula for a three-year subsidisation package (see Table 11.2).

Regulating the funding of service delivery is only one of the immediate problems facing the federal government and the new Länder. The physical state of many of the health facilities is extremely poor. East German hospitals have overcrowded wards, low quality buildings and ineffective heating systems. They are particularly deficient in terms of high-technology medicine. The old GDR method of funding hospitals provided an incentive for the oversupply of inpatient beds to the neglect of day and community-based care facilities. This had a particular impact on the frail elderly, many of whom were hospitalised because of a lack of alternative residential or day care. The same applied to long-term psychiatric patients. The Unification Treaty allocated monies for an immediate emergency renovation programme for the inpatient sector, but it is generally admitted that the upgrading process will be a long-term effort. Impressionistic estimates by the official 'concerted action' committee on health care suggest that up to DM 40,000 million could be required over the next ten or fifteen years to renovate about half the inpatient capacity. Such a sum, which normally should be funded by the Länder under West German regulations would be financially crippling in the East and, at least in the middle term, the federal government will unavoidably be called on to provide the largest share of the funds (Meier and Walzik, 1991).

The urgency of injecting additional funds into East Germany has raised, once again, the question of cross-subsidisation among the sickness schemes. This issue forms part of a wider – and now all-German – debate that preceded the health care reform legislated in 1987, principally to reinforce cost containment efforts. The plurality of sickness funds means that for more or less the same access to health care contribution rates vary from between 8 and 16 per cent of income, depending on whether the subscriber is a member of a 'contracted out' scheme or the local general scheme that, typically, has a heavier risk profile in terms of an older and more chronically ill membership. However, cross-subsidisation continues to have low political feasibility, giventhe persistent resistance of richer funds and those federal states where local general schemes bear a more favourable risk loading.

Blüm's 1987 reform programme was designed to stabilise over the long term what had been rapidly rising health expenditures. Principal components of his strategy included raising the level of patient contributions to direct treatment costs and to prescriptions. Non-essential treatments and 'comfort' medication were excluded from future reimbursement. Expenditure on drugs, which was one of the highest in the EC countries, was to be controlled by the creation of an approved prescription list. Of the projected DM 14,000 million to be saved, half was allocated to a new community care programme for the elderly and severely disabled and the remainder was reserved for a reduction in the sickness insurance contribution.

For varying reasons, the reforms – though scarcely radical – upset almost everyone and this was reflected in the subsequent poor showing of the CDU in Länder elections. The pharmaceutical industry, in particular, lobbied to restrict the application of the approved list.

By the early 1990s under 50 per cent, and not the projected 90 per cent, of drugs were on the list. Expenditure trends in recent years reveal that the impact of the reform was short-term and by 1990 health budgets were on the increase again. The assimilation of the former GDR into the system can only accelerate this trend. There have been fresh calls from the SPD for a further policy review with the aim of giving serious consideration to the implementation of global budgeting for the whole of the health care system. But, so far, Blüm has proposed only ad hoc reforms such as revising patient prescription costs to reflect the total price of the drugs supplied.

'Pflegenotstand': The Crisis of Care

Apart from cost containment, a prominent health issue in the 1980s – which has similarly remained a topical item on the policy agenda – was the 'crisis of care'. Long-term care, as opposed to active treatment, is not a risk adequately covered by German social security and sickness funds attempt to restrict their liabilities to those judged to require strictly medical intervention. The chronically disabled, the mentally ill and the frail elderly do not easily conform to these criteria and, in many cases, social assistance is called upon to indemnify the costs of their care with the client or his near family being required to make a contribution based on their disposable means. The problem has been growing in significance and has attracted considerable media attention since it incorporates such contemporary concerns as the position of women (who compromise the majority of informal carers) and the problem of social marginalisation (people 'warehoused' in remote long-stay institutions).

In the mid-1980s the government rejected the idea of an additional insurance premium to provide for the eventuality of the need for chronic nursing care, largely because it was felt that it could inflate demand for services, once an entitlement had been established. Insted, as mentioned earlier, a community care package was included in the 1987 health reform. Informal carers were offered tax incentives, pension credits, an attendant's allowance, regular relief support and an annual holiday relief. The measures were intended to provide an incentive to maintain people in the community and thus reduce the need for institutionalisation.

Nonetheless, even before it was implemented (the measures are being phased in during the early 1990s), the inadequacy of this package as a long-term solution became apparent. Clearly, demand for forms of long-stay care was going to remain high, in the face of a rapidly ageing population, which the annexation of the GDR did little to ameliorate. Moreover, there is an urgent need for major infrastructural investment in the care sector, all the more so since unification. Staffing levels, too, leave a lot to be desired, estimates being that an additional 20 per cent of nursing staff are required, partly to offset the loss of nursing input due to the reduction in the conscription period which meant that men opting for alternative 'civil duty' are now available to the care sector for five months less than previously.

The idea of compulsory care insurance was taken up again by Blüm and canvassed in the election campaign of 1990. His scheme had the broad support of the SPD, who had proposed something similar, but it seriously upset the FDP who wished to promote voluntary private insurance. Because of differences of opinion within the coalition an ultimate decision was deferred. In the subsequent inter-party negotiations on drafting a bill the FDP became increasingly truculent, Count Lambsdorff even alluding to the fragility of the coalition if legislation were forced through. A definitive statement of policy intent is awaited.

The Future of Pensions

The negotiations on pensions in the Union Treaty proved problematic, chiefly because they account for the largest single item of social expenditure. In the centre of the dispute was the question of the retention of a national minimum pension available in the GDR. Of equal importance was the problem of how to finance a rapid improvement of the generally low level of pension entitlements being inherited from the old East German scheme where the average benefit amounted to about one-third of previous income and, furthermore, was not index-linked (although many East Germans took out voluntary 'top-up' supplementary insurance).

The Treaty made provision for a long-term adjustment of GDR pensions to Western levels. Pension schemes on the lines of those in the West were to be in operation by 1992 and were to be more strictly earnings-related than had been the case in the outgoing system. Indexation was also introduced, but according to Eastern rather than national wage developments. State subsidies of the Eastern schemes were incorporated at the same level of those available to the Western funds.

The pensions question unleashed a fresh debate among politicians that had been particularly prominent in West Germany in the mid-1980s: namely, what are the present and future social purposes to which benefits should be harnessed? At issue were arguments about citizenship, social equity and gender equality. Social policy experts in the SPD, supported by Eastern politicians, pressed for the preservation of the basic pension offered by the GDR system. This benefit, they argued, should provide a guaranteed minimum which would secure a reasonable living standard in old age. They criticised the prevailing West German earnings-related principle for carrying into old age the income inequalities of working lie, to the detriment of the low wage earner. These inequalities are most clearly evident in the unfavourable pensions profiles of west German women when compared to men although women were also disadvantaged in the East German scheme (Schmähl, 1990). Moreover, the Western system has meant that pension levels for many recipients are below subsistence levels and, therefore, need to be supplemented by means-tested social assistance, although the stigma attached to this has, it is claimed, deterred many potential claimants.

In 1990, two-thirds of East German pensioners (the majority women) were receiving the minimum pension. Their anxieties raised by the warnings of GDR politicians about the likelihood of an immediate and massive application for social assistance, which was only then being established by local authorities, the government adopted an exceptional measure. A federally-funded 'social supplement' was to be made available automatically to East German minimum pension holders, without test of need, to bring their benefits up to subsistence level. In 1990 one in six Eastern pensioners were receiving the supplement, 95 per cent of them being women.

The 'social supplement' is a novelty in German social security, since it created a *de facto* needs oriented minimum pension in contradistinction to means-tested assistance. A universal benefit – admittedly introduced only to prevent overburdening local authorities in the East with social assistance claimants – was therefore replacing discretionary welfare. In fact, this sort of citizenship benefit was precisely what the CDU had rejected in the 1980s as being unlikely to secure cross-party consensus, since it moved away from the insurance principle to a notion of universalism. The government was accused of crude opportunism: of doing the right thing for the wrong reason. In the wake of criticism that Easterners were getting preferential treatment, while their Western counterparts had to apply for a means-tested and discretionary benefit, Labour Minister Blüm was at pains to insist that the supplement would be available only for five years and, moreover, would not be index-linked. Although CDU social policy specialists and the employers' organisation, the CDA, urged a serious reconsideration of a minimum pension to be available throughout Germany, the party did not include it in its 1990 election manifesto, unlike the SPD and the Greens.

The 'social supplement' is part of a wider effort on the part of the government to raise Eastern pension levels rapidly, thus reducing the differential with Western pensions. Within one year of the Social Union the average Eastern pension had been increased by over 70 per cent, but even so it still amounted to only half of the Western equivalent. Full parity will take years to achieve. Bäcker (1991) for example, calculates that, even if pension in the East were to rise annually by 20 per cent and those in the West by only 5 per cent, it would still require seven years before parity was attained. There are urgent reasons why the federal government is taking speedy action, since delay will incur additional funding of the supplement or radically increased social assistance expenditure after its expiry in 1995.

The future of pensions – East and West – awaits long-term resolution. In the East it is a question, at least initially, of compensatory funding on a massive scale: semi-official estimates of the costs of full assimilation suggest the sum required could be as much as DM 10,000 million, but this does not take into account the sharp increase in uptake of social assistance after 1995. In both East and West the future of pensions is threatened by long-term demographic trends. These two factors have prompted opposition politicians and the trade unions to advocate a review of the pensions reform of the late 1980s which was implemented in 1992. So far, their arguments have not impressed the Labour Minister.

Blüm's package increased the retirement age to 65 years for both men and women and made early retirement less financially attractive. Although the new pensions formula reduced projected increases in contribution rates, the revised indexation procedure meant that future pensions would be less generous than those currently received. On the positive side, credits for child care and for those tending the elderly and severely disabled were improved. Although a consensus on pensions was achieved at the time of enactment, the SPD were unhappy about several aspects of the reform and some social policy oriented CDU politicians shared their view that the package was strong on short-term palliatives but weak on means of confronting the fundamental and long-term issue of inter-generational equity. For them, Blüm's formula simply transfers the burden to future generations, since, quite simply, pensioners in the twenty-first century will fare less well than current recipients, although they are being required to foot the bill for today's pensions. As with the case of health policy, the government continues to bide its time and, at least in the short run, they can exploit a respite because the western funds are currently benefitting from a temporary budgetary surplus.

The 'Two-thirds' Society

In the 1980s the recrimination that Kohl's *Wendepolitik* had created a 'two-thirds' society of the 'haves' versus the 'have nots' gained currency among critics of the regime. Since the incorporation of the GDR this division in German society had taken on a regional dimension of massive proportions. It is generally conceded that the West German welfare state has been relatively weak in terms of vertical redistribution. 'Solidarity' has been conceived of as appropriately achieved through the operation of the insurance and earning-related principles. East Germans bring into the union a different concept of solidarity and, in the urgency of their situation, they are less enamoured of the self-help and strong ecological input into social policy that was espoused, among others, by the Greens in the 1980s. Social equity as a legitimising goal of the social state becomes suspect when, over the long term, the earned and the social income are paid merely according to the region where one is resident.

The social consequences of a two-tier state in the 'united' Germany will be experienced into the next millenium. Prized welfare principles which were the mainstay of the old FRG – subsidiarity, the insurance principle, and so forth – and the newly espoused policies of the *Wendepolitik* – self-help, privatisation and community care rather than institutionalisation – will be sorely tested. Some will have to be partially surrendered to safeguard that overarching social goal that has been pre-eminent in a comparatively young country such as (West) Germany: the preservation of social stability. There are worrying signs in the East that this is breaking down, with frequent reports of serious delinquency and violent racism.

A change of direction of welfare objectives of the dimension being proposed here will necessarily have consequences for the style of German policy-making, where importance has always been attached to securing broad cross-party consensus centrally and a 'concerted federalism' among the Länder. This approach, whilst having ensured that the policy line is fairly stable over time – even the *Wendepolitik* was more rhetoric than reality – does have its limitations. It has often been complained that the search for solutions that are '*Konsensfähig*' (consensus generating) thwarts innovative policy reform. Commentating before unification was a remote possibility, Bulmer (1989) speculated on the dangers of this political immobolism. Events subsequent to 1990 can only reinforce his position. His reservations are shared by Bäcker and Steffen (1991) who suspect that the political effort involved in unification will stifle any impulse to improve the welfare system as a whole, and not simply due to costs. The delay in resolving the problem of care insurance, they believe, is part of this phenomenon.

In 1991 GDP in the former GDR amounted to only 8 per cent of that of West Germany. The '*Aufschwung Ost*' has been slow to take-off and, in the plannable future, Easterners' access to total welfare (in terms of the earned and the social income) will remain chronically below that of the West, raising questions of constitutional legality. The two-thirds society in Germany coexists with a growing dualism within the new federal states. Income differentials there are intensifying and the old securities of the 'niche society' are rapidly falling away. In its stead a plural, and to a growing extent atomised society is forming, from which sectors of the population feel increasingly alienated.

Social equity, the guarantor of social stability, will require a greater role for the federal government. Existing transfer mechanisms have relied heavily on cooperation among the Länder, the federal government taking a back seat in the process. This comfortable position may have to be surrendered, sooner rather than later, since the old federal states are regrouping to protect their fiscal futures. Besides, federal subsidies in one form or another will be required over the long term, despite initial declarations to the contrary. Subsidiarity and concerted federalism could be sound principles in a country where serious regional income disparities did not exist. That situation no longer pertains and intransigent social and economic problems may produce irresistible pressures on the federal level to assume a more central and directive welfare role than was the case in the Bonn Republic.

12

Rethinking Environmental Policy

ECKARD REHBINDER

West German Environment Policy before Unification

After twenty years of institutionalised environmental policy, the FRG had come to conceive of itself – together with Japan and some smaller countries such as the Netherlands, Sweden and Switzerland – as in the vanguard of environmental policy in Europe. Indeed, following the occurrence of widespread forest damage and other conspicuous episodes of environmental damage, such as the nuclear incident at Chernobyl, the chemicals accident at Basle and algae pollution in the North Sea, environmental politics in West Germany in the 1980s underwent profound changes. Public pressures, in particular the emergence of the Green Party as a factor in politics, forced all established parties to accord environmental issues more weight in their programmes and their policies (Weidner, 1989, 16–27; Paterson, 1989, 271–88).

The response of the CDU/FDP coalition government was the introduction of regulations that provided for, and ultimately achieved, a drastic reduction of some air pollutants that were thought to contribute to forest damage. Programmes for the reduction of other air pollutants as well as of total discharges of nutrients and hazardous substances into the water were initiated later. In the field of nuclear energy, a controversial issue in West Germany, the reaction to Chernobyl was the establishment of the Federal Ministry of the Environment and a stiffening of safety requirements as an alternative to the abandonment of nuclear power ('*Ausstieg*') demanded by the Green Party and – in a less radical form – by the Social Democrats (Paterson, 1989, 276–83).

Finally, some hazardous chemicals were banned on the basis of the Chemicals Act, although a true '*Chemiepolitik*' entailing a pro- gramme of reducing the flows of all hazardous substances in the environment has never been envisaged by the coalition government.

The more recent past of West German environmental policy was marked by a growing Europeanisation and globalisation. Particularly since the insertion of environmental policy as a common policy in the Treaty of Rome by the Single European Act, involvement by Brussels gained momentum, although in general it has seldom really hampered, rather promoted, national environmental policies. The global dimension of environmental policy attracted public attention with the publicity given to ozone layer depletion, the greenhouse effect and deforestation of tropical forests. After some hesitation, the coalition government actively promoted the conclusion of the ozone convention and protocol of 1985–87 and took national mea- sures that went beyond the obligations assumed internationally. Since 1989, Germany has belonged to a small group of advocates of an effective world climate convention and it developed a national concept for reduction of carbon dioxide emissions.

To be sure, the image of West Germany as being in the vanguard of environmental policy one-sidedly emphasises the stringency of control measures as well as greater public awareness of environmen- tal problems at the expense of the burden of pollution per km^2 or *per capita* which remains high, and there are clear deficiencies in some areas. For example, air pollutants, such as nitrous oxides and hydrocarbons which are also held responsible for forest damage, could not be reduced because of the increase of car traffic, the rooted aversion to speed limits on highways, and the dependence of national requirements on EC policy decisions. In the field of waste manage- ment, prevention and recycling of waste were given priority only recently with the adoption of a crackdown programme on one-way containers, packing materials, and waste paper. The Achilles heel of water-pollution control has remained agriculture. Although the number of farmers and others employed in agriculture has been decreasing continuously, farmers constitute a stable bloc in German politics which is difficult to overcome. Hence, the extremely harmful effects of modern agricultural practices, especially overuse of manure and widespread spraying of herbicides, have never been tackled effectively. This has led to creeping pollution of ground water. Modern agricultural practices are also mainly responsible for the alarming pace of species extinction in West Germany.

The Council of Environmental Experts (Rat von Sachverständigen für Umweltfragen), in its 1989 report on the state of the environment in West Germany, considered the measures and effects of environmental policy as ambivalent, finding major progress but also deficiencies and failures (SRU, 1988), an opinion shared even in governmental circles.

Some authors attribute to the FRG in the period between 1970 and 1985 only an average ecological modernisation capability considering its capacity for innovation, consensus formation, and development and implementation of environmental protection strategies (Jänicke and Mönch, 1988; Jänicke, 1990). However, in view of an evident improvement of environmental quality, major reductions of emissions and discharges, and the increasing use of environmentally friendly technology in the more recent past, in an international comparison a characterisation of the FRG as an 'environmental state' is generally correct (Weidner, 1989, 25–7).

German unification has posed new challenges to environmental policy. Due to the high degree of pollution in the new Länder the German record of environmental protection abruptly deteriorated, and the environmental restoration tasks are enormous.

The response of the coalition government has been to organise an environmental crisis management for the East which implies a shift of emphasis of environmental policy from West to East and – more important – from prevention to restoration. This development and its background will be analysed below. Whether a united Germany will be able to maintain momentum with respect to both objectives – effective cleaning-up in the East as well as further development of preventive policy in all Germany and meeting the global challenges – has also to be considered.

Environmental Issues in the Unification Process

In the process of German unification, environmental protection did not, at first, play a prominent role. The Draft Treaty for the establishment of the German currency union originally did not include environmental protection. It was then decided to extend the Treaty and create, in addition to a currency union, an environmental union. The major reason for this change was the – economically motivated – decision of preventing East Germany from becoming a pollution haven for West German industry. Article 16 of the Currency Union Treaty of July 1990 provided that East Germany would soon adopt domestic legislation to introduce in practice some important West German environmental laws especially in the field of air pollution, waste, and nuclear safety. But, except for nuclear safety, this was limited to new plants and products. With regard to existing activities, adjustment periods were to be provided in keeping with the principle of proportionality and social considerations. The general concept underlying Article 16 of the Treaty was that in the future a new, common environmental policy and law should be developed which were to be guided by principles of environmental policy and law already recognised in West Germany, namely the principle of prevention, the 'polluter pays' principle and the cooperation principle. It was also considered important at that time that there should be no diminution in the status quo established by both sets of environmental legislation (Rublack, 1991, 24). The East German Environmental Protection Framework Law (Umweltrahmengesetz) of 20 July 1990 reflects the principles set forth in the Currency Union Treaty.

With the unexpectedly rapid unification which followed less than three months after the conclusion of the Currency Union Treaty, this idea of developing a new common environmental policy and law for all Germany was not pursued further. Article 34 of the Unification Treaty simply extended the environmental statutes, regulations and administrative rules of West Germany to East Germny, although subject to exceptions with respect to existing plants and products. Furthermore, it established environmental clean-up and development programmes in order to achieve equal environmental conditions in the old and new parts of the united Germany. Development of a new environmental law is identified as a task that lies in the distant future.

Parallel to developments in Germany, discussion proceeded in the European Community. While at the beginning of the unification process there was a widespread belief that an amendment of the EC Treaty would be necessary, with the simple accession of East Germany to the FRG, the opinion gained ground that, except for some institutional changes, the Treaty could be left intact and only changes of secondary law of the Community made.

Independent of the legal form of East Germany's integration into the Community, German unification created problems that are similar to those arising when a new member joins the Community. In the field of environmental protection, more than 200 regulatory texts were to be instantly applicable. The problems of transition arising out of these framework conditions were somewhat mitigated by an important factor: the East German Environmental and Protection Law of July 1990 and then the German Unity Treaty had already extended much of West Germany's legislation to East Germany, and insofar as this was in conformity with EC law, the formal question of transposition of EC law into national law (local law of East

Germany) was resolved. However, this transfer, generally speaking, was limited to new plants and products while both pieces of legislation provided for relatively long transition periods for existing facilities. Without parallel empowerments by Community law, this would constitute a violation of the Treaty. Looking at the contents of the transition directive of the Community in the field of environmental protection, it is safe to say that the Community recognised the need for a generous transitional regime.

The final EC transition rules with respect to environmental protection of October 1990 may be summarised as follows:

- New facilities and new products/substances are fully subject to Community environmental law.
- Existing products/substances that do not meet EC requirements can be put on the market only in East Germany and only until the end of 1992; in the meantime, they must be notified to the Commission for classification where such systems exist under Community law.
- With respect to existing facilities and quality standards, the Community grants the FRG – limited to East Germany – differentiated transition periods running from 1991 up to 1996. A shorter period is provided for the preparation and submission of restoration programmes and plans, and a longer period exists for meeting the substantive EC requirements (quality standards as well as permit requirements for existing facilities). The deadlines are different with respect to the different directives.
- Where a particular directive sets out an emission reductions quota (in particular, the Major Combustion Plants Directive), both the quota and the deadlines for meeting them have been extended. For example, the previous reduction targets for SO_2 were 1.3 million tonnes per year by 1992, 0.89 million tonnes by 1998 and 0.668 million tonnes by 2003. The new quota is 2 million tonnes per year by 1996 and 1.5 million tonnes by 2003. In view of 5.2 million tonnes of total emissions in the united Germany this target will require enormous effort.

In setting forth the adjustment periods, the Community took account of the considerations put forward by the West and East German governments as well as precedents established in the Greek Accession Treaty.

East German Environmental Problems and their Causes

The environmental problems encountered in East Germany, especially in the highly industrialised south, are enormous. The EC Commission, when submitting its proposal for transition regulations to the Council, correctly stated that the question was not so much restoration and protection of the environment, but rather the creation of an ecological minimum of elementary conditions for human life (Commission of the EC, 1990, 117–19).

Some figures (BMU, 1990; Naujoks, 1991, 67) may highlight the environmental situation in East Germany:

- Due to the massive use of sulphur-rich lignite for the generation of electricity and for heating, SO_2 pollution was four times the Community average (related to West Germany alone, the figures are even farther apart: while West Germany, in 1990 emitted 1.05 million tons, East Germany, with 20 per cent of West Germany's population and 50 per cent of its territory, emitted 5.2 million tons per year, and some areas in the South had annual averages 7 to 10 times higher than the West German Ruhr area; the extent of forest damage was twice as high as in West Germany; in the vicinity of the chemical industry in the South, there was high pollution by carcogenic substances.
- Only 68 per cent of all households were connected to sewerage systems; many municipal sewage treatment facilities did not meet minimum standards; 12 per cent of all sewage was discharged without any, and 36 per cent after simple, mechanical treatment.
- 50 per cent of drinking water is not fit for human consumption as measured by Community standards; since 95 per cent of industrial waste water was discharged without any treatment, pollution of rivers by hazardous substances was extremely high.
- The industrialisation of socialist agriculture has led to a widespread overuse of manure mineral fertilisers, contaminated sewage sludge and pesticides with disastrous effects on the quality of ground water, rivers and lakes, as well as soil.
- 60 per cent of industrial waste was deposited without any control; there was heavy soil and ground water pollution beneath and in the vicinity of industrial sites, especially in Saxony and Saxony–Anhalt, and municipal waste dump sites.
- Nuclear safety was extremely low; uranium mining and processing caused extremely dangerous soil and ground water pollution by radioactive substances.
- East Germany in the year 1987 emitted roughly 358 million tonnes

of CO_2 which means 22.4 tonnes *per capita* as compared to West Germany with 715 million tonnes, but only 11.7 *per capita*.

Indeed, the East Germany regime left an environmental mess; it had exploited the environment in a manner similar to old-style capitalism – despite the teachings of Karl Marx and Friedrich Engels that a socialist society should treat natural resources like a *paterfamilias*, a good housekeeper – and despite environmental legislation which, in international comparison, was relatively developed; East Germany was in the forefront of modern environmental legislation. Its environmental code of 1968 – the Act on Socialist Environmental Management (Landeskulturgesetz) – was based on a comprehensive concept of rational management of environmental resources (Oehler, 1990; Kloepfer and Reinert, 1990). In contrast to West Germany legislation, it did not regulate separate environmental sectors but viewed the environment in its entirety. Moreover, besides traditional command and control regulation and the socialist appeal to the environmental responsibility of state enterprises, economic incentives were provided. This Act was implemented in the 1970s by several regulations, and a new wave of improvement to environmental legislation, especially in the field of air and water pollution, took place in the 1980s.

However, East German environmental law and policy contained major deficiencies (BMU, 1990, 9; Kloepfer and Reinert, 1990, 13–16). A major flaw of East German environmental legislation, was that it unilaterally relied on 'rational use' of natural resources. By denying conflicts between ecology and economy and by implying the possibility of exploiting these resources up to their absorptive capacity aspects of prevention were neglected. Consequently, an ambient quality oriented policy, which is always fraught with the problem of scientific uncertainty and of translation into requirements for particular sources, prevailed. The systematic reduction of emissions did not play a major role. Secondly, the obligations imposed upon existing sources were formulated in such a vague way that they amounted to merely appellative rules. Thirdly, the 'tonnage' philosophy of a planned economy and the attempt to build an economy on an autarchic basis which prevented the importation of advanced production and emissions control technology played a role.

But the most important factor was the deficient implementation of the environmental legislation. From the late 1970s, the government had become convinced that the ambitious target of reaching the West German standard of living and maintaining the subsidisation of basic food products and housing could, at best, be achieved only by sacrificing the environment. Therefore, the implementation of the environmental legislation was systematically decreased, especially by the State Planning Commission's denial of investment funds for environmental protection in major industries, renunciation or lowering of pollution charges, and non-enforcement of existing control requirements. This deliberate policy of dismantling environmental regulation through non-implementation and non-enforcement for about fifteen years, which was made possible by the system of the planned economy as well as the priority of the party over law, seems to be the decisive cause of the disastrous environmental situation East Germany was confronted with when the regime collapsed.

Of course, not everything was, and is, bad about the East Germany's environment. Consumer-related pollution was much lower than in the West due to the lower level of consumer-related activities. For example, NO_2 emissions that primarily originate with cars and trucks amounted to only 610,000 tonnes per year as compared with 2.7 million in West Germany. The generation of household waste *per capita* was much lower than in the West, and an elaborate highly subsidised system of recycling, which was motivated by the needs of resource economy rather than environmental protection, kept the amount of wastes that were deposited relatively low. Finally, East Germany could boast of large natural spaces, especially in the north, where conservation was good because of their use as hunting grounds for state and party officials as well as the low degree of industrialisation in that area. However, on balance, the environmental situation in East Germany is so bad that it needs a massive and long-lasting effect at cleaning-up that is technically difficult, financially expensive and fraught with considerable social problems. In view of all these circumstances, the formal transfer of West German and EC environmental law to East Germay by itself does not mean much; it has merely a symbolic value.

A Restoration Policy for the East

Already before formal unification, especially after the conclusion of the German Currency Union Treaty in July 1990, some heavily polluting industrial plants in the chemical industry, in the production of ferro-silicon and in copper and silver mining, as well as three blocks of a nuclear reactor in East Germany were closed or their production reduced (BMU, 1990, 19–29). These measures were taken partly because of the lack of competitiveness of the relevant enterprises in the newly established all-German market system; partly they were taken for environmental reasons at the instigation of the West German Minister of Environment. Moreover, several pilot projects of environmental investigation and restoration in extremely heavily polluted areas were financed and a programme for technical assistance to municipalities and enterprises was initiated.

Immediately after formal unification the Minister of the Environment set out a first programme for 'ecological restoration and development in the new Länder' (BMU, 1990). This programme describes the environmental situation in East Germany and makes proposals and recommendtions for future action. Based on the premise that the damage inflicted on the East German environment during forty years of mismanagement can be remedied only gradually, the programme distinguishes between urgent measures for the removal of dangers for public health which must be taken and become effective immediately, measures for restortion of the environment which will also be started immediately but will have only mid-term impact, and preventive measures for the future. In this latter context, it discusses the prospects of an ecological modernisation of East Germany industry, energy production, infrastructure and agriculture.

Apart from some concrete measures, the programme contains many non-binding commitments, recommendations and policy proposals which must be firmed up at a later stage, especially after the question of financing has been resolved. With respect to financing, the programme admits that the strict application of the 'polluter pays' principle to restoration measures (i.e. the attribution of the costs of the necessary environmental protection measures to enterprises, households and municipalities) is not possible because this would result in incalculable economic, employment, social and environmental risks. The financial burden resulting from the high restoration expenses would endanger the development chances of enterprises and municipalities. Hence, an adequate contribution of the federal government in the enviornmental restoration costs is considered justified.

In February 1991 the 'Action Programme for Ecological Reconstruction' in the new Länder (BMU, 1991) was published. The programme lists a variety of urgent measures in the fields of water pollution, air pollution and abandoned waste dump and old industrial sites. In particular, the following measures are envisaged:

- Construction or retrofitting of 35 municipal and 24 industrial waste-water treatment plants in the Elbe basin and of 27 municipal and 30 industrial waste water treatment plants at the Baltic Sea and in the Oder–Neisse basin.
- Construction of 6200 km and restoration of 5000 km of sewerage canals.

- Reduction of water pollution caused by extensive and inappropriate use of manure and pesticides.
- Closure of contaminated drinking water wells and retrofitting of 1500 water works with modern treatment equipment.
- Cleaning-up 278 major fuel-burning combustion plants (10 lignite-burning plants, 142 industrial and 126 heating power plants) by 1 July 1996; this will result in a reduction of particulate matter emissions by 1.3 million tonnes per year and of SO_2 emissions by 4.2 million tonnes per year.
- Retrofitting of 6735 listed air polluting facilities according to the requirement of the (West German) Technical Rules for the Control of Air Pollution of 1986 by, as a rule, 1 July 1994.
- Conversion of other commercial and of household heating installations from lignite to less polluting fuels and regular control of these installations.
- Establishment of 6 soil treatment centres in the Halle/Leipzig conurbation and of 5 plants for thermal treatment of polluted soils.
- Establishment of 40 household waste, 10 industrial waste and 2–3 underground waste deposits.
- Restoration of abandoned waste dump and old industrial sites according to priorities set forth by the Länder, and investigation of the potential dangers presented by other sites.
- Restoration of uranium mining areas.

The programme also contains an indication of the envisaged costs of some, not all, measures and the possibilities of financing them (BMU, 1991, 11–24). As regards industrial air pollution and new waste deposits, the financial burden will be borne by the relevant operators. In all other cases, use will be made primarily of the existing financing mechanisms, such as the municipal financing programme of the Bank for Reconstruction and the German Compensation Bank (volume: DM 15 billion between 1991 and 1993, interest rate: 6.5 per cent), the ERP credits for industrial investment in the new Länder (volume: DM 7 billion, interest rate: 7.5 per cent), the Common Task Programme 'Improvement of Regional Economic Structure' (volume with respect to East Germany including EC structural financing: DM 4 billion per year) and the Common Task Programme 'Improvement of Agricultural Structure and Coastal Protection' (volume with respect to East Germany: DM 4.5 billion between 1991 and 1993, among them DM 800 million in 1991). The total sum of these credit and subsidisation facilities amounts to DM 17 billion.

Beyond these means of direct financing, the utilisation of the existing programme for the promotion of employment, also in the field of environmental protection, subsidisation of urgent restoration measures that have a great employment impact, and mobilisation of private capital by abolishing obstacles to privatisation and introducing improved tax incentives for environmental investment, are envisaged. For the future, the programme calls for the introduction of a waste and a carbon dioxide charge the primary purpose of which will be the prevention of waste and the reduction of CO_2 emissions, but the proceeds of which can also be used for financing restoration tasks in the East.

Prospects for Achieving the Goals

Because of the magnitude of environmental problems in East Germany, it is doubtful whether the clean-up targets set by the Community are realistic. Of course, major reductions of emissions will result – and have already resulted – from plant closures, many of which have occurred for purely economic reasons; others will be necessary because retrofitting would be too expensive or technically impossible. Indeed, even in the short period between July 1990 and the end of August 1991, the pollution of the ambient air and water in major agglomerations has improved due to plant closures. East Germany's economy is characterised by an outdated industrial structure – a large share of primary industry – which will have to change, at least in the long run. This process, which already is under way, will be aided by the inclusion of structurally weak economic regions in East Germany in the system of transfer payments under the EC Regional Fund. But even if one considers these mostly gratuitous effects of economic change, they will account only for a relatively small part of overall reduction of pollution required.

The obstacles that impede massive clean-up in the short- or even the mid-term are enormous. First there is the depressed economic situation in the East. The introduction of the Deutschemark in itself did not produce a second economic miracle – quite the contrary – and even the massive financial aid the federal government poured into the East has not caused an immediate turnaround, although it has stabilised the economic situation (see Chapter 10 in this volume). To be sure, the necessary ecological modernisation of East Germany's economy offers great economic prospects in the long run. It will increase the competitiveness of industry on future markets for environmentally friendly production processes, control equipment and products. But this effect appears remote and does not motivate enterprises and municipalities at present.

Second, the high and uncertain costs to be incurred for cleaning up existing industrial sites hampers new investment. Theoretically, this probem should have been resolved by the introduction of a 'relief clause' in the German Unity Treaty (as amended by the 1991 Act for Promotion of Investments). This clause provides that the competent state agencies may release any new investor who acquires polluted industrial premises in the East from the legal obligation to clean it up or to pay for the cleaning up (Rehbinder, 1991, 421); a recent amendment even extended this provision to private law liability. However, the financial burden of cleaning up would then fall on the new Länder which suffer from chronic budgetary problems. The financial responsibility of the Treuhandanstalt is doubtful and arguably does not exist. Therefore, the state agencies are reluctant to exercise their powers of releasing investors from their responsibility. This, in turn, creates a vicious circle because neither a restoration of polluted sites nor investment to replace outdated, heavily polluting equipment will occur. A related problem is presented by the fact that a literal application of air pollution control regulations in heavily polluted areas where ambient air quality standards are already exceeded might exclude all future investments. This problem has been resolved by an 'offset' provision in the German Unity Treaty (codified as Para 67a of the Federal Emission Protection Act). In non-attainment areas new sources will be permitted if they cause only minimal additional pollution, and a considerable reduction of pollution is to be expected within the next five years. Alternatively, additional emissions may be offset by emission reductions twice their amount from plant closures in connection with the new project (Rublack, 1991, 25).

Third, while the scientific and technical knowledge is quite well developed in East Germany, there is a marked lack of administrative infrastructure that could tackle the difficult problems East Germany is confronted with. This deficiency can be attributed to a mix of administrative inertia, even obstruction from old public officials, non-existence of an adequate administrative organisation, over-legalisation of the West German type of environmental management which was simply transferred to the East, and lack of familiarity with the new administrative procedures now subject to the rule of law. It is further aggravated by the conversion of East Germany from a central to a federal system of government. Especially at the lower – municipal and county – levels there are conspicuous gaps in the administration, whereas the situation is somewhat better at the middle level (which, however, will be, or already has been, abolished). All this, of course, concerns not only environmental administration, but administration in general.

In order to mitigate the adverse effects presented by the administrative deficit, two measures have been taken. The East German

Länder policy of hiring public officials from the West is hampered by lower salaries and the widespread shortage of housing. However, the German Unity Treaty provides that the West German Länder may grant the East German Länder administrative assistance. Permit applications for major facilities in East Germany require that a West German counterpart agency be given an opportunity to comment on the application; in practice, it is this latter agency which processes the application. Similar arrangements have been taken with respect to cleaning up abandoned waste-dump sites and existing or old industrial sites, construction of sewage treatment plants, and the retrofitting of existing facilities. The West German Länder concluded an agreement dividing up the responsibilities among them; in practice, each East German district has one or two West German counterparts that are competent for, and obliged to, grant administrative assistance. Nevertheless, the administrative difficulties encountered in East Germany remain great. It may be questioned whether it was prudent to simply transfer West German administrative law, which is characterised by a high degree of legalisation and formalisation, to East Germany which was not used to implementing laws but, rather, party directives. The structure of West German administrative law makes it difficult to set priorities and address the most urgent problems first, while tolerating temporarily less important violations of law.

Fourth, enviromental awareness and environmental values are still underdeveloped in the East. This is true both of the public at large and of the elites. Although there is now awareness that the environmental situation is bad, all polls show that economic development is a clear priority for the great majority of East Germans. This priority was, in particular, expressed in the voting behaviour of East Germans. The victory of the CDU in the Länder elections in 1990 and the federal election of December 1990 reflects these economic preferences. The East Bündnis '90/Grüne group is less environmentally oriented than that of its West German counterpart. Although the love affair of East Germans with the Christian Democrats has somewhat cooled off in the meantime, the Bündnis '90/Grüne will most probably not profit from this shift of public opinion. It also is revealing that the plans of the West German nuclear power industry to build two new nuclear power plants in East Germany did not fail because of a lack of public acceptance but were abandoned for reasons unrelated to local conditions. By the same token various steps taken by the federal government to streamline administrative procedures in the field of structure and local planning, construction permits and planning of infrastructure facilities, potentially at the expense of environmental concerns, did not meet with much opposition in the East.

Fifth, East German plant managers will yet have to learn that environmental law is binding and not negotiable. With the low value placed on law in the socialist society, the dominance of the Communist party over legal rules and the dependence of environmental investments on decisions taken by the State Planning Commission, plant managers in the past did not really feel – and did not need to feel – bound by environmental laws and regulations. They are now amazed that this situation should have changed so suddenly. To be sure, with the acquisition of many enterprises by investors from the West and the associated substitution of West German managers for the present ones this problem will diminish.

All told, there are many obstacles to a speedy improvement of environmental conditions in East Germany, and it will take strong efforts to meet the deadlines set out in the EC transitional rules on the environment. The target laid down in the German Unity Treaty of achieving equal environmental conditions throughout Germany is far away. Politicians now aim at the year 2000 rather than 1996 – the ultimate deadline for meeting EC ambient quality standards set forth in the transitional rules.

Future of Environmental Policy

The question remains in which direction German environmental policy will develop in the future. The new tasks in the East require considerable budgetary and private means; the figure of more than DM 200 billion in the next ten years has seriously been advanced. They absorb administrative personnel, and managerial activities. They exert a considerable strain on contruction capacity for treatment plants, desulphurisation equipment, and waste disposal sites. In view of the selectivity of public attention, they may also deflect the media and the political public from environmental objectives previously considered to be priorities. As yet, the general 'as if nothing had happened' attitude that characterises the approach of West Germans towards unification seems to prevail. The new environmental challenges in the East are considered as an additional burden which should not deflect the drive towards better environmental quality in the West. An indication of the correctness of this statement is the fact that the coalition government, in the year after unification, adopted stringent measures designed to curb the volume of product waste, achieve a better control of the incineration and deposit of wastes and ban the production and use of some hazardous chemicals; it also continued endeavours to tackle global environmental problems. Internationally most significant are the setting of an extremely stringent emission standard of 0.1 nanograms for dioxin emissions from waste incineration plants and a total ban on CFCs and halogens.

The generally favourable framework conditions for an active and preventive environmental policy have not been fundamentally changed by German unification. The relatively high degree of organisation of environmental interests, the active involvement of mass media, a widespread public acceptance for environmental policy, a diminishing resistance of industry and trade unions against cost-relevant measures for environmental protection, and a certain 'ecological transformation' of existing environmental law by the administrative tribunals (Weidner, 1989, 25–6) – all contribute to a continued viability of environmental policy in the united Germany. The disappearance of the West German Green Party from the Bundestag had all the signs of an 'accident' and does not mark the beginning of a decline of environmentalism in German politics. Apart from the attractiveness of the environmental ticket of the SPD Party, the defeat of the Green Party was the response of voters to the anti-unification stance of the party.

Environmental politics in the united Germany is dominated – and will perhaps continue to be dominated – by West Germany. Given the preference of East Germans for economic development, the political weight of environmentalists from the East is low. Demands for more public participation, for strengthening the rights of environmental associations in relation to administrative tribunals and direct democracy as developed by the East German Round Table, which could create more openness of environmental decision-making and strengthen environmental policy, have not, as yet, gained wide public acceptance. The work of the Round Table will perhaps play a role in the debate on a revised all-German constitution. Attempts in West Germany to insert a state obligation for environmental protection in the federal constitution have failed due to disagreement between the CDU and the SPD about the binding force of the new provision and the future role of parliament in environmental policy-making. These obstacles may be overcome since the new constitution will have to reflect some elements of East German constitutional thinking. But in general, the East German input into environmental policy-making is low which, on the one hand, ensures continuity, but, on the other, deprives environmental policy of new impulses.

This is not to say that German unification will not leave traces on the direction of German environmental policy. First of all, economies of scale considerations may lead to a redistribution of environmental quality. In West Germany, further reductions of air and water pollution will be extremely costly because, given an already existing high control rate, marginal costs will increase, while in the East comparatively much higher reductions of emissions and discharges can be achieved at lower costs. Therefore, it makes sense temporarily to freeze further preventive measures in the West and offset them by increased restoration measures in the East. For example, there is now a discussion on reducing, or at least slowing down, the introduction of tertiary treatment of effluents in the West in favour of more stringent clean-up measures in the East; indeed, comprehensive introduction of secondary treatment of waste water in the East would make a contribution to preventing further pollution of the North and Baltic Seas by nutrients and hazardous substances that would be ecologically more effective and economically more efficient than what could be achieved by tertiary treatment in the West. The same is true of reduction of CO_2 emissions where the reduction potential at given cost is much higher in the East than in the West.

Some negative effects of German unification on environmental policy in the West may also be expected from changes in administrative procedure law in the field of local structure and planning, construction permits and the planning of infrastruture facilities which were introduced or proposed in the new Länder in order to speed up necessary investments but which, although they may partly also promote a speedy introduction of less polluting facilities and equipment in the East, do not adequately take environmental considerations into account; speedy decisions often are bad decisions from an environmental viewpoint. Although these measures were adopted or proposed as transitional measures, a domino-effect cannot entirely be ruled out. But, overall, it is realistic to expect that the united Germany will be able to maintain momentum with respect to both objectives – effective cleaning up in the East as well as further development of preventive policy in all Germany and, with respect to global problems, worldwide.

It is another question whether it will be possible to avoid mistakes in environmental policy in East Germany that have previously been made in West Germany, in other words, whether beyond restoration an enlightened policy of prevention of future environmental harm will have a chance. As already stated, due to a much lower degree of consumption, car ownership, road transportation of goods, tourism and leisure activities and low population density in the north, some environmental problems West Germany had and has to cope with are much less in East Germany. Since the aspirations of East Germans are directed at reaching the West German standard of life as quickly as possible, there is no chance that in East Germany a new, environmentally friendly life-style could be introduced. High consumption, car ownership, tourism – including tourism from West Germany – and leisure, together with the environmental problems associated with these activities, will soon be normal in East Germany. Any attempt to induce East Germany to play a pioneer role in conservation and environmental protection that would entail sacrifices in terms of standard of life is bound to be a failure. Therefore, an increase of pollution and 'consumption' of open spaces for roads, housing and tourist facilities seems to be inevitable. It is also not likely that the present relationship between transportation of goods by rail and by road of 80 to 20 that exists in East Germany (AGU, 1990, 17–18) can be maintained; in a single market, two entirely different structures of public transportation of commercial goods is not feasible. What may realistically be expected is mitigation of the adverse effects of development based on negative experience in the West. However, perhaps the most important ecological impact of reconstruction of industry in East Germany will be the establishment of a modern, low-pollution industrial structure which will give a strong push to future environmental friendly development all over Germany.

PART FOUR

Current Issues

13

German Migration Policies

BARBARA MARSHALL

Dimensions of the 'Migration Problem'

Roughly 25 per cent of the 80 million inhabitants of the new Germany are 'immigrants' of different kinds. About 12 million Germans came into the territory of the former FRG as a result of World War II because they had been expelled from their home areas in the east. Their integration and their contribution to West Germany's economic recovery is considered one of the outstanding achievements of German post-war history. The fast growing German economy also made it possible to absorb the steady influx of citizens of the former GDR. Once their numbers declined after the construction of the Berlin Wall in 1961, further labour was attracted into the Federal Republic by a series of treaties concluded between the Germans and the governments of southern Europe and of Turkey. However, a ban on further recruitment of these *Gastarbeiter* (guestworkers) was imposed in 1973 because of the oil crisis of the early 1970s and the ensuing economic downturn, but also because of the growing awareness of the difficulties involved in integrating a sizeable foreign minority. But the ban, far from reducing the numbers of foreign workers in the country, actually increased them. Those foreign workers already inside Germany remained for fear of not being able to return and increasingly brought their families to Germany. There are thus at present nearly 5 million foreigners in the country (about 4.8 million in West and 100,000 in East Germany).

There has also been a steady flow of asylum seekers from all parts of the world but especially from Eastern Europe and the Soviet Union. Emigration from the east was of course encouraged by Western governments during the Cold War as proof of the superiority of the West, and 'free travel' for people in the Soviet Bloc as a basic human right was one of the standard Western demands which was put forward with particular emphasis at the 1975 CSCE conference in Helsinki and regularly repeated. The numbers of asylum seekers in the FRG have grown steadily over the years but have exploded since the mid-1980s (with a hiatus in 1987) mainly for two reasons: the overall numbers of refugees world-wide has grown dramatically to between 15 and 17 million. Europe as a whole and in particular Germany, with over half of all asylum seekers coming to Europe, are receiving a (small) percentage of this figure. In addition there has been a growing exodus from the Eastern bloc which grew into a flood after the collapse of communism. Migrants from this area now make up by far the greatest percentage of asylum seekers in Germany. While nowadays only a small number are ultimately recognised as political refugees (except for Yugoslavs and Rumanians), under German asylum law their individual claims nevertheless have to be examined, and the processing of their applications, their accommodation and general upkeep while these are pending confronts the Federal Republic with serious problems.

However, even greater pressure on resources comes from a different group of migrants, the ethnic Germans. These are Germans who have lived in Eastern Europe and the former Soviet Union, often for many generations, but who nevertheless were persecuted by Stalin as 'German Fascists'. The Federal Republic therefore traditionally felt a special responsibility towards them. Under Brandt (1970) and particularly Schmidt (1977) agreements were concluded with Poland for the repatriation of ethnic Germans, but their numbers always remained small. However, greater freedom to travel in the east has led to very large numbers of new arrivals in the FRG, despite the fact that in the wake of *perestroika* greater freedom to display their national characteristics has increasingly been granted to those ethnic Germans still living in the east (*Info-Dienst*, 22/1991, 29). Unlike asylum seekers, ethnic Germans are considered Germans and therefore have automatic access to the German housing and job markets, which puts increasing strain on the system.

The situation is further aggravated by the massive influx, since 1989, into the territory of the old FRG of inhabitants of the former GDR. Over the last three years a total of over 2 million people has sought to settle permanently in Germany (see Table 13.1), although it is estimated that about 40 per cent of asylum seekers do not stay in Germany. There are, however, no precise figures for those who are *leaving* the Federal Republic, (Gugel, 1991, 92).

TABLE 13.1   *Migrants into Germany; 1985–91*

Year	Asylum	Ethnic	Resettlers
1991	256 112	220 000	–
1990	193.063	397.075	238.384 (Jan.–Jun.)
1989	121.318	377.055	343.854
1988	103.076	202.673	39.832
1987	57 379	78.523	18.961
1986	99 650	42.788	26.178
1985	73 832	38.968	24.912

Source:
Info-Dienst Deutsche Aussiedler (December 1990); Bundesanstalt für Arbeit,
Bundesausgleichsamt, 'Innenpolitik', VI. 1991

As the scramble for resources intensifies, the pressures to curtail the influx of asylum seekers has grown: the needs of the German economy are filled by citizens of the former GDR and by ethnic Germans for all but the humblest jobs. Asylum seekers therefore depend mainly on the goodwill of the host country, but their large numbers and the potentially even larger influx in the future strengthens the already existing concerns about the integration of 'foreigners' with their 'alien cultures' into German society.

Compared to these figures, other categories of migrants into the FRG such as contingent refugees (e.g. Vietnamese boat people), unaccompanied minors, Jews or travellers are so small that they will be disregarded in this study. However, all categories present the German government with difficult policy choices to which so far it has found no coherent response. But they are urgently required in the light of a possible mass influx from the former Soviet Union, of the planned harmonisation of European policies, and of growing discontent inside Germany where the lack of action by the government and by all parties generally is increasingly criticised.

There are broadly two aspects to the overall problem: (1) the treatment or integration of those foreigners who have a right to live in Germany; and (2) the admission into, or possibilities of keeping out of, the country of further migrants. For the first category the tenet of successive German governments, that Germany is 'not a country of immigration', has become all important. It has meant that, although for a variety of reasons foreigners have come to Germany, their status remains that of 'non-Germans'. The second category applies to the arrival in Germany of very large numbers of asylum seekers and ethnic Germans who come on the basis of certain clauses in the German constitution, but although both categories claim persecution in their home areas, their treatment in Germany is quite different.

The Legal Framework: 'Not a Country of Immigration'

Although the 5 million foreigners living in Germany make up only 6.25 per cent of the population of contemporary Germany (as against 8 per cent in France; 9 per cent in Belgium; 16 per cent in Switzerland – excluding their seasonal foreign workers – and 23 per cent in Luxembourg (Funke, 1991, 7), there has been a long-standing consensus between the federal government and the Länder that access to the FRG by foreigners from outside the EC should be controlled by all possible legal means (*Pressedienst des BMI*, 24 June 1988). The problem of how to deal with those foreigners already settled in the country has provoked public controversy between the parties particularly at election times. However, no action was taken and this contributed to the increase in votes for the right-wing Republican Party in the Berlin and Hesse elections in 1989; this in turn provided the impetus for the Aliens Law which came into force on 1 January 1991. There are three areas which illustrate German policy towards foreigners: (1) the right of foreigners to vote in local elections in Germany; (2) foreigners and German nationality; and (3) the new Aliens Law of 1 January 1991.

A recent survey showed that 70 per cent of foreigners living in Germany would be in favour of having local voting rights (Pehle, 1988, 26). Foreigners would be able to influence developments in their local communities where they pay tax and where they are directly affected. For this reason, but also because they are on the whole expected to vote for 'left' parties, this right was introduced in the two SPD-led Länder Schleswig-Holstein and Hamburg in 1989 and others such as Bremen, North Rhine–Westphalia and Berlin were planning to do the same. However, in a unanimous verdict of 30 October 1990 the Federal Constitutional Court ruled these measures to be irreconcilable with the constitution, on the grounds that only 'Germans' were entitled to vote. In the opinion of the Court only future EC legislation could oblige the FRG to make changes to the German constitution. Voting rights in local and European elections for nationals of other EC states were in fact agreed at the Maastricht Conference in December 1991. The Court's other suggestion, that foreigners who wished to take part in local elections should adopt German nationality and thus become part of their host society, is not in practice an easy option.

The law which regulates nationality is still the *Reichs- und Staats-*

bürgergesetz of 22 June 1913 in which nationality is based on the principle of the *ius sanguinis*, i.e. the nationality of the father (or, since 1974, in accordance with equality between the sexes' legislation, of either parents) is transmitted by 'blood' to their offspring. This contrasts with the practice of countries such as France or the USA where *ius solis* applies, i.e. children who are born in the country automatically obtain its nationality. Children of foreigners born in Germany thus remain foreigners and candidates for German nationality must exhibit a 'positive attitude to German culture'. This definition precludes the possibility of dual nationality which for many foreigners would be a useful 'half-way house'. A survey of 1989 showed that 41 per cent of foreigners were worried that by giving up their old nationality they would abandon important rights (such as inheritance rights in Turkey) in their old countries (Hoffman, 1990, 90). This explains the comparatively small number of annual naturalisations in Germany of 14 per cent of foreigners (Funke, 1991, 21) although 44 per cent of all foreigners and 49 per cent of Turkish residents expressed the desire to acquire German nationality (Hoffmann, 1990, 90).

The new Aliens Law of 1 January 1991 underlines the impression that foreigners can only with difficulty become part of German society. The law has been in gestation over several years and eventually replaced the one of 1965. A first draft was leaked to the public in the Spring of 1988 but its hostility to foreigners led to widespread protests, and its withdrawal contributed to the replacement of the interior minister by the more flexible Schäuble (CDU) at the beginning of 1989. The revised draft of September 1989 had lost much of the nationalist flavour of its predecessor but was generally considered only a 'modified improvement'. It became law in April 1990 while public attention was absorbed in the process of German unification, despite the protests by numerous welfare groups, trade unions and churches. However, the Federation of Local Communities (*Bundesvereinigung der Kommunalen Spitzenverbände*) argued that the law was so 'soft' on foreigners, that it demanded a reiteration of the principle that the FRG was 'not a country of immigration' (Bade, 1990, 64). Other observers agreed that the law started from the assumption 'that [all] foreigners are undesirable' (*Der Spiegel*, 49/ 1990).

The improvements lay in the clauses which enable wives and children to obtain a separate residence permit. Young people who are returning to their family's country of origin are given the right to return to Germany, if their links with the latter prove stronger. But the ban on dual nationality remains in force, and the clauses which regulate residence rights of foreigners have been made more restrictive, requiring eight (previously five) years in the FRG and contributions to German insurance schemes for 60 months in order to qualify. A foreigner also has to prove 'sufficient living space', the lack of which will not only prevent a residence permit but, together with one infringement of the law and unemployment for longer than two years, also provides sufficient grounds from expulsion from the country.

These latter clauses were singled out by the Bundesbeauftragte für Ausländische Arbeitnehmer (Federal Officer for Foreign Workers) as highly discriminatory (Funke, 1991, 11). This official indifference towards the problem of foreigners, made worse by the government's and the political parties' preoccupation with the problems of national unification led to her resignation in July 1991. Her successor, the former general-secretary of the FDP, took over only at the beginning of November 1991. Although she was given wider responsibility for *all* foreigners (except asylum seekers) and an increased budget (by DM 400,000, to just over DM 500,000), it took four months to negotiate this 'package' and the funds still seem modest for the task. There is still no automatic access to the cabinet (*Das Parlament*, 20/27 December 1991). Like her predecessor she works in an honorary capacity in the Ministry of Labour. Plans to upgrade the office to place it on a par with the Ombudsman for Defence would require a change in the constitution for which there would not at present be a clear majority.

Different Principles: Aslyum Seekers and Ethnic Germans

Both asylum seekers and ethnic Germans are admitted on the basis of provisions in the German constitution: ethnic Germans are provided for in Article 116. An individual right to asylum is guaranteed under Article 16/2. Of the two groups the legal provision for asylum seekers is much stronger. Article 16 describes one of the Basic Rights which can be altered only by a change of the constitution with a two-thirds majority in parliament. This right is moreover protected by special provisions in Article 19 and by the commitment to preserve the dignity of the individual of Article 1. These Basic Rights embody the fundamental legal principles of the German state, the '*Rechtsstaat*'. Article 116, by contrast, is in one of the later sections of the constitution which deals with specific problems resulting from Germany's military defeat in 1945. It can be changed by a simple law. There are thus two different legal principles involved in the same constitution: one deals with a human right which is universally applicable: 'Persons persecuted on political grounds shall enjoy a right to asylum'. The other gives specific rights to Germans or – and this is the difficulty – to those whom it considers to be German. Both provisions have to be seen in their historical context. Article 16 was a reflection of the experience of Nazi persecution. Article 116 made provisions for those Germans who at the end of the war found themselves outside the new, much smaller, Germany but who had lived within the boundaries of the Germany of 1937.

However, Article 116 also perpetuates the notion of a special ethnic bond of *all* Germans (*'Volkszugehörigkeit'*) which had first been given legal expression by the Nazis and which still forms the basis on which ethnic Germans come to the Federal Republic from areas which had never been within the German boundaries of 1937, as stipulated by Article 116. Moreover, the claim of third or fourth generation descendants to be German can often be dubious, and the use of the so-called *Volkslisten* (Nazi lists in which Poles, Soviets or Germans were often forced to enter their names to show their desire to become German) as proof of German descent has been highly controversial. German legislation assumes that all ethnic Germans and their descendants live under the pressure of persecution (*'Verfolgungsdruck'*) when this assumption is often no longer valid. This contrasts with the persecution which *genuine* asylum seekers suffer.

The Treatment of Asylum Seekers

In the absence of an immigration policy, access to the FRG for all kinds of would-be immigrants is possible only by making an application for asylum. There is thus a great variety of people making use of the asylum procedure ranging from the politically persecuted to those escaping from deprivation, ethnic disturbances, civil war, sexual or religious harassment to 'economic migrants' who would not normally apply for 'asylum'. Even those ethnic Germans whose ethnicity is open to doubt can apply for asylum. Successive governments have not disentangled the problems involved, and by their own statements and views have tolerated or even encouraged the impression that Germany is 'swamped' by waves of would-be immigrants and that the country has reached the limits of what it can absorb (*'das Boot ist voll'*).

The growth in the number of applicants has been the main reason for the increasingly restrictive handling of asylum in Germany (as in most other European countries). A whole gamut of measures have been introduced to make entry to the Federal Republic more difficult, with such measures as visa requirements, the fining of carriers and the refusal of asylum to a person coming from a 'safe' country. There have also been the extensive refusals of entry at the border;

applications for asylum for reasons of economic or general distress have been deemed 'obviously unjustified', and there has been an intensification of pressure to depart after an unsuccessful appeal against a first, negative application. In 1988 a speeding-up of 'unjustified' asylum applications was introduced and central *refoulement* (expulsion) centres in the Länder established. In 1985 a special agreement was reached with the GDR authorities which blocked access to the FRG for asylum seekers entering via East Berlin. The current policy on asylum is based on the *Asylverfahrengesetz* of April 1991.

Thee measures have been accompanied by an ever-decreasing rate of recognition of political persecution (see Table 13.2). However, the definition of what nowadays constitutes 'political persecution' has become extremely narrow. It now applies only to persecution perpetrated by state governments and in the past applied mainly to communist governments. For example, massive cruelty such as torture, civil war, ethnic persecution leading to genocide, sexual or religious harassment do not constitute 'persecution', in the interpretation of the German courts. To some observers there therefore exists an 'erosion of the Geneva Convention' in Germany (Bade, 1990, 90).

Once inside Germany and with an asylum application pending, applicants are distributed among the Länder according to a 'distribution key'. Since unification the new Länder in the East are obliged to take in 20 per cent of the total, a decision which may have been a serious mistake: it has only marginally lightened the burden of the Western Länder but has been a contributory factor in the outbursts of violence against foreigners in the former GDR. Moreover, as there is as yet no infrastructure of specialist lawyers, social workers, etc. in the East – with greater hostility from the population – accommodation there is highly unpopular with asylum seekers (and with ethnic Germans). Since 1 July 1991 asylum seekers have been allowed to earn their living after a five-year ban on work introduced in 1987 was lifted. If they are unemployed, they live on social security which is now increasingly paid 'in kind' to make payments to carrier organisations more difficult and in order to reduce the attraction (the 'pull-factor') of Germany to further migrants. However, even these provisions are often more generous than the incomes which asylum seekers could aspire to in their home countries. Asylum seekers receive no help with language classes as integration into German society is not intended, but basic health care is provided. While the children of asylum seekers can attend school in some Länder, there is no federal mandatory provision. Without help with

TABLE 13.2   *Asylum seekers: applications, recognition and origins*

(a) Applications and recognition rates

Year	Applications	Recognition rates (%)
1988	103 076	8.6
1989	121 318	5.0
1990	193 063	4.4
1991	256 112	6.9

(b) (Main) countries of origin

Countries	1988	1989	1990	1991
Romania	2 634	3 121	35 345	40 504
Yugoslavia	20 812	19 423	22 114	78 854
Turkey	14 837	20 020	22 082	23 877
Iran	7 867	5 768	7 271	8 643
Vietnam	n/av	984	9 428	8 133
Bulgaria	n/av	429	8 341	12 056
Poland	29 023	26 092	9 155	
Sri Lanka	3 383	7 758	4 361	5 623
Pakistan	2 390	2 673	3 983	
Afghanistan	1 462	3 650	7 348	
Palestine	n/av	984	9 428	

Note:
The percentage of Europeans among asylum seekers declined from 69.3 (1988), to 60.4 (1989), to 52.6 (1990)
Source:
Statistik des Bundesamtes für die Anerkennung ausländischer Flüchtlinge.

the language, their progress remains problematical, even when eventually a qualified right to a longer residence is obtained.

Decisions about asylum can often take many months, if not years, because only a fraction of cases are heard each year and because of the lengthy appeal system which both the state authorities and the asylum seeker can resort to if a decision is negative (Article 19 of the Basic Law). As the courts are moreover often understaffed, it is this system which is responsible for the great number of asylum seekers in Germany at any one time. Even when an application has been turned down, rejection does not automatically lead to an asylum seeker having to leave the country. An analysis of what happened to 57,605 unsuccessful asylum seekers in 1989 shows that only 6 per cent were sent back to their home countries; 15 per cent left the

FRG of their own accord, and the fate of 18 per cent was unknown
– many of them stay on illegally. The rest remained in the FRG
legally: 6 per cent put in a further appeal; 34 per cent were allowed
to stay as *de facto* refugees on humanitarian grounds. They obtain
a limited right of residence in Germany after two years in the country
and a permanent one after eight years. Of the unsuccessful asylum
seekers, 16 per cent were allowed to stay on temporarily. Since 1
July 1991 their cases are to be re-examined every six months (ZDWF,
1991). This means that 56 per cent, or over half of the unsuccessful
asylum seekers, were allowed some form of residence. This figure
puts the official claim of a 'massive abuse' of the asylum system,
which is suggested by the recognition rate of 4 per cent, into perspective. Abuse does take place by means of criminal organisations
specialising in bringing migrants into Germany. However, this practice is seldom referred to in government pronouncements, undoubtedly so as not to give the impression of generosity towards asylum
seekers which would attract even greater numbers and because this
situation does not fit in with the official attitude towards 'foreigners'.

The Integration of Ethnic Germans

The unexpectedly large numbers of ethnic Germans (*Aussiedler*)
arriving in Germany for a variety of reasons meant that their originally generous treatment was increasingly replaced by more stringent measures. Thus a first '*Sonderprogramm Aussiedler*' of 31
August 1988 allowed ethnic Germans free access to the FRG and,
once there, complete equality with Germans. They were free to
travel and to settle at a place of their choice, and this resulted in a
clear preference for certain German states such as North Rhine–
Westphalia (for ethnic Germans from Poland) or Bavaria and Baden-
–Württemberg (for those from Rumania) which led to a higher intake
for these states than they were meant to have under the distribution
formula. Less than a year later the government had to modify the
Programm and then on 1 January 1991 a new, more restrictive
'Ethnic German Reception Law' came into force.

Whereas previously *Aussiedler* would automatically become eli-
gible for German citizenship on arrival in the FRG, an application
for acceptance ('*Aufnahme*') has now to be made before leaving
their home countries, either through the embassies and consulates
of the FRG (whose personnel have been drastically increased) or via
members of families or friends already in Germany. Moreover, the
proof required of connections with German 'culture' have been made
more stringent. Ethnic Germans are still given a choice of accommodation where possible but if they apply to a Land whose capacity is

full (and this applies to about 10 per cent of ethnic Germans a year), they are simply allocated to a given area where they have to stay for the subsequent three years. If they nevertheless move, they forego substantial benefits and are treated like 'normal' foreigners. Some ethnic Germans who have been allocated to the new Länder in the East which are taking in 20 per cent from 1 December 1990 prefer this option to remaining in the original area. The benefits obtainable in the new Länder are of course much lower (*Info-Dienst* 24/1991).

Aussiedler receive a number of benefits, which although they have been scaled down, are still considerable. These range from an *Eingliederungsgeld* (integration money) on arrival, to help with the purchase of furniture and clothing and cheap loans for the construction or purchase of accommodation. As Germans, they are naturally entitled to all forms of insurance benefits and, if of a pensionable age, to the normal state pension. They have the immediate right to work and the state gives help with the finding of jobs either directly through the services of the Labour Exchanges or in the form of language classes. Finally, as Germans, their children are obliged to attend German schools, and the latter have to provide for their special needs. In theory, the social integration of ethnic Germans should be unproblematical; in practice however, the fact that they are treated like Germans without being so either subjectively (too much in the real Germany is different from what ethnic Germans expected it to be) or objectively in the eyes of the average Germans (who see little evidence that they are dealing with 'Germans'), makes their social integration a slow and difficult task.

Economic and Social Aspects

Of the three categories of 'migrants', the considerable contribution by foreigners to the German economy is well known; indeed, certain sectors could no longer function without them (Bunzenthal, 1989). Ethnic Germans are welcome because they tend to be younger than the German population and offer skills in areas which have become unpopular with the Germans (see Table 13.3). A government-sponsored study therefore saw the benefits to be derived from ethnic Germans in a highly optimistic light. Even the most modest scenario showed that the social services would benefit from 1990 onwards and would by 2010 have a surplus of DM 67 billion (IdW, 1989) – welcome news at a time when the ageing German population seemed to make both increases in contributions and the cutting of benefits inevitable. However, while there seems to be a consensus among politicians and leading industrialists on the long-term benefits for the

TABLE 13.3   *Ethnic Germans: age, employment and religious structures*

(a) Age structures: ethnic Germans and German population, %

	Ethnic Germans			Germans
	1988	1989	1990	1989
Under 6	11.95	13.09	10.36	6.3
6–18	20.46	18.37	18.04	11.9
18–20	2.59	3.28	3.54	2.7
20–25	8.07	9.95	9.23	8.5
25–45	37.00	36.24	33.46	29.4
45–60	12.59	11.64	14.81	20.4
60–65	3.29	3.68	5.03	5.5
65 and older	4.05	3.75	6.01	15.3

(b) Employment structure: ethnic Germans and Germans, %

	Ethnic Germans			Germans
	1988	1989	1990	1988
Industry/ Crafts	48.7	49.29	46.67	36.5
Service Industries	39.76	37.19	35.11	54.3
Technical	7.48	6.49	6.28	6.9
Mining	2.29	3.33	1.84	0.6
Agriculture	1.66	2.57	4.25	1.5
Others/undecided	0.06	1.14	5.85	0.2

(c) Religious structure: ethnic Germans and Germans, %

	Ethnic Germans		Germans
	1989	1990	1988
Roman Catholic	72.6	53.1	43
Protestant	15.7	32.5	41
Other	9.5	11.2	16
No religion	0.9	1.5	n/a
No information	1.3	1.7	n/a

Source:
Info-Dienst Deutsche Aussiedler (31 December 1990).

German economy (Kraushaar, 1990), their rapid influx in recent years has created the problem of '*Aussiedlerstau*' (a 'bunching' of ethnic Germans) both in the labour and housing markets. As far as employment is concerned, their greatest impediment in finding work has been the language, with as many as 90 per cent of ethnic Germans from Poland and two-thirds of those from the Soviet Union unable to speak German, whereas those coming from Rumania on the whole have good German (Leciejewski, 1990, 57). For this reason the provision of language classes of ten (from July 1990, eight) months and retraining has been a priority for the *Bundesanstalt für Arbeit* (BfA) in Nürnberg and the local Labour Exchanges.

Although there is general willingness to employ ethnic Germans, the latter are entering the German labour market at a time when unemployment among foreigners (10.2 per cent at the end of June 1991), is already considerably higher than that among Germans (5.6 per cent at the end of August 1991) (BfA). Available figures do not yet allow a precise calculation of unemployment among ethnic Germans, but it is certainly considerably higher than that for foreigners. Fears that they take jobs away from Germans are almost certainly at present misplaced.

One area where ethnic Germans compete directly with the poorer sections of German society is for cheap housing where they have moved into a situation of already existing shortage. A mixture of miscalculation of population trends and ideological preoccupation with privatising the housing market led to a stop in the construction of council housing which created serious scarcities in cheap accommodation from 1987 onwards. The situation deteriorated further in 1989 after the opening of the Berlin Wall and the influx of thousands of East Germans in addition to ethnic Germans. By the middle of 1991 the National Tenants' Association calculated a deficit of 1.5 million homes in the West and another one million in the East. There is a particularly serious problem in the big cities into which foreigners and ethnic Germans are drawn for a variety of reasons. In Cologne some 10 per cent of the population, or 100,000 people – 'with trend sharply rising' – are at present either roaming the streets or cramped together in emergency accommodation (*Independent*, 26 August 1991). In all about 1 million people are at present living in some form of emergency housing.

As far as asylum seekers are concerned, they enter the job market at the bottom of the employment 'pecking order' because they can be employed only if no German is available. They will thus find work only with difficulty, but giving them the *right* to work constitutes a welcome development for a number of reasons. For the local communities it removes them from their budgets into those of the (centrally financed) Labour Exchanges who ultimately pay unemployment benefits. For the German public it is important that asylum seekers are seen to be working in view of their huge costs to the state (DM 5 billion in 1990). For asylum seekers there is the psychological benefit which they derive from being able to earn their living. A less favourable development for asylum seekers is that, once in gainful employment, they can be charged rent for their accommodation by private and public landlords. In the city of Munich for example, asylum seekers are charged, or rather overcharged, DM 810 a month for often not more than 6 m^2 in a room which is being shared by up to four others. Local authorities in charge of finding accommodation are increasingly seen as benefactors of landlords of 'problem housing'. ·

Searching for Solutions

As we have seen, the biggest problem which Germany faces as a result of its migration policies is that of the great number of ethnic Germans. Although numbers declined to 220,000 in 1991 this was a result of the delay of the processing of applications (*Süddeutsche Zeitung*, 7 January 1992) rather than any real decline in the number of those still wishing to come. On the contrary, the number of the latter has been estimated to be potentially huge with between 2 and 3 millions 'sitting on their suitcases', ready to move westwards (Otto, 1990). A change of policy towards ethnic Germans has therefore repeatedly been called for, notably by the SPD, but resisted by the government. It has so far preferred to deal with the problem by administrative means, but also by providing incentives to ethnic Germans to stay in their home areas, such as support for German cultural establishments and the possible creation of a 'home' for ethnic Germans in some part of the former Soviet Union. But, as the situation there deteriorates, these methods are likely to be even less effective. Moreover, there is opposition from the Russian population to the setting up of a new 'Volga Republic' (*Süddeutsche Zeitung*, 27 November 1991).

Public attention, by contrast, has always focused far more on asylum seekers in Germany. In 1991 their numbers increased by a further 32.7 per cent to 256,112 from the previous year's record high (192,056) and with the authorities processing only 168,000 applications, this means a backlog of almost 100,000 cases carried forward into 1992. The civil war in Yugoslavia is reflected in a threefold increase of asylum seekers from there to 78,854 and 40,504 came from Romania (*Süddeutsche Zeitung*, 7 January 1992). These figures might increase even more dramatically as a result of the break up of the Soviet Union.

The search for means to stem the influx has, of course, polarised the political parties for years, with the Bavarian CSU and a majority of the CDU demanding an amendment to Articles 16 and 19 of the

Basic Law. This change would allow more strigent checks at the borders and would replace the legal appeal system guaranteed in Article 19 by 'Appeal Commissions' whose judgements would be final. The SPD, Greens and sections of the FDP have opposed this alteration on the grounds that Germany, because of her past, has a moral obligation of tolerance towards asylum seekers. They also fear that a change of Article 19 in this context might set a precedent for altering the constitution for other purposes. They believe moreover that administrative measures of this kind will not ultimately reduce the flow of migrants. To ease the existing problems they propose instead a more efficient handling of the asylum procedure. Growing discontent at local level – where asylum seekers after all have to be housed and provided for – is now putting increasing pressure on all parties and this has led to the so-called 'party compromise' of 10 October 1991. In it the Länder undertook to set up camps for a minimum of 500 asylum seekers by the beginning of 1992 in exchange for the federal government providing more executive staff. This would make decisions in cases where applications were 'obviously unfounded' possible within six weeks. As 40–50 per cent of applications would fall into this category, a noticeable improvement could be achieved. However, the practicability of this proposal has been questioned. Only few Länder were able to offer the large camps, with even the Bundeswehr reluctant to relinquish its vacated barracks for this purpose (and where this is the case, the Finance Minister decided to charge the Länder rent for them). Moreover, the government seemed unable to find sufficient staff and claimed lack of support from the Länder. The 'party compromise' has thus fallen into disarray.

An Answer at the European Level?

One reason for the government's seemingly half-hearted approach to this formula has been the ongoing negotiations at European level. The German government has repeatedly called for a common policy on borders and asylum and the Europe-wide distribution of asylum seekers. Some progress has been made with the Schengen Agreement (1985) and the Dublin Convention (April 1990). Both aim for the removal of internal borders and the introduction of controls at the common external border, and these objectives were reiterated at the Maastricht summit of December 1991. However, in this sphere countries like Britain have voiced their strongest opposition (Douglas Hurd in *Die Zeit*, 15 November 1991) and even the early full implementation of the Schengen agreement for the abolition of border controls between five of the six original EC members has been delayed for two years (*Das Parlament*, 29 November 1991). There has been marked reluctance on the part of the other European countries to take in asylum seekers from Germany whose system is seen as too 'soft' and would have to be changed if a common European asylum policy were to be achieved. Pressure on a European level might well be the basis on which an internal German compromise was made possible.

European and German policies thus seem closely linked in this area but could also prove divisive for Europe in the coming years. All governments are facing growing xenophobia in their own countries, most visibly in the election successes of the National Front in France, but also in previously particularly liberal countries such as Holland.

German Attitudes and Public Opinion

There is a growing realisation that Europe's prosperity could be threatened by the world's and notably the East's poor and her culture by militant creeds such as Islamic fundamentalism. Germany's attitudes to foreigners have to be seen in this context. We have already noted the unease with which foreigners have been treated on the questions of voting in local elections, of German nationality and in the new Aliens Law. A Memorandum by the Head of the 'Constitution Department' of the German Ministry of Interior (Extracts in *Der Spiegel*, 40/1991) on the problem of foreigners in German society reflects the concern that 'German culture' and 'identity' are being threatened by an ever-growing influx of foreigners of all kinds.

This position of *Abwehr*, of defence against everything foreign, is particularly noticeable in the formmer GDR where anti-foreign sentiments serve as one means of identification as 'German' (Berger, 1991, 1). In the old FRG an opinion survey of September 1991 (*Der Spiegel*, 38/1991) revealed that 76 per cent of those asked favoured a change of the Basic Law to prevent the misuse of asylum; 69 per cent wanted to change the asylum provisions altogether. A staggering 96 per cent wanted to keep out 'economic migrants'. Moreover, 73 per cent were in favour of changing the constitution to prevent the entry into the country of ethnic Germans. In other words, the population is increasingly weary of *all* those people it perceives as being 'foreign'. It is also not surprising in this context that 36 per cent expressed sympathies with right-wing tendencies where 'action against foreigners' is a main platform. In the September 1991 election in Bremen the right-extremist DVU polled 6.2 per cent (the SPD lost its absolute majority) and the potential for right-wing radicalism in youth, particularly in the East, is considered to be high (Runge, 1990).

There can be little doubt that Germany (and Europe) is facing difficult problems for which no easy solution is in sight. However, the debate on the issues appears to be often irrational and serving party political purposes. Thus the important economic role which foreigners play contrasts with the distrust and distance with which they are officially treated. This applies also to the general impression that Germany is inundated by migrants of different kinds without any rational assessment of the number of people which Germany has taken in in the past and could, to her own benefit, take in in the future. There are also the problems of an almost unrestricted intake of ethnic Germans on the basis of an anachronistic understanding of ethnicity which contrasts with the lack of adequate practical provisions. Whereas in the past the policy could be defended on the grounds that this 'bringing home' of Germans living outside the FRG was a means of reuniting the German people as long as the unification of their country remained impossible, with the FRG acting as a kind of Israel for the dispersed Germans, the recent changes in the Eastern bloc have made such a substitute role unnecessary.

There is also the contradiction in the way the government seeks to stem the flood of asylum seekers. Here the problem seems to be that access to the country is possible only by means of the asylum procedure. The most recent figures again reveal the weaknesses of this system: the majority of Yugoslavs, for example, have come as temporary refugees and are determined to return to their homeland once the situation there has reverted to normality. In the absence of other mechanisms these people are forced to apply for asylum as a means of gaining entry to and accommodation in the Federal Republic. The repeated rejection of a consistent and comprehensive immigration policy – for a variety of reasons – which would remove refugees and 'economic migrants' from the asylum process precludes any more flexible response and magnifies Germany's problems. Long-term solutions to counter her attraction for 'the world's poor and persecuted' (Willy Brandt) will remain a major problem, and although the government has begun to address the subject with its '[World] Refugee Concept' of September 1990, little concrete action has so far followed. Ultimately only a world-wide approach can bring solutions. Of this there is so far little sign.

14

Women in the New Germany: The East–West Divide

EVA KOLINSKY

Two Models: West and East Germany

Women in East and West Germany entered the post-war period with the same history and similar opportunities; by the time German unification brought the post-war period to a close, their worlds had become distinctive and different (Weidenfeld and Zimmermann, 1989). In 1950, just over one in three women East or West of the German–German border were in employment. Women, then, were very much the second gender: the majority had obtained only basic education and had not completed vocational or professional qualifications. Although National Socialism had imposed a cult of motherhood and dismantled most of the political and social rights women had begun to accumulate during the Weimar years, the war years and the dislocations of the immediate post-war period forced women to cope without men and husbands, manage their own and their family's affairs, work in industry, construction or agriculture (Mommsen, 1986; Edwards, 1985). Forced by circumstance, women added employment to their traditional family roles. In the West, women experienced opportunities and limitations in choosing between employment and family roles or combining the two; in the East, women's life was prescribed as encompassing both. For women, unification brought two contrasting societies together.

In the 1950s, West German women returned to full-time home-making as soon as their own family situation and standard of living permitted them to do so (Kolinsky, 1989; Helwig, 1987). Normalisation in the post-war years consisted of a life as wife and mother. Of course, the decimation of the male population by the war left more women than in the past unmarried. Alongside the role as mother and wife, that of the working woman gained in social prominence and attractiveness. By the end of the 1950s, younger women hoped they could avoid having to choose and might be able to combine employment and family roles. This type of expectation has remained in force into the 1990s with more impatient demands from women under fifty about the balance between the two worlds, and the nature of women's opportunities in society.

Before examining the meaning of equal opportunities on the eve of unification, we need to look at the history of East German women. For them, the return to homemaking did not happen (Voigt, Voss and Meck, 1987). The establishment of a socialist political order treated women in line with socialist ideology: their equality, their opportunities and rights were deemed to be achieved in and through the world of work. Equality as *Werktätige*, as working people, was declared the precondition and the guarantor of equal opportunities. Thus the right to work which was enshrined in the GDR constitution as the *Recht auf Arbeit* was synonymous with a *Pflicht zur Arbeit*, an obligation to work (Weber, 1985, 327 ff.). With its dual meaning as a right and as a duty, employment formed an integral part of GDR citizenship for women as well as for men.

On the eve of unification, 49 per cent of the East German labour force was female compared to 38 per cent in the West. In 1950, 49 per cent of East German women of working age were in employment, on the eve of unification, that figure had risen to near 90 per cent; in the West, it had just topped the 50 per cent mark (*Datenreport*, 1989; *Frauenreport '90*, 1990). In both societies, women of the post-war generations increased their participation in the educational and training system. In the West, families could soon afford to let girls stay on at school, enter university, learn a profession or trade. In the East, state regulation stunted individual educational motivations. In both Germanies, education and employment had emerged as key issues in women's lives – as prescribed activities in the East, as motivations and goals in the West beyond the traditional realms of homemaking and motherhood.

Equality: An Unmet Promise in the West

In the 1970s, women obtained better qualifications in schools than men, but failed to break even in higher education, vocational qualifications and employment opportunities. Discrimination was one hurdle. The other was a matter of circumstances. Just as the educated young women of the post-war generations began to enter the labour market, unemployment had become an endemic problem and restricted their chances. It hit women harder than men at all levels of qualification but especially at the lower end. Women who found work were often employed at a level below their qualifications, at the lower levels of seniority and tended to cluster in a narrow range of occupations: hairdressing, retailing, office work, receptionists, bank clerks, or at the professional level in teaching or health care. Moreover, the majority of working women in West Germany (84 per cent) have taken one or more career breaks, normally for family reasons; the need to find a private solution to combining the roles of wife, mother and career woman has forced West German women to remain adaptable, move in and out of part-time work or change career halfway through their lives.

In our context of comparing women's issues at the point of unification, two developments in West Germany should be stressed. The first concerns the salience of women's issues. The discrepancy between women's educational qualifications and employment motivation on the one hand, and on the other the experience of unequal opportunities, which may have been tolerated by past generations, not least since only few women would qualify at the higher levels; in the 1970s, the persistence of inequality was castigated as a violation of the constitutional promise of equality, and as an infringement of women's right to self-realisation. Women of the post-war generations developed a new assertiveness in demanding their rights and publicly articulating their issues – women's issues. This new focus on women's issues gave rise to the new women's movement.

The second development concerns institutional and policy change. In the 1970s, West German women began to change their voting preferences (Hofmann-Göttig, 1986). Parties were increasingly selected for their competence – or publicly perceived competence – to address specific issues. Party preference by issues displaced voting in line with social background or tradition. The issue of equal opportunities emerged as one of the politically salient issues. Moreover, as women gained educational and vocational mobility, they became politically more interested and prone to change party preferences at a time when none of the larger parties enjoyed a large enough cushion of votes or seats to be secure in government and in a position to ignore women's issues (Kolinsky, 1991a; Brinkmann, 1990). The 1980s and early 1990s reaped the fruits of these developments. Equalisation offices at regional and local level secured an institutional base for women's issues and their impact on policy. Ministries with special responsibility for women have been created at central and regional government level. The European Community directives on equal opportunities inspired the West German Labour Promotion Legislation, which advocates special measures to promote equal opportunities in recruitment, career development and retraining. Several of the West German Länder went further and introduced positive discrimination or quotas in order to reduce the women's deficit in employment, especially at the upper end of the career spectrum (*Frauenforschung*, 3, 1987). Women's occupational opportunities improved significantly in public service and administration. Since the mid-1980s, quotas have also been considered by political parties and instituted in the Greens and the SPD. They are intended as a device to enable women to reach leadership positions in their political party, enter parliaments and make politics their career.

Also in the late 1980s, a programme of social legislation was introduced with the twofold aim of encouraging women to bear more children and looking after them at home but also of facilitating reintegration into the labour market (*Frauenforschung*, 4, 1990). The main provisions consist of pension rights for mothers who gave up their employment; improved maternity leave; leave from employment at 70 per cent of the salary for either women or men; and a guarantee that a place of employment at the same level will be available up to three years after taking a career break.

The thrust of women's policies in West Germany since the late 1980s has been to increase choices for women or men and modify the conflict which traditionally arose for women who strove to combine the role of wife and mother with a career. Despite improved opportunities and provisions, discriminatory practices have persisted (Gerhard and Limbach, 1988). More equality, better career chances, a gender balance in education, training, employment had not been accomplished in the West when the two Germanies joined into one, but they seemed no longer entirely out of reach.

Women in the East before Unification

Viewed across the German–German border, women in socialist Germany seemed a fair way ahead on the path towards equal opportunities. Participation in the labour market was higher than in other advanced industrial societies (83 per cent; 91 per cent including full-time education). The ideological axiom of moulding socialist personalities did not appear to prescribe specific gender roles (Lemke, 1991). On the contrary, the GDR prided itself on having instituted equal chances for all and to have eradicated social disadvantage incurred by social origin or gender (*Frauen in der DDR*, 1985). In the education system, women seemed to hold their own: prior to unification, more than half the university students and over 80 per cent of students at technical colleges (*Fachschulen*) were women. Of the girls who left full-time education after the compulsory ten years, 99 per cent entered vocational training. Since the educational reforms in the 1960s made entering professional or vocational training obligatory in the GDR, the high participation rates suggest that women simply complied with the state instructions. Yet there is no evidence of reluctance; women of the post-war generations accepted that training to obtain vocational or professional qualifications was a normal part of their lives. Since the early 1970s, women's qualifications improved significantly; by 1989, just 12 per cent of women in employment did not hold a qualification, 88 per cent did. On the eve of unification, the majority of women below retirement age were qualified in a trade or profession: training, like working, had become part of their lives.

Despite such strides in professional and vocational qualifications, a gender gap remained. In everyday life and schools, gender stereotypes persisted, not merely in the allocating of household chores, but also in perceptions of personal roles and competence. Women were less likely than men to set their sights on obtaining leadership positions or on being the head of household and main breadwinner (Table 14.1).

Offical GDR statistics presented the situation of women as one of decreasing disadvantage. Equality, so it seemed, was just a matter

TABLE 14.1   *Role expectations of men and women*

Issue	Predominantly relevant for					
	Men		Both men and women		Women	
	m	f	m	f	m	f
Professional advancement	20	15	79	82	1	2
Leadership positions	23	15	74	84	3	1
Breadwinner in family	59	45	40	53	1	2
In charge of household chores	1	2	40	48	56	50
Head of household	65	49	33	49	2	2

Note:
The data are based on surveys conducted by the former Central Institute for Youth Research in Leipzig.
Source:
Bertram (1989) 172.

of time and would follow as more better qualified women entered the labour market. Table 14.2 records the official picture for 1987: at the basic level of skilled worker, women appeared to have achieved near-equality, at the intermediate level they had gained the advantage, while at the top levels they continued to trail behind.

TABLE 14.2 *Women in employment, by selected positions 1987*

Type of position	Women (%)	Men (%)
Skilled worker*	48	52
Advanced skilled (*Meister*)	12	88
Leadership functions** in the Technical School Sector (*Fachschulkader*)	62	38
Leadership functions in the University Sector (*Hochschulkader*)	38	62

Notes:
* In accordance with the ideological precepts in the GDR, the majority or people in employment were classified as 'workers' regardless of the specific function they performed.
** 'Kader' in the GDR terminology referred to individuals or groups who were entrusted with leadership functions on the strength of their special political and professional competence.
Source:
Frauen in der DDR (1987), 14.

A closer look at the nature of women's employment, their access to leadership positions, and their earnings reveals, however, that equal opportunities were less within reach than official pronouncements and statistical profiles had claimed. In the GDR, women had been lured into a false sense of equality. Vocational qualifications tended to be bunched as 60 per cent of women trained in 16 out of a possible 259 occupations (*Frauenreport '90*, 1990, 43). The persistence of typical women's jobs was obfuscated by terminology as a typist became a 'Specialist in Writing Technique', a seamstress a 'Clothing Specialist', or a carpenter a 'Specialist for Wood Technology'.

The narrow range of occupations corresponded to a narrow employment pattern: as in the West, women tended to concentrate in certain economic sectors such as trade, services, textiles, communications.

There is some evidence that GDR women preferred traditional female occupations to placements in industrial production but were forced to train in industry since placements of their choice were not available (*Frauenreport '90*, 1990, 48). In fact, women were more likely to acquire advanced vocational qualifications (*Meister*) or rise to managerial positions within traditional women's fields than in the men's fields of engineering or manufacturing.

Statistical data which were suppressed during the lifetime of the GDR and have been published after its collapse paint an alarming icture of administered, institutionalised, inequality. Generally speaking, women in the GDR occupied the lower rungs of the professional ladder. In the socialist economy, just one in three women held a managerial position; only 2 per cent could be regarded as in top managerial positions. In the university sector, 15 per cent of management positions were held by women but only 3 per cent of those at the top (*Frauenreport '90*, 1990, 95). Although most women worked, although their earnings contributed significantly to the overall income of GDR households (43 per cent) and although they valued employment as highly as men (Bertram, Job and Friedrich, 1988, 82) discrimination against women was built into the system. Employment throughout the GDR economy was grouped into three broad bands (*Leistungsgruppen*) of seniority and pay. Regardless of the area of employment or whether women worked in the industrial or service sector, in fields traditionally dominated by men or by women, women were underrepresented throughout the economy in the top groups. Moreover, even those women who had broken the mould and held positions in the top band (*Leistungsgruppe I*) were paid less than men in the same band. (*Monatsberichte*, June 1991, 58ff.; *Monatsberichte*, July 1991, 58ff.). On average, women's earnings were pegged at 12–25 per cent lower than those of men (Einhorn, 1991, 1). A study of occupational mobility revealed in 1990 that men who changed their employment tended to gain seniority and pay, even if they entered an area outside their original qualifications. Women, by contrast, tended to stay on the same level and move to a new employment without stepping up from one *Leistungsgruppe* to another (*Frauenreport, '90*, 1990, 51).

Yet, during the lifetime of the GDR there was little public awareness of such inequalities. The paucity of women at the helm of political power, in the leadership positions of the state, the party or the politburo was obvious; in the closing days of the GDR, the only woman to hold ministerial office was the wife of Erich Honecker. Yet, women in the GDR seemed to enjoy better access to political institutions and participate more actively than women in the West: in 1987, 30–40 per cent of party members were women, compared with about 22 per cent in the FRG. The membership of the East German Free German Trade Union was 53 per cent female, compared to just over 20 per cent in the West. In the East, women held 32 per cent of the seats in the Volkskammer and around 40 per cent in regional and local assemblies. In the West, women's representation in the Bundestag had stagnated at 10 per cent or below until 1983 and has since shot up to 20 per cent. In regional parliaments, the recent emphasis on women's candidacies boosted their representation to near 25 per cent on average, a considerable gain but still behind the GDR figures (Kolinsky, 1991b).

The social composition of parliaments was as predetermined by the state as the provision of places in training or education. The women's quota here pertained to the official women's movement; like other member organisations of the so-called National Front, it delegated the required number of people to take the seats reserved for women. Participation, like employment and training, seemed to be assured for women; pressures for more or a different kind of representation did not exist. Indeed, the freely elected parliaments which succeeded the collapse of state socialism in the GDR included fewer women than their imposed predecessors: 21 per cent in the last Volkskammer and 16 per cent on average in the new Land parliaments.

Women in the GDR did not have as keen a sense of disadvantage as that which had emerged in the West. East Germans were inclined to accept the state administered place of women as securing equal opportunities at least in the public sphere. Even after unification, a majority continues to believe that equality had been achieved (Table 14.3).

TABLE 14.3   *Did woman have equal chances in the GDR?*

Question: Did women in the GDR have the same opportunities at work as men, provided they worked as efficiently or did men generally enjoy preferential treatment?	
Women did have equal opportunities	54%
Men enjoyed preferential treatment	34%
Do not know	10%

Note:
Values for men and women nearly identical.
Source:
Harenberg (1991) 64.

Equal Opportunities of Motherhood?

The hidden agenda of GDR socialism was inspired by the intention of achieving a maximum integration of women into the labour force together with maximum population growth. Integration into the labour force served several purposes. Throughout its short history, the GDR suffered a population loss as people of working age fled the country or applied to resettle in the West. Compulsory employment for the whole adult population was intended to ensure a sufficient supply of labour. Since the GDR operated with outmoded technology and generally low productivity, a larger workforce was required than might have been the case in a more modern country. The right and duty to work also allowed the state to integrate its population through employment into the polity, since the social environment of GDR citizens was, above all, defined through their employment, inside and outside working hours. It has been suggested that since the early 1980s, compulsory employment was no longer an economic necessity but served above all the political purpose of controlling people's lives (Flockton, 1992). One of the revelations after unification concerned the vast overmanning in industry, administration and services, and the key role of the workplace for the informers' culture and Stasi networks which characterised and destroyed the GDR.

Integrating women into the labour market was, therefore, expected to integrate them into the decreed state socialism. In order to achieve this, the GDR government undertook to support women in their role as housewives and mothers. As mentioned earlier, equal pay or conditions were denied. Instead, East German women were humoured with exceptions, privileges, special measures and financial bonuses to embrace their family roles and especially motherhood more willingly (Enders, 1986; *Frauenreport '90*, 1990). Married women were entitled to a 'housework day' every month, working mothers could take paid leave when their children were ill. The employer, not the woman, was obligated to provide child care facilities throughout the year. Fees were nominal, and care provision was on a daily basis from 6 a.m. to 6 p.m. for babies and children up to the age of ten. For East German mothers, the use of public child-care facilities became the rule rather than the exception. In 1960, for instance, 14 per cent of children up to the age of three were looked after in a creche; in 1989, 80 per cent. On the eve of unification, 95 per cent of all pre-school children over the age of three attended a kindergarten; in 1960, 46 per cent had done so. Also in 1989, 81 per cent of school children between the ages of six and ten received all-day care after school; before the collapse of the GDR,

90 per cent of all pupils attended organised holiday camps under the auspices of the Free German Youth or, more frequently, their mother's place of work at a cost of only 4 East German Marks per week.

Child care in the GDR was freely available and cheaper than looking after a child at home. The low cost of provision for children tallies with the generous child allowances which could contribute significantly to the monthly family income, and especially to the relatively low incomes of women.

The adjustments in the level of child allowances reflect the efforts of the state to use financial incentives to encourage child-bearing. In 1950, only families with four or more children were entitled to receive child benefit. Since 1958, benefit was payable for every child, with higher rates for large families. In the 1980s, encouraging child-bearing seemed to displace the traditional notion of supporting large families. Between 1981 and the collapse of the GDR in 1990, child benefit for larger families doubled while it rose sevenfold for every second child and nearly fivefold for every first child. The steepest increase for small families occurred after 1987 (*Frauenreport*, '*90*, 1990, 140). Although financial incentives for child-bearing failed to encourage a return to family sizes of the past, the decline in the size of families in the GDR was halted; the average family size of 2.2 had been propped up by the blend of administered employment security and multiple bonuses. Since unification, the birth rate in the new Länder has dropped sharply. Child benefits will be reduced to the Western level from 1992.

Child bonuses and special rights softened the harsh reality of low incomes. The majority (82 per cent) of women in the GDR worked above all to earn money (Harenberg, 1991, 65). Given the low income levels of the average GDR citizen and the exorbitant prices of so-called luxury goods in the socialist version of consumer society, most households could make ends meet only if women went out to work. As mentioned earlier, women contributed an average of 43 per cent to the household budget; moreover, an increasing number of households consisted of one parent and children as families split up through divorce or women chose to remain unmarried. For single mothers, employment constituted the only source of income, backed by the state benefit and child-care system outlined above. Although some East German women regarded work as self-realisation, most worked to make ends meet. In the former GDR, economic and social conditions for women were too harsh to foster more subjective, postmaterialist values.

By the late 1980s, one in three women dodged their decreed role as *Werktätige* and opted for part-time work, although this was discouraged by the state (Belwe, 1989, 129–30). Unpublished surveys revealed that eight out of ten East German women would have preferred to work part time (interview with Barbara Bertram, DJI Aussenstelle Leipzig, 22 August 1991). To some extent, GDR women had remained housewives at heart: they continued to cook an evening meal, although hot midday meals were provided at work and for children at their school or nursery. They preferred to save up for their own, expensive washing-machine although apartment buildings offered communal facilities (Einhorn, 1991:5). The partial retreat from the prescribed role as *Werktätige* suggests that many GDR women expected a different lifestyle and different patterns of recognition and self-realisation than the socialist working environment was able to deliver. The detachment from the social system was particularly evident among women without university education who had been by-passed by the socialist culture of privilege and prerogatives, and who looked towards the West as offering a better lifestyle and fairer opportunities.

Unification and its Impact on Women

In social or economic terms, unification had a limited impact on women in the Western regions of the new Germany: it could be argued that competition in the labour market and for vocational training places intensified as women arrived from the East. Ever since the generation of the *Pillenknick* entered the labour market – the first age cohort to reflect the decline in the West German birth rate after oral contraceptives became readily available in the early 1960s – chances for young women to gain equal qualifications and employment improved, and in the key sector of vocational training, places on offer outnumbered applicants. The economic boom which followed unification ensured that women's transition from school to training and from training to employment did not deteriorate, and female unemployment in the Western regions fell into line with unemployment generally. For women who had arrived from the East since 1989 unemployment tended to be transitional (*Probleme und Perspektiven*, 1991). In the West, the social and economic repercussions of unification concerned awareness and debate rather than the living conditions of women. In direct contact, East German women seemed surprisingly conformist to young West Germans, keen to redress the gender balance of society, promulgate feminist values and advocate self-realisation. East German women seemed to bring with them a broad acceptance of West German society, its institutions and practices while West German women had found a corporate voice which criticised the persistence of inequality.

Different priorities also surfaced with regard to more specific issues. In the 1960s and 1970s, the East German model of state sponsored child care facilities for all had been the envy of women in the West, and demands for improved provisions had persisted. After unification, the issue of child care in the East became the specific problem that facilities were closed or under threat of closure as state subsidies dried up and the economy was put on a market footing. As we saw earlier, nearly 90 per cent of all East German children up to the age of ten attended full-time day-care facilities; closure threatened the established child care arrangements of working mothers and would have forced women or families to take on child-care roles which they had previously delegated. While East German women regarded full-time child care as a prerequisite of their lives, West German women had come to reject institutionalised child care as detrimental to the wellbeing of the child. The government pledged itself to provide nursery places (morning only) for 90 per cent of pre-school children between the ages of three and six, while discussions in the SPD, the Greens and the women's movement concentrated on *Tagesmütter*, a system of care where children would be placed during the day in private homes and cared for as individuals. To East German women, neither the word nor the concept of *Tagesmütter* were meaningful. The misunderstandings about child care point to the hiatus which has arisen between women at both sides of the former German–German border. In the West, unification left women's social and economic situation untouched but brought some issues more forcefully on political agenda, foremost among them the issue of abortion (see below). In the East, unification engendered the threat that women's personal environment might collapse, or had already done so.

Unemployment hit women more forcefully than men in the new Länder (Belwe, 1991b). One year after unification, 60 per cent of the unemployed were women; women's working contexts were less often protected through short-time working, and they were less successful than men in finding new jobs in the emergent East German labour market. Since women tended to be less skilled and had held less senior positions in the GDR economy, women have come into the front line of unemployment and the back row of re-employment.

Initially, unemployment seemed to leave women in the new Länder no worse off than they had been in employment since benefit levels were adjusted to Western standards, and the general level of wages in the former GDR had been pegged at 60 per cent of those in the West. Since state subsidies on foodstuffs, energy, housing and child care were phased out and costs adjusted to market prices by the autumn of 1990, unemployment created a new poverty trap as women were phased out of the revamped economy into long-term unemployment. Women over 40 in particular, the generations who grew up in the GDR and were the first to benefit from improved access to education and qualifications, face the bleak future of being unemployable.

In West Germany, the adverse effects of unemployment had often been hidden as women devoted more of their time to their families. East German women, whether employed or unemployed, continue to send their children to full-time day-care facilities and delegate family roles to public institutions. Immediately after unification, it seemed as if child-care facilities would disappear with the factories or offices that maintained them. Interim funding from central government enabled regional and local governments to keep the facilities open. In 1991, legislation was passed to transfer responsibility for child care to the communities, and moves are under way to make child care self-financing. At full cost, however, it would be out of reach for most women in East Germany, especially for single mothers who need it most, and public subsidies will be required if the network of child-care provision in the East is to survive (Engelen-Kefer *et al.*, 1990).

One of the legacies of the GDR has been to link social environments, leisure pursuits and activities to employment. In the new Länder, the unemployed find themselves isolated from their familiar social networks while replacements have been slow to emerge. Isolation had already been the dominant experience of women during the so-called Baby Year. Isolation and despondency seemed to be the dominant impact of unemployment as women struggled to cope with the post-socialist uncertainties.

The new climate of personal uncertainties also stifled women's political involvement after unification. During the *Wende*, the period between the system collapse in October 1989 and formal unification in October 1990, women were actively involved in the demonstrations and debates which forced the GDR to abandon socialism and in the efforts of the Round Table in recasting it. Modelled on the new women's movement of the West and in emphatic opposition to the official German Women's Federation (DFG), a women's movement emerged in the East and for a time became a hive of political and social activity. Against the Stasi, the Leipzig groups for instance could mobilise 40,000 women; safe houses, equalisation bureaux, women's bookshops and women's centres were founded throughout the former GDR. They articulated the new sense of participation but they also diffused women's issues and activities. By the time protest was needed to halt the closure of child-care facilities, the independent women's movement seized the initiative: the demonstrators, however, were not the mothers who wanted their children looked after but the nursery nurses and teachers who feared for their employment. The blend of economic dislocation and fears of declining personal circumstances extinguished the spark of participatory politics. Women refrained from joining political parties or political participation. They opted for a contemporary replica of the traditional women's deficit in politics, retreating from activity and waiting for change.

The Abortion Law Controversy

The treaty which sealed the unification of Germany constituted a formidable blueprint for institutional and legislative change in one major direction: that from West to East. Since the Eastern regions joined the West, the task of unification was perceived as extending proven practices to the East, and considering how they could be implemented there. The only exception to this formula pertained to abortion legislation: its unification was postponed for two years after the treaty came into force, and was to be decided by the Bundestag in a free vote.

On the surface, the issue was straightforward enough: in West Germany, abortion was in principle illegal and the legislation specified the circumstances under which it could be permitted; in East Germany, abortion during the first 12 weeks of pregnancy had been legal since 1972.

This clash in legislative practice might not have turned into an obstacle to proposing a unified legislation had it not been for the fact that abortion had been a controversial issue in the West since the early 1970s, with a flare-up of public debate in the late 1980s. To both sides, unification seemed to provide a chance to effect the desired changes. In the East, on the other hand, abortion had acquired a symbolic meaning as an area where individuals were free to choose without interference from the state.

The background can briefly be sketched: the East German legislation of 1972 conferred a right of abortion (Para. 218, 1991). Although not intended to replace birth control, and although oral contraceptives (the pill) were available free of charge, East German women made extensive use of abortion. In 1973, 3 per cent of women of child-bearing age (15 to 45) terminated at least one pregnancy; in 1988 amidst a declining birth rate, 2 per cent of potential mothers had abortions (*Frauenreport '90*, 1990, 167). It has been estimated that since 1972 at least one in three pregnancies have been terminated. Initially, the use of oral contraceptives lowered the abortion rate but it rose again after the side-effects of oral contraceptives became public knowledge.

The rights or wrongs of abortion were not discussed in the GDR. Deemed legal, facilities to conduct it were instituted by the state, and used by women who felt they needed them. Abortion seemed to be only about self-realisation and diverse lifestyles of people, a right rather than a problem: 'I am a citizen of the GDR, I am 57 years old and a mother of three grown up children. I cannot for the life of me understand that there are always some people who think they can pass judgement over the most intimate aspects of their fellow human beings. They punish people, who are the only ones to judge what is good and right for them. Nobody else can do so, since only the person who lives through the experience is in a position to decide how much he can bear' (*Die Zeit*, 2 June 1989, 20).

After unification, abortion acquired an additional symbolic meaning: a progressive legacy of the GDR which could and should be salvaged. At a time of personal dislocation, the abortion right signified an element of continuity and recognition of an acceptable GDR heritage. There is, however, no groundswell of popular demand. Early protests could mobilise large numbers of women and could defer an immediate decision in the unification treaty. Since then, apathy has followed unemployment or the fear of unemployment. The public voice in support of the old GDR abortion law and against the West Germany format has virtually fallen silent.

In the Western part of unified Germany, the situation is even more complicated. Until recently, the East German law was hailed (by the new women's movement and the Greens) as the blueprint for legal reform: to abolish Section 218 of the penal code which dated back to Bismarck's Germany and rendered abortion a criminal offence. In the 1970s, West German legislation came close to legalising abortion; under the auspices of an SPD–FDP government, the Bundestag introduced in 1975 a reformed law which stipulated only how many weeks into a pregnancy it could rightfully be terminated (*Fristenlösung*). In 1976, however, the Federal Constitutional Court ruled that this violated the right to life laid down in the Basic Law (Berghahn, 1991). Under the replacement legislation, abortion remained a criminal offence. Pregnancies could, however, be terminated if authorised by a medical doctor; this formula has been termed the *Indikationslösung*. The change of recorded reasons for legal abortions underlines a general change from restrictive to liberal: in 1977, one in three abortions were carried out for specifically medical reasons; in 1988, less than one in ten. The less clearly defined reason 'general hardship' rose from 58 per cent to 68 per cent in the same period (Kaiser, 1990, 23).

At the time of unification, abortions were at least as frequent in the West as in the East, about one in four pregnancies. Despite the liberalisation in practice, illegal terminations continue; it has been estimated that legal abortions in West Germany constituted only two-fifths of all abortions.

While abortion seemed to have been as common in the West as in the East, East Germans and women endorse it most. In 1991, 57 per cent of West German and 69 per cent of East German women thought that abortion should be legalised altogether, or at least within the first three months of pregnancy. This view was held more strongly among women under 30 than among older women, and more strongly also among SPD voters than among CDU voters (Harenburg, 1991, 64).

In West Germany, abortion entered the policy agenda through the women's movement, which identified self-realisation with a right to terminate pregnancies and demanded the complete elimination of abortion from the criminal code. Inside political parties, notably the SPD and FDP but also the liberal wing of the CDU, the discussion focused on women's right to choose whether or not to bear a child, and the small print of regulations to specify when abortions should be permitted. On the other hand, the Catholic wing within the CDU and CSU, but also the church reacted to the decrease in the birth rate with an intensified anti-abortion campaign, and the Bavarian state undertook to prosecute doctors who had conducted abortions without the prescribed advisory procedure (Frommel, 1991).

Unification coincided with a new controversy about abortion in West Germany between conservative and clerical forces calling for a more restrictive code, and those in favour of legalising abortions within the early stages of pregnancy. Calls to make all abortions legal were silenced as the debate within the women's movement, the Greens and the left-liberal political strands in the West developed a new sensitivity for the protection of human life in rejection of gene technology, and selective abortions to eliminate babies with unwanted characteristics – illnesses, disability, even gender. Increasingly, abortion was perceived not just as a liberating right women should enjoy, but as a potentially dangerous device of social engineering (*Bevölkerungspolitik und Tötungsvorwurf*, 1988). The East German model also lost its glamour as reports revealed the humiliating and uncaring manner in which abortions had been carried out.

In the Bundestag, members of all political parties will be given a free vote to decide how the abortion legislation in the new Germany will be shaped. The Free Democrats, and the former minister for women's affairs, Rita Süssmuth appear to have coined the winning formula when they advocated a compulsory process of counselling which should precede an abortion (*The Times*, 14 May 1991). If women then wished to go ahead, they should have the right to do so without special medical permission or assessment, provided they had not reached too advanced a state of pregnancy. The practical solution will, of course, constitute an important dimension of women's rights in the new Germany. The symbolic value, however, of abortion as a natural right of self-realisation has faded: in the East, the state-administered and institutionalised life of women has lost its function with the collapse of state socialism; in the West, the advocates of full legislation themselves had second thoughts and now tend to stress the value of human life and the need to protect it. In their terminology at least, they have come closer to conservative and church positions. The multifaceted views of abortion have smothered most of the explosive force the issue seemed to have when the unification treaty was formulated. In the case of abortion, as in so many issues of German politics, change will be incremental and based on incorporating diverse positions into a legislative package. Although discontent about losing rights in the East or not gaining enough rights in the West will not cease, abortion will not take central stage as an issue for women. Their concerns now are to recast their lives in a new and harsher environment, to salvage their expectations and to realise their opportunities in the new Germany.

15

Labour Market Problems and Labour Market Policy

CHRISTOPHER FLOCKTON AND JOSEF ESSER

A Dual Economy

The hasty incorporation of the GDR on 1 July 1990 into the market system and currency region of the FRG brutally exposed the lack of international competitiveness of the GDR's centrally planned economy, at a time when its post-war historic links with COMECON were also becoming dislocated (see Chapter 10 in this volume). The Eastern state was however not only absorbed into a single trading and currency area with its developed Western neighbour: it joined a social union, whereby it came to form part of a single labour market with the West, and so adopted Western social and labour legislation and industrial relations practices. Indeed, the prime motive for the forced pace of monetary, economic and social union was the desire to prevent the collapse of the GDR through the haemorrhage by migration westwards of its young and skilled labour in search of remunerative work. However, if the creation of this single labour market were to lead to a uniform level of wage costs throughout unified Germany, when labour productivity in the East was perhaps only 30 per cent of that in the West, this equalisation would raise the spectre of continuing long-term high unemployment in the less developed region. The very high labour costs of Western Germany, justified by the high productivity there, would be imposed on an Eastern Germany very different in structure and level of development. There has therfore been intense debate over the appropriate longer-term labour market policy to be pursued by government, employers' organisations and trade unions, which

281

would promote the required high level of investment in the East, while at the same time stemming the migration flow.

In the short term of course, we have the split or dual economy, where the extremes of labour shortage in the West and the spectre of mass unemployment in the East reflect the boom and slump which have, respectively, been the immediate consequences of economic and monetary union. In response, as Chapter 10 in this volume makes clear, the federal government has not only had to reverse its ideological stance at the macroeconomic level, engaging in Keynesian deficit financing without post-war parallel in Germany, but it has also had to adopt a far more interventionist stance in the labour market, an approach which has tended to run counter to the 'supply-side' labour market reforms of the earlier 1980s. The threat of mass unemployment in the East elicited a crisis management response from Bonn, which has had to rely on its traditional armoury of labour market instruments ill-suited to the scale and nature of the problem in the East. The rules have been interpreted liberally, but such programmes appear merely very costly short-term palliatives, when the need is for jobs which will survive in the competitive marketplace.

From Autumn 1990 onwards, the challenge of wage harmonisation has been posed. It was of course inevitable that with social union the West German industrial relations system, with its centralised wage bargaining, its extensive participation rights for employees and the legal underpinning which ensures the broad application of negotiated wage contracts through whole branches of the economy, would be applied unchanged in Eastern Germany. Here, one might postulate, conditions required a direct link between (low) productivity and wage rates. The federal government itself willingly extended its own system of national wage bargaining to the public services in the East, and it accepted without demur the initial wage increases of 20–30 per cent throughout the East in Summer 1990. This turned to alarm, however, when the West German unions took over negotiating rights in Autumn 1990 and then signed agreements at the beginning of 1991 (in the case of IG Metall and the public services union ÖTV) which would introduce a phased wage equalisation by 1994. In July 1991 the Bundesbank expressed its concern over the consequences for employment, inflation and public expenditure. Through mid- and late 1991 the public debate became heated over the appropriateness of the wage policies being pursued in the East, especially in the face of escalating wage claims and settlements in the West, to which the East would align. Without any doubt, German trade unions are well aware of the pay–productivity link (having pursued pay moderation throughout the 1980s), but all the organisational pressures are toward wage harmonisation throughout the federal territory. Recruitment of union members in the East demands it, the aim of broadly equal living conditions could be construed as doing so, and above all the threat to Western German wage earners by a low wage region to the East could not be tolerated. Much evidence (*Wirtschaftswoche*, 46/1991, 17) also points to an unwillingness by German employers to countenance price competition by a lower production-cost region. The acknowledgement of market forces does not extend to allowing a competitive threat of that magnitude.

This rapid rise in wage costs in the East, and the programme of equalisation within three years, removes Eastern Germany's one absolute advantage – its abundant, cheap (and well-trained) labour. The large-scale redundancies which were anyway in prospect will be severely exacerbated by this phenomenon, and the growth of small and medium-sized firms to compensate will be seriously constrained. Herein lies the dilemma for government employment policy. The first Kohl government of the first half of the 1980s sought some deregulation of the labour market to improve the supply side of the economy– such changes took legal form in the 1985 *Beschäftigungs-förderungsgesetz* (BFG) (Employment Promotion Act) and the 1986 *Arbeitsförderungsgesetz* (AFG) (Work Promotion Act), this latter being first passed in 1969 by the SPD–FDP coalition but whose instruments were never brought fully into effect. Some greater flexibility in employment contracts (part-time and fixed-term), some dilution of the social plan redundancy provisions, and a limitation of strike pay, were all the result of the 1985 legal changes. In 1986, the AFG provisions were strengthened regarding job creation programmes, early retirement, labour subsidies for recruitment of the older and long-term unemployed, so as to improve the labour market instruments required to manage the historically high unemployment of the early and mid-1980s. The Kohl government is now faced with a parting of the ways in its economic philosophy: in response to the economically unjustified wage harmonisation pressures, there are calls for wage subsidies; the labour market intervention instruments of the AFG law have been called upon to an unforeseen degree, and in a way which probably damages the emergence of a competitive economy in the East; in contrast, economic liberals, the government's own expert advisers, and its Deregulation Commission all proposed a return to liberalisation, to the supply-side economics of the early Kohl years. In the real world, a political management of the forbidding employment situation in Eastern Germany will be needed, but there is no doubt that this will be very costly to public budgets, that the emergence of a market economy will be more delayed, and that overall growth will suffer because of the weight of public debt. In later sections of this chapter, we turn in detail to the labour market strategies, and more briefly to the structural policy strategies of the federal government. However, the facts of the labour market evolution in this 'dual' economy will first be elucidated.

Table 15.1 gives output and employment data for the two halves of Germany, and reveals the contrasting evolution in this dual economy. Even before the 'unification bonus' to growth at the end of the decade, West Germany had benefited from a relatively slow but sustained recovery from the trough of the recession in 1982. By 1988 and 1989, record growth rates and current account surpluses were achieved and so finally the unemployment of 2.25 million, which had stayed consistently high from mid-1983, fell below 2 million in 1990. Already, signs of overheating of the economy were apparent from the boost to demand coming from the East, and so the stream of immigrants (of Eastern and ethnic German origin) amounting to 1 million in each of the years 1989 and 1990, alleviated labour shortages and further stimulated demand and investment. (The registered unemployed in West Germany at that date must therefore be regarded as 'mismatch', or structural, unemployment.) The Bundesbank (MRDB, October 1991) reports that the 'unification bonus' to West German growth may have accounted for one-half of the expansion in the eighteen months from 1 July 1990 (2 and 2½ percentage points respectively in the half years 1990:H2 and 1991:H1). Half of the 1.7 million new jobs created in the two years since the 1989:Q4 arose from this effect, and most were filled by immigrants, since registered unemployment in the West fell by only 250,000.

The counterpoint in the East has of course been profound economic and social dislocation and a slump in output. The impact is now readily apparent from Table 15.1 The collapse of output may have stabilsed in 1991:Q3 (bolstered by private services and especially by construction programmes, where orders stand 77 per cent higher than one year earlier), but this still leaves manufacturing value-added at scarely more than half of its pre-unification level. GNP may have fallen by 20 per cent in 1990, with perhaps a further fall of 5–10 per cent in 1991. The attendant labour market difficulties are only too apparent. the following qualifications to the data may be made:

- Perhaps only half of pre-unification full-time jobs now remain as full-time. The more recent fall in short-time working is not complemented by an equal rise in unemployment (which points to the impact of labour market measures, discussed below).

TABLE 15.1 *Labour market and output*

(a) Western Germany

Year	Employed	Vacancies (000)	Short-time (000)	Unemployed	Unemployment rate* (%)
1985	26593	110	235	2304	9.3
1989	27733	251	108	2038	7.9
1990	28444	314	56	1883	7.2
1990:Q3	28568	325	30	1802	6.9
1990:Q4	28812	296	46	1719	6.6
1991:Q1	28891	324	121	1687	6.7
1991:Q2	29019	338	140	1680	6.0
1991:Q3	29129	342	136	1704	6.2

* % of dependent civilian labour force.

(b) H1 = half-year

Year	Employed Manuf., constr.	Vacancies (000)	Short-time (000)	Unemployed	Unemployment rate* (%)
1990 Aug	–	20.0	1500	361	4.1
1990:Q4	–	24.0	1736	589	6.7
1991:Q1	2208	21.8	1926	757	8.6
1991:Q2	2130	24.8	1962	835	9.5
1991:Q3	–	40.4	1464	1023	11.6

* % of dependent civilian labour force.

Value added	In manufacturing (1990:Q3=100)	In construction (orders) (1991:H2=100)
1990 July	108.5	76.5
1990:Q3	100.0	98.4
1990:Q4 .	89.8	101.6
1991:Q1	63.4	86.1
1991:Q2	61.1	134.5

H2=half-year.
Source:
Deutsche Bundesbank, Statistical Series.

- The data exclude cross-'border' commuting. The Bundesbank (MRDB, November 1991) judged this to amount to 415,000 by July 1991. In contrast, the sizeable migration flows of 540,000 persons over the period Summer 1989 to mid-1990, shrank to 200,000 in the twelve months following unification.

The Labour Market Situation in Eastern Germany

The fact that output may have stabilised in Autumn 1991, and that the seasonally-adjusted unemployment rate for October 1991 at 11.9 per cent was well below the high point of 12.1 per cent for July and August, should not, however, detract attention from the fact that the rapid expansion in special labour market measures (particularly job creation) have absorbed what would otherwise be a large rise. The much-feared rise in unemployment at the end of June (when short-time working provisions were due to expire, but were then extended for a further six months) did not transpire, even though the waiting queue of civil servants employed in organs of the communist state and suspended on 70 per cent of pay, together with job protection in the metal-working branches, came to an end. However, looking ahead, short-time working provisions for 150,000 expired at the end of 1991, and the Treuhandanstalt planned to make 300,000 job cuts then. Unemployment will continue to rise, unless fully absorbed by special measures, since redundancies far exceed the rate of spontaneous job creation.

Officially, the breakdown of those in receipt of various types of labour market aid was as follows (MRDB, November 1991):

	thousands
unemployed	1050
short-time work	1200
job-creation schemes	350
retraining	90
special early retirement	280

However, other estimates indicated far higher numbers in the last three categories. With those remaining in full-time employment now amounting to only 4.78 million, the number of full-time jobs appears to have halved since the breaching of the Wall. To lend greater balance to these kinds of assessment, one must bear in mind the very substantial disguised unemployment which existed in the GDR, and which may have approached 15 per cent of total employment. Klauder and Kühlewind (1991) point out that were West German standards of productivity to be applied, then 70 per cent of the former East German jobs would have been superfluous.

Two groups in particular are directly threatened by the slump in employment, namely, apprentices and women workers generally. There is now a chronic shortage of apprentice training places, representing perhaps two-thirds of total demand, which has arisen because of the dislocation and of the adoption of the longer, dual system of training which prevails in the Federal Republic (Belwe, 1991). There is an almost virtual absence, historically determined, of training in medium-sized enterprises and in services (DIW, 25/ 1991). As discussed below, this represents an area of priority action by the federal government and Federal Labour Office.

Secondly, it was always suspected that females would be more than proportionately affected by the restructuring and slump (see Chapter 14 in this volume). Having, at 90 per cent (FRG, 63 per cent), the highest female participation rates in the world, the GDR considered as a major social achievement the provisions for 'socialist equality' for women in the workplace: kindergarten provision, sick leave for the care of children, assured reintegration into the workplace after maternity leave, were all socialist gains now at risk of harmonisation down to the West German level (which in an international comparison remains good). 58.5 per cent of the unemployed in mid-1991 were female. It is not only the 350,000 single or divorced working mothers who will be badly hit, since typically females contributed 44 per cent of total household earnings (DIW, 30/1991; Belwe, 1991; Bäcker and Steffen, 1991). Of course, the child-care facilities formerly provided by all firms and organisations have since been drastically reduced for financial reasons, which limits the mobility of women. More generally, it appears that the victims of this massive deindustrialisation process are unequally distributed socially and regionally within the East. The social and regional divisions of West German society observed during the 1970s and 1980s (Esser, 1986) may now be repeated in the East, but with a broader gap within the 'two-thirds society'.

Table 15.2 shows the shift in employment structure since mid-1989. If we take the twelve months from 1990:Q1, employment fell by 24 per cent, with industry (30 per cent) and agriculture (33 per cent) especially badly hit. By branch, deindustrialisation has hit hardest consumer goods, metallurgy and engineering. Difficulties in shipbuilding, automobiles, farm machinery and furniture arose in particular because of the ending of specialisation and cooperation agreements with COMECON. In textiles and chemicals, well over half of employees are on short-time working (DIW, 12/1991). The Treuhandanstalt decided to close the Wartburg and Trabant car works as well as letting the state airline, Interflug, and the Pentacon camera works collapse. Cuts by 50 per cent of the workforce at the giant Buna and Leuna chemicals complexes are now programmed, and the shipbuilding and optical branches face planned job losses of more than half. Finally, there is no shortage of assessments which postulate the survival of a mere rump of the original jobs: an internal Finance Ministry study cited by *Der Spiegel* (16/1991, 126) forecasts that only 20 per cent of the original jobs will remain. This is very far from the conclusions reached by studies prepared at the time of monetary union, which postulated that the terms were not greatly onerous for the competitiveness of East German industry (DIW, 20/1990; MRDB, July 1990)!

TABLE 15.2   *Employment structure in Eastern Germany*

	Mid-1989 (%)	1991:Q1 (%)
Agriculture, forestry	10.8	8.44
Mining, energy, manufacturing	43.1	36.79
Contruction	6.6	5.33
Distribution	10.3	8.16
Transport	6.0	7.88
Public services	(23.2)	21.65
Private services	–	11.75

Sources:
Statitisches Jahrbuch der DDR; DTW, *Wochenbericht* (30/1991).

Labour Market Policy

The federal government's actions to remedy at least part of this forbidding employment situation in Eastern Germany can be grouped under the three broad sub-areas of labour market policy. 'Structural policy' encompasses direct intervention using public industries or, more frequently, the indirect means of financial incentive programmes to influence the supply of jobs in an area or branch of industry. In the present context, therefore, the Treuhandanstalt and the '*Gemeinschaftswerk Aufschwung Ost*' regional aid package serve this purpose, although at least five public budgets have transferred funds of an estimated DM 165 billion in 1991 to support activity and consumption in the East. Secondly, wage policy and labour market regulation at the aggregate level seek internal economic balance, namely, the optimal level of employment consistent with price stability. Here the territorial authorities in Germany are negotiating partners only in the wage-setting of their own employees, free wage-setting having the status of a constitutional principle in

Germany. However, in terms of regulatıon, the Kohl government has been active in promoting 'supply-side' reforms designed to promote greater flexibility in the labour market. As a third policy area, also one of direct intervention, the federal government, through the agency of the Federal Labour Office, promotes the supply of trained labour using the instruments of the *Arbeitsförderungsgesetz* and *Beschäftigungsförderungsgesetz* legislation. There is provision here also for short-term employment creation programmes.

Each of these policy areas is discussed below, but let it first be said that the federal government, alarmed at the unfolding magnitude of the problem, has been essentially reactive in its approach to these labour market issues. Chancellor Kohl's coalition government consistently professed great optimism, throughout the succession of election campaigns during 1990, that market forces, and the strength of West German firms' investment efforts, would provide a timely and sound basis for rapid rebirth in the east. 'Defeatism' was the charge laid at the SPD opposition, which consistently warned of the danger to output in the East, as well as to federal finances, of rushed unification.

When the Treuhandanstalt first announced major plant closures in the Autumn of 1990, when the magnitude of short-time working (often with zero output) and delays in inward investment became apparent, policy adjustments and palliatives came under consideration. In the Spring of 1991, in response to street demonstrations over unemployment and closures, the federal government announced three major policy innovations: in March, the Treuhandanstalt was enjoined to take regional and social issues more explicitly into consideration in its restructuring and closure programmes, which effectively gave Eastern Länder a right of veto over major plant closures. Almost concurrently, the '*Gemeinschaftswerk Aufschwung Ost*' programme of enhanced regional development assistance was announced. Finally, legislative changes were introduced to resolve in the short term the conflict of interests over property rights between restitution to a previous owner and sale to a new investor, which had had such a baleful effect on inward investment. As we shall see, these programmes, aimed at creating long-term employment, can exert a beneficial effect only after some delay. In the short term, the pressure is for wage support (short-time working assistance was extended a second time from July to December 1991) in its various guises. In addition to the very heavy burden for public finances which this creates, it can also harm investment and delay adoption of market principles.

Structural Policy

In its Monthly Report of March 1991, the Bundesbank discussed the great number and range of programmes for the restructuring and integration of the new German Länder. The Federal Posts and Railways budgets, for example, bore considerable costs of infrastructure renewal (and the associated construction employment), while the German Unity Fund, a 'shadow' budget endowed with DM 100 billion to 1994, had among its tasks support to local authority budgets in Eastern Germany, which will finance much of the rehabilitation of the housing stock and of social and health facilities. Of prime interest in their direct employment impacts, however, are the operations of the Treuhandanstalt and the Aufschwung Ost programme (see also, Chapter 10 in this volume).

When first created as a holding company of state enterprises under the Modrow government in early 1990, the Treuhandanstalt grouped together 9000 businesses, and at the time of union, it had 8000, employing 4 million people. Through its operations from the second half of 1990, to break up the monopoly combines (often creating thereby many medium-sized firms), to restructure, privatise or close, and so create a competitive productive sector, its total workforce fell to 3.4 million at the end of 1990. By September 1991, its number of businesses had been reduced to 6000 approximately, and the fall in employees was forecast to go down to 1.7 million by the end of 1991 (IAB, 1991). The Treuhandanstalt took its present organisational structure in January 1991, which also granted minimum code-termination rights (since it is not a public company) to four trade union representatives on its administrative council. The change in strategy in March 1991 away from privatisation and closure to an emphasis on restructuring and the financial recovery of enterprises brought an enhanced role for union and Land representatives. 'Structural, industrial and labour market aspects' were henceforth to be considered before a plant's future was decided. The Länder, responsible for the regional and social consequences of closures, formed Economic Councils, which had to be given early information of closure proposals, and so what one now sees is a corporate system of cooperation between the Treuhandanstalt, Länder, unions and local authorities, whose aim is to take the regional employment interest directly into account.

If one takes the view that it was wholly unrealistic for the productive sector in Eastern Germany to adopt market structures and behaviour in a short time-scale, and that the forced closure of plant which might achieve financial viability in the longer term is economically and socially wasteful, then this shift in priorities is to be welcomed. Plants in heavy industrial sectors remain afloat on the basis of huge subsidies, but at least have avoided full closure (Christ, 1991). Yet the costs of such commitments appear daunting. The Treuhandanstalt probably incurred net losses of DM 21 billion in 1991 after privatisation sales of about DM 14 billion. It retains huge overmanning (though, as discussed below, the surplus manpower may be shifted to job creation schemes) and, if it is to invest to a degree sufficient to equip each worker at the average level for manufacturing in West Germany, then DM 300 million in investment will be needed. According to inside information, the financial needs of the Treuhandanstalt enterprises have been estimated by the federal government at DM 400 billion by the year 2000, net of asset sales (Christ, 1991).

Private investment flows into Eastern Germany have been slow (see Chapter 10). In order to encourage the essential contribution by private capital to economic restructuring, an enlarged package of measures was announced on 8 March 1991 which buttresses the existing regional development programmes of federal and Land governments (the 'Gemeinschaftsaufgabe: Verbesserung der regionalen Wirtschaftsstruktur'). The new package entitled 'Gemeinschaftswerk Aufschwung Ost' (Joint project for Eastern recovery) encompassed a DM 24 billion two-year budget with a threefold purpose: payments to local authorities for essential repairs to schools, hospitals and dwellings; an expansion of job creation schemes (see below); and an expansion of investment incentives. These latter are detailed by Ragnitz (1991) and MRDB (March 1991), but it is clear that private investors now have to pay less than half of the investment cost in the first year. Meanwhile the attractiveness of this huge development area, compared with the old Länder, is increased with the announcement of the phased withdrawal of regional aid to West Berlin and the old inner-German border areas.

Wage Harmonisation, Differentiation and Subsidisation

As discussed in Chapter 10, the terms of German monetary union, in permitting the translation of current transactions (and therefore of wages and prices) at 1:1, represented in practice a much more formidable challenge to the East's competitiveness than was realised at the time. Concerning subsequent wage adjustment, in part to the new all-German price level and to the Western income tax and social insurance systems, it was the view in official circles that wage differentiation would proceed apace, reflecting the market reality of relative productivity growth and relative demand for products. To expect East Germany to maintain its absolute advantage as a low wage economy, competing with Southern Europe, would be inappropriate not least because high investment levels would generate a rapid rise in productivity levels and therefore of labour demand. In contrast to this expected wage differentiation process, the adoption of West German union representation and negotiating procedures has led to a programmed wage harmonisation, and so raises the prospect of a *'Mezzogiorno* effect' in the eyes of market economists (see Chapter 10 in this volume). Here, long-term structural unemployment (and substantial outmigration) will prevail because inappropriately high production cost structures (wage, social insurance and job protection) have been imposed on a lower-productivity workforce. Such critics therefore foresee in Eastern Germany an accelerated rate of job losses through closures, missed opportunities for rationalisation and job retention, failing inward investment and an inappropriately high level of capital intensity, given the labour abundance (Härtel, 1991).

There can be little doubt that Western German employers and unions have sought to emasculate the potential competitive challenge of the East by imposing there a Western level of production costs. The arguments which have been marshalled in favour of wage harmonisation (other than 'social justice') focus on staunching the migration flow, raising purchasing power there (and therefore employment), compensation for tax increases and subsidy removal, and the 'efficiency' wage (Donges, 1991). It is of course incontrovertible that many sections of the East German population have faced the loss of familiar organisational structures and social identity, and that pensioners, single parents and the older, potentially unemployed must be facing an uncertain future with considerable anxiety. Putting a floor under their real incomes by compensating wage rises is one approach, but by raising the cost of labour, it may generate job losses as well as a wage–price spiral. In practice, these claims for upward wage revisions are really claims for an appropriate social policy, since economically the arguments are poorly founded:

- Wage differentiation, targeted on the younger, skilled and potentially mobile worker, offers more effectiveness than a generalised wage increase for all, which by raising the level of unemployment, must speed outmigration.
- A full wage compensation for price increases generates an inflationary spiral: partial compensation is all that can be promised.
- The raising of purchasing power by raising wages does not raise real incomes because of the rise in the price level.

- Wage compensation for tax increases thwarts government decisions over redistribution of income.
- Generalised wage increases are a poorly-targeted incentive to efficiency.

Of course, the phased harmonisation of wage rates will not by 1994 thereby achieve harmonisation of effective wages, rather it is thought that engineering workers in the East, for example, will gain effective wages 20 per cent lower than their Western counterparts if working-time differences, holiday entitlement and fringe benefits are included. One might add that the impact of such agreements will also be ameliorated to the extent that small- and medium-sized companies refuse membership of their employers' association, and so escape the legal requirement to pay the negotiated wage contract rate.

Liberal economists have of course grasped this opportunity to point out the high costs in terms of unemployment and budget deficits, which will result if wage rates in the East, like any other price, do not adjust to reflect the huge excess supply of labour. Both Donges (1991) and Härtel (1991) point to the need for much greater differentiation in wage rates, by firm, sector and region, to reflect relative variations in productivity, and therefore the demand for labour. In doing so, they take up the proposals of the Deregulation Commission (Reports I and II, 1990 and 1991) and of the Committee of Expert Advisers to the Federal Economics Ministry (13, 14 July 1991) concerning a liberalisation of the German labour market. Such proposals merely restate longstanding liberal economic criticisms of the inflexibilities in German wage-setting and in recruitment–redundancy provisions. Such criticisms focus on the breadth of coverage of the negotiated wage contract, and the narrow skill and geographical differentials provided in it; but employment law also reduces speed of adjustment by costly and cumbersome redundancy provisions, and by forbidding private employment agencies from acting as intermediaries.

In the case of one legal provision of particular interest to Eastern German employers and investors, namely Para. 613a of the BGB (Civil Code), which insists that in the case of a takeover the legal responsibilities of the previous employer to its workforce are assumed in their entirety by the purchaser, the federal government is considering a relaxation for East Germany. It will be of no surprise that market liberals favour the introduction in Eastern Germany of exceptions to this German system of close labour market regulation, by favouring an enterprise-level wage contract with provision to pay less than national rates, performance-related and profit-related pay, the greater application of fixed-term employment contracts, the establishment of private employment agencies, and a relaxation of Para. 613a (Donges, 1991).

Others, who accept that wage differentiation on this scale is incapable of achievement in German conditions within any acceptable time frame, and who accept that wage differentials of the magnitude required to reflect relative productivity are simply impossible in a unified labour market, have favoured wage subsidies to employers so as to raise the demand for labour. Household income and labour cost to firms are thereby separated. Typical of such proposals are those by Akerlof *et al.* (1991) and Engels (1991):

- Akerlof *et al.* estimated the effects of the economic and monetary union on each of 116 East German combines, using GDR planning data. On the basis of DM wage levels pertaining in October 1990, they estimated that only 8.2 per cent of manufacturing jobs in enterprises belonging to the Treuhandanstalt could survive. Clearly the proportion is now lower, given the intervening wage inflation. Were, however, wage subsidies of 50 per cent to be paid, then 36.6 per cent of jobs might be saved, and 77 per cent of jobs saved at a three-quarters subsidy level. Akerlof *et al.* are conscious of the need to avoid unions' building the subsidy into their wage claims, and so postulate two approaches to subsidisation: either the subsidy rate varies in direct relation to the wage gap between East and West, so favouring the maintenance of a gap, or the subsidy be fixed in time and overall amount so that proportionately less is paid as the number of jobs expands or as wage inflation proceeds.
- Engels suggested a labour subsidy which was degressive over time, and would be paid according to the relationship of value-added in the East to the Western German wage contract rate. Were this relation zero (i.e. zero value-added) then 68 per cent of the wage contract rate would be paid as a subsidy (exactly as under the Arbeitsförderungsgesetz, see below). Were the relation to reach 110 per cent then no further wage subsidy would be needed.

Elegant though these formulations are, and while manifold subsidies are already paid in Eastern Germany, it remains the case that such labour subsidies are a very costly and undifferentiated instrument. By applying to all labour, the charge to the public budget may be heavy indeed, having interest rate and exchange rate effects: the immediate need is to prevent only the most mobile and highly-qualified from migrating. Incentive-based pay would surely achieve this at a fraction of the cost. A further drawback of such schemes lies in the fact that, by raising household incomes to West German levels, this will feed into asset prices (housing and land) and into the wages of those offering local services, so exacerbating the price spiral. A policy which deliberately delayed rent, transport and domestic fuel price rises might be more cost-effective as it would raise real incomes while allowing a nominal wage gap to remain.

Job Creation, Retraining and Redeployment

The federal government appears largely to have taken a reactive stance, as the true scale of the restructuring needed, and the employment challenge, unfolded. To accompany the measures taken in March 1991 to buttress the collapsing enterprise sector and to attract inward investment, the federal government announced a substantial expansion in job creation and retraining assistance, in anticipation of a wave of unemployment following the ending of the short-time working and job protection agreements at the end of June. In the event, the short-time working provisions were extended to the end of 1991. The Arbeitsförderungsgesetz (AFG) (Work Promotion Act), last modified in 1986, specifies the labour market instruments which can be applied in Germany for the retraining and redeployment of workers unemployed or threatened with redundancy; in addition, the law provides for job creation measures. Financial assistance takes the form of wage-related payments to the trainee, and these are borne by the Federal Labour Office's budget, any deficit thereby falling to the federal government. Typically, an unemployed worker could receive training assistance for one year at between 63 and 68 per cent of the relevant wage contract rate or, if still in employment, could be trained for 10 per cent of his working time, the salary cost being borne by the Labour Office. Job creation measures provided work for normally one year for an unemployed person, at these wage-related rates, and the work created had to meet strict criteria, so as not to pose a subsidised threat to firms in the competitive economy. Typically, organised in association with a local authority or with a large employer in structural decline, a programme would have to create tasks which were additional to those normally undertaken by the authority, and would have to be of general public utility. Clearly, many environmental improvements, community care, creation of leisure areas, and demolition of closed factories, would come within this remit. As we shall see, in spite of the fact that the terms of these labour market instruments have been considerably relaxed in Eastern Germany, much of the debate has focused on the unsuitability of the AFG law to a situation of mass unemployment, while others see it as a major threat to the emergence of a thriving entrepreneurial sector there.

That the unfolding employment crisis in the East was gravely underestimated is evidenced from the fact that, at the outset, the Federal Labour Office budgeted for only 130,000 job-creation places in the East. This was later raised to 285,000 (see Table 15.3) and a further 120,000 were added, paid for by the federal budget at a cost of DM 2.5 billion. The extra federal subvention for 1992 was estimated at DM 3 billion. The instruments of the AFG law grant more favourable conditions in the new Länder: job-creation measures may last two years per individual, and if a permanent job is being created, up to three years; up to 100 per cent of the wage rate may be borne; retrainees in employment may spend 20 per cent of their working time in publicly-financed training; grants and loans from federal ERP (European Recovery Programme) funds may be used to cover 100 per cent of the fixed and working capital costs of a job-creation or training programme; the requirement that recipients (other than retrainees in employment) be unemployed and also in receipt of unemployment benefit is relaxed.

TABLE 15.3   *Key targets for the labour market policy intruments of the Arbeitsförderungsgesetz (AFG) in 1991 (no. of assisted persons in a yearly average)*

	West	East	Total
Training, retraining, further training	466900	445800	912700
Rehabilitation	185220	47000	232220
Entering employment aid	366500	101000	467500
Job creation (of which: Gemeinshaftwerk Aufschwung Ost)	101500	285000 (150000)	386500
Short-time	65000	1370000	1435000
Language courses for ethnic German immig.			90400
Total (exclud, lang.)	1185120	2248800	3433920

Source:
Bundesanstalt für Arbeit.

It was clear that the government placed great emphasis on job-creation schemes as having the most immediate impact on employment, while it also saw retraining for those in post as a useful secondary measure. So-called 'employment enterprises' (*Beschäfti-*

gungsgesellschaften) which had been used in exceptional circumstances in the SPD governed Länder of the West, such as in the run-
down of the Saar steel industry or in coalmining areas, were seen as
a further option. They were not countenanced, though, to anything
like the extent to which they have now been used. The basic idea of
these 'employment enterprises' is that they should offer the chance
to the potentially unemployed to continue working and to be
retrained in their home environment.

Criticisms from the trade union side (Engelen-Kefer, 1991) of the
government's employment policy focus on poor organisation, as well
as on the inappropriateness of the AFG instruments. Apart from
delay, the government is accused of misjudging the financial crisis of
territorial authorities in the East, their poor administrative ability,
and the lack in particular of trained personnel to coordinate and
initiate schemes drawing on a variety of development assistance
programmes. Since it falls to local authorities to play a major role
in job-creation schemes, including borrowing to help finance them,
these are indeed critical shortcomings. The terms of the job-creation
schemes as specified in the AFG law have also attracted considerable
criticism for their unworkability: how can the tasks fulfilled be
'additional' and of general utility (including non-profit making) when
the public authorities in the East have inherited responsibilities in
infrastructure, housing and public service provision on an unim-
agined scale? However, as will be seen, in practice job-creation
schemes seem to have been introduced for a wide range of purposes
and tasks, many of which would normally be expected to be undertaken by private enterprises. More generally, it has to be said that
such labour market measures offer only short-term assistance, and
to individuals, their purpose is not to create long-term jobs which
would survive in a competitive market.

It is around the role of '*Beschäftigungsgesellschaften*' ('employment enterprises') that the recent debate has crystallised. It is true
that from April 1991, the federal government did contemplate a
much more active role for these organisations in avoiding a mass of
unemployed and inactive workers: the trade unions and, seemingly,
the population in the East, attribute a far more ambitious role to
them in absorbing potential unemployment and promoting an interventionist employment policy. An 'employment enterprise' is a
pseudo-firm which employs otherwise unemployed workers for a
wide variety of tasks, of which training to meet future labour market
requirements was clearly the prime task in the eyes of the founders.
Its financing derives from the AFG provisions previously described,
and other related labour market instruments have been called upon,
such as the 75 per cent wage subsidy for two years for firms employ-

ing the longer-term unemployed, and aid for the employment of someone previously unemployed to replace an early retiree. In other words, 'employment enterprises' draw on the full battery of labour market programmes by offering to the otherwise unemployed full-time employment at the full wage contract rate. Here lies the rub, for instead of paying up to two-thirds of the rate, as under a job-creation or training measure, these enterprises pay 100 per cent of the rate negotiated in national wage agreements. In addition, the recipient is in paid employment for two years, and when that expires, will then benefit in most cases from the full length of unemployment benefit and social assistance for up to two years, earnings-related. In the eyes of its detractors, therefore, it is a mechanism for maintaining income growth in the East, at taxpayers' and social insurance contributors' expense. It clearly also stops the East from undercutting wage rates in the West.

In the first half of 1991, there were many examples of Treuhandanstalt firms forming 'employment enterprises', where full or partial closure of the plant was envisaged, and so making the termination of employment socially tolerable. In the interim, such transferred employees could, for example, clear the obsolescent plant and prepare an industrial estate, or they might commence an environmental clean-up. The biggest such examples relate to the chemical industry:

- The demolition of the Riesa steelworks, and the associated environmental improvements employed 600 workers in an employment enterprise; other East German steel plants have adopted this model.
- The Bitterfeld Training and Planning Company was created to eliminate the catastrophic soil and water pollution in the area. 12,000 unemployed workers are expected in the medium term to work on this project, which alone has ordered DM 340 million of equipment. Today there are about 300 such 'employment enterprises' (*Wirtschaftswoche*, 42/1991, p. 66).

Negotiations between the trade unions and the Treuhandanstalt headquarters over the future role of 'employment enterprises' reached a crisis point in June 1991, as it became clear that the privatisation and financial health objectives of the Treuhandanstalt clashed with the ambitious, interventionist aims of the unions. To avoid mass redundancies, when short-time working provisions were due to expire at the end of June, the unions (especially IG Metall) wished that employees affected be transferred, without termination of employment, to such an 'enterprise', whose major shareholder would remain the Treuhandanstalt, and in which the unions would exercise codetermination rights. Covering several hundred thousand employees, these arrangements would act as the bridge to a later permanent post once more – all the more so if such enterprises could draw on programme aid from the Federal Research and Technology Ministry for forward-looking training in the skills of the future. The 'employment enterprises' should be nominated 'manufacturing and technology centres' for this purpose (Meyer, 1991). Other commentators saw the framework for new industrial structures in a coalition between 'employment enterprises', the Treuhandanstalt and the Länder (Ullmer, 1991).

The framework agreement finally agreed between the unions, Eastern Länder and Treuhandanstalt on 17 July 1991 represented a compromise which IG Metall could accept only with the greatest reluctance. At the centre of debate was the role of the Treuhandanstalt, and the employment contract position of the recipients. The outcome allowed the Treuhandanstalt to take a 10 per cent stake in the umbrella organisations at East German and regional levels, and its enterprises could supply plant, machinery and premises, but it would not be a participant in the 'employment enterprises' themselves. These were now designated 'Gesellschaften für Arbeitsförderung, Beschäftigung und Strukturentwicklung' (ABS). Equally, when Treuhandanstalt employees were transferred to an ABS, their previous employment contract was therefore terminated, which clarified·the rights and obligations of the parties concerned. In particular, this prevented a continuing responsibility of the Treuhandanstalt for its ex-workforce well into the future.

As an exercise in crisis management, and to make profound structural change socially tolerable, this outcome may be considered appropriate. It also has ancillary advantages that Treuhandanstalt enterprises may divest themselves of surplus labour and so be prepared for sale, while at the same time this surplus labour can be retrained, rather than retained under short-time working provisions with little or no work to do. However, key criticisms by market economists of the use of the ABS focus on their anti-competitive role, which may prevent the emergence in the East of a class of entrepreneurs and of a raft of small firms. By paying the full wage contract rate, the ABS pay well above that of a normal job-creation scheme, and are said in cases to pay 50 per cent more than small firms there are able to pay. They then prevent a flow of labour into small firms: likewise, they can harm the growth of small firms, because over many tasks they compete (though subsidised) with them for contracts.

This mechanism clearly perpetuates for up to two years the job protection which Easterners have traditionally enjoyed. It serves as a buffer between labour-shedding enterprises and unemployment. One may ask, however, whether it prevents East Germany from operating as a lower-wage economy (since it sustains the national wage level), and whether it delays even further the operation of competitive market mechanisms in the East. Clearly, such ABS accomplish many socially useful tasks and one assumes that the training does offer some perspective for the future. The cost falls directly to the Federal Labour Office and federal government, while indirectly the economic cost is one of a delay in labour market adjustment.

The Policy Conundrum

The collapse of activity and the demand for labour in Eastern Germany does of course have its roots in the abrupt ending of COMECON and the rapidity and terms of economic and monetary union with the West. But the associated social union of two states of such different economic structure and productivity poses a continuing and highly costly policy conundrum. For, if social union entails the achievement of a broad uniformity of living standards in a short time-scale, does this necessarily mean wage rate uniformity, with its highly damaging effects on jobs and investment? Could not an acceptable approximation of post-tax real incomes in the two halves of Germany be achieved by subsidisation in some other form than by wage subsidy, perhaps by holding down rents and transport fares? Given that the adjustment to a market economy, ultimately by the restructuring of Treuhandanstalt enterprises into competitive firms and by inward investment, will take far longer than the optimistic pronouncements of coalition politicians foresaw, then political management of the threatening job losses in the East is obviously needed. But one cannot deny that many of the mechanisms presently in place serve to delay the adjustment to market relations while at the same time obstructing the emergence of new firms. For the defensive, wage equalisation strategies which Western trade unions and employers have applied to the East remain in force even as the mass of surplus labour is transferred to a raft of labour market programmes, designed to make restructuring socially tolerable. If the wages at which the unemployed will accept work never fall below the West German level, from where will the supply of new jobs, in vast numbers, come? Proponents of continued subsidisation must acknowledge that this harms firms in the competitive sector, while posing public debt and interest rate burdens whose ramifications feed through exchange rates into an international deflation.

PART FIVE

Ideology and Identity

16

Political Ideology

PETER PULZER

The Revival of Ideological Conflict

Writing an introduction to Walter Laqueur's history of the German Youth Movement in 1962, Richard Crossman, future Labour cabinet minister and himself no mean ideologue, observed:

> There are many complaints that youth in the Federal Republic is material-
> istic, egotistical and unwilling to accept any civic or political responsi-
> bilities. In themselves these characteristics are unattractive. But in the
> case of Germany they may well be a stage on the road to normality. A
> healthy democracy is impossible without a healthy scepticism, constantly
> corroding the adulation of leaders and uncritical acceptance of ideology
> on which totalitarian rule depends (Laqueur, 1972, xxii).

It reminded one of the mythical German student of the reconstruction period who, when asked which two books had influenced him
most, replied: his father's cheque book and his mother's cookery
book. A few years later a seminal book, Ralf Dahrendorf's *Society
and Democracy in Germany*, first published in 1965, argued that the
road to normality had been largely completed. Thanks to the pattern
of post-war economic development, thanks also to Hitler's destruction of many of the traditional elites, Germans had abandoned their
'special path', the *Sonderweg* that had diverted them from evolving
as a normal liberal society:

> The chances of liberal democracy in a German society have never been
> as great as they are in the German Federal Republic . . . authoritarianism
> of the traditional kind has become impossible in German society (Dahren-
> dorf, 1968, 442, 438).

Scarcely was the ink dry on this verdict than its opposite was forcibly asserted. Ideological offensives generally arise out of a combination of causes. They need the exhaustion of an older set of ideas, the retirement of a generation of opinion-leaders, perhaps an external impulse. They also need spectacular events to detonate public receptivity to what would otherwise remain obscure pamphlets or esoteric café debates. Only then can we speak of ideas whose time has come. The reply to Dahrendorf, in effect if not in intention, came in 1966 from Karl Jaspers, a distinguished philosopher and veteran nonconformist. The occasion was the prospect of a Great Coalition between Social and Christian Democrats and speculation that this, or another government would pass emergency legislation to acquire special powers in the event of war or an international crisis. But his challenge to the complacency of his fellow citizens, *Wohin treibt die Bundesrepublik?* was clearly the outcome of long reflection. For Jaspers, who remembered the Weimar Republic and the Empire, nothing of substance had changed since 1945. The Federal Republic's rulers, like their predecessors, wanted to exclude the citizen from the political process:

> We see the possible path: from the party oligarchy to the authoritarian state; from the authoritarian state to dictatorship; from dictatorship to war (Jaspers, 1966, 174).

Jaspers's denunciation of West German politics was not an expression of specific discontents. He did not simply complain that institutions failed to live up to the expectations placed in them, or that otherwise honourable politicians had pursued mistaken policies. On the contrary, despite its parliamentary form of government, 'the structure of our state rests on fear of the people, of distrust of the people' (Jaspers, 1966, 167). The critique is unqualified and unconditional. It was the first example of a new genre that was to become commonplae in the following twenty years, the *Totalkritik*, the fundamental rejection of everything the Federal Republic stood for:

> The turn-around of the Federal Republic's policies, whether in foreign or domestic policy, cannot come about on this or that special issue. If it is to be successful it must happen in its entirety (Jaspers, 1966, 258).

In other words: Everything must change before anything can change.

Totalkritik is distinguished by style as well as substance. It is by definition ideological, since it presupposes an all-explanatory model of what is wrong and an all-encompassing model of what ought to be. Beyond that it can cover an almost infinite range of utopias. Jaspers's own was that of an idealised liberal democracy. But the apocalyptic tone and the all-or-nothing prescription were a common feature of the re-ideologisation of West German politics in the late 1960s.

The Great Coalition of 1966–9, which seemed to symbolise the ultimate stage in the post-war West German consensus, and the emergency legislation duly passed in 1968 (which did no more than transfer to the federal government powers hitherto exercised by the allied military authorities), were not the only factors causing many to question the achievements of the post-war period. Some of these were peculiar to Germany, others world-wide. There were large-scale trials of concentration camp guards in 1965, which publicised in detail what many had only vaguely known, and which added to the distrust that the post-war generation had of their parents. There was the war in Vietnam, tacitly supported by the West German government, which changed the image of America for many: the great protector, the home of the New Deal and author of the Marshall Plan, became the great oppressor. There was the wave of the 'New Politics', the campus revolt that spread across the United States from Berkeley to Harvard, in response not only to the Vietnam war but to the sudden expansion of higher education. Universities doubled and tripled in size, without changing their structures or adapting to first-generation students who had not imbibed the traditional academic ethos from their families. This explosion, common to America and France, to Britain and Germany was more intense in Germany, and the fall-out more extensive, because the intergenerational divide was deeper and the post-war ideological vacuum was more in evidence.

The Quality of Political Life

One did not have to accept Jaspers' *Totalkritik* to appreciate that post-war West Germany was somewhat defective in the quality of its political life. To be sure, Bonn was not Weimar (Allemann, 1956). Government was stable, cabinets did not collapse in crisis, there were no major parties determined to overthrow the system, no generals, judges or civil servants who were secretly – or openly – disloyal. Political violence was virtually unknown. But these were negative virtues. The men who had led Germans out of the rubble and ashes of Year Zero were foxes, not lions. Konrad Adenauer and Kurt Schumacher, Jakob Kaiser and Theodor Heuss were the generation that had failed to stop Hitler. All were burnt children who knew what the fire was like. Their vision after 1945 was one of disaster-avoidance, not a new heaven and a new earth.

The political consensus that emerged in these years was liberal—conservative: capitalist with a social conscience. Above all, it was anti-Communist. With the collapse of the Third Reich and the arrival of the Red Army on the Elbe, it was the present, not the past tyranny that posed the threat. It did so especially for the Churches which were, however undeservedly, the chief repositories of moral authority after 1945. They saw National Socialism not as a counter-revolutionary movement or a capitalist conspiracy, but as the perversion of secular and materialist ideas, a bastard child of the French Revolution. For Cardinal Frings, Archbishop of Cologne and one of the main patrons of a new, inter-confessional Christian Democratic Union, 'the enemy stands on the left, that is in the camp of the materialist *Weltanschauung*' (Schmidt, 1987, 240).

Such a development was a grave disappointment to re-emergent forces of the Left, who had assumed that they would be the heirs of any revulsion against the Third Reich and the beneficiaries of the proletarianisation of the German people after the collapse. Yet the Left, too, were burnt children; they shared the new-born Right's suspicion of popular sovereignty, or at least of their fellow-citizens' ability to exercise it. They, too, saw political life as St Augustine had done, in terms of the burden of Original Sin. It was not some sceptical Catholic conservative but Georg-August Zinn, Social Democratic Prime Minister of Hesse, who told the Parliamentary Council in the debates on the Basic Law: 'We cannot afford to rely on the masses' (Merkl, 1963, 81). In any case any Social Democrat hopes of a fruitful anti-fascist alliance with the Communists were soon dashed by the forcible amalgamation of the two workers' parties in the Soviet zone into the Socialist Unity Party (SED) and the rapid establishment of a single-party dictatorship there. The Social Democrats, like the Christian Democrats, in the end committed themselves to a pro-Western orientation, even if not at first to its military implications. The ideological spectrum in the infant Federal Republic was thus further narrowed.

The early years of West German politics, both before and after the formation of the Federal Republic, were not free from political polarisation. Industrial relations were far from peaceful and in the mid-1950s there was a major confrontation on the question of German rearmament within the framework of Western integration. Petitions and mass demonstrations, supported by the trade unions and parts of the Evangelical Church under the slogan *Kampf gegen den Atomtod* ('struggle against nuclear death') were the last great challenge to the consensus that Adenauer had set out to create. That consensus became complete in 1959 at the SPD's Bad Godesberg conference, at which the Social Democrats finally accepted Western economic integration and the mixed economy and in 1960 military integration with the West. They abandoned Marxism as the sole inspiration of their programme, claiming to be rooted instead in Christian ethics, humanism and classical philosophy. Practice had in any case preceded proclaimed principle for some years. In economic matters, consensus had, if anything, arrived earlier and gone further still. The unified post-war trade union federation, the DGB, suprapartisan but *de facto* closer to the Social Democrats than to any other party, accepted, from the early 1950s onwards, a role of maximising its benefits from the re-established market economy. It fought for, and got, codetermination in heavy industry. But codetermination entailed the abandonment not only of nationalisation but of the class struggle. Indeed labour law imposes on works councils the obligation to maintain industrial peace (*'Friedenspflicht'*) as long as a contract remains in force (Markovits, 1986, 40, 44).

The Demand for Democratisation

It was this farewell to conflict, which in any case corresponded with deep-seated German desires for harmony in state and society, that most disturbed the new generation of critics. They saw a Germany that continued to be divided between rulers and ruled, between the few who decided and the many who accepted. Little seemed to have changed since Kurt Tucholsky had asserted in the 1920s that it was the ambition of every German to sit behind a counter and the fate of every German to stand in front of one. The watchword of all critics, whether radical or reformist, was therefore democratisation. For Willy Brandt, leader of the SPD, democracy needed 'to embrace the whole of social life' (Brandt, 1969). The social philosopher Jürgen Habermas, chief mentor but also critic of the new radical generation, defined 'the democratic form of will-formation' even more explicitly: it would enable decisions 'to derive from a consensus achieved in a discussion without domination' (Habermas, 1969, 127). When Brandt became Chancellor in September 1969 he announced that 'we are not at the end of our democracy, we are only just beginning' (von Beyme, 1979, 281). What all the critics had in common was the feeling that even if German constitutional life had now been democratised, German society had not been. And even where the critics agreed on the ends to be achieved, there was often conflict on means.

The demand for democratisation had three basic components.

First, the creation of the 'mature citizen' ('*mündiger Bürger*'), no longer deferential towards authority. Secondly, the creation of equality of opportunity, especially through educational reforms. Thirdly, the creation of greater tolerance for nonconformity and of a greater variety of 'social spaces', in which different life-styles could flourish. All of these any conscientious, liberal-minded person could agree with; all of it was consistent with the existing political order, as defined by the Basic Law. It was the realisation of at least some of these objectives that the Brandt government had in mind when the new Chancellor told his fellow-citizens to lose their fear of experimentation – a universally understood allusion to the CDU's 1950s election slogan 'No experiments'.

Some democratisers, however, wanted to go a great deal further. For them there could be no emancipation without the transformation, or indeed destruction, of the existing distribution of wealth and power. This presupposed both a radical critique of the existing state of affairs and a blue-print for the post-revolutionary order: in other words, a re-ideologisation of politics. Democratisation meant *knowing why* one needed to democratise. This call adopted the tone, if not the content, of Jaspers's *Totalkritik*.

In one form or another, the radical democratisers were Marxists. The revival of Marxism was the most important event in the ideological history of the Federal Republic in the late 1960s. Few of the Marxists of this period were orthodox. They disliked, and in many cases strongly opposed, the Communist regimes of Eastern Europe; indeed, one of the main figures of the Marxist revival, Rudi Dutschke, had grown up and studied in the GDR and had left for West Berlin to escape the stifling orthodoxy East of the Iron Curtain. Some were inspired by the Italian heterodox Marxist Antonio Gramsci, others by the Frankfurt School, founded before the war by Theodor Adorno and Max Horkheimer and whose leading post-war German representative was Jürgen Habermas. Many of them were influenced by Herbert Marcuse, a member of the Frankfurt School who had stayed in America and who argued that under modern capitalism the proletariat could no longer be expected to initiate a revolution; that task now fell to intellectuals, in particular to intellectual youth, i.e. students (Marcuse, 1969). This idea was very attractive to students. *Totalkritik* and total protest, in so far as it came from the Left, was largely the property of students broadly defined, ranging from the senior classes of *Gymnasien* to the younger generation of graduates, mostly in the arts and the social sciences and concentrated in teaching, the media and the social service professions.

The incubation period of this protest was quite long; its eruption sudden. Marxism had never quite disappeared from the West German ideological map. A handful of academics, of whom the most prominent was Wolfgang Abendroth of Marburg University, continued to proclaim themselves Marxists. But until the late 1960s they were a sect on the margin of public consciousness. What mobilised them was the coincidence of the Great Coalition, the emergency legislation and the war in Vietnam. What served as a flare to rally mass support was the killing of a student by the West Berlin police in 1967 in the wake of a demonstration against a visit by the Shah of Iran. Here was proof, for anyone that needed it, of the essential oppressiveness of the state, of the kid-glove fascism inherent in the existing order. As the scope of protest broadened and the causes of discontent multiplied, the bearers of the counter-politics became a movement, the extra-parliamentary opposition (*Ausserparlamentarische Opposition*, APO). If many of its followers had no clear ideological motivation, its leaders, inspirers and – as time went on, its cadres – undoubtedly had one. This was especially true of one of the movement's main journals, *konkret*, edited for a time by Ulrike Meinhof. All subsequent ideological developments in the Federal Republic are either an extension of the APO or a reaction to it.

The APO was the extreme, on occasion violent, expression of a much wider desire for change and reform in the Federal Republic which is to be explained as much by the passage of time and of generations as by specific events. The change was to take the form of the liberalisation of many public institutions and social processes, but also of a revised attitude to the partition of Germany and the acceptance that the GDR had come to stay. Symbolic of the shift in the climate of opinion was the changing of the guard in the FDP, which had been excluded from power by the formation of the Great Coalition. Under the leadership of Walter Scheel it transformed itself from a socially conservative, rather nationalistic party of nineteenth-century free enterprise and anti-clericalism into a vehicle for legal reform and non-collectivist middle-class social concern. The new programme was codified in the Freiburg Theses of 1971, which also talked of democratisation (Flach *et al.*, 1972, 62–4); the FDP showed its inclination early by contributing to the election of the Social Democrat Gustav Heinemann to the Federal Presidency in the spring of 1969, and by the speed with which Free Democrats and Social Democrats formed a government when their parties gained a narrow majority in the Bundestag election of September 1969. This alternation, the first transfer of power in the history of the Federal Republic, was in itself symbolic. The reconstruction generation handed over to those who had been liberated by the successes of the early years.

Unlike many of the APO, the new Brandt government believed that change could and should take place within the framework of the existing order. What they shared with the APO, indeed what held together the whole spectrum of reformers and radicals, was a revived political optimism: a recovery of the belief that progress was possible, that happiness could be enhanced and evil diminished by rational human beings acting in concert. The most clear-cut success of the Brandt government lay in foreign policy, with the revision and stabilisation of relations of Eastern Europe under the general cover of detente and known as Ostpolitik. Its domestic programme, like many schemes of reform, caused more frustration than satisfaction. For instance, ambitious schemes to let everyone have a say in large educational institutions could – and did – lead either to chaos or the domination of the participatory process by hard-line cliques. By the time Brandt resigned in 1974 the climate had once more begun to change, and faith in progress been shaken.

Doubt and Disillusionment

As before, the impulses were external as much as domestic. The oil shock of 1973 put an end to the assumption that continuing growth could supply a continuing expansion of social benefits. But even before that, doubts had begun to arise about the wisdom of giving priority to economic growth, without regard to the social, cultural and environmental consequences. The Club of Rome's report, *Limits to Growth* (1972), had a more profound effect in Germany in this respect than in many other developed countries. Brandt's successor, Helmut Schmidt, with his emphasis on managerial competence, signalled not only a response to the harsher international economic climate but a changed style in political expectations and solutions. As the era of reform came to a close, new ideological alignments emerged in the Federal Republic. These can be divided into three broad categories. The first may be called limited liberal disillusionment, the second augmented radicalism, the third revived conservatism. None of these has one recognised spokesman or a distinctively coherent programme. But most of those who have sought to influence West German opinion since the mid-1970s fit into one or other of these categories.

That the enthusiastically-launched reform programme of the Brandt government achieved less than it promised, or even its most moderate adherents expected, was widely acknowledged. Typical of the disappointed utopian was Winfried Vogt who confessed:

The abolition of the domination of man over man has not advanced one step . . . indeed the demand itself nowadays has an almost embarrassing, romantic-pathetic sound (Habermas, 1979, 381 ff.).

Perhaps more significant was the verdict of an eminent non-utopian, Ralf Dahrendorf, who saw a more profound ideological revolution at work than the rude awakening of a naïve dreamer. What the oil shock, the declining growth rate in the capitalist world and the escalating costs of Brandt's reforms signified was the 'end of the Social Democratic century'. Social Democracy was, for him, not the programme of a party, but the theme of an epoch. Its components were growth, equality, work, rationality, state and internationalism. But what happens, he asked, when growth cannot be achieved at an adequate rate; when the level of welfare can no longer be maintained; when a 'society based on work runs out of work'; when entirely new attitudes gain ground – the return of the sacred, or a new social ethic, let alone fear; when people no longer see the state as benevolent but as an expensive failure; when the hopes placed in international cooperation are reversed in the direction of smaller units? (Dahrendorf, 1983, 16–24). All of Dahrendorf's questions have proved timely, though the answers to them have not necessarily been: 'social democracy comes to an end'. The policies and priorities of Helmut Schmidt showed the limits that social democracy had reached, but also how firmly it remained entrenched. True, beating inflation now took priority over maintaining full employment and the expansion of the welfare state came to a halt. But the role of the state as adjudicator of social claims and provider of safety nets remained in West Germany, even with the departure of the SPD from office – certainly in comparison with some other Western countries. Indeed, with the unificiation of Germany in 1990 and the urgency of preventing the economic collapse in the Eastern Länder, the debate on the state versus the market has revived. Nevertheless, even if there was not a reversal of policy, a *Wende*, there was a change of emphasis; an end, if not of the social democratic century, then of progressivist euphoria, of that faith in the ability of politicians to increase human happiness that marked the year 1969.

The Environment, Terror and Peace

Beside this liberal disillusionment there arose an augmented radicalism. Some of the protest of the late 1960s had been absorbed by SPD and FDP and this had been one of Brandt's main aims. But the potential remained, as did the habit and style of *Totalkritik*.

What disappeared was the faith in progress. As the theme of protest moved from the emergency legislation and the Vietnam war to the environment and the arms race, as the student-dominated Marxist wave of protest ebbed, a mood of despair and the language of the apocalypse took over. The temporal coincidence of the Club of Rome's report and the oil shock reinforced the anti-capitalist suspicions of the protestors. Not only was capitalism threatening the very future of the universe, it was not even any longer capable of delivering on its own terms. As early as 1972 the growing number of local, ad hoc environmental citizens' groups formed themselves into a national federation, Bundesverband Bürgerinitiativen Umweltschutz. Some of its leaders were, or became, prominent in the SPD, though in the main the new body was the ancestor of the Green Party. Its ideologues, whether they leaned to the Left or the Right, shared a sense of imminent doom. For the ecologist Herbert Gruhl, who came from the CDU, 'the total war of man against the earth is in its last phase' (Gruhl, 1975, 219). For Erhard Eppler, the former acting president of the lay assembly of the German Evangelical Church and for many years chairman of the SPD in Baden-Württemberg, 'Mankind has arrived at frontiers of which it either knew nothing, or did not want to know anything in the two preceding centuries' (Eppler, 1979, 9). This was a long way from Rudi Dutschke's conviction of 1967 that mankind had never been closer to fulfilling the dream of the Garden of Eden (Dutschke, 1980, 13).

Though the mood of the *Totalkritiker* had changed, their prescription did not. They were guided, then as earlier, by Hegel's observation that once the realm of the imagination was revolutionised, the real world would not be able to resist for long. What was needed was a *Bewusstseinswandel*, a transformation of the imagination. Just as Rudi Dutschke claimed to have begun 'breaking through this false consciousness . . . by our enlightenment, by our provocations and mass actions' (Bergmann, 1968, 89), so the celebrated fantasy fiction writer Michael Ende, a German Tolkien, insisted that 'We must all, whether we want to or not, learn to think prophetically' (Eppler, 1981, 70).

While many graduates of the protest generation turned to apocalyptic words, some turned to apocalyptic deeds. One of the children of the age of political reawakening and its disappointments was terrorism. There were never more than a handful of terrorists, known to themselves as the *Rote Armee Fraktion* (Red Army Column, RAF) and to their enemies as the Baader–Meinhof gang, or more than a few thousand active supporters. The justification for the 'propaganda of the deed' is simple. It is the extreme means to the transformation of consciousness. It aims to stir the masses out of their apathy by demonstrating how vulnerable the existing order is, and how repressive when it responds. In West Germany the intensity of both the challenge and the response has to be seen in the light of the post-war history of the Republic. By the early 1970s it had been in existence for a mere quarter of a century. It was, according to the Basic Law, a provisional structure pending a peace treaty with a reunited Germany. Its relatively weak legitimacy, its heavy dependence on the existing geopolitical alignment, the uncertainty surrounding the future of Germans as a nation, all helped to make it an easy target. This weak legitimacy also explained the *grande peur* that gripped many West Germans as a small group of *kamikaze* activists succeeded in spectacularly kidnapping or murdering a series of highly-placed public figures with apparent impunity: first Jürgen Ponto of the Dresdner Bank, then Siegfried Buback, the chief Public Prosecutor and finally Hanns-Martin Schleyer, president of the West German employers' federation. The climax of their activities came in 1977, with the kidnapping and murder of Schleyer and the hijacking of a Lufthansa airliner with the aim of securing the release of imprisoned RAF members. With the storming of the airliner, the capture of Schleyer's murderers and the collective suicide of the imprisoned RAF leadership, the effectiveness of terrorism was at an end. Sporadic acts of violence have continued and new recruits lay claim to the RAF mantle, but they are a shadow of the original RAF.

Violence of another sort has characterised one of the other developments of the protest movement. From within the largely pacifist–anarchist consensus of the alternative politics there emerged a hard core of Marxist–Leninist fanatics of various leanings – Stalinist, Maoist, pro-Albanian – known collectively as the K-groups. Their numbers were negligible, but their tight and dedicated cadre organisation enabled them to infiltrate the loose and more broadly-based coalitions that existed on many campuses and that organised large-scale demonstrations against nuclear power installations, urban redevelopment schemes (often involving mass squats) and environmentally insensitive construction projects like the new runway at Frankfurt airport. The premeditated violence that occurs at the margin of most of these, culminating in the shooting of a policeman in 1987 results, as in no doubt intended, in governmental curtailments of the right to demonstrate.

The final great wave of protest was that of the 'peace movement'. Here, too, the conjuncture of intellectual antecedents and external political impulses was crucial. Anti-militarism was a natural reaction to the experience of the Third Reich and had already surfaced in the 1950s when a German contribution to NATO was first instituted.

To it was added the fear that in the event of a war between the superpowers Germany, East and West, would be the main battle-field. The more weapons were stationed in West Germany, the more vulnerable it seemed. In a more direct political sense the peace movement reflected disillusionment with the outcome of detente. From the mid-1970s on relations between the superpowers again deteriorated: the Soviet invasion of Afghanistan in 1979 and the election of President Reagan in 1980 seemed to confirm that. But the biggest single stimulant was the twin-track policy launched by Helmut Schmidt in 1979: NATO would install medium-range cruise and Pershing II missiles in Western Europe, including West Germany, unless the Soviet Union withdrew the SS-20 missiles that had recently been added to its arsenal.

The peace movement appealed to all those whose guiding principle since the 1960s had been distrust of established power-holders and official politics, enhanced by a dislike, amounting at times to a hatred, of America. It also appealed to those who were convinced that unless their prescription was accepted, imminent disaster would follow: 'The destruction of mankind has begun', Günter Grass wrote at the height of the anti-missile campaign (Grass, 1982). But it did not appeal to those alone. As in the 1950s, the hundreds of thousands who converged on Bonn in 1981 and 1983 were united by a fear that they were witnessing a mindless arms race in which neither of the antagonists was interested in dialogue. Like all the waves of protest this one subsided, too. The missiles were installed and the world did not come to an end. Indeed in 1987 they were dismantled by the mutual agreement of the Great Powers. Of all the legacies of twenty years of protest only one has maintained staying power: concern over the environment.

The ideologues of reform and *Totalkritik* have undoubtedly affected the political agenda of the Federal Republic. In particular, after 1974 the battle over conventional versus alternative politics, whether on nuclear power or defence policy, was carried on within the SPD and eventually led to the fall of the Schmidt government, as the Chancellor lost the confidence first of some of his own party and then of his FDP coalition partner. But the long-term stabilisation of a protest movement has also institutionalised it. There is now an established counter-culture, consisting largely of students, young graduates and the artistic–literary intelligentsia in all the larger urban centres. They are united by a rejection of the dominant social con-formity of the Federal Republic, its hierarchical organisations and the policies it has pursued since 1945; they are divided by whether to participate at all in conventional politics and on the question of violence. In the end, having begun to contest local elections with 'alternative lists' they formed themselves into a political party, the Greens. They entered the Bundestag in 1983, having previously succeeded in entering the majority of Landtage. Though their name implies an emphasis on ecology, they are best understood as a coalition of the radical urban Left, embracing neutralists, feminists, gay liberation groups, minorities and the discriminated against in general. Their failure to be elected to the first all-German Bundestag in 1990 was a setback, but not a defeat. As a counter-culture they survive.

The GDR: An Ideological Graveyard

While Marxism in its many guises enjoyed an intellectual revival in the Federal Republic and became the guiding principle of numerous opposition groups, it became the official ideology of the GDR. The consequence of that was, in the words of one of the GDR's foremost Socialist critics,

> . . . the dogmatic paralysis and distortion of its ideas, the transformation of Marxism into 'official opinion', whose content is determined from one instance to another by the authorities (Havemann, 1970, 181).

Though the GDR was founded under the aegis of the Soviet occupation authorities and was from the beginning dominated politically by the SED, it only gradually evolved into an orthodox Marxist–Leninist state. The 1949 constitution, like the Basic Law of the Federal Republic, claimed validity for the whole of Germany: 'Germany is an indivisible democratic Republic' (Article 1). It also guaranteed the economic freedom of the individual (Art 19) and the sanctity of private property (Art 22) (Weber, 1986, 156–63). The national anthem spoke of 'Germany, the united fatherland'; the division of Germany was blamed on the anti-Socialist politicians of the West.

One by one the regime of the GDR departed from these positions. From the early 1950s onwards industry and commerce were nationalised, from the late 1950s agriculture was collectivised. In August 1961 the Berlin Wall was built to stem the ever-growing flow of refugees and the GDR was physically sealed off from the West. The political and diplomatic isolation of the GDR came to an end in the course of Ostpolitik, when the two German states signed a treaty of mutual recognition (1972) and became members of the UN (1973). The rapprochement of the two German states was a political triumph for the GDR, but an ideological danger. Easier travel, better communications and the penetration by Western media threatened to undo the stabilisation that the Berlin Wall had made possible. The regime's defence against the new developments was *Abgrenzung* (demarcation). German unification was no longer the aim of the regime; the social and economic development of the GDR had advanced so far that they had created a new nation and a new citizenship, incompatible with that of the West. Where the 1968 constitution still talked of the GDR as 'a Socialist state of the German nation', that of 1974 spoke of 'a Socialist state of workers and peasants . . . under the leadership of the working class and its Marxist–Leninist party . . . indissolubly allied to the Union of Societ Socialist Republics' (Weber, 1986, 345–7).

Against this doctrine, or at any rate its implementation, there was from time to time dissent. The Evangelical Church expressed unease about educational policy and the liberalisation of divorce and abortion, but was careful to avoid an open breach with the regime. The most dangerous opposition came from the Marxists within the SED who, stirred by Krushchev's revelations in 1956, thought they knew better than the regime, but retained the assurance that scientific Socialism would one day triumph. The philosopher Wolfgang Harich, sentenced to a long term of imprisonment in 1957, had hoped that:

A radically de-Stalinised Eastern economic structure in the USSR and in the People's Democracies will in the course of further development gradually influence the capitalist West . . .

In a re-united Germany there must not be a capitalist restoration (Weber, 1986, 228–9).

The physicist Robert Havemann, for whom the crushing of the Prague Spring in 1968 was the last straw, aware that 'Marxism is suppressed precisely in those countries that claim to be based on it', nevertheless,

. . . affirmed this state as a decisive step forward in German history and regard[ed] it as that part of Germany that contributed decisively towards overcoming capitalism and fascism (Havemann, 1970, 198, 253, 301).

How many citizens of the GDR cared either for its 'official opinion' or its Socialist critics cannot now be established, though it is worth remembering that in its early years the state could still count on a stock of anti-fascist goodwill and a tradition of Socialist and Communist activism dating from before 1933. What developed in the course of time was an inner emigration, a protective shell of indifference towards the public realm, a *Nischengesellschaft*, a society of private corners, one in which sport, hobbies, family and personal friendships substituted for a vacuum of public norms.

Conservative Counter-attacks in the West

Protest creates counter-protest; change gives birth to reaction. It would be surprising if the rise of an ideological Left had not met with a response on the Right. For the first twenty years of its existence the Federal Republic was a conservative state, but the conservatism was implied, not explicit. It was a conservatism of social and moral values, not of the legitimacy of inherited structures. It could hardly have been otherwise: the traditional components of German conservatism – nationalist rhetoric and authoritarian government – were too discredited. Whatever the long-term hopes of German reunification, the basis of the Federal Republic's foundation was the separation of state and nation. This, too, affected the kind of conservatism that dominated the early Republic. Until 1945 Germany's foreign policy and Germany's sense of national mission had been related to the centre of Europe: Germany was not part of the barbaric East, but neither was it part of Western civilisation. After 1949 such an option was not available. The Federal Republic belonged to the West: economically, strategically, politically, intellectually. That was part of its definition. On the one hand that implied an instinctive anti-Communist consensus and nothing could be more welcome to conservatives. But it also meant a farewell to traditional German conservative suspicions of rationality, industrial society and parliamentary government – all the things that went with Western civilisation. Slowly, but from the 1950s onwards irrevocably, West Germany became conservative in a Western way: it became a stable, capitalist parliamentary republic.

To be sure, there was some nostalgia for other pasts, whether monarchical or totalitarian. There was a sizeable neo-Nazi wave in the early 1950s, associated with the Socialist Reich Party of Major Remer, who had personally helped to foil the plot against Hitler in 1944. There was another in the mid-1960s, associated with the National Democratic Party, at the time of the first serious post-war economic turn-down and the Great Coalition, i.e. in the absence of a legitimate opposition party. But none of these reappearances had any staying power and none had a political message that had not been heard before. The one item of continuity on the radical Right is a newspaper, the *Deutsche National- und Soldatenzeitung*, whose circulation of between 100,000 and 150,000 indicates the size of the hard core of this constituency. Full-blown Nazism is too discredited a creed to serve as a receptacle for anti-progressive sentiment, even at a time when the violent Left is on the offensive. And the politicisation of personal and social life that characterised National Socialism makes it an unsuitable refuge for those fleeing from similar ambitions proclaimed by the Left.

The first reaction to the reform wave was a response to its democratisation programme. In part this simply expressed the outrage of a number of academics, many of them formerly on the Left, at the chaos caused by student revolutionaries and their allies in various universities. They came together in the *Bund Freiheit der Wissenschaft* (League for the Freedom of Scholarship) to resist the assault on rationality in much of the revolutionary sloganising. Richard Loewenthal, one of the League's prominent SPD members and a veteran of Weimar, recognised the ambiguity of the Left's 'romantic relapse':

> Today's radicalisation in the commitment of left-wing intellectuals is not *only* a conscious counter-blow to the ideas of National Socialism . . . It is *also* the unconscious continuity of the intellectual currents that made these horrors possible . . . The old passions of anti-liberal and anti-Western romanticism [have] broken through again in an apparently rational and 'enlightened' guise (Löwenthal, 1970, 13–18).

It was also a response to the claims that the democratisers – or at least some of them – made to possessing a monopoly of enlightenment as an 'intellectual priesthood' (Schelsky, 1975, 15, 402). But above all it sought to deny that the demands for democratisation were theoretically valid or socially beneficial. The political scientist Wilhelm Hennis argued that the 'democratisation' of the social sphere would merely result in its total politicisation. It ignored the distinction between the public and the private sphere, between the state and civil society (Hennis, 1970, 24, 27): democracy relates to the choice of government, not to the running of a factory or a school. Conservatives like Arnold Gehlen, Eugen Forsthoff and Helmut Schelsky defended the manager, the expert and the wealth-creator against 'moralising intellectuals' (Gehlen, 1974, 9; Schelsky, 1975, 180). What present-day conservatives admire about technocracy is the authority that it gives to the expert. As early as 1961 Schelsky had maintained that 'nowadays it is often not the politicians who represent the public interest, but the experts of the scientific-technical state' (Schelsky, 1961, 29).

These critics of the gospel of progress were the prophets of the partial policy revision that took place at the hand-over from Brandt to Schmidt: the emphasis on the possible rather than the desirable. But most spokesmen of conservatism wanted more than this: a recovery of faith in capitalism, a renewed recognition that it was capitalism that was truly progressive. At the very moment that the Left, disillusioned by the Brandt years, overwhelmed by environmental concerns and the arms race, began to sense disaster in its nostrils, the Right re-occupied the ground of confidence and optimism. What inspired the Right was West German economic achievement and, even more, West German economic potential. It is therefore not surprising that the slogan of the Bavarian Christian Social Union, in many respects the most conservative of West Germany's major parties, is 'Der Fortschritt spricht bayrisch' ('Progress speaks Bavarian'). The achievements of Bavaria's high-technology industry and export leaders, like Siemens, Audi and BMW, were eminently compatible with law and order, Church and family, anti-Communism and compulsory Aids-testing. Nor is it surprising that the campaign slogan of the CDU in the 1983 election, following the fall of the Schmidt government, was 'den Aufschwung wählen' ('vote for recovery'). Conservative confidence was to replace the doubts and pessimism of the final Schmidt years. This was to be the *Wende*, the great turn-around.

National Identity and National Unification

The new West German conservatives were traditional also in the rediscovery of the nation. Not that the idea of German national aspirations had ever entirely gone away. In its extreme restorationist form it was largely an underground phenomenon, associated with neo-Nazism. Just as in the 1970s the homeless electorate of the NPD was for the most part absorbed by the mainstream parties, so small ultra-nationalist terrorist groups emerged to parallel those on the Left – *Wehrsportgruppen* (military sporting groups) – rather on the lines of 'survivalist' groups in other Western countries. Though they engaged in much rhetoric about national revival and reversing moral decay, their main recruiting agent was xenophobia. Their hatred and resentment was directed at immigrant workers, asylum seekers and the increasingly cosmopolitan appearance of West Germany's cities, a new and disorientating development in a country that, unlike America, France or Britain, had no experience of acting as a melting-pot. There has been a party-political revival of this constituency in the form of the Republican Party, which polled 7 per cent in the European elections of June 1989 and has had other local successes but fell when real unification took the place of cost-free nostalgia.

However, the mere existence of these groups, the fact that minor ultra-right parties began fighting elections again, as well as the pan-German tones of some neutralists on the Left – Günter Grass, for instance, talked of the anti-missile movement as an 'all-German responsibility' (Bracher, 1986, 399) – caused some concern to conservatively-inclined politicians, historians and publicists. For some decades the Federal Republic's integration with the West, and in particular its leading role in pushing for European unification, seemed to provide a satisfactory alternative to nationalist sentiment. As disillusionment set in with the way the European Community was developing, as national sentiment survived or revived in Europe to an extent that many, especially Germans, had not anticipated in 1945, the question of a West German political identity once more became salient. There was a fear that a new generation might grow up that felt neither European nor German, or whose only knowledge of the German past was, in Ernst Nolte's phrase, a 'negative myth', with an emphasis on the origins and crimes of the Third Reich. Such a state of affairs could easily lead to anarchy and disintegration: 'In a country without memory, everything is possible', the conservative historian Michael Stürmer warned (Stürmer, 1986). It is this concern that gave rise to the so-called '*Historikerstreit*' – the historians' dispute which burst upon the public in 1986 but had been bubbling within the historical profession for some time before. At the core of this dispute was the question whether German history was to be 'normalised' or not: was it the story of a thousand years, interrupted by a thirteen-year horror alien to its tradition, or was the Third Reich the central, traumatic experience of the German past that made the history of Germany different from anybody else's? (Piper, 1987; Maier, 1988). Both sides agreed that an understanding of history was the key to political consciousness. The conservatives saw this in a recoupling with the traditions of the nation-state, the radical, 'critical' historians in a permanent reassessment of the past, leading to an acceptance of the democratic Federal Republic as a new model. This is what Jürgen Habermas called '*Verfassungspatriotismus*', constitutional patriotism (Habermas, 1987, 135).

What the historians' dispute has once more emphasised is the extent to which the Federal Republic was a child of the German past. Both in its institutions and in its thinking it defined itself negatively in terms of the Third Reich, the Weimar Republic and even the Empire of 1971. For the founding fathers of the Parliamentary Council and for the reconstruction generation the Federal Republic was to be what the Third Reich and Weimar had not been. The first nineteen articles of the Basic Law, with their guarantee of civil rights, and the creation of a Constitutional Court (Articles 93,

94) to guard these rights, were designed to shut the stable door on the democratic horse. So was the legal prohibition of political parties that threatened the liberal–democratic order (Art 21). But if Bonn was not to be the Third Reich, it was not to be Weimar either. The articles of the Basic Law that regulated the appointment of the Chancellor, votes of confidence and the dissolution of the Bundestag (Articles 63, 67, 68) as well as the various versions of the electoral law, with their increasingly severe discrimination against splinter parties, were all meant to ensure that the new republic should not suffer from the instability of its predecessor.

The historians' dispute was rooted in a divided Germany. The question it raised was: what should it mean to be German at a time when there was little prospect of a German nation-state? It is therefore not surprising that this dispute disappeared from the scene as unification became first a realisable prospect and then a reality. But unification was something that happened to Germany; it was not a course of events initiated by its political leaders. Its proximate cause was the crisis in the Soviet bloc and, in particular, in the GDR. In the Federal Republic politicians of the Right spoke as if they still hoped for unification one day, but probably did not expect it. Those on the Left no longer even hoped for it. Both the SPD and the Greens were committed to the 'two-state theory' of the German Question, which they saw as the logical outcome of Ostpolitik. Much of the West German Left, including large parts of the SPD and the trade union movement, while not approving of the GDR, were not inclined to oppose it, or the division of Germany, actively. They shared the embarrassment of the European Left generally when faced with nationalism; they were unwilling to be associated with the militant anti-Communism that they associated with Cold War propaganda. Some writers and intellectuals of the Left did indeed accept the 'negative myth' of the German past. Günter Grass said three months after the fall of the Berlin Wall:

> The horrific and incomparable experience of Auschwitz, which we have made, and the peoples of Europe with us, exclude a united German state (Grass, 1990, 60).

Thus the Left as a whole was taken unawares when it emerged that the population of the GDR wanted one German state, not two, and a state on the Western model (Kitschelt, 1991; Markovits, 1992).

Nor was there much demand for national unification among the increasingly articulate opposition groups in the GDR, who began to dominate the political debate from the beginning of 1989 onwards. As in the 1950s they were to be found either inside the SED itself or were concerned with the betrayal of the GDR's founding principles, not with disputing the (presumed) principles themselves. The Leipzig demonstration in January 1989, on the seventieth anniversary of the murder of the Communist leaders Rosa Luxemburg and Karl Liebknecht, called for 'the democratisation of our Socialist state' (Mittler and Wolle, 1990, 13). The September 1989 manifesto of the most significant of the opposition groups, the New Forum, called on citizens 'to collaborate in the transformation of our society' (Schüddekopf, 1990, 31). In the same month Demokratie Jetzt (Democracy Now) wanted to 'develop and ensure the future of the Socialist revolution which has come to a halt through nationalisation' (Schüddekopf, 1990, 34–5). Demokratischer Aufbruch (Democratic Awakening), which allied itself with the CDU in the Volkskammer election of 1990 and was then absorbed by it, declared that:

> The critical attitude of . . . DA towards real existing Socialism in no way signifies a renunciation of the vision of a Socialist social order. We are participating in the debate about the concept of Socialism . . . Our point of departure is the existence of two German states (Schüddekopf, 1990, 163–5).

Only some time after the breach of the Berlin Wall, as new parties rather than informal groupings began to emerge, were the first programmatic calls for unification heard, in particular from the reconstituted SPD on the left and the German Social Union (DSU) on the right.

If anything, the end of the Berlin Wall on 9 November 1989 and of one-party rule in the GDR (7 December) reinforced the GDR identity of the dissidents. The prospects of a reformed GDR corresponded with their aims and justified their courageous efforts. The state was no longer the private property of the party elite, but the public property of its citizens. Jens Reich, one of the leaders of New Forum, said that only after 9 November did he feel himself to be a GDR citizen (Fenner, 1991, 307). Behind this reluctance to embrace the large nation-state lay other considerations. Some were practical – the fear of becoming 'the backyard and low-wage reserve of the West' (Reich, 1991, 202–3). But the ones that mattered most were ideological. The GDR opposition was inspired by the same utopianism of direct democracy and small political units that had guided the West German New Left twenty years earlier, the same distrust of representative government and of the organs of the modern state – parliaments, lobbies, bureaucracy. They sought, in the words of Wolfgang Ullmann of Democracy Now, 'a future to be realised not through force and competition, but in common discourse and joint decision' (Thaysen, 1990, 210).

Those who spoke thus spoke for a minority. The calls of the crowd 'We are the people' before 9 November became 'We are one people' after that date. The motivation for this was not chauvinist emotion but pragmatic. Unlike Jens Reich and Wolfgang Ullmann, most GDR citizens did not now feel a new loyalty to their state. They were glad it was about to disappear and wanted to join the real world – the Federal Republic – with the least delay. They wanted freedom of speech and the rule of law. They also wanted the Deutschemark. The impetus towards national unity was a consequence, not a cause of the coming down of the Berlin Wall (Fulbrook, 1991).

Sober Rationality and Pragmatic Reflection

Unification came because the population of the GDR demanded it. There was no enthusiasm for it in the Federal Republic, no street chants of 'We are one people', only a rueful counting of the costs. Unification came in accordance with Article 23 of the Basic Law, under which the GDR sought accession to the Federal Republic. Legally, economically and even politically the West took over the East. Constitutionally the new German Federal Republic is an enlarged version of the old German Federal Republic. What remains uncertain is whether its political character will remain unchanged.

The Basic Law was framed to ensure that Bonn would not become Weimar. But what no constitution and no Act of Parliament could ensure was an end to the ideological polarisation of the earlier years of the twentieth century. Yet that is precisely what did happen: sober rationality and pragmatic reflection replaced the pursuit of fanciful, naïve and, in the end, murderous ideals. And it is that which made an increasing number of the second generation of West Germans dissatisfied with their republic, a discontent that flourished particularly in the vacuum between the Adenauer and the Brandt eras. Having failed to run a democracy once, Germans were understandably sensitive to the fear that they might fail again – not, this time round, through physical disintegration, but through the incapacity to breathe the spirit of democracy into authoritarian institutions. The Federal Republic was not only the self-conscious negation of the recent past, it was also its heir and successor; whatever else 1945 had been, it was not Year Zero. This German sensitivity to the imperfections of their democracy is understandable: the new democratic consensus 'was the product not of a long history, but the experience of *one* formative succession of catastrophes and resurgence' (Löwenthal, 1982).

In the West the coincidence between the incipient failure of Brandt's reform programme, the oil shock and growing concern about the environment and in the East the failure of 'real existing Socialism' created nothing less than a crisis of the idea of progress. Where *Totalkritik* had originally been based on limitless faith in man's capacity for self-improvement, it became obsessed with the imminence of global disaster. The revolution of declining expectations came with Helmut Schmidt's assumption of office. Along with it came a growing scepticism towards world-reforming gospels and indeed of the capacity of the state or society to implement them. A loose party of alternative politics continued to exist. National unification has the potential for putting many of these assumptions back into the melting pot, though in the first year of unity there were few signs of this. The ending of the country's division has not resulted in a Fourth Reich. The Gulf War of 1991 demonstrated the desire of both the government and the public to remain a military and diplomatic pigmy while accepting economic superpower status. The costs of unification and the gap in affluence and expectations between the Western and the Eastern Länder certainly threaten the carefully-crafted social consensus of the old Federal Republic. The urgent needs of the ex-GDR economy have diminished the appeal of the market as the solution to structural disequilibria. A CDU–FDP government has been obliged, however temporarily, to practise Social Democracy through the back door.

An Ideological Vacuum

In the aftermath of unification there is an ideological vacuum. The collapse of Communism, the electoral defeat of the SPD and the demoralisation of the Greens, overrun by a process that they neither expected nor wanted, mean that for the first time since the French Revolution the Left is no longer the party of hope. The continuing traumatic legacy of the Third Reich means that the integral national-ism of the traditional Right also remains at a discount. The political consensus of the new Germany is that of the old Federal Republic writ large. There is a majority, which reaches well into the SPD, in favour of a market economy. There is a majority, which reaches well into the CDU, in favour of a strong welfare state. There is a majority that encompasses all the major parties in favour of further European integration, given that the degree of integration so far has been to Germany's manifest advantage. Nevertheless, this consensus is weaker than it was in the relatively homogeneous society of the old Federal Republic. Unification has generated resentments that arise out of the disparities between the Eastern and the Western Länder. There are widespread suspicions in the West that East Germans want something for nothing and want it instantaneously, and in the East that West Germans are lacking in solidarity and in a readiness for sacrifices. Market economies bring costs as well as benefits, costs that had been absent in the calculations of many. The pains of restructuring, the spectre of unemployment and the threat of inflation combine to give the politics of redistribution a higher place in the agenda of the 1990s than in that of the 1980s or 1970s. Above all, after unification the German present is as much haunted by the past as before: indeed, doubly so. Germans must now not only confront the National Socialist past, which may be receding but refuses to disappear. They must also face the more recent Communist past, which confronts them with the same accusations of indifference, double-think and collusion. The very weakness of post-unification German nationalism means that an over-arching integrative force that most advanced states can take for granted is not present.

In the early stages of unity the political and economic leadership lies with Westerners. Many East Germans feel strangers in their own land. For the 1990s there are four possible directions of development. (1) The ideological hegemony of the West is confirmed and the belief systems of the old Federal Republic become the norm for the whole of Germany. (2) The traditions of the GDR population make some impact on the dominant ideology, with the result that German political thinking becomes more Protestant, more moralistic, more socially orientated, less interested in a world role. (3) There is a growing cleavage between East and West, resulting in an ideological dissensus. (4) Only if the process of European integration results in serious disappointments is there a major risk that self-assertive nationalism will return.

Under either (1) or (2) there will be a balance of continuity with the Germany of the West: a broad spectrum from the moderate Left to the moderate Right which accepts that the Federal Republic is a modern, industrial state firmly anchored in the West. The Socialist Jürgen Habermas spoke for it when he asserted, 'The unconditional opening of the Federal Republic to the political culture of the West is the great intellectual achievement of our post-war epoch' (Habermas, 1987, 135); the Liberal Ralf Dahrendorf, in his confidence that 'in the end modernity is useful to man and will appeal to him' (Sontheimer, 1983, 120); and the more conservative Karl-Dietrich Bracher when he concluded that though most of his fellow-citizens identified with both the German nation and the Federal Republic, they live in a 'post-national democracy' (Bracher, 1986, 406).

17

A New German Identity

PETER H. MERKL

Ambivalence and Escapism

In the Spring of 1990, when the former British prime minister, Mrs Thatcher, assembled the so-called Chequers Seminar – in anticipation of a meeting with Chancellor Helmut Kohl – to give her an assessment of German 'national character', the renowned academics painstakingly examined a list of alleged attributes gleaned from German history between 1871 and 1945. Perhaps they began with 'aggressive' and 'angst-ridden', but then may have paused, realising that with the rest of the alphabet to consider, there was a formidable list of negative adjectives that they might have to add.

A national sense of identity in times of great and rapid change is impossible to pin down, and in the German case may still be as disjointed today as that of any superficially and recently united nation. How can we expect the diverse groups of Germans, whose different generations and social or political groups are miles apart in quiet times, to share the same sense of who they are and where they are going, when their very geographic configuration and their foreign policy are undergoing such drastic changes? In the 1980s we could still describe the forty-year evolution of elements of the West German sense of identity, its geographic uncertainties and cultural--historical conundrums, and relate the political relevance of it all to the political behaviour of the masses and the elites of the old Federal Republic (Smith, Paterson and Merkl, 1989, 6–21).

But then came the gradual disintegration of the communist empire in the Soviet Union and throughout Eastern Europe, the mass exodus of East Germans via Hungary and Czechoslovakia, and the ever-larger demonstrations in Leipzig and other East German elites with placards saying '*We* are the people' and eventually, 'We are *one* people'. West Germans were so surprised by the long-desired but quite unexpected gift of German unification, they vacillated between joy and dismay: dismay about the sudden East German refugee demand on scarce West German jobs and housing, and later about the enormous cost to them of this unexpected present. A never-ending series of grim revelations about the communist dictatorship, its 'Stasi octopus' with its army of informers, the broken-down economy, desolate inner cities, and vast environmental degradations made the gift look like a Trojan horse of troubles. On 3 October 1990, within less than a year from the unexpected opening of the Berlin Wall and other borders, the Germans found themselves actually united and yet beginning to dislike each other – for opposite reasons. East Germans wanted to be received and supported as long-lost brothers while their West German countrymen would much rather have treated them as distant cousins – the more distant the better – and without the financial sacrifices that majorities of West Germans refused from the beginning. Young West Germans, in particular, were widely quoted as saying that they felt that East Germans were no closer to them than Czechs and perhaps less so than the Italians and the French. The writer, Patrick Sueskind, complained in a popular magazine that the old FRG had been such a pleasant and harmonious community; why did the East Germans have to spoil everything with their reunification? Since Chancellor Kohl's government insisted that 'no new taxes' would be necessary to consummate unification, moreover, opposition spokesmen had a field day speculating about unification costs running up to a level of DM 100 billion a year for the next ten years (von Dohnanyi, 1990, in a *Spiegel* series).

By mid-1991, the dire economic consequences of German unification had reached full strength on both sides. The East Germans were headed for the highest level of unemployment expected – perhaps as much as 30 per cent of the employables, not counting the large numbers forced into early retirement or migrating to the West by the tens of thousands a month. The West Germans at last – *after* the national elections of 2 December 1990 – had been hit with hefty tax increases of their mineral oil (petrol) and value-added (VAT) taxes and were vengefully turning on the '*Steuerlügner* (tax liar) Kohl.' Far from a euphoria of national unity, prominent East Germans responded with a wave of nostalgia for the 'good old days' of the GDR and a communist utopia that had never existed. Just as if there had been no revelations whatsoever about the realities and dismal legacies of the dictatorship, old communist leaders, members of the unsuccessful democratic opposition of 1989, and nostalgic exiles conjured up a *Trotzidentität* (identity of spite), as civil rights leader Jens Reich (Bündnis '90) called it. They bewailed their inability to establish an independent reform–communist regime in late 1989 and blamed betrayal by the old 'bloc parties' of the communist state party (SED) and greedy West German capitalists for their failure, conveniently forgetting that both the old regime and the small reformist movements were pushed aside by the East German people in massive demonstrations and in the decisive East German elections of 18 March 1990 (*Der Spiegel*, 19 August 1991, 46–7).

Not to be outdone in escapism, the West Germans, too, showed the strain of living with the burdensome changes. Responding to a public opinion poll of the *Süddeutsche Zeitung*, asking how they envisaged Germany in the year 2000, 40 per cent answered 'like Switzerland' and another 29 per cent 'like Sweden', both small neutral but wealthy countries, geographically tucked away from the brunt of world conflicts. West Germans also responded to the outbreak of hostilities in the Gulf War with paroxysms of pacifism, massive peace demonstrations of people as young as in their midteens, blocking roads and entrances of American bases and consulates – East Germans were less active, but according to the polls, agreed strongly that Germany ought to stay out of the war. West Germans hid behind a clause of the Basic Law they interpret as barring the deployment of German troops 'outside the [NATO] theatre' and strongly preferred to buy their way out of the impasse with monetary contributions to the allied efforts and to affected front-line states such as Israel, Egypt, and Turkey. Only later and gradually did German majorities accept the obligation that such a strong and enlarged state as theirs ought to participate more actively in maintaining collective security.

How can we pin down the evolving German sense of identity under these changing conditions and in such a way as to create a recognisable image? Perhaps the best way is to rely heavily on public opinion polls that measure change and are representative of the masses of people rather than of a handful of eloquent elite persons. Rather than giving mere statistical averages of the changing attitudes of the whole German people, nearly 80 million of them, that conflict with each other, perhaps we should instead give distinctive group opinion profiles, say of the young and the old, of German nationalists and of the dying breed of GDR socialists, in the hope that these glimpses may add up to a memorable compound image of how Germans see themselves – no fewer than *six groups of senses* of German identity, all in search of a nation in rapid change.

The Dying of a Faith

The GDR, like the FRG, started out as a creation of the Cold War and both were tied into the rival military blocs, NATO and the Warsaw Pact. But beyond this, and especially after the construction of the Berlin Wall, the communist part of Germany was also the realm of a militant, quasi-religious faith, communism or revolutionary socialism, that ruled for three decades with a combination of indoctrination and coercion under the protection of the Soviet empire. A generation of militant old communists had founded it, including many veterans of the communist parties of the 1920s and 1930s, the Spanish Civil War, Nazi jails and concentration camps, and of bitter exile outside Germany, including the Soviet Union. These founders believed they were establishing a new German identity far from the feudal oppression, Prussian militarism, and capitalist exploitation of German history. In fact, they rejected most of that history, except for the sixteenth century peasant wars and the radical democratic traditions of 1848, and oriented themselves instead towards such international guideposts as the French Revolution and the Paris Commune of 1870, communism in the Soviet Union, and Third World liberation movements around the world (*Der Spiegel*, 22 April 1991, 146–64).

Over the years, much of their crusading enthusiasm began to fade in the crucible of everyday realities and, by the 1970s they had begun to settle for a 'realistic socialism' (*realexistierender Sozialismus*) rather than their dreams in the name of which their own oppression and coercion had been justified. Gradually, and of course without acknowledgement by the communist (SED) rulers, the system slipped into a somewhat more relaxed mode of 'party patrimonialism', based on quasi-feudal party bosses, their sinecures, cronies, and corruption. The communist leaders acted as if they 'owned' the whole system – hence the label 'patrimonialism' – and began to resist modernisation, let alone, democratisation of their authority, and all this while the great propaganda machine continued to spread the faith in public life, in the schools and mass organisations like the state youth (FDJ). By the mid-1980s, and following a decade of economic crises and reverses, the communist theocracy was showing signs of the dying of the faith, in particular among younger East Germans who were exposed to the new social movements from the West: ecological and pacifist protest, alternative life-styles, individual autonomy and spontaneity were the new messages, all anathema to communist orthodoxy. The communist regime reacted with punitive repression to stirrings of youthful autonomy, sometimes turning harmless groups of apolitical and non-communist youth into seething neo-Nazis. But none of this constituted a serious challenge to the regime until the 'new thinking' of Mikhail Gorbachev cut satellite regimes like the GDR – in the midst of new streams of exodus and popular rebellion – loose from their Soviet moorings in the last quarter of 1989. For the GDR where even the small civil rights and democracy movements still identified emphatically with a 'socialist' future, the alternative was unification with the much larger and more powerful FRG which hitherto, in the communist vocabulary, had been the capitalist and monopolistic class enemy, the spearhead of aggressive West German revanchism and Western imperialism, in short the old German identity from which the communists had wanted to depart.

We have already mentioned the ageing of the communist elites and their faith. What about the masses? GDR public opinion polls prior to the opening of the borders are few and highly unreliable, but we have information on the erosion of the faith from that time on. For example, in early December 1989, the Mannheim polling group asked East German adults whether they 'thought a great deal of' or 'set some store by' socialism, or 'thought hardly anything' or 'nothing' of the political faith that was the old identity of the GDR. 30.1 per cent said 'a great deal' and 41.2 per cent 'set some store by' socialism, for a positive total of nearly three-quarters. One-quarter thought little or nothing of it. By the time of the March elections in East Germany, the positive total was still a bare majority while the negative views added up to 45.2 per cent of the respondents (FGW Meinungen, 1989, 122–3, 126, 287). As might be expected, three-quarters of supporters of the communist PDS (formerly SED) thought 'a great deal' of socialism while up to two-thirds of the adherents of the CDU-led Alliance for Germany and a majority of Free Democrats regarded it with disdain. The Alliance and FDP then went on to capture a majority of the popular vote in the GDR elections while the PDS only received 16.4 per cent. Its membership had already lost eight of every ten members.

The change of East German mass opinion from the defence of the old system to its surrender to the FRG, i.e. reunification, also emerges clearly from a set of GDR surveys conducted in November 1989, in January–February 1990, and in February–March of the same year. In November, following the opening of the Wall, a majority of 52 per cent was 'rather' or 'completely against' surrender to the class enemy, while 16 per cent were 'completely' and 32 per cent 'rather for' unification. Towards the end of January, after massive demonstrations had first championed unification and then attacked Stasi headquarters, those 'completely for it' had risen to 40 per cent and the total majority for unification to 79 per cent. On the other hand, only 21 per cent were now opposed, and by February–March, they too were down to 16 per cent, while the eager supporters rose to 44 per cent and their combined majority to 84 per cent of all East Germans over 15 years of age. The great change in the East German sense of identity had evidently occurred during December and January, still before Gorbachev indicated to GDR premier, Hans Modrow, that he accepted unification 'in principle'.

Divided Support for German Unification

For the West Germans – that is, by far the bulk of the population of a united Germany – the endorsement of German unification was by no means a matter of unanimity from the start. To be sure, for four decades West Germans had responded positively, four out of five, to the simplistic question whether they would like the great trauma of the German division healed. But the polls of the last twenty years usually paired the question with a kind of reality test: 'Do you believe that within the foreseeable future a reunification of the FRG and the GDR will occur?'. Fewer and fewer would say yes: 13 per cent in 1968, 5 per cent in 1984, and 3 per cent in 1987 when 72 per cent thought it 'unlikely' and 25 per cent 'uncertain'. Until 1989, reunification was a disembodied issue of high ideological symbolism, but it had no policy content other than the Ostpolitik initiatives of the 1970s which really aimed at amelioration of conditions in the GDR and not unity. German identity simply meant carrying a large scar from a long-healed wound. As early as 1967, in fact, a majority said they had become used to the division – only one-third still found it 'intolerable' – and in 1976, two-thirds agreed that 'East and West Germany would never be united'. Among respondents under 30 it was even 73 per cent (Institut für Demoskopie, 1968–1973, 505–6). Even the voices and movements of the radical right were at best half-hearted in using such a 'dead issue' for their agitation.

When reality overtook the 'reality test', in the dramatic months from October to December 1989, West Germans at first refused to recognise the handwriting on the wall. In a telephone poll in the midst of the growing October demonstrations in the GDR, only 24 per cent 'expected to see reunification within the next ten years'. This finding was more or less confirmed by an Allensbach poll after the fall of the Berlin Wall (9 November) which ascertained that 30 per cent believed that 'it would occur within their lifetime', while 46 per cent still thought it would not, in spite of the emotional scenes at the Wall and Willy Brandt's solemn declaration that 'what belongs together will grow together again' (Bergsdorf, 1990, 13–19). *Time* magazine (27 November 1989, 40–1) declared that 'reunification is not on the current agenda – not on East Berlin's nor on Bonn's'. An Emnid poll ascertained that over two-thirds of West Germans approved of the 100 Deutschemarks 'wecome money' their government gave to every East German refugee and a similar percentage favoured financial aid to the GDR as long as it would not raise their taxes. Only 22 per cent were willing to pay higher taxes for this purpose which was probably a major reason for the Kohl government's later promise that unification would not require increased taxes (*Der Spiegel*, 20 November 1989, 16–17). West Germans were ambiguous in their reaction to the East German exodus – 57 per cent expected it to aggravate unemployment and 81 per cent the housing shortage in the West – and their support for it dropped dramatically from two-thirds in November to a quarter in January and to one-tenth in April, while pressure groups and some SPD politicians demanded a reduction of the government handouts that allegedly fuelled the exodus. By then, of course, the East German population had turned away from the idea of perpetuating a socialist GDR, and away from the small elite of intellectuals, ministers, and artists of the opposition. After the March election, all East German parties and their adherents were heavily (91 per cent of all partisan supporters) in favour of German unity, even the opposition groups (84–88 per cent) and the PDS (77.3 per cent) (Roth, 1990, 369–93).

In early May 1990, West German polls on unification revealed that three-quarters endorsed (and 94 per cent of East Germans), while 10 per cent opposed unification (IPOS, 1990, 68–9). This level of support was all the more remarkable because by that time West Germans had emphatically rejected personal financial sacrifices – only 28 per cent were willing. Three out of five felt that the Bonn government 'put the emphasis of its work too much on the GDR' (*Der Spiegel*, 28 May 1990, 34–44). Fortunately two-thirds of East Germans already knew they could not expect much willingness to make financial sacrifices from the 'Wessis' (West Germans). At this point, it had also become clear that younger Germans on both sides, under 45 and particularly under 30 years of age, were only lukewarm about German unification while the older generation supported it with considerable emotion. In September, another Emnid poll confirmed the divided pattern of West German support for unification: only 71 per cent were in favour while 29 per cent were 'against' or 'somewhat against'. The positive majority, in fact, was divided between being 'very much for it' (25 per cent), 'in favour' (23 per cent), and 'rather for it' (23 per cent), which was hardly a pattern of fervent nationalism as, for example, Conor Cruise O'Brien had pictured it in his 'Fourth Reich' article (*The Times*, 31 October 1989). The level of dissatisfaction has changed only incrementally since. On the one hand, the East German pains of transition increased and transformed into a more general dissatisfaction with what Bonn had done to cope with East German economic problems, especially in February–March 1991. On the other hand, while open West German opposition became rather pointless after the union was completed, West Germans were more unhappy than ever when the feared tax increases became a fact.

Identification with the Nation

A rather obvious way to determine a country's sense of identity has always been the extent to which its citizens exhibit pride in their nationality and identify with such national symbols as the flag. In the German case, of course, the succession of recent regimes, each with a different sense of identity and flag, complicates such assessments. The Weimar Republic, the Third Reich, the FRG, and the GDR in this respect differ profoundly from one another; the last two, in fact, were diametrical opposites in many respects. Some studies have therefore preferred to avoid direct reference to Germany or the Germans and concentrated instead on West German pride in the country's institutions. The 'civic culture' survey of 1959, for example, asked respondents in five countries in 'which aspect of their nation' they felt pride. The researchers discovered that Germans had a much lower level of appreciation of their own political institutions and social legislation than, say, Britons did. Only 7 per cent of West German adults were proud of their democratic institutions (85 per cent in the United States, 46 per cent in Britain), whereas 33 per cent took pride in their economic system (23 per cent in the United States, 10 per cent in Britain), and 36 per cent in their national character (7 per cent in the United States, 18 per cent in Britain) (Almond and Verba, 1963, 102). What they meant was also revealed in a series of questions asked by the Institut für Demoskopie between 1955 and 1965: 'whether Germany would ever again be a great power?' In 1954, 38 per cent said yes and 41 per cent no, but by 1965 it was 17 per cent yes and 52 per cent no.

Fortunately, German confidence and pride in their political institutions grew prodigiously over the years, and never more dramatically so than in confrontation with the communist GDR in its state of dissolution. Between mid-1989 and May 1990, West German 'satisfaction with our democracy' rose from 73 per cent 'satisfied' citizens to 85 per cent, a considerable rise and very likely a reflection of the inevitable comparisons with the sorry state of politics and the economy in East Germany (IPOS, 1989, 48–9 and IPOS, 1990, 21–3). In December 1989, nine out of ten East Germans also 'esteemed democracy as in the FRG' either 'greatly' or had 'some respect for it', although their response to another question might raise doubt. East Germans were asked whether they thought the GDR was being 'taken over' (*vereinnahmt*) by the economically superior FRG. Only a narrow majority rejected such an interpretation; 45 per cent agreed, although one in four of them regarded such a 'takeover' as 'a good thing' (FWG Meinungen, 1989, 1, 122–3, 126). Respondents over 60 particularly stood out in this double-barrelled reaction.

The same survey also asked East Germans if they considered themselves 'Germans' or 'GDR citizens' and received a vote of three-fifths for 'Germans'. Six months later, in May 1990, they were asked if they were glad whenever they saw the West German flag (!) and half of them responded 'yes' (43 per cent expressed indifference) which was nearly as high as the West German reaction to their own flag. On that occasion GDR citizens were also polled on whether they were 'proud to be German' and 79 per cent said yes (8 per cent said no), a level considerably ahead of that of the old FRG where a year earlier, before the onset of all the changes only 70 per cent agreed (13 per cent said no). When we recall the internationalist indoctrination of the East Germans in schools and mass organisations, this degree of national identification is a surprise (IPOS, 1990, 74–6).

In the old FRG, German national pride has always been a point of great debate and partisan division because of Germany's past (Merkl, 1974, 26–35). Even after forty years of non-aggressive, democratic behaviour, in the 1980s, German nationalism has been more subdued than elsewhere in Europe, witness the 86 per cent in 1985 who indicated their belief that 'exaggerated nationalism is bad, but a healthy national identification is worth striving for' (Honolka, 1987, 199). In 1970, for example, only 38 per cent of West Germans pronounced themselves 'very proud to be German', as compared to 66 per cent of French, 62 per cent of Italians, and an EC average of 55 per cent. Another 33 per cent (EC average 27 per cent) of West Germans were 'rather proud' while 23 per cent were 'not very' or 'not at all' proud (EC average 13 per cent). In the early 1980s, after a decade of declining confidence in political institutions in most Western countries, the number of 'very proud' West Germans (22 per cent) could be compared with 56 per cent among the British and 76 per cent among the Greeks (EC average 37 per cent). As Eurobarometer surveys showed, in the years of the great peace demonstrations against the deployment of new missiles, the 'very proud' percentage among the Germans – but not elsewhere – drifted even lower, 17–20 per cent, while the 'not very' and 'not at all' proud rose to 30–33 per cent.

The upshot of all this for the current German sense of identity appears to be that, aside from the confusion of whether national pride refers to both or just one Germany, contrary trends seem to have stabilised the responses. On the one hand, since 1949, there has been growing identification with the old FRG and its institutions which now include also those of the united Germany. On the other hand, deliberate moderation and the postindustrial attitudes of younger Germans have kept national pride and confidence in institutions at a comparatively low level, far from the flag-waving patriotism of the United States and Great Britain. There is also a geographic reason for confusion about whether the old GDR and the old FRG were 'two states in one nation' – the underlying principle of Brandt's Ostpolitik – or were separate nations. 70 per cent still spoke of one nation in 1974 whereas 29 per cent denied that the Germans of East and West were of the same nation. By 1984, a majority of 53 per cent held the latter view, while only 42 per cent still thought of Germans as 'one nation'. This gives us an idea of the situation just before the two Germanies were actually merged (Emnid-Informationen, 3/4, 1984, 8). To complicate the reference point of national identity still further with geographical details, an Allensbach poll asked West Germans in 1981 and 1986 what they meant by 'the German nation today,' or, 'German culture'. The 1981 answer was the old FRG (43 per cent), the two Germanies (32 per cent), the same plus German ethnic areas in the east (12 per cent), or all German-speaking areas (7 per cent). The 1986 answers were very similar (Institut für Demoskopie, 1981; IFD-Umfrage, 4076, 1986). It will be many years before the two populations of the GDR and the old FRG really grow together and share a national identity that is not confused by the legacy of recent history.

German Memories of the Past

In the week of 22 June 1991, a number of joint German–Russian exhibitions – for example, 'Topography of Terror in Berlin' – television features, and historians' conferences marked the fiftieth anniversary of the unprovoked Nazi German invasion of the Soviet Union, dubbed Operation Barbarossa. It started as a savage campaign to win *Lebensraum* (living space) in the East from its 'subhuman' population, to destroy the alleged Jewish–Bolshevik conspiracy, and to force World War II to an early conclusion favourable to the Third Reich. It ended with immense suffering on all sides, first visited on millions of Soviet soldiers, prisoners of war, and civilians – with a genocidal campaign against Jews and Gypsies, but also other Soviet citizens, and plans to starve another 30 million. An estimated 27 million Soviet people died, including 8.5 million soldiers. Then, as the fortunes of the war turned, Soviet vengeance was wrought on German soldiers and civilians, prisoners of war, refugees, and conquered villages, and on millions of their own Soviet citizens, especially those captured by the Germans, those suspected of collaboration, and even the forced labourers the German army had pressed into service in Germany. For the German side, historians clearly established that the responsibility for all that killing and brutality was by no means limited to special SS units, but involved the entire Wehrmacht in the East which had been penetrated by racism and Nazi ideology. Millions of officers and soldiers had known and participated, and lied about it to their families back home. The burden of guilt of this 'second holocaust' of the war generation was heaped upon that of the first one. But instead of trading bitter mutual recriminations, both German and Soviet representatives now assured each other of their sincere desire not to let the horrors of the past keep the new generation from cooperation and friendship.

Given the cataclysmic history of Germany in the last hundred years, it should not surprise us that historical events and their current interpretations play a major role in how Germans see themselves. Having fought and lost two world wars and lived through a murderous, totalitarian dictatorship which enjoyed their enthusiastic support has left a confusing array of memories, guilt feelings, and nostalgic distortions differentiated by partisanship and distinctive generations in their sense of identity. The range of partisan views goes from the communists associated with the GDR through the guilt-ridden left, i.e. the moderate anti-fascist and anti-communist Social Democrats and the Free Democrats, and through the broad range of the bourgeois and conservative Christian Democrats to the ever-changing gaggle of neofascist, radical-right groups, such as the DVU and Republicans, which still orient themselves in spite of everything by the lodestar of the Third Reich. The range of generations begins with the World War II and Nazi generation – defined by when its members were in their formative years, between about 15 and 25 years of age – and older generations, all over 65 today and therefore including only about one in five Germans. It is important to remember that the broad brush of generational analysis accounts only for the bulk of a particular generation, and in this case misses the many victims and opponents of this Third Reich generation who of course shared little of their attitudes. After all, are not Willy Brandt (78),

Helmut Schmidt (73), Richard von Weizsäcker (71) and Hans-Dietrich Genscher (64) also members of the war generation as we have defined it here?

After the war and Nazi generation, there are three or four post-war generations beginning with the birth cohorts of about 1927–8. The first of these is Chancellor Kohl's generation who, in his controversial phrase, thanked the Lord for having been 'born too late (*die Gnade der späten Geburt*)' to have become involved in the deeds of the Nazis and soldiers of his generational predecessors. The second post-war generation are the student and other rebels of 1968 (born between about 1940 and 1955) who shared a completely different outlook on social life and politics from Kohl's generation, the 50–65-year-olds. The 1968 generation is between 35 and 50 today and beginning to move into leadership positions throughout German society. In fact, there have been major problems of generational renewal in some German organisations such as Kohl's CDU/CSU, where it has been lagging among the party leadership. Finally there is one younger generation, perhaps even two, who grew up during the energy crises of the 1970s and the pacifist agitation of the early 1980s and the Gulf War. All of these generations, by reason of their different birth cohorts and formative periods, perceive German history in very different ways.

Over the forty years of the FRG, the dying-off of the older generations and maturing of new generations can account for most of the changes. To illustrate with an example, West German attitudes regarding, 'Who is to blame for World War II?' have changed dramatically since the early 1950s when the adult population of the FRG consisted almost exclusively of the war generation whose aggressive nationalistic and imperialistic views and participation in the war may have hardened their hearts against the victims and antagonists. In 1951, only six years after the end of the war, therefore, one out of four of a representative adult sample responded 'the others' are to blame, 18 per cent said 'both sides', and a mere 32 per cent admitted that it was Germany's fault. By 1967, 22 years later, enough people of the next generation had attained adulthood and older cohorts died off to raise the admission of German responsibility gradually to 62 per cent, while only 8 per cent still claimed it had been 'the others' and 8 per cent said 'both' (Institut für Demoskopie, 1967, 146). Of course, it is not easy for adults to admit guilt or that they have been wrong, and Germans are no exception.

In the same way, West Germans changed their minds about the restoration of monarchy – probably dear only to members of the pre-World War I and World War I generations who still remembered the Kaiser – 33 per cent for it in 1951 to a mere 11 per cent in 1965 while the opposition rose from 36 per cent to 66 per cent. The appreciation of Adolf Hitler as 'one of Germany's greatest states-men' similarly declined from nearly half in 1955 (against 36 per cent opposed) to 31 per cent (56 per cent opposed) in 1978 even though young neo-Nazi groups and opinions were replacing some of the earlier, dying supporters. In early 1989, on a 10-point scale of a *Spiegel* poll, only 14 per cent gave Hitler a positive vote as a historical figure, scattering their marks over a range of 1–5 points. 74 per cent rated him negatively, including 36 per cent as the worst (-5) and 27 per cent as next to worst choice (*Der Spiegel*, 10 April, 1989, 150–60). In 1951 people favouring one-party rule still made up 25 per cent of the respondents even though a majority of 53 per cent championed multiparty politics. But by 1978, the pluralistic majority had grown to 92 per cent, leaving a mere 5 per cent to dream of one-party rule as in the Third Reich (Conradt, 1989, 54). Obviously, it took the coming and going of generational cohorts to facilitate the learning process by which the FRG became a stable democracy, the younger generations being a far better bet to make pluralist democracy work in Germany than their elders.

Can one tell to what extent members of the war generation after forty years have learned from their experience? A test issue is the recognition of the finality of the loss of the once-German Oder—Neisse area to Poland which was officially accepted by the Brandt administration of the early 1970s after a quarter of a century of West German denials and furious resistance on the part of German refugees who had been expelled from there in 1945. In 1951, 80 per cent of West Germans agreed (8 per cent did not) 'we should not reconcile ourselves to the Oder–Neisse border' and two years later in the face of their fears of the Soviet colossus – West Germany had not yet been brought into NATO and felt at the mercy of the power politics between East and West – two-thirds insisted that, someday, 'Pomerania, Silesia, and East Prussia would once again belong to Germany', and 'not be lost forever' (Institut für Demoskopie, 1955, 313 and 1964, 482–3, 504–5). This was mostly the war generation talking, including some 10 million German refugees, a majority from the Oder–Neisse area and Poland. By 1962, the percentages had changed dramatically as half of the West Germans agreed (26 per cent did not) that Germans should resign themselves to the Oder–Ne-isse line, thus preparing the ground for Chancellor Brandt's Ostpoli-tik. The GDR government had recognised the new Polish border already in 1950, immediately after its own establishment by the Soviets.

In Winter 1989–90, the collapse of the communist regime in the GDR and the prospect of a united Germany bordering on Poland revived the Oder–Neisse issue as Chancellor Kohl and other CDU/ CSU politicians once more tried to pacify the refugee organisations with a pretended reluctance to accept the border line. This manoeuvre probably failed to convince the refugees to vote CDU/ CSU rather than for the right-wing Republicans – but it certainly raised alarm bells from Warsaw to Paris and Washington, as well as among the opposition in the FRG and GDR. The masses of Germans, at any rate, have long been on record with their opinions: in 1990 81 per cent of West Germans accepted the Oder–Neisse line (17 per cent did not) and the same was true of 91 per cent of East Germans of whom only 7 per cent were still opposed. The differences in East and West reflected, among other things, the larger numbers of refugees and of the older generation in the FRG. For those over 60, the percentages of rejection were 25 per cent in the West and 15 per cent in the GDR. In other words, even among the older West Germans of 1990 (who were 20 years and older in 1951) at least two-thirds had learned to accept the inevitable. The large numbers of refugees from the Oder–Neisse to the old FRG made it possible to separate responses by people who themselves had fled from the Oder–Neisse area or were the children or grandchildren of such refugees: of the war generation respondents who personally experienced the hardships and brutality of the expulsion, only 56 per cent were prepared to recognise the Oder–Neisse line created by the war. 43 per cent were opposed. Among the children and grandchildren of refugees, 24–28 per cent opposed recognition, evidently reflecting family indoctrination, while 72–75 per cent accepted the new border, not all that different from the popular averages (IPOS, 1990, 87).

The Third Reich Generation

'Born after a [world] war that later was dubbed the first. Raised for an even crueller second world war', reads the caption under a picture of a row of milk-faced 13-year olds in the winter uniforms of the Jungvolk (Junior Hitler Youth) gathered around their flag in a book on German Gymnasium graduates of 1939, of the Dreikönigschule for Boys in Dresden. Born in 1920–1, of the class of 54 boys, all but one served in the war, 23 fell in battle, two died from their injuries soon after the war, and a few more later. Quite a few returned to the ruins of their home town, Dresden, where allied bombers had killed and incinerated at least 40,000 – some estimates name five times that many – in a few days in mid-February 1945. One slashed his wrists upon seeing the ruins of his parents' house there. 23 of the survivors were interviewed by the author, Helga Gotschlich, now the director of the Berlin Institute for Contemporary Historical Youth Research, who sought to fathom the great urge of German youth to kill and be killed in World War II (Gotschlich, 1990, 7–11, 32). What she found was the legacy of the 'great patriotic war' of 1914–18, passed on to immature boys in the 1920s and 1930s by their parents and older siblings, often World War I veterans, teachers, and in schools dominated by the pre-war patriotic Right, memoirs of war heroes, youth groups such as the Bündische, the old bureaucratic and military establishment, and of course the Nazi party, once it was in power, through its hydra-headed propaganda machine. This particular cohort reached the age when youth is most directly impressed by dramatic political events just in time for the great wave of popular pro-Nazi enthusiasm, 1933–9, and for the Goebbels' propaganda apparatus to use all its resources to inculcate militaristic values: the schools, Hitler Youth, papers, radio, books, movies, the party, Nazi-subverted organisations and public festivals of every kind, not to mention the role of patriotic parents (Gotschlich, 1990, 129–44).

It was the crest of a generational wave of enthusiasm for renewing the German struggle for European hegemony to which both younger – by 1945 the Nazi government had drafted all birth cohorts down to the year of birth 1928, and even younger males were pressed into service to assist the anti-aircraft brigades – and older men and many women rallied. After all, the parents of the birth cohorts from 1920 to 1928 had already been enthusiastic nationalists. The crucible of terrors of World War II, both those they suffered and those they visited upon others bound them together until the bitter end.

But even the defeat and the disclosure of their deeds at the War Crimes Trials in Nuremberg – the holocaust of the European Jews, the deaths of an estimated 25–29 million Soviet citizens and of millions of Poles, Yugoslavs, and many others – did not exactly break the nationalistic attitudes of the survivors, witness the American occupation zone (OMGUS) surveys of 1945–7. In spite of the War Crimes Trials and denazification, the views of the adult respondents then were not much different from those of the Nazi period: 33 per cent held racist views regarding Jews, blacks, and Poles, justifying persecution with the claim that 'it was necessary for the security of the Germans'; 50 per cent insisted that 'Danzig, the Sudetenland, and Austria should be part of Germany proper'; 15–29 per cent expressed authoritarian views extolling dictatorship and the suppression of dissent, and 12–19 per cent attributed stories of German atrocities and the war itself to foreign conspiracies and propaganda. In 1945, half of the respondents also characterised National Socialism as 'a good idea badly carried out'. This percentage rose to 55 per cent in 1947 and 66 per cent in the 1950s – only the maturing of new generations in the 1960s finally lowered it drastically. But in spite of a high level of anti-semitism, 60 per cent of the respondents also agreed on what was carried out so badly: the persecution of the Jews and other minorities (Merritt and Merritt, 1970, 31, 146–8).

In 1991, the birth cohort of 1920 was 71 years old and the entire war generation (born before 1928) over 64. It amounted to about 20 per cent of the voting population over 18, and two-thirds were women. Our opinion polls distinguish only the group of Germans over 60, but they distinguish them from the younger cohorts in significant ways. For example, 85 per cent of this group in the FRG (as compared to an average of 70 per cent) professed to be 'proud to be German' and only 4 per cent said they were not (average 12.1 per cent) – both values are similar to the 86.6 per cent and 6.2 per cent, respectively, of today's Republicans. Ten years earlier (1980), in fact, 91 per cent of the same people (then aged over 59) had expressed national pride – two-thirds were 'absolutely proud to be German' – while only 4 per cent were not (Hübner-Funk, 1985, 495). This was indeed the crest of the nationalist generational wave. In 1991, they also differed from today's average, with similar margins, in their rate of approval at hearing the national anthem and seeing the national flag (IPOS, 1989, 137–41). As we shall see, there is a striking contrast in this respect between the oldest and the youngest generation of today's voters, those under 25.

Since these percentages vary rather continuously if not evenly from one age cohort to the next, it is worth noting that respondents in their fifties, i.e. Kohl's generation, are much closer to those over 60 than they are to their juniors (in their forties) whom we have dubbed the 1968 generation. Some scholars have described Kohl's generation the 'Hitler Youth generation' which was exposed to the contagion although too young to serve in the war (Hübner-Funk, 1990, 84–98). But we need to consider that the formative years (15–25) of the fifty-something cohort were the years of catastrophic defeat, of the division of the country (1945–9) – and, following this, of painful and slow rebuilding. Kohl's generation grew up politically in mortal fear of the Soviet threat which, by the way, offered many of the old nationalists a new means of displacement, communism, just as the 'fascist' FRG was the displacement target for the GDR. The formative experiences of the first decade after the war were likely to produce a tougher, more conservative, and more defensive pattern of political ideas than the years of prosperity from 1955.

Whither German Youth?

At the opposite end of the age-scale from the older age-groups, when the drama of 1989–90 began, were the West German voters between 18 and 24 years: among them, only 42 per cent expressed national pride – half the rate of their elders – 30 per cent were indifferent (against 4.3 per cent) and 28.1 per cent 'did not know' (against 10.7 per cent). Even fewer (35.8 per cent of the young) liked to see the flag (57 per cent did not) or hear the anthem (38 per cent yes, 50 per cent no). A year later, after the most important decisions on German unification had been made, national pride among West Germans under 25 had risen to a level of 56 per cent (IPOS, 1989, 137–41 and IPOS, 1990, 109). This did not prevent the young voters from being substantially more dissatisfied with their own political institutions than were the older age-groups. Still more revealing was their indifference in endorsing German unification. Whereas older people were heavily for it (84 per cent), followed closely by Kohl's generation (81 per cent), respondents under 30 could muster only 64 per cent in favour as against 18 per cent against and 18 per cent indifferent (IPOS, 1990, 114). The younger set was also considerably more tolerant of liberal issues, such as suffrage for resident foreigners and of the right of political asylum. They are obviously far removed from the nationalism of the war generation.

Young East Germans, by way of contrast, were considerably prouder to be German than their Western cousins (65 per cent versus 56 per cent), but also less so than the East German average (79 per cent), not to mention East Germans over 60 (89 per cent). When asked whether they favoured German unification – in May–June 1990 – young East Germans went for it 89 per cent (versus 5 per cent against it and 5 per cent indifferent). While 95 per cent of older people endorsed it as 'very important', however, only one-third of the youngest cohort called it that (IPOS-DDR, 1990, 10, 54, 59). Some of this surprising nationalism coming out of communist closets was also mirrored in the prominent upsurge of radical right groups and xenophobia in the former GDR. Leipzig opinion researcher Walter Friedrich speaks of 'a strong right wing extremist potential with distinct nationalist attitudes' among East German youth, 'with national arrogance, worship of authoritarian leaders, ostentatious rituals, xenophobia, anti-semitism, and aggressiveness towards non-conformists' (Friedrich and Förster, 1991, 349–50). There has been violence against foreigners, anarchist and 'alternative' youth, and gays by young neo-Nazis, and hooligans. Some of the manifestations may look like the early Nazi party, but without the clear political purpose and the quasi-military organisation and operations of the old stormtroopers.

The East German radical right is a very disorderly scene. The handful of real neo-Nazis, often led by West Germans or Western-'trained' activists, are having a hard time organising the hooligan rabble; the Nazi slogans and symbols common among the latter are as deceptive as a swastika on the leather jacket of a Hell's Angel or soccer hooligan (Merkl, 1986, 229–33). Another reason for East German nationalism may be the high rate of participation of East German youth in the big demonstrations in Autumn and Winter 1989–90. Three out of five East Germans under 25 claimed to have been so involved in October–November and one out of three to have been associated with one of the new opposition groups. They were also far more impatient for free elections in the GDR – the survey was taken in the first week of December 1989 (FGW Meinungen, 1989, 5, 7, 11, 52 and 93). A third reason, of course, is the perception of East German marginality, as compared to prosperous, well-ordered West Germany, which compels the 'Ossis' (East Germans) to grasp the cloak of the common national identity. Other surveys of young East and West Germans confirm the low levels of nationalism, especially in the West, and the transient surge of political interest and national identification during the Autumn of 1989–90.

Germans View the Future

These then are the six features in search of the new German identity, East and West, young and old, burdened with memories of the past and divided on German unification, though of increasing self-confidence as a nation that has overcome its trauma of division and shown its readiness to 'mention the war' (against the Soviets). Some of the elements of the present German identity, especially those dealing with guilty persons of the older generations – whether from the Nazi past or the yet barely understood one of communist Germany – call more for the assessment of punishment where it is due than for a debate about the principles of right or wrong. Others, such as the attitudes of young Germans and the direction in which a united Germany might go, are much more suitable for discussion.

It makes sense for the Germans, East or West, to look forward into the future, say, until the year 2000. How do the Germans envisage their future and their role in the world? In the Germany 2000 poll of Infratest (p. 329 above), in which 40 per cent saw their country as another Switzerland and 29 per cent another Sweden (*Süddeutsche Zeitung*, 4 January 1991, supplement). The Germans' one-time idol, the United States only rated 6 per cent and this after Italy (10 per cent) and Japan (8 per cent), a split between *joie de vivre*, economic and military power. An ample majority of Germans evidently likes the idea of a future multicultural society as long as it does not cost much or attract streams of foreign 'economic refugees': half of them would like to see more tolerance towards foreigners and more foreign residents (a third are satisfied with the current numbers), and yet large numbers would stop 'economic refugees' (79 per cent) from coming – even ethnic German ones (52 per cent), and seekers of political asylum (43 per cent). At least one-third is haunted by the vision of too many foreigners in the year 2000. Germans also want to continue living in traditional cities and with a diversity of means of transportation, streetcars, buses, cars, bicycles, and not with supermodern magnetic (Maglev) people movers and other technological marvels; 82 per cent opt for traditional living. They also would like to see industrial areas well separated from their dwellings.

The German visions of the future also concentrate on the domestic scene: 85 per cent rate environmental protection as the highest goal and would like the state and the schools to commit more resources to this task which preceded such goals as a better welfare state (77 per cent), economic prowess (55 per cent) and technology (45 per cent), not to mention culture or sports (each 7–8 per cent). People would prefer to live close to nature, only a few steps away (92 per cent), as long as this does not mean curbs – by means of higher taxes – on their energy consumption. They would like to have hiking trails, bicycle paths, and walks in natural greenery nearby. And they prefer well-cultivated agricultural landscapes to unkempt meadows and forest wilderness.

They also want to take it a little easier, perhaps retire at 57, and have art everywhere around them as well as in museums and galleries. Unlike the Wessis, moreover, who evidently fear the authoritarian state, the Ossis would prefer more police and law and order in the streets and more discipline in the schools, evidently motivated by the rise of crime and violence in the five new Länder. They also call for 'more respect for state authority' (40 per cent as compared to 22 per cent in the West), a telling manifestation of statism in spite of their great faith in personal economic success in the GDR. German social life in the year 2000, two-thirds and more of all respondents agree, should be characterised by mutual helpfulness (78 per cent), respect for the aged (67 per cent), and both the courage to speak up and tolerance for nonconformists (64 per cent and 63 per cent, respectively).

There can be no future, alas, without some awareness of the past:

29 per cent of the respondents believe that a sense of 'shame about the crimes of fascism' should be an important part of the German future. In East Germany, it was nearly 50 per cent, perhaps a legacy of the carefully nurtured displacement of the old GDR. 18 per cent of Germans, however, oppose this (21 per cent in West Germany). One-third, on the other hand, would like the 'shame of the crimes of [GDR] socialism' to be kept alive, no doubt including many old Cold Warriors in the West. Surprisingly, the respondents also broke with some well-established German trends and patterns such as sticking to one's calling and a W. C. Fields-like aversion to small children. In the survey, a majority thought it would be desirable for a person to pursue several careers in succession and another 9 per cent feels ready to tackle several careers simultaneously. Up to 75 per cent also seem prepared to reverse the long-standing trend away from families with children. They want neighbourhoods full of kids, plenty of child care centres – many East German ones have survived the old regime and, in the West, there is a terrible shortage – and state support for combining motherhood with a career. Two-thirds want to see the man more involved in a couple's household chores (four of five women agree). On the explosive issue of legalising abortion, a majority of 60 per cent favours a woman's free choice, 34 per cent of them during the first three months and 24 per cent are for the total elimination of the relevant articles (Article 218) of the criminal code – even the CDU/CSU supporters endorsed these positions, thereby disagreeing with their conservative representatives in Bonn. Only 28 per cent of the respondents agree with the present law which permits abortion within three months only if certain 'indications' are present (danger to the health of the mother or baby, cases of rape, and socioeconomic hardship). Only 13 per cent wish to outlaw abortion altogether.

And what about Germany's role in the world by the year 2000? The German future in the eyes of the respondents is a peaceful one: 75 per cent want the country to stay out of international conflicts – hence the choice of neutral Switzerland and Sweden rather than of the superpower America. Only 25 per cent were in favour of becoming militarily involved. Their choice in favour of 'staying out', of course, was sorely tested within a month of the survey by the hot phase of the Gulf War. The aerial bombardments triggered vast youthful peace demonstrations, split the German Left, and sparked a spirited debate. The pacifist side finally admitted as the chief German reason for a possible intervention, the fear that Israel might be drawn into the conflict. Otherwise, they remained adamant about staying out and preferred to pay large sums (Politbarometer, January 1991, 54–6) to buy their way out.

By the year 2000 Germans hope to be part of a European federation. They envisage their country as a 'state with open borders, no
barriers and no controls' (83 per cent). In their relationship to other
nations, the three countries to which Germans would give 'priority
in good and close relations' were the Soviet Union (59 per cent),
the United States (44 per cent), and France (36 per cent). Their
friendly feelings towards the Soviets were already demonstrated with
vast sums pledged in aid and credit ($32 billion) and with a grand
care package campaign in Autumn and Winter 1990–1. The Kohl
government spared no effort to enlist other Western countries in
aiding Soviet economic reconstruction. To quote President von Weizsäcker, 'Our European humanity and peace depend to an extraordinary degree upon Soviet developments and their impact upon
Europe. Gorbachev's most important motive for agreeing to German
unification, in my opinion, was the desire not to be left out of the
[European House], to overcome the distance . . . I think we need
to respond to that'.

All the border fortifications between East and West Germany
along the nearly 1000 mile (1378 km) border have been removed,
and the wide strip once guarded by border guards, dogs, and lethal
devices is to become a series of nature parks – in Berlin bicycle paths
run along where East German Border Police vehicles used to control
attempts to cross the Wall. Many of the tall border towers, however,
from which army soldiers rushed out to stop refugees with automatic
weapons, are still there to haunt the landscape, reminding people of
what once divided them. Today, the issues that divide are different
and nobody is mauled by a dog or shot to death. But there is an
'inner wall' between people, East and West, who have learned to
despise each other. To quote the new director of the Institut für
Demoskopie, 'We're too mesmerized by the economic problems of
unification to take notice of the human dimension, for example the
lack of West German sympathy for the East Germans as a people'.
East Germans feel exposed and embarrassed, deeply offended by
some '*Besserwessi*' – a new portmanteau word combining Wessi
(West German) with the German schoolmasterly propensity to know
everything better – telling them they need to learn again how to
work. Ossis despise themselves for being *westgeil* (too eager to join
the West) and simply accepting everything instead of working for it.
The Wessis' arrogance makes their sense of humiliation even worse.
No wonder an Infas poll in May 1991 among East Germans disclosed
that as many as one in three 'very frequently' (6 per cent) or 'frequently' (26 per cent) wishes the times before the opening of the
borders were back. Another one-third 'vaguely' thinks along these
lines.

West Germans rarely feel such nostalgia for the days of the Berlin Wall. East and West have grown apart over the decades of division and yet, East and West Germans both may recognise their sense of present identity in the musings of the East German dissident poet Guenter Kunert about 'the myth of Germany', or rather 'that impenetrable confusion of several myths of the most diverse origins' – six characters in search of a national identity (Keller, 1991, 46–54) – including those of Prussia, the World War I army, the Weimar traditions, the Third Reich, 'realistic socialism', and Adenauer's capitalist democracy. 'These myths always stem from . . . a dead yesterday, where they rise, like Count Dracula to delight in the blood of the living . . . and to promise an extraordinary life above the everyday evidence to those who accept their leadership'. With many images Kunert conjured up the rising myth of life in the old GDR, 'freed of the last memories of oppression, need, fear, and hatred', so that 'tears will well up in the eyes of the oldsters'. The nostalgic myth of the old GDR aside, it was the past myth of the German nation that 'in part turned the traditional ethical norms inside out, and in part suspended them, which in the end made possible the catastrophe of the real, non-mythical Germany' (p. 54–61). Today's young Germans, we hope, may have learned to live without such myths.

Appendix: The Legal Context of Unification

HANS-WERNER LOHNEIS

Unification in the Post-1945 Era

Since German unification had been one of the most important issues of post-1945 European politics, there have been an abundance of proposals for a solution. The Cold War made certain that they were usually of a nature that disregarded the other side's interests. It is, nevertheless, instructive to compare – in a formalised way – the proposed steps towards unification of the 1950s with the reality of 1990.

	Proposals of the 1950s		1990/91 Events
	USSR/GDR	Western Powers	
First Step	International recognition of borders (esp. Oder–Neisse line). Agreement on German neutrality and level/type of German armaments	Free elections (Right of self-determination)	Revolution in the GDR 'Round Table', Changes of GDR constitution, Free elections in the GDR
Second Step	Definition of internal structures ('anti-fascist', 'peace-loving', etc.)	Establishing an all-German government with the right to choose between alliances	Monetary, economic and social union (economic unification)

	Proposals of the 1950s		1990/91 Events
	USSR/GDR	Western Powers	
Third Step	Elections, Setting-up an all-German government	German government signs a peace treaty. Agrees on borders, reparations, etc.	Recognition of borders and other external aspects: 'two-plus-four' treaty. Unification treaty (political unification). GDR joins FRG and ceases to exist
Fourth Step	Withdrawal of all foreign troops		All-German elections. First all-German government emerges. Beginning of Soviet troop withdrawal. Germany remains in NATO

Unification and the Basic Law: Articles 23 and 146

The original text of the constitution of the Federal Republic made it clear that it was designed as a provisional arrangement pending unification; all governments and state organs were constitutionally bound to pursue a policy leading to unification. This 'unification imperative' derived from the Basic Law's preamble as well as Articles 16, 23, 116 and 146. In 1973 the Federal Constitutional Court reinforced this imperative on the occasion of a ruling on the constitutionality of the 1972 Basic Treaty (with the GDR): the German state had not ceased to exist in 1945 but continued as a single entity, even though it was unable to act for want of a state structure and state organs. The FRG and the GDR were regarded merely as reorganisations of part of the territory of the single German state, within its 1937 borders. Germany's continued existence meant that there could be only one German citizenship as well as only one German nation. While recognising the GDR's autonomy and state character in 1972, the relations between the two German states would have to be (as emphasised by the Brandt–Scheel government at the time) of a special nature. Under the Basic Law, West Germany was unable to recognise East Germany as a completely separate, fully independent sovereign state. The Basic Treaty (1972) was therefore accompanied by the 'letter on German unity' in which the federal government reaffirmed its political goal as 'aiming at a state of peace in Europe in which the German people will regain their unity by an act of self-determination'.

It was the events in Hungary and Czechoslovakia, follwed by the East German revolution and the mass immigration from East Germany, that made the unification articles of the Basic Law suddenly highly relevant again. Two constitutional ways of achieving unification were envisaged. Article 23 simply stated that 'other parts of Germany' could accede to the Federal Republic (the Saar accession in 1957 had set a precedent), while Article 146 said that the Basic Law would cease to be in force once a new constitution, accepted by the 'free decision of the German people', had been adopted. Article 23 meant that the GDR as a whole, or the newly created Länder, could accede to the Federal Republic, West Germany not being in a position to veto this step short of repealing Article 23. Article 146 envisaged a quite different procedure: a full-scale constitutional debate, possibly elections to a constitutional assembly, and then conceivably a referendum on the draft constitution. This procedure would arguably have provided a greater degree of legitimacy but would have been a more lengthy process than that under Article 23. As long as the East German revolution was in the initial phase of 'democratic socialism', most observers expected the GDR to continue to exist for a considerable period and early unification unlikely. Prime Minister Modrow spoke of a 'contractual community' with West Germany, and while Helmut Kohl's '10-point plan' of November 1989 treated unification as the ultimate goal, the proposals foresaw a number of intermediate steps. Apparently the time-span for achieving unification was years, rather than months, although this was not spelt out.

Amendments to the GDR Constitution

At its first meeting (on 7 December 1989) the Round Table charged a committee with drawing up a new constitution for the GDR. Its purpose was twofold: to provide a new democratic constitution for the period until unification and a bargaining counter in negotiations with the FRG, so that some of the features of the GDR would be preserved in an all-German constitution. Soon it became clear, however, that the GDR with an open border to the Federal Republic could not survive for any length of time unless it received massive economic support from West Germany (there were 360,000 *Übersiedler* from East to West Germany between November 1989 and March 1990). On 28 November Kohl stated:

Economic improvement can only occur if the GDR opens its doors to Western investment, if conditions of free enterprise are created, and if private initiative becomes possible.

After Modrow's visit to Bonn in February 1990 negotiations got under way that eventually led to the first State Treaty. These negotiations were accelerated after the outcome of the GDR March elections. The East German voters opted for the fastest route to unity, disregarding the 'citizens movements', and supporting those parties that had been lukewarm in their endorsement of a separate constitution for the GDR. When the draft constitution of the Round Table was published in April it had been effectively superseded by events. It was debated by the Volkskammer but (by 179 votes to 167) it was decided not to refer it to committee stage.

Prior to April 1990 there had been six amendments. The best-known is the first: the abolition of the leading role of the SED on 1 December 1989. In January 1990 private ownership of the means of production was permitted as well as joint foreign ventures. In February, the constitutional provisions for elections were changed, thus making free elections in March possible. In March, the freedom of trade unions was recognised, and finally in April the preamble was repealed, the state council (Staatsrat) abolished and its functions transferred to the presidency of the Volkskammer. These piecemeal amendments did not find favour with the new de Maizière government. On 17 May 1990, a bill was introduced (and adopted on 17 June) that described in Article 1(1) the GDR as a free, democratic, federal, social and ecologically orientated state under the rule of law. Constitutional provisions or laws not in harmony with these principles would no longer be valid. There then followed a catalogue of basic and human rights similar to those in the Basic Law. The independence of the courts was also assured. Important, too, was Article 8 because it established a new procedure for concluding treaties with West Germany, in requiring a constitutional law passed by a two-thirds majority in the Volkskammer. Henceforth sovereign rights could be transferred to institutions of the Federal Republic without making specific amendments to individual articles of the GDR constitution. Both state treaties achieved two-thirds' majorities in the Volkskammer and were designated as constitutional laws. (In the West the treaties were passed by two-thirds' majorities in the Bundestag and the Bundesrat.)

The First State Treaty: Monetary, Economic and Social union

The first state treaty was signed on 18 May and came into force on 1 July 1990. It is a complex document consisting of 38 articles, a protocol on guidelines (*Leitsätze*) and with 11 Appendices. Its complexity is unsurprising because it achieved the economic unification of Germany and was intended as a major step towards full unification. The preamble makes it clear that German unification would be achieved on the basis of Article 23 of the Basic Law. The GDR's accession would mean, however, that all the economically relevant laws of the Federal Republic would also apply to the GDR. The preamble also stated that the external aspects of unification were at that time under discussion with the governments of the four Allied wartime Powers (see 'Two-plus-four' Treaty below).

The aspect of immediate importance in the State Treaty was monetary union. The Bundesbank would be responsible for the monetary policy in the whole of Germany, and the East German Mark would be replaced by the Deutschemark on 1 July 1990. The debts of the GDR would be reduced by 50 per cent and then shouldered by the Bundesbank. The conversion rate for all recurrent payments such as wages, salaries, scholarships, old-age pensions, rents and leases was at the rate of 1:1; for personal savings (and liabilities of the GDR) it was 2:1, though with a special 1:1 provision for small savers: 2000 Marks if aged under 15, 4000 Marks if under 60 and 6000 Marks for the over-sixties. The West German taxation system was to be introduced in stages, for example VAT rates applied from 1 July 1990, income tax rates from 1 January 1991. The sting in the tail was the new system of public finance, tucked away in Articles 26–28. These provisions made it clear that subsidies from the state budget for industrial goods, agricultural products and food, transport, heating and rents had to be reduced to conform with EC rules. In addition, the expenditure on the staff employed in the public services had to be cut. This meant that hefty price rises in all these sectors as well as redundancies were to be expected. Article 28 stated that significant subsidies from the Federal Republic would be made to the GDR (in the second half of 1990: 2 billion) in order to balance the budget. There would also be start-up finance provided for the insurance schemes, such as old-age pensions and employment.

Economic union extended the 'social market economy' to both parts of Germany. The State Treaty characterised the principles as: the right to private ownership, competition, free pricing, and the free movement of goods, services, labour and capital (Article 1(3) of the State Treaty). A framework was to be created for the liberalisation of market forces that would first benefit small and middle-sized businesses and the liberal professions. As the 'social market economy' is defined in a document that has constitutional force, it thus bestows a quasi-constitutional recognition on this type of economy, something not enshrined in the Basic Law. Foreign trade links were immediately affected as the whole of Eastern Europe had in future to pay for East German goods in hard currency.

Undoubtedly the biggest problem involved in economic union was the question of restoring private ownership. The principles of a solution were outlined in a joint declaration by the two governments on 15 June 1990: property that had been expropriated after the foundation of the GDR (October 1949) would be returned to the original owner. (The unified German state was unwilling to pay compensation for the huge number of claims that would inevitably arise. By October 1991 more than 1 million claims had been filed.) However, expropriations that had taken place under the jurisdiction of the Soviet Military Government (1945–9) would not be reversed, although the Bundestag could in the future agree on compensatory payments if it wished. The numerous claims for the return of property and the fact that for many properties no clear title of ownership existed, has severely hampered private investment. In March 1991 the government introduced a new law to resolve this problem, but only for property that was purchased from the public trustee (Treuhandanstalt – the body entrusted to implement privatisation). Once investment plans and job security for three years had been agreed with the purchaser or major investor, the Treuhandanstalt was empowered to issue a clear title to the property acquired. It would then be up to the previous owners to take the Treuhandanstalt to court for compensation. Restitution of the property in these cases would not be allowed.

Article 16 of the State Treaty refers to environmental protection. (In the Bundestag committee on 'German unity' the SPD and the Greens had demanded an 'Environmental Union'.) The GDR guaranteed that the safety and environmental protection laws of the Federal Republic would immediately apply to new installations. Existing installations would adopt the West German standards as soon as the necessary adjustments could be made.

Finally Social Union (Articles 17–25) meant that the West German labour and codetermination laws would immediately come into force in the East. East Germany also adopted all the insurance schemes relating to old age pensions and health, accident and unemployment. The 'Arbeitsförderungsgesetz' (Retraining and Job-Creation Act) also came into force in East Germany. Initially, the finance for economic unification was provided by the Federation and the Länder together ('*Fonds Deutsche Einheit*'). Subsequently it transpired that these funds were inadequate and other sources had to be found. Most came from federal funds which means – as the new 'Länder are now financially dependent upon the Federation – that unification has not strengthened the federal nature of Germany: on the contrary, the centre has been strengthened and Länder autonomy weakened.

The 'Two-plus-four' Treaty: the 'Substitute' Peace Treaty

The 'two-plus-four Treaty (signed on 12 September 1990) refers to the two German states and the former, four former occupying Powers (Soviet Union, United States, Great Britain and France). It is in reality a substitute peace treaty as indicated by its subtitle, 'Final Settlement in relation to Germany'. The two German states, however, were not interested in the holding of a formal peace conference which would have given rise to reparation demands. Such a conference would also have had a polarised character: the victorious powers and the defeated. Given that the two Germanies had been allies of their respective superpowers for decades, a conventional 'peace conference' would have been impossible.

The Treaty itself deals with three major issues. It defines Germany's borders, it restores her full sovereignty, and it specifies the conditions under which this newly won sovereignty would be exercised. Article 1 defines the territory of Germany as that of East and West Germany plus Berlin. This definition means that any claims on territory east of the Oder–Neisse line are henceforth impermissible in international law. To make absolutely certain of this interpretation Poland and Germany undertook to sign a separate treaty to this effect. In addition, under Article 1(4), Germany has to ensure that the German constitution 'does not contain any provision incompatible with these principles'. (This explains the repeal of Article 23 of the Basic Law in the Unification Treaty.)

The restored sovereignty is referred to in two articles. According to Article 7, the four wartime allies 'hereby terminate their rights and responsibilities relating to Berlin and Germany as a whole'. These 'reserve rights' of the allies had always given them an effective veto over the unification issue. Article 6 states that a united Germany may belong to any alliance she chooses. Obviously this provision is closely linked to the security question. On 16 July 1990 Chancellor Kohl and President Gorbachev reached a preliminary agreement that made unification within NATO dependent on the following conditions: the German armed forces would be reduced within three to four years to 370,000 (the Bundeswehr and the Nationale Volksarmee together had comprised about 600,000 men). The armaments of the German forces would permanently exclude the ABC weapons – nuclear, biological and chemical weapons. Furthermore, following the phased Soviet troop withdrawal, only German troops without any nuclear carrier weapons could be stationed on the territory of the former GDR. In return for these disarmament and arms limitation measures, the Soviet Union made her greatest concession: a united Germany could remain within NATO if she wished to do so. Continued membership within NATO had not only been demanded by the Western allies and West Germany but also by Poland, Hungary and Czechoslovakia. For Germany's neighbours, a sovereign Germany securely within the NATO alliance seemed greatly preferable to a neutral Germany left to herself.

The Unification Treaty

By the time the draft version of this 'two-plus-four' Treaty was published, it was clear that all major obstacles for signing the Unification Treaty had been overcome and that German unification was soon to be realised. In its three Appendices the Treaty (signed on 31 August 1990) is a monument to the labour of senior civil servants who (in Appendix II) painstakingly enumerated all the East German laws that needed changing. Thus the Unification Treaty completed the legal unity of Germany that the State Treaty had begun. It meant that the five new Länder (at that time not in existence) and Berlin would have to adopt virtually all the laws of the old Federal Republic.

Article 1 of the Unification Treaty specified the conditions of accession of the GDR to the Federal Republic on the basis of Article 23 of the Basic Law. Five new Länder (Mecklenburg–Western Pomerania, Brandenburg, Saxony, Thuringia and Saxony–Anhalt) were to come into existence, and the 23 districts of East and West Berlin would form the new Land of Berlin. On 22 July 1990 the Volkskammer passed an 'Introduction of Länder' law which meant that five new Länder would be established on the date of the first Länder elections, 14 October. But this date was brought forward to 3 October, the day the Unification Treaty came into force. The Volkskammer's electoral laws for these Land elections specified proportional representation, much like the federal election law. The number of deputies for each Landtag is dependent on the number of voters. There are, for example, 66 MPs in the Mecklenburg Landtag but 160 in Saxony. The territory of the five Länder is largely identical with the territory of the five Länder that previously existed from 1945–52. The Unification Treaty makes provision for Berlin and Brandenburg to merge by way of agreement between the Länder, thus avoiding the complicated procedure envisaged in Article 29 of the Basic Law.

Changes to the Basic Law

In the old Federal Republic there had been a long-standing debate on constitutional changes, and as a concession to those in the SPD and the Greens who had demanded a debate and a referendum (the SPD votes were necessary for a two-thirds majority in the Bundestag for the Unification Treaty), Article 5 of the Treaty advised consideration by the legislative bodies of a unified Germany of the following matters within two years:

- the relationship between the Federation and the Länder;
- the possible merging of Berlin and Brandenburg;
- the provision of additional state objectives (*Staatsziele*);
- the question of applying Article 146 of the Basic Law and the holding of a referendum on the constitutional changes.

By October 1991 a constitutional commission had been established but the outcome of its deliberations were expected only late in 1992.

Another thorny question was that of the location of the capital city and the seat of government. Article 2 of the Unification Treaty stated that 'Berlin is the capital of Germany', but the seat of government was left undecided. After a heated public debate, the Bundestag in June 1991 decided by 337 to 320 votes that Berlin should also become the seat of government, although the time-scale for the move to Berlin was left undetermined. Some days later the Bundesrat decided 'for the time being' that it would remain in Bonn.

Six changes of the Basic Law were incorporated in the Unification Treaty, including the deletion of Article 23. The preamble was amended in such a way as to claim the whole German people's authority for the amended Basic Law, a claim that was contested in view of the absence of direct consultation with the people by referendum. One effect of the 'two-plus-four' Treaty was the abolition of Article 23, signifying that all German territories were now united within Germany. The new Article 51(2) changed the distribution of votes in the Bundesrat according to the size of the Länder. In future all the Länder with a population of more than 7 million will have six votes. Those in question are Bavaria, Baden–Württemberg, North Rhine–Westphalia and Lower Saxony, all of them 'old' federal Länder. Article 135 was amended so that the new Federal Republic accepts the liabilities of the GDR. In Article 43 it is laid down that legal unification should be completed by December 1992 but making allowance in some exceptional cases for extended time-limits. One such case was the discrepancy between the abortion laws in the two parts of Germany, and this was to become a highly contentious political issue.

Article 146 was amended to reflect the validity of the Basic Law for the entire German people. But the possibility of adopting a new constitution by a free decision of the German people remains open. What concerns constitutional lawyers is the possibility that the existing German constitution can now be changed in two ways: by two-thirds majorities in the Bundestag and the Bundesrat, or by a simple majority through a referendum. The perceived danger in the referendum procedure is of manipulation and far-reaching changes of the Basic Law by a simple majority vote.

Just as some financial provisions of the State Treaty failed to last even for a year, so the details of Article 7 of the Unification Treaty on the distribution of finances were soon superseded. Now the distribution of VAT among the Länder is made simply according to population size (thus giving far higher receipts to the new Länder) rather than according to the sliding scale laid down in this Article. Further, Article 25 of the Treaty, relating to the Treuhandanstalt was modified by a law in March 1991. Originally the Treuhandanstalt was charged to privatise only state property and restructure firms to make them saleable; the new law, however, emphasises the need to preserve as many jobs as possible which makes the task of the Trehandanstalt even more difficult.

The Unification Treaty extends the validity of the Basic Law to the new Länder where new federal structures and local government administrations had to be set up, and the same laws – with some exceptions – are now valid for Germany as a whole. In addition to the wide disparity in the economic development and performance of the two parts of Germany, it is apparent that the introduction of new structures of government and administration in the new Länder will cause continuing problems which were initially greatly underestimated.

Guide to Further Reading

Chapter 1   German Unity

Offe (1992) analyses unification as a 'natural' experiment. Noelle-Neumann (1991) and Scheuch (1991) provide insights into the changing moods of public opinion in the two parts of Germany. Thaysen (1990) assesses the significance and shortcomings of the 'Round Table' in the period of transition. The best account – an insider one – of how unification was negotiated is given by Schäuble (1991). The monetary/economic handling of unification is critically examined by Priewe and Hickel (1992). Fulbrook (1991) and Roberts (1991) look at some aspects of the cultural and social problems resulting from unification. By far the best account of the international context is given by Kaiser (1991). The attitudes of the Soviet Union and Britain are analysed in Adomeit (1991) and Padgett (1990) respectively. The integration of the new Länder into the European Community is well documented in Spence (1991).

Chapter 2   The Nature of the Unified State

Standard accounts of the German political system prior to unification are still of use, such as Johnson (1983) and Smith (1986), since all of the structural features of the Federal Republic are essentially unchanged. Reference to the first version of *Developments* (Smith, Paterson and Merkl, 1989) should also prove helpful as will Merkl (1989). Account is taken of the post-unification situation by Paterson and Southern (1991), and on federalism, see Jeffery and Savigear (1991). In German, von Beyme (1991a) is an up-to-date text. For the Chancellor, see Padgett (1992) and Smith (1991); specifically on Helmut Kohl, Vogel (1991) contains a variety of views and assessments, and Glotz (1989) supplies a sharply critical analysis. Guggenberger *et al.* (1991b) is of interest for proposals on how the German constitution should be revised.

359

Chapter 3   Two German Electorates?

Kendall Baker and his colleagues (1981) provide a comprehensive overview of the evolution of German public opinion and voting behaviour from the early 1950s to the late 1970s; this research has been updated in a comparative framework in Dalton (1988). Klingemann (1985) explores the various components of volatility in German voting behaviour. The German language literature on West German public opinion and voting behaviour is exceptionally rich and sophisticated. For an introduction to current research see Bürklin (1988) and the collection of edited volumes prepared by Kaase and Klingemann (1990) and Klingemann and Kaase (1986). Weidenfeld and Korte (1991) provides an excellent overview of public opinion in the two Germanies. Finally, Dalton *et al.* (1992) analyse party actions and voter responses in the 1990 Bundestag elections.

Chapter 4   The 'New' Party System

For the development of the parties and party system, see Padgett and Burkett (1986) and Smith (1986). On individual parties, refer to Padgett and Paterson (1991) for the SPD, Schmid (1990) and Chandler (1989) for the CDU, and Kirchner and Broughton (1988) for the FDP as well as Søe (1989). The theory of the *Volkspartei* is analysed in Smith (1982). For the Greens, good treatments are to be found in Kolinsky (1989) and Hülsberg (1988). Padgett (1989) examines the party system changes in the period prior to unification. Derbyshire (1991) provides an excellent, concise guide to party-related events in the recent past. Analyses of recent elections are made by: Fitzmaurice (1990) and Müller-Rommel (1991) both for East Germany; for the 1990 all-German election, refer to Irving and Paterson (1991), James (1991), and Kitschelt (1991), in particular, is recommended for a wide-ranging analysis.

Chapter 5   Government at the Centre

The stream of literature on the government of the new Germany has just begun to flow. A first general overview is provided by the standard textbooks of von Beyme (1991a) and Ellwein and Hesse (1992). More has been published on the process of bringing about unification (Rauschning, 1990; Schäuble, 1991). Schäuble gives an account of the negotiations on the unity treaty as an insider, as minister responsible. Guggenberger and Stein (1991) have collected the published opinions on the constitutional consequences of German unity. A more general picture of the problems and prospects of German unity is drawn by Lehmbruch (1990). Special attention to the problems of an all-German public administration is paid to by Derlien (1991) and König (1991).

Chapter 6 The Changing Territorial Balance

With German unification most of the older German literature on federalism has become obsolete. A fortieth-year appraisal of a wide range of policy fields in which German Federalism operates can be found in the *Publius* special issue: *Federalism and Intergovernmental Relations in West Germany* (1989). Some of the German standard texts have been updated (Laufer, 1991), and quite a number of new volumes have been edited often with the support of the Länder (Hanns-Seidel-Stiftung 1991; Hesse and Renzsch, 1991). They deal with the double challenge to the Länder's future: German and European integration (for these see also Sturm, 1991 and 1992). The volume by Jeffery and Savigear (1991) is the most recent effort in English to come to grips with federalism in its new clothes.

Chapter 7 Gulliver Unbound: The Changing Context of Foreign Policy

Helmut Kohl's speech 'Our Future in Europe' is the best short guide to German foreign policy priorities. Those who read German should consult the recently published book *329 Tage* by Horst Teltschik (1991), Kohl's former foreign policy adviser. Also useful is *Das Ende der Teilung Der Wandel in Deutschland und Osteurope* (1991). The 'dominance issue' is analysed at length by W. E. Paterson in his contribution to Jonathan Story's *The New Europe* (in press). Ronald Asmus is the author of a very perceptive study, *German Unification and its Ramifications* (1991).

Chapter 8 Uncertainties of Security Policy

A good source of articles on current developments in German security policy is the journal *Aussenpolitik*. For a recent English-language study of German security policy is Szabo (1990); for German-speakers, Fritsch-Bournazel (1990), Weidenfeld (1990) and Enders, Siebenmorgan and Weisser (1990) are highly recommended. Rotfeld and Stützler's edited volume (1991) contains a number of interesting papers on the security dimension of German unification, along with the key documents and speeches of the period from late 1989 to November 1990. Anglo–German defence cooperation is examined by Kaiser and Roper (1988), whilst Franco–German security relations by Kaiser and Lellouche (1986). The socio-economic problems arising from the stationing of US forces in Germany have been studied by Nelson (1987). A good introduction to the debate on the participation of Bundeswehr troops in UN peace-keeping operations is provided by Bardehle (1989). CDU approaches to security policy have been analysed by Clemens (1989), and SPD approaches by Schlauch (1990). For the broader European context of German security policy, see Hyde-Price (1991) and Buzan (1990).

Chapter 9 The EC: Seeds of Ambivalence

The early period of West German involvement in integration is covered in Willis (1965). The period 1969–86 is examined in Bulmer and Paterson (1987), with particular emphasis on the origins of the sectorised, and occasionally, contradictory, nature of European policy. The essays in Morgan and Bray (1986) examine both the Franco–German relationship and the Anglo–German one in the triangle of contacts between Bonn, Paris and London on European matters. Saeter (1980) explores the wider European context, including the Ostpolitik and defence. A review of West Germany and the EC, on the eve of the 1988 presidency of the Council of Ministers, is given in the conference papers edited by Wessels and Regelsberger (1988). Kirchner (1989) offers an interpretation of forty years of the Federal Republic and European integration. He also deals with the implications of German reunification on EC–German relations (forthcoming, 1992). The possibility of a reunified Germany becoming hegemonic is explored by Markovits and Reich (1991). The edited collection by Schweitzer and Karsten (1990) attempts a cost–benefit analysis of German membership of the EC. Of the German-language material, Hrbek and Wessels (1984) consider West German interests in most of the key areas of European cooperation and integration, while May (1985) attempts to evaluate the costs and benefits of German membership of the EC.

Chapter 10 The New German Economy

For an account of the political economy of the Federal Republic before unification, see Katzenstein (1987). The standard literature on the GDR economy tends to underestimate the extent of its weakness, but for readers of German, Merkel and Wahl (1991) give an account which draws on the insights opened up by unification. A satisfactory English language coverage of the new German economy has yet to emerge, but see Lipschitz and McDonald (1991) on the economic issues raised by unification. Singer (1992) gives an acocunt of the political debate accompanying currency union. Valuable German sources are the monthly reports of the Deutsche Bundesbank (1991), and the excellent series of *Unification Issues* produced by the Deutsche Bank, as well as the DIW weekly reports. The German economic press is also a useful source, especially *Wirtschaftswoche*.

Chapter 11 Social Policy: One State, Two-Tier Welfare

Literature on the impact of unification on social policy is only now consolidating and all of it is in German. A helpful collection of papers has been published by Humboldt University in Berlin: *Eine politische Heilslehre auf dem Prüfstand* (1991). Inter-Nationes press agency regularly publishes social report updates. These are normally available from German Embassies.

Three key papers well worth consulting are Bank and Kreikebohm (1991), Bäcker (1991) and von Maydell (1990).

Chapter 12   Rethinking Environmental Policy

There is as yet no satisfactory account of German environmental policy and politics after unification available in English. West German environmental politics before unification are analysed in Paterson (1989). Environmental politics in both German states immediately prior to and during the unification process are discussed in Hager (1992). The role of economic principles on environmental politics in West Germany is discussed in Miller and Miller (1988). The references given there even to date afford the reader much insight into conditions and trends that will dominate environmental policy and politics also in the united Germany. Even literature in German on post-unification environmental policy and politics is sparse and its content not always satisfactory. Those who read German could consult Naujoks (1991) and Wicke (1990) regarding the objectives, restraints and instruments of the ecological clean-up policy for East Germany as well as potential economic impacts on all Germany. The official policy is outlined in BMU (1990, 1991).

Chapter 13   German Migration Policies

Comparatively little work has so far been done on German migration policy and most works which have appeared are collections of articles. A useful introduction to the international aspects is provided by Loescher and Monahan (1990) and Collinson (1992). The most comprehensive introduction to the many aspects of Germany's problems can be found in Bade (1990), whereas Otto (1990) gives a good insight into the problems concerning ethnic Germans. Germany as a country which is still in search of its identity as either an '*Einwanderungsland*' or a German *Nationalstaat* is analysed in Hoffmann (1990). A short guide through the main manifestations of xenophobia (in the old Federal Republic) is provided by Gugel (1991).

Chapter 14   Women in the New Germany: The East–West Divide

The changing situation in post-war Germany has been explored for the West by Kolinsky (1989) and described by Edwards (1985) for the East. Helwig (1987) offers a readable East–West comparison, while Weidenfeld and Zimmermann (1989) discuss the situation of women in the broader context of parallel chapters on social change in East and West Germany. Voigt, Voss and Meck (1987) and Lemke (1991) draw on official and non-official sources on social structure and socialisation in the former GDR. Both conclude that women were less than equal, despite ideological assurances to the contrary.

Since unification, the Frauenreport (1990) has made extensive data available on the position of women in GDR society, including data on hidden inequalities, institutional and legislative provisions for women before unification. Harenberg (1991) reports survey results on the impact of unification on women's attitudes and expectations in the new and old parts of the FRG.

Chapter 15   Labour Market Problems and Policy

Details of labour market policy and data can be found in English in the *Monthly Report* of the Deutsche Bundesbank, and in the accompanying *Reports of Statistical Series*. The five economic research institutes publish regular studies of labour market evolution and policy; DIW – *Wochenbericht*; *Wirtschaftsdienst*; *Konjunkturbericht*; all contain valuable assessments. Official publications are the *Monatsbericht* of the Bundesanstalt für Arbeit, *Wirtschaft und Statistik* by the Statistisches Bundesamt, and the studies by the Institut für Arbeitsmarkt und Berufsforschung of the Bundesanstalt für Arbeit.

Chapter 16   Political Ideology

There are relatively few English-language books on this topic, though there are plenty that deal in passing with the ideological components of party programmes. These include Pridham (1977) and Miller and Potthoff (1986). The best introduction, despite its age, is still Dahrendorf (1968), first published in German in 1965. Useful information will also be gleaned from Baker, Dalton and Hildebrandt (1981) and the comparative data in Kaase and Barnes (1979). The most comprehensive coverage of alternative politics is in Burns and van der Will (1988) and Kolinsky (1989). Much the most important works in German are Greiffenhagen and Greiffenhagen (1974), Sontheimer (1982) and Bracher (1986). On the ideas of the East German revolution, consult Thaysen (1991).

Chapter 17   A New German Identity

There are few sources in English on the subject of a new identity, aside from Baker, Dalton and Hildebrandt (1980) and Conradt (1980). See also, Weilemann (1985) and the literature cited in this chapter as well as the references given in the earlier *Developments* (Merkl, 1989).

Bibliography

Adams, P. (1990) 'The unity of economic and social policy in the GDR', in Deason, B. and Szalai, J. (eds), *Social Policy in the new Eastern Europe*, Aldershot: Avebury Press.

Adomeit, H. (1991) 'Gorbachev and German Unification', *Problems of Communism*, 39 (4) (July–August) 1–23.

AGU (1990) *Arbeitsgemeinschaft für Umweltfragen, Umweltunion in Deutschland, Das Umweltgespräch*, Aktuell: Presseinformation '90, Bonn: Schriftenreihe der Arbeitsgemeinschaft für Umweltfragen.

Akerlof, G. A. *et al.* (1991) 'East Germany in from the cold. The economic aftermath of currency union', paper presented to the Conference of the Brookings Panel on Economic Activity, Washington, D.C. (4–5 April) 12.

Allemann, F. R. (1956) *Bonn ist nicht Weimar*, Cologne: Kiepenheuer & Witsch.

Almond, Gabriel A. and Verba, S. (1963) *The Civic Culture: Political Attitudes and Democracy in Five Nations*, Princeton, N.J.: Princeton University Press.

Almond, G. and Verba, S. (eds) (1980) *The Civic Culture Revisited*, Boston: Little, Brown.

Asmus, R. D. (1991) *German Unification and its Ramifications*, Santa Monica: Rand.

Atlantic Council (1990) 'The United States and United Germany: Task Force on German Unification', Policy Paper, Washington, D.C.: 31 October.

Bade, K. (1990) *Ausländer, Aussiedler, Asyl in der Bundesrepublik Deutschland*, Hanover: Landeszentrale für politische Bildung.

Bäcker, G. and Steffen, J. (1991) 'Reichtum im Westen – Armut im Osten?', *WSI-Mitteilungen*, 44 (5/1991) 292–307.

Bäcker, G. (1991) 'Sozialpolitik im vereinigten Deutschland', *Aus Politik und Zeitgeschichte*, 3–4, 3–15.

Baker, K. L., Dalton, R. J. and Hildebrandt, K. (1981) *Germany Transformed. Political Culture and the new Politics*, Cambridge, Mass.: Harvard University Press.

Bank, H.-P. and Kreikholm (1991) 'Einige Anmerkungen zu sozial-politischen Trends im vereinten Deutschland', *Zeitschrift für Sozialreform*, 37, 1–15.

Bardehle, Peter (1989) '"Blue Helmets" from Germany? Opportunities and Limits of UN Peacekeeping', *Aussenpolitik*, 40 (IV) 372–84.

Bauer, Joachim (1991) *Europa der Regionen. Aktuelle Dokumente zur Rolle der deutschen Länder im europäischen Integrationsprozess*, Berlin: Duncker & Humblot.

Beck, P. (1981) 'The Dealignment Era in America', in Dalton *et al.* (1984).

Belwe, K. (1989) 'Sozialstruktur und gesellschaftlicher Wandel in der DDR', in Weidenfeld, W. and Zimmerman, H., *Deutschland Handbuch. Eine doppelte Bilanz 1949–1989*, Munich: Hauser.

Belwe, K. (1991a) 'Noch fehlen wirtschaftspolitische Konzepte', in *Probleme und Perspektive der deutschen Einheit. Themenausgabe Das Parlament*, 41 (9) (22 February) 10.

Belwe, K. (1991b) 'Zur Beschäftigungssituation in den neuen Bundesländern', *Aus Politik und Zeitgeschichte* (29/1991) 27–39.

Berger, A. (1991) 'Würzelbehandlung – Überlegungen zu den Ursachen der Fremdenfeindlichkeit und den Ängsten vor dem Andersartigen', in *Asylbewerber als Sündenböcke, Dokumentation Evangelischer Pressedienst*, Frankfurt (10 June).

Berghahn, S. and Fritzsche, A. (1991) *Frauenrecht in Ost und Westdeutschland*, Berlin: Basisdruck.

Bergmann, U. et al., (1968) *Rebellion der Studenten oder die neue Opposition*, Reinbek, Rowohlt.

Bergsdorf, W. (1990) 'Wer will die deutsche Einheit?', *Die Politische Meinung*, 248 (January–February) 13–19.

Bergsdorf, W. (1991) 'German–American Relations in Public Opinion', *German Comments*, 22, 18–94.

Bericht der Kommission (1990) *Erhaltung und Fortentwicklung der bundesstaatlichen Ordnung innerhalb der Bundesrepublik Deutschland – auch in einem vereinten Europa*, Düsseldorf: Landtag North Rhine–Westphalia.

Bertram, B., Job, K. and Friedrich, W. (1988) *Adam und Eva heute*, Leipzig: Verlag für Frau.

Bertram, B. and others (1989) *Typisch weiblich – Typisch männlich*, Berlin: Dietz.

Bevölkerungspolitik und Tötungsvorwurf (1988) *Dokumente zweier Foren der Grünen Frauen im Bundestag. Series: Argumente*, Bonn: Die Grünen.

Beyme, K. von (1979) *Die grossen Regierungserklärungen der deutschen Kanzler von Adenauer bis Schmidt*, Munich and Vienna: Hanser.

Beyme, K. von (1991a) *Das politische System der Bundesrepublik Deutschland nach der Vereinigung*, München: Piper.

Beyme, K. von (1991b) *Hauptstadtsuche*, Frankfurt am Main: Suhrkamp.

Bundesanstalt für Arbeit (1991) Nürnberg: BfA Statistics.

Blackwill, R. D. (1991) *The Security Implications of a United Germany: Paper II, America's Role in a Changing World*, Adelphi Paper, 257, London: Brassey's for the IISS, 92–5.

BMU (1990) Bundesminister für Umwelt, *Naturschutz und Reaktorsicherheit, Eckwerte der ökologischen Sanierung und Entwicklung in den neuen Ländern* (November).

BMU (1991) Bundesminister für Umwelt, *Naturschutz und Reaktorsicherheit, Aktionsprogramm ökologischer Aufbau* (19 February).

Boldt, H. (1991) 'Wiedervereinigung und föderative Ordnung', in Wildenmann, Rudolf (ed.), *Nation und Demokratie Politisch-strukturelle Gestaltungsprobleme im neuen Deutschland*, Baden-Baden: Nomos, 35–50.

Bracher, K.-D. (1986) 'Politik und Zeitgeist. Tendenzen der siebziger Jahre', in Bracher, K.-D., Jäger, W. and Link, W., *Republik im Wandel 1969–1974. Die Ära Brandt, Geschichte der Bundesrepublik Deutschland*, vol. V/I.

Bradley Scharf, C. (1987) 'Social Policy and Social Conditions in the GDR', in Rueschemayer, M. and Lemke, C. (eds), *The Quality of Life in the German Democratic Republic*, Armonck, N.Y.: Sharpe.

Brandt, W. (1969) 'Die Alternative', *Die Neue Gesellschaft* (Sonderheft) May.

Brandt, W. (1991), in Lölhöffel, H., *Die Geplagten dieser Erde, Frankfurter Rundschau* (3 July).

Brinkmann, H. (1990) 'Zeigen Frauen ein besonderes Wahlverhalten? *Frauenforschung*, 3, 55–75.

Bürklin, W. (1988) *Wählerverhalten und Wertewandel*, Opladen: Leske & Budrich.

Bulmer, S. (1990) 'Efficiency, Democracy and West German Federalism: A Critical Analysis', *EPRU Working Paper*, University of Manchester.

Bulmer, S. (1989) *The Changing Agenda of West German Public Policy*, Aldershot: Dartmouth.

Bulmer, S. (1989) 'Territorial Government' in Smith, Paterson and Merkl (1989).

Bulmer, S. and Paterson, W. (1987) *The Federal Republic of Germany and the European Community*, London: Allen & Unwin.

Bundesministerium des Innern (1989) *Aufzeichnung zur Ausländerpolitik und zum Ausländerrecht der BRD* (July).

Bunzenthal, R. (1989) 'Ausländer in der BRD – Wichtige Stütze für die Wirtschaft', *Frankfurter Rundschau* (6 May) reprinted in Bade (1990), 165 *passim*.

Buzan, B., Kelstrup, M., Lemaitre, P., Tromer, E. and Waever, O. (1990) *The European Security Order Recast: Scenarios for the Post-Cold War Era*: London, Pinter.

Chandler, W. (1989) 'The Christian Democrats', in Merkl, P. H. (ed.) *The Federal Republic of Germany at Forty*, New York and London: New York University Press.

Christ, P. (1991) 'Zum Sündenbock gestempelt – Detlev Karsten Rohwedder und die Treuhand – eine Bilanz', *Die Zeit*, 15 (5 April) 17–18.

Clemens, C. (1989a), *Reluctant Realists: The CDU/CSU and the West German Ostpolitik*, Durham and London: Duke University Press.

Clemens, C. (1989b) 'Beyond INF: West Germany's Centre-Right Party and Arms Control', *International Affairs*, 65 (1) 55–74.

Collinson, S. (1992) *International Migration*, London: Chatham House Publishers.

Commission of the European Communities (1990) *The Community and German Unification*, COM (90) 400 Final, vol. 1.

Conradt, D. (1980) 'Changing German Political Culture', in Almond and Verba (1980).

Conradt, D. (1989) *The German Polity*, New York: Longman, 4th edn.

Converse, P. (1969) 'Of Time and Partisan Stability', *Comparative Political Studies*, 1, 139–71.

Dahrendorf, R. (1968) *Society and Democracy in Germany*, London: Weidenfeld and Nicolson.

Dahrendorf, R. (1983) *Die Chancen der Krise. Über die Zukunft des Liberalismus*, Stuttgart: Deutsche Verlags-Anstalt.

Dalton, R. (1984) 'Cognitive Mobilization and Partisan Dealignment in Advanced Industrial Democracies', *Journal of Politics*, 46, 264–84.

Dalton, R. (1988) *Citizen Politics in Western Democracies*, Chatham, N.J.: Chatham House Publishers.

Dalton, R. (1989) 'The German Voter', in Smith, G. *et al.*, *Developments in German Politics*, London: Macmillan.

Dalton, R. (1992) *Politics in Germany*, New York: Harper Collins.

Dalton, R. and Rohrschneider, R. (1990) 'Wählerwandel und die Abschwächung der Parteieigungen von 1972 bis 1987', in Kaase, Max and Klingemann, H.-D. (eds), *Wahlen und Wähler*, Opladen: Westdeutscher Verlag.

Dalton, R. *et al.* (1984) *Electoral Change in Advanced Industrial Democracies*, Princeton: Princeton University Press.

Dalton, R. *et al.* (1992) *Germany Votes 1990: Unification and the New German Party System*, Oxford: Berg Publishers.

Datenreport (1989)

Dennis, M. (1988) *The German Democratic Republic: Politics, Economics and Society*, London: Pinter.

Derbyshire, I. (1991) *Politics in Germany*, London: Chambers.

Derlien, H.-U. (1991) *Regimewechsel und Personalpolitik*, Hamburg: Verwaltungswissenschaftliche Beiträge.

Deutsche Bank (1991a) Economics Department, Unification Issue, 50 (18 June).

Deutsche Bank (1991b) Economics Department, Unification Issue, 51 (24 June).

Deutsche Bundesbank (1990) 'The monetary union with the GDR', *Monthly Report* (July) 13–27.

Deutsche Bundesbank (1991a) 'Promoting economic activity in the new Länder', *Monthly Report* (March) 15–26.

Deutsche Bundesbank (1991b) 'One year of German monetary, economic and social union', *Monthly Report* (July) 18–30.

Deutsche Bundesbank (1991c) 'The West German economy under the impact of unification', *Monthly Report* (October) 14–20.

Deutsche Bundesbank (1991d) 'Die Wirtschaftslage', *Monatsbericht* (November) 10–12.

DIW–Deutsches Institut für Wirtschaftsforschung (1991a) 'Gesamtwirtschaftliche Auswirkungen der deutschen Währungs-, Wirtschafts- und Sozialunion auf die BRD', *Wochenbericht* (20/1990) 269–77.

DIW–Deutsches Institut für Wirtschaftsforschung (1991b) 'Gesamtwirtschaftliche und unternehmerische Anpassungsprozesse in Ostdeutschland', *Wochenbericht* (12/1991) 123–42.

DIW–Deutsches Institut für Wirtschaftsforschung (1991c) 'Zu knappes Angebot an Ausbildungsplätze in den neuen Bundesländern und Berlin (Ost)', *Wochenbericht* (25/1991) 347–52.

DIW–Deutsches Institut für Wirtschaftsforschung (1991d) 'Einkommen und Verbrauch der privaten Haushalte in den neuen und alten Bundesländern', *Wochenbericht* (29/91).

DIW–Deutsches Institut für Wirtschaftsforschung (1991e) 'Der Arbeitsmarkt ein Jahr nach Beginn der Währungsunion', *Wochenbericht* (30/1991) 427–33.

DIW–Deutsches Institut für Wirtschaftsforschung (1991f) 'Frauenpolitische Aspekte der Arbeitsmarktentwicklung in Ost- und Westdeutschland', *Wochenbericht* (30/1991) 421–6.

Deutsches Jugendinstitut e.V. (DJI) (1990) 'Deutsche Schüler im Sommer 1990 – Skeptische Demokraten auf dem Weg in ein vereintes Deutschland', *Deutsch–deutsche Schülerbefragung 1990, DJI Arbeitspaper 3–019*, Forschungsgruppe Wahlen e.V., Politbarometer (monthly).

Deutsches Jugendinstitut e.V. (DJI) (1991) *Survey Jugend und Politik*, Munich (5 July).

Dohnanyi, K. von (1990) *Das deutsche Wagnis: Über die wirtschaftlichen und sozialen Folgen der Einheit*, Munich: Knaur Verlag.

Donges, J. B. (1991) 'Arbeitsmarkt und Lohnpolitik in Ostdeutschland', *Wirtschaftsdienst* (1991/VI) 283–91.

Dutschke, R. (1980) *Mein langer Marsch. Reden, Schriften und Tagebücher aus zwanzig Jahren*, Reinbek: Rowohlt.

ECRE (European Consultation on Refugees and Exiles) (1991) Participants' Meeting, Budapest (8–9 March).

Edwards, G. E. (1985) *GDR Society and Social Institutions*, London: Macmillan.

Einhorn, B. (1991) 'Emancipated Women or Hardworking Mums? Women in the former German Democratic Republic', in Corrin, C. (ed.), *Women's Changing Experience in the Soviet Union and Eastern Europe*, London: Pinter.

Ellwein, T. and Hesse, J. J. (1992) *Das Regierungssytem der Bundesrepublik Deutschland*, Opladen: Westdeutscher Verlag.

Enders, T., Siebenmorgan, P. and Weisser, U. (1990) *Schlüssel zum Frieden Sicherheitspolitik in einer neuen Zeit*, Bonn: Bouvier Verlag.

Enders, U. (1986) 'Kinder, Küche, Kombinat – Frauen in der DDR', *Aus Politik und Zeitgeschichte*, B 6–7.

Engelen-Kefer, U. (1991) 'Die Arbeitsbeschaffungsmassnahmen müssen ausgeweitet werden', *Wirtschaftsdienst* (1991/III) 114–17.

Engelen-Kefer, U., Beyer, M., Maintz, G. and Schmidt, R. (1990) *Frauenpolitische Forderungen für Gesamtdeutschland. Gesprächskreis Frauenpolitik*, Bonn: Friedrich Ebert Stiftung.

Engels, W. (1991) 'Offensiv vertreten. Subventioniert der Staat einen Teil der Löhne im Osten, spart er Geld und macht die Unternehmen wettbewerbsfähig', *Wirtschaftswoche* (26/1991) 109–14.

Eppler, E. (1979) *Ende oder Wende? Von der Machbarkeit des Möglichen*, Stuttgart: Kohlhammer.

Eppler, E. (1981) *Wege aus der Gefahr*, Reinbek: Rowohlt.

Ernst, W. (1991) 'Gedanken zur Neugliederung des Bundesgebietes', *Gegenwartskunde*, 40(1), 5–15.

Esser, J. (1986) 'State, Business and Trade Unions in West Germany after the Political *Wende*', *West European Politics*, 9(2) (April) 198–214.

(1989) 'Federalism and Intergovernmental Relations in West Germany: A Fortieth Year Appraisal', Special issue of *The Journal of Federalism*, 13(4).

Feist, U. and Kreiger, H. (1987) 'Alte und neue Scheidelinien des politischen Verhaltens', *Aus Politik und Zeitgeschichte* (21 March) 33–47.

Fenner, C. (1991) 'Das Ende des Provisoriums Bundesrepublik, oder: Reaktionen einer postnationalen Gesellschaft auf die Anmutung des Nationalen', in Süss, W. (ed.), *Die Bundesrepublik Deutschland in den 80er Jahren*, Opladen: Leske.

Fitzmaurice, J. (1990) 'Eastern Germany', *Electoral Studies* (special issue on Elections in Eastern Europe, vol. 9) (December) 327–36.

Flach, K. H., Maihofer, W. and Scheel, W. (1972) *Die Freiburger Thesen der Liberalen*, Reinbek: Rowohlt.

Flockton, C. (1992) 'The Failure of the East German Economy', in Kolinsky, E. (ed.), *Recasting Germany*, Oxford: Berg.

Forschungsgruppe Wahlen FGW. (1989) *Meinungen der Bürger der DDR*, Mannheim (December).

Franklin, M. *et al.* (1992) *Social Structure and Party Choice*, New York: Cambridge University Press.

Frauen in der DDR (1987) *Auf dem Weg zur Gleichberechtigung?* Bonn: Friedrich Ebert Stiftung.

Frauen in der DDR (1985) *Bilanz der Erfüllung*, Ministerrat der Deutschen Demokratischen Republik (ed.), Berlin: Zeit im Bild.

Frauenforschung 3/1987 (1987) 'Themenschwerpunkt Kommunale Gleichstellungsstellen', Institut Frau und Gesellschaft, Bielefeld: Kleine.

Frauenforschung 4/1990 (1990) 'Vereinigung der Ungleichheiten – die Frauenfrage im deutschen Einigungsprozeß', Institut Frau und Gesellschaft, Bielefeld: Kleine.

Frauenreport '90 (1990) 'Im Auftrag der Beauftragten des Ministerrates für Gleichstellung von Männern und Frauen', G. Winkler (ed.). Berlin: Die Wirtschaft.

Friederich, W. and Förster, P. (1991) 'Ostdeutsche Jugend 1990', *Deutschland Archiv*, 24 (4) (April) 349–60.

Fritsch-Bournazel, R. (1990) *Europa und die deutsche Einheit*, Bonn: Verlag Bonn Aktuell.

Frommel, M. (1990) 'Lebensschützer auf dem Rechtsweg', *Aus Politik und Zeitgeschichte*, B14.

Fulbrook, M. (1991) 'Wir sind ein Volk? Reflections on German Unification', *Parliamentary Affairs*, 44/3 (July) 389–404.

Funke, L. (1991) *Bericht der Beauftragten der Bundesregierung für die Integration der ausländischen Arbeitnehmer und ihrer Familienangehörigen*, Bonn.

Gehlen, A. (1974) *Sinn und Unsinn des Leistungsprinzips*, Munich: Deutscher Taschenbuch Verlag.

Gerhard, U. and Limbach, J. (1988) *Rechtsalltag von Frauen*, Frankfurt: Suhrkamp.

Gesetz über Finanzhilfen des Bundes gemäss Artikel 104a, Abs.4 GG für Investitionen zur vorläufigen Unterbringung von Aussiedlern und Übersiedlern (5/7 July).

Glotz, P. (1989) *Die deutsche Rechte: Eine Streitschrift*, Stuttgart: Deutsche Verlags-Anstalt.

Gluchowski, P. (1986) 'Wahlerfahrung und Parteiidentifikation', in H-D. Klingemann and M. Kaase (1986).

Gluchowski, P. (1987) 'Lebensstile und Wandel der Wählerschaft in der Bundesrepublik Deutschland', *Aus Politik und Zeitgeschichte* (21 March) 18–32.

Gotschlich, H. (1990) *Reifezeugnis für den Krieg. Abiturienten des Jahrgangs 1939 erinnern sich*, Berlin: Verlang der Nation.

Grass, G. (1982) *Die Zeit*, 3 December.

Grass, G. (1990) *Ein Schnäppchen namens DDR. Letzte Reden vorm Glockengeläut*, Frankfurt: Luchterhand.

Greiffenhagen, M. and Griffenhagen, S. (1974) *Ein schwieriges Vaterland*, Munich: List.

Gruhl, H. (1975) *Ein Planet wird geplündert*, Frankfurt: Fischer.

Grunenberg, N. (1990) 'Der richtige Riecher. Helmut Kohl, Kanzler der Einheit', *Die Zeit* 28 September 3.

Gugel, G. (1991) *Ausländer, Aussiedler, Übersiedler. Fremdenfeindlichkeit in der Bundesrepublik Deutschland*, Tübingen: Verein für Friedenspädagogik.

Guggenberger, B. and Stein, T. (eds) *Die Verfassungsdiskussion im Jahr der deutschen Einheit*, Munich and Vienna: Hanser.

Guggenberger, B., Preuss, U., Ulmann W. (eds) (1991), *Eine Verfassung für Deutschland. Manifest, Text, Plädoyers*, Munich and Vienna: Carl Hanser Verlag.

Habermas, J. (1969) *Protestbewegung und Hochschulreform*, Frankfurt: Suhrkamp.

Habermas, J. (1987) 'Eine Art Schadensabwicklung', *Die Zeit* (11 July 1986), reprinted in *Eine Art Schadensabwicklung*, Frankfurt: Suhrkamp.

Habermas, J. (ed.) (1979) *Stichworte zur geistigen Situation der Zeit*, 2 vols, Frankfurt: Suhrkamp.

Hager, C. (1992) Environmentalism and Democracy in the Two Germanies', *German Politics*, 1 (1), 96–118.

Hancock, M. D. (1989) *West Germany: the Politics of Democratic Corporatism*, Chatham, N.J.: Chatham House Publishers.

Hanns–Seidel–Stiftung (ed.) (1991) *Die Zukunft der kooperativen Föderalismus*, Munich: Seidel Stiftung.

Harenberg, W. (1991) 'Das Profil der Deutschen', *Spiegel Spezial*, Hamburg: Spiegel Verlag.

Härtel, H.-H. (1991) 'Lohnpolitik im vereinten Deutschland', *Wirtschaftsdienst* (1991/I) 7–10.

Havemann, R. (1970) *Fragen, Antworten, Fragen. Aus der Biographie eines deutschen Marxisten*, Munich: Piper.

Helwig, G. (1987) *Frau und Familie, Bundesrepublik Deutschland – DDR*, Cologne: Wissenschaft und Politik.

Hennis, W. (1970) *Demokratisierung. Zur Problematik eines Begriffs*, Opladen: Westdeutscher Verlag.

Hennis, W. (1973) *Die missverstandene Demokratie, Demokratie-Verfassung-Parlament. Studien zu deutschen Problemen*, Freiburg: Herder.

Hennis, W. (1990) 'Die Chance einer ganz anderen Republik. Zur Verfassung der zukünftigen Deutschland', *Frankfurter Allgemeine Zeitung* (10 March) Supplement.

Herz, W. (1991) 'Aus eins mach zwei. Alte und neue Bundesländer streiten um Milliarden Steuergelder', *Die Zeit*, 21, 17 May.

Hesse, J. J. and Renesch, W. (eds) (1991) *Föderalstaatliche Entwicklung in Europa*, Baden-Baden: Nomos.

Höhnen, W. (1991) 'Die Finanzierung der deutschen Einheit: eine Zwischenbilanz', *WSI Mitteilungen*, 5, 307–14.

Hoffmann, L. (1988) *Deutsche Interessen und die Ausländer. Die Pläne des Bundesministeriums für eine neue Ausländerpolitik und ein neues Ausländerrecht*, Brakel: Referate der Fachtagung der Friedrich Ebert Stiftung.

Hoffman, L. (1990) *Die unvollendete Republik. Zwischen Einwanderungsland und deutschem Nationalstaat*, Cologne: Papy Rossa.

Hoffman, L. (1991) 'Steps on the Road to Economic Salvation', *Financial Times* (25 February).

Hofmann-Göttig (1986) *Emanzipation mit dem Stimmzettel*, Bonn: Neue Gesellschaft.

Honolka, Harro (1987) *Schwarzrotgrün: Die Bundesrepublik auf der Suche nach ihrer Identität*, Munich: Beck, 1987.

Hrbek, R. and Wessels, W. (1984) *EG-Mitgliedschaft: ein vitales Interesse der Bundesrepublik Deutschland?*, Bonn: Europa Union Verlag.

Hubner, B. (1991) 'Work and the Unions', *German Politics and Society*, 23 (Summer).

Hübner, S. (1991) 'Women at the Turning Point: Socio-Economic situation and prospects of Women in the Former German Democratic Republic', *Politics and Society in Germany, Austria and Switzerland*, 3 (3).

Hübner-Funk, S. (1985) 'Nationale Identität', Deutsches Jugendinstitut (ed.) *Immer diese Jugend: Ein zeitgeschichtles Mosaik*, Munich: Kösel, 495–508.

Hübner-Funk, S. (1990) 'Die "Hitler-jugend Generation": umstrittenes Objekt and streitbares Subjekt der deutschen Zeitgeschichte', *Prokla*, 20 (3) 84–98.

Hülsberg, W. (1988) *The German Greens: A Social and Political Profile*, London: Verso.

Humboldt University (1991) 'Eine politische Heilslehre auf dem Prüfstand, *Geister- und Sozialwissenschaften*, 2, Berlin: Humboldt University.

Hyde-Price, A. (1991) *European Security Beyond the Cold War: Four Scenarios for the Year 2010*, London: Sage.

IAB (Institut für Arbeitsmarkt- und Berufsforschung der BAA) (1991) 'Noch starker Abbau in Treuhandunternehmen', *Kurzbericht* (11 July).

Info-Dienst (Deutsche Aussiedler) (1990), (1991) published by the federal government's Ombudsman for Foreigners.

Inglehart, R. (1984) 'The Changing Structure of Political Cleavages in Western Society', in Dalton *et al.* (1984).

Inglehart, R. (1990) *Culture Shift in Western Society* Princeton: Princeton University Press.

IdW (Institut der deutschen Wirtschaft) (1989) *Gutachten: Die Integration deutscher Aussiedler-Perspektiven für die BRD*.

IdW (Institut der deutschen Wirtschaft) (1991) *Informationdienst* (29 August).

Institut für praxisorientierte Sozialforschung (IPOS) (1990) *Einstellungen zur aktuellen Fragen der Innenpolitik in der BRD und in der DDR*, Mannheim.

Internationes Bonn (1991) *Sozial Report. Soziale Sicherheit im vereinten Deutschland*.

Irving, R. and Paterson, W. (1991) 'The German General Election', *Parliamentary Affairs*, 44 (July) 353–72.

Jänicke, M. (1990) 'Erfolgsbedingungen von Umweltpolitik im internationalen Vergleich', *Zeitschrift für Umweltpolitik*, 13, 213–32.

Jänicke, M. and Mönch, H. (1988) 'Ökologischer und wirtschaftlicher Wandel im Industrialändervergleich', in Schmidt, M. G. (ed.), *Staatstätigkeit. International und historisch vergleichende Analysen, Politische Vierteljahresschrift*, special issue, 389–405.

James, P. (1991) 'Germany United: The 1990 All-German Election', *West European Politics*, 14 (July) 215–20.

Jaspers, K. (1966) *Wohin treibt die Bundesrepublik? Tatsachen-Gefahren-Chancen*, Munich: Piper.

Jeffery, C. and Savigear, P. (eds) (1991) *German Federalism Today*, Leicester: Leicester University Press.

Joffe, J. (1991) *The Security Implications of a United Germany: Paper I, America's Role in a Changing World, Adelphi Paper*, 257, London: Brassey's for the IISS, 84–91.

Johnson, N. (1983) *State and Government in the Federal Republic of Germany* Oxford and New York: Pergamon.

Kaase, M. and Barnes, S. (eds) (1979) *Political Action and Mass Participation in Five Western Democracies*, Beverley Hills: Sage.

Kaase, M. and Klingemann, H.-D. (eds) (1990) *Wahlen und Wähler*, Opladen: Westdeutscher Verlag.

Kaase, M. and Schrott, P. (1991) 'Political Information in the 1990 German General Election', paper presented at the annual meeting of the American Political Science Association, Washington, D.C.

Kaiser, G. (1990) 'Was wissen wir über den Schwangerschaftsabbruch?', *Aus Politik und Zeitgeschichte*, B14.

Kaiser, K. (1991) 'Germany's Unification', *Foreign Affairs*, 70 (1), 179–205.

Kaiser, K. and Lellouche, P. (eds) (1986) *Deutsch–Französische Sicherheitspolitik*, Bonn: Europe Union Verlag.

Kaiser, K. and Roper, J. (eds) (1988) *British–German Defence Co-operation: Partners within the Alliance*, London: Jane's for the RIIA and DGAP.

Katzenstein, P. (1987) *Policy and Politics in West Germany: the Growth of a Semi-Sovereign State*, Philadelphia: Temple University Press.

Keillenmann, P. H. (ed.) (1985) *Aspects of the German Question*, St Augustin: Konrad Adenauer Stiftung.

Keller, Dietmar (ed.) (1991) *Nachdenken über Deutschland*, vol. 4, Berlin: Verlag der Nation.

Kennedy, E. (1991) *The Bundesbank: Germany's Central Bank in the International Monetary System*, London: Pinter.

Kerr, H. (1990) 'Social Class and Party Choice', in Saankiaho, Rist (ed.), *People and their Politics*, Helsinki: Finnish Political Science Association.

Kirchner, E. (1989) 'The Federal Republic of Germany in the European Community', in Merkl, P. (ed.), *The Federal Republic of Germany at Forty*, Cambridge: Cambridge University Press.

Kirchner, E. (1992) 'The Maturing of German–EC Relations', in Hodge, Carl C. and Nolan, Cathal J. (eds), *Shepherd of Democracy? America and the German Question*, Westport: Greenwood Publishing.

Kirchner, E. and Broughton, D. (1988) *'The FDP in the Federal Republic of Germany: The Requirements of Survival and Success'* in Kirchner, E. (ed.), *Liberal Parties in Western Europe*, Cambridge: Cambridge University Press.

Kitschelt, H. (1988) *The Logics of Party Formation*, Ithaca: Cornell University Press.

Kitschelt, H. (1991) 'The 1990 Federal Election and the National Unification', *West European Politics*, 14 (October) 121–48.

Klatt, H. (1986) 'Reform und Perspektion der Föderalismus in der Bundesrepublik Deutschland. Stärküng der Länder als Modernisiersungskonzept', *Aus Politik und Zeitgeschichte*, 28, 3–21.

Klatt, H. (1991) 'Deutsche Einheit und bundesstaatliche Ordnung. Das föderale System der Bundesrepublik Deutschland im Umbruch', *Verwaltungsarchiv*, 29 (3) 430–58.

Klauder, W. and Kühlewind, G. (1991) 'Arbeitsmarkttendenzen und Arbeitsmarktpolitik in den neunziger Jahren', *Aus Politik und Zeitgeschichte*, 34–35, 3–13.

Klopfer, M. and Reinert, S. (1990) 'Aspekte des Umweltschutzes in der DDR', *Zeitschrift für Umweltpolitik*, 13, 1–17.

Klingemann, H.-D. (1985) 'Germany', in Crewe, I. and Denver, D. (eds.), *Electoral Change in Western Democracies*, New York: St Martin's Press.

Klingemann, H.-D. and Kaase, M. (eds) (1986) *Wahlen und politischer Prozess*, Opladen: Westdeutscher Verlag.

Kohl, H. (1991) *Our Future in Europe*, Edinburgh and London: Europa Institute/Konrad Adenauer Stiftung.

Kolinsky, E. (1989) *Women in West Germany. Work, Life and Politics*, Oxford: Berg.

Kolinsky, E. (1991a) 'Women's Quotas in West Germany', *West European Politics*, 14 (1) (January).

Kolinsky, E. (1991b) 'Women in the New Germany', *Politics and Society in Germany, Austria and Switzerland*, 3, (3).

Kolinsky, E. (ed.) (1989) *The Greens in West Germany: Organisation and Policy Making*, Oxford and New York: Berg.

Kommers (1989) 'The Basic Law of the Federal Republic of Germany', in P. Merkl (ed.) (1989).

König, K. (1991) *Die Transformation einer real-sozialistischen Verwaltung in eine klassisch-europäische Verwaltung*, Speyer: Forschungsinstitut für öffentliche Verwaltung.

König, K. (ed.) (1991) *Verwaltungstrukturen der DDR*, Baden-Baden: Nomos.

Kraushaar, D. (1990) 'Politik, Wohnungssituation und Arbeitsmarkt. Veränderte Rahmenbedingungen für die soziale Arbeit mit Aussiedlern', *IZA* (2/90).

Krautkrämer-Wagner, U. (1989) *Die Verstaatlichung der Frauenfrage, Gleichstellungsinstitutionen der Bundesländer*, Bielefeld: Kleine.

Krell, G. (ed.) (1991) *Searching for Peace after the Cold War. Conceptual and Practical Problems for a New European Peace Order*, Frankfurt (PRIF Report 19/20) (May).

Kuechler, M. (forthcoming 1992) 'Ossies and Wessies: Truly United?' *Public Opinion Quarterly*.

Lampert, H. (1990) 'Die soziale Komponente im vereinten Deutschland', *Zeitschrift für Bevölkerungswissenschaft*, 16, 397–405.

Laqueur, W. (1962) *Young Germany. A History of the German Youth Movement*, London: Routledge & Kegan Paul.

Laufer, H. (1991) 'Der föderative system der Bundesrepublik Deutschland', Munich: Bayerische Landeszentrale für politische Bildung, 6th edn.

Leciejewski, K. (1990) 'Zur wirtschaftlichen Eingliederung der Aussiedler', *Aus Politik und Zeitgeschechte* (3/1990).

Lehmbruch, G. (1990) 'Die improvisierte Vereinigung: Die dritte deutsche Republik', *Leviathan*, 18, 462–86.

Lemke, C. (1991) *Die Ursachen des Umbruchs. Politische Sozialisation in der ehemaligen DDR*, Opladen: Westdeutscher Verlag.

Leyendecker, L. (1990) 'Constitutional and Legal Costs and Benefits', in Schweitzer, C. and Karsten, D. (eds) *The Federal Republic of Germany and EC Membership Evaluated*, London: Pinter, 148.

Lhotta, R. (1991) 'Verfassung, Bundesstaatsreform und Stärkung der Landesparlamente im zeichen der deutschen Einheit und der europäischen Integration', *Zeitschrift für Parlamentsfragen*, 22(2), 253–88.

Lijphart, A. (1984) *Democracies*, New Haven: Yale University Press.

Lipschitz, L. and McDonald, D. (eds) (1991) *German Unification: Economic Issues*, Washington, D.C.: International Monetary Fund.

Löbler, F. (1991) 'Friktionen im Bundesstaat als Folge der Vereinigung', in Löbler, F., Schmid, J. and Tiemann, H. (eds), *Wiedervereinigung als*

Organisationsproblem. Gesamtdeutsche Zusammenschlüsse von Parteien und Verbänden, Bochum: Brockmeyer, 186–201.

Loescher, G. and Monahan, L. (eds) (1990) *Refugees and International Relations*, Oxford: Clarendon Press.

Loewenberg, G. (1979) 'The Remaking of the German Party System', in Cerny, Karl (ed.), *Germany at the Polls*, Washington, D.C.: American Enterprise Institute.

Löwenthal, R. (1982) in *Das Parlament*, 32/33.

Löwenthal, R. (1970) *Der romantische Rückfall*, Stuttgart: Kohlhammer.

Lübkemeier, E. (1991) 'The Political Upheaval in Europe and the Reform of NATO Strategy', *NATO Review*, 39 (3) 16–21.

Maier, C. S. (1988) *The Unmasterable Past. History, Holocaust and German National Identity*, Cambridge, Mass.: Harvard University Press.

Mangen, S. (1989) 'The Politics of Welfare,' in Smith, Paterson and Merkl (1989).

Mangen, S. (1991) 'Social Policy, the Radical Right and the German Welfare State', in Glennerster, H. and Midgley, J. (eds), *The Radical Right and the Welfare State: An International Assessment*, Hemel Hempstead: Harvester Wheatsheaf.

Marcuse, H. (1969) *An Essay on Liberation*, Boston: Beacon Press.

Markovits, A. (1986) *The Politics of West German Trade Unions. Strategies of Class and Interest Representation in Growth and Crisis*, Cambridge: Cambridge University Press.

Markovits, A. (1992) 'The West German 68-ers Encounter the Events of 1989', *German Politics* I (1). 13–30.

Markovits, A. S. and Reich, S. (1991) 'Should Europe Fear the Germans?', *German Politics and Society*, 23 (Summer).

Marx, R. (1990) 'Die Neuregelungen zum Asylrecht aufgrund des "Gesetzes zur Neuregelung des Ausländerrechts",' unpublished manuscript (25 May).

May, B. (1985) *Kosten und Nutzen der deutschen EG-Mitgliedschaft*, Bonn: Europa Union Verlag, 2nd edn.

May, H. and Rühle, M. (1991) 'German Security Interest and NATO's Nuclear Strategy', *Aussenpolitik*, 42 (1) 20–30.

Maydell, B. von (1990) 'Auf dem Wege zu einer einheitlichen deutschen Sozialordnung', *Zeitschrift für Sozialreform*, 8, 515–28.

Meier, M. and Walzik, E. (1991) 'Das Gesundheitswesen im Vereinten Deutschland', *Soziale Fortschritt*, 3, 57–62.

Merkl, P. H. (1963) *The Origins of the West German Republic*, New York: Oxford University Press.

Merkl, P. H. (1971) 'Politico–cultural Restraints on West German Foreign Policy: Sense of Trust, Identity and Agency', *Comparative Political Studies*, 3 (4) (January) 443–67.

Merkl, P. H. (1974) *German Foreign Policies, West and East*, Santa Barbara: Clio Press.

Merkl, P. H. (1989) 'The German Search for Identity', in Smith, Paterson and Merkl (1989) 6–21.

Merkl, P. H. (1992) *German Unification in the European Context*, Boulder, Col.: Westview.

Merkl, P. H. (ed) (1989) *The Federal Republic at Forty*, Cambridge: Cambridge University Press.

Merkel, W. and Wahl, A. (1991) *Das geplünderte Deutschland. Die wirtschaftliche Entwicklung im östlichen Teil Deutschlands*, Bonn: Institut für Wirtschaft und Gesellschaft.

Merritt, A. J. and Merritt R. (1970) *Public Opinion in Occupied Germany*, Urbana, Ill.: University of Illinois Press.

Meyer, W. (1991) 'Welchen Beitrag können Beschäftigungsgesellschaften leisten? Anforderungen aus gewerkschaftlicher Sicht', *Wirtschaftsdienst* (1991/VIII) 385–8.

Miller, J. R. and Miller, L. (1988) 'Principles of environmental conomics and the political economy of West German environmental policy', *Governance and Policy*, 6, 457–74.

Miller, S. and Potthoff, H. (1986) *History of the German Social Democratic Party from 1848 to the Present*, Leamington: Berg.

Mittler, A. and Wolle, S. (1990) *Ich liebe euch doch alle! Befehle und Lageberichte des MfS, January–November 1989*, Berlin: Basis Druck.

Möller, J. M. (1991) 'Attitudes and Temperaments: How Eastern Germans are Reacting to the Gulf War', *German Comments*, 22, 36–8.

Mommsen, M. (1986) 'Die Politische Rolle der Frau in Ost und West', *Aus Politik und Zeitgeschichte*, B6–7.

Morgan, R. and Bray, C. (1986) (eds) *Partners and Rivals in Western Europe: Britain, France and Germany*, Aldershot: Gower.

Müller-Rommel, F. (1991) 'The Beginning of a New Germany? The GDR Elections of 18 March 1990', *West European Politics*, 14 (January), 139–47.

Naujoks, F. (1991) *Ökologische Erneuerung der ehemaligen DDR*, Bonn: Dietz.

Niethammer, L. (1972) 'Traditionen und Perspektiven der Nationalstaatlichkeit für die BRD', *Aussenpolitische Perspektiven des westdeutschen Staates*, 2: Das Vordringen neuer Kräfte', Forschungsinstitut der Deutschen Gesellschaft für Auswärtige Politik, Munich: Oldenbourg, 72.

Noelle-Neumann, E. (ed.) (1980) *Institut für Demoskopie, The Germans 1967–1980*, Westport, Conn.: Greenwood Press.

Noelle-Neumann, E. 'The German Revolution', *International Journal of Public Opinion Research*, 3/3, 237–259.

Nötzold, J. and Rummel, R. (1990) 'On the Way to a New European Order', *Aussenpolitik*, 41 (3), 212–24.

Norpoth, H. (1983) 'The Making of a More Partisan Electorate', *British Journal of Political Science*, 14, 53–71.

OECD (1991) *Economic Outlook*, 49 (July).

Oehler, E. (1990) 'Umweltschutz und Umweltrecht in der DDR', *Deutsches Verwaltungsblatt*, 105, 1322–33.

Offe, C. 'German Reunification as a "Natural Experiment" ', *German Politics* 1/1, 1–12.

Ölmez, M. A. (1988) 'Wehret den Anfängen. Wende in der Innen- und Rechtspolitik der neuen Ausländerpolitik', in Hoffman (1988).

Otto, K. A. (1990) (ed.) *Westwärts – Heimwärts? Aussiedlerpolitik zwischen Deutschtümelei und Verfassungsauftrag*, Bielefeld: AJZ Verlag, 1990.

Padgett, S. (1989) 'The Party System', in Smith, Paterson and Merkl (1989).

Padgett, S. (1990) 'British Perspectives on the German Question, *Politics and Society in Germany, Austria, Switzerland*, 3, 22–37.

Padgett, S. and Burkett, T. (1986) *Political Parties and Elections in West Germany*, London: Hurst.

Padgett, S. and Paterson, W. (1991) *A History of Social Democracy in Post-War Europe*, London and New York: Longman.

Padgett, S. (ed.) (1993, forthcoming) *Adenauer to Kohl: the Development of the German Chancellorship*, London: C. Hurst.

Pappi, F.-U. (1984) 'The West German Party System', *West European Politics*, 7 (October) 7–26.

Pappi, F.-U. (1986) 'Das Wahlverhalten sozialer Gruppen bei der Bundestagswahl im Zeitvergleich', in Klingemann and Kasse (1986).

Pappi, F.-U. and Terwey, M. (1982) 'The German Electorate', in Döring, H. and Smith, G. (eds), *Party Government and Political Culture in Western Germany*, New York: St Martin's Press and London: Macmillan.

Paterson, W. (1989) 'Environmental Politics', in Smith, Paterson and Merkl (1989) 267–88.

Paterson, W. (1989) *Foreign and Security Policy Developments I*, 192–210.

Paterson, W. and Southern, D. (1991) *Governing Germany*, Oxford: Basil Blackwell.

Payne, K. B. and Rühle, M. (1991) 'The Future of the Alliance: Emerging German Views', *Strategic Review* (Winter) 37–45.

Pehle, H. (1988) 'Das Schwedische Modell. Erfahrungen mit dem Kommunalen Wahlrecht für Ausländer', *Aus Politik und Zeitgeschichte* 24 (10 June).

Perger, W. A. (1991) 'Bühne frei für den grossen Konsens', *Die Zeit* (12 April) 3.

Piper, E. R. (ed.) (1987) *Historikerstreit. Die Dokumentation der Kontroverse um die Einzigartigkeit der nationalsozialistischen Judenvernichtung*, Munich: Piper.

Poettering, H.-G. (1991) 'The EC on the Way Towards a Common Security Policy', *Aussenpolitik*, 42 (2) 147–51.

Pridham, G. (1977) *Christian Democracy in Western Germany. The CDU/CSU in Government and Opposition*, London: Croom Helm.

Priewe, J. (1991) 'Logik des Kahlschlags. Die Aufgaben der Treuhand sind unlösbar', *Blätter für deutsche und internationale Politik*, 36, 208–315.

Priewe, J. and Hickel, R. (1991) *Der Preis der Einheit: Bilanz und Perspektiven der deutschen Vereinigung*, Frankfurt/Main: Fischer.

Probleme und Perspektiven (der deutschen Einheit), Themenausgabe, Das Parlament, 41 (9) (22 February).

Pulzer, P. (1989) 'Political Ideology', in Smith, Paterson and Merkl (1989).

Ragnitz, J. (1991) 'Regionalpolitische Aufgaben in den neuen Bundesländern', *Wirtschaftsdienst* (1991/VIII) 411–15.

Raschke, J. (ed.) (1982) *Bürger und Parteien*, Opladen: Westdeutscher Verlag.

Rauschning, D. (1990) 'Der deutsch–deutsche Staatsvertrag als Schnitt zur Einheit Deutschlands', *Aus Politik und Zeitgeschichte*, 33, 3–16.

Reese, H. and Weyrather, I. (1990) 'Die Spitzenverbände der deutschen Wirtschaft begrüssen vorbehaltslos den Aussiedlerzustrom. Anmerkungen zur Haltung der deutschen Wirtschaft zur Aussiedlerfrage', in Otto (1990).

Rehbinder, E. (1991) 'Die Freistellung von Anlagenerwerbern von der Verantwortlichkeit für die Sanierung von Altlasten in den neuen Bundesländern', *Deutsches Verwaltungsblatt*, 106, 421–7.

Reich, J. (1991) *Rückkehr nach Europa. Zur neuen Lage der Nation*, Munich and Vienna: Carl Hanser Verlag.

Renzsch, W. (1991) *Finanzverfassung und Finanzausgleich. Die Auseinandersetzungen um ihre politische Gestaltung in der Bundesrepublik Deutschland zwischen Währungsreform und Deutscher Vereinigung (1948 bis 1990)*, Bonn: Dietz.

Risse, H. (1990) 'Germany's Federal State Organisations' in Schweitzer, C. and Karsten, D. (eds) *The Federal Republic of Germany and EC Membership Evaluated*, London: Pinter.

Roberts, G. (1991) 'Emigrants in their own Country', *Parliamentary Affairs* 21/3, 353–72.

Roose, A. (1989) *Die bundesrepublikanische Asylpolitik in den 80er Jahren*, unpublished dissertation, University of Marburg: 1989.

Rose, R. and McAllister, I. (1986) *Voters Begin to Choose*, Beverley Hills: Sage.

Rotfeld, A. D. and Stützle, W. (eds) (1991) *Germany and Europe in Transition*, Oxford: Oxford University Press for SIPRI.

Roth, D. (1990) 'Public Opinion Before the First Federal Election in Unified Germany', Paper presented at The American Institute for Contemporary German Studies, 9 November.

Rublack, S. (1991) 'Environmental Law for the New German States', *Environmental Policy and Law*, 21, 23–5.

Runge, I. (1990) *Ausländerfeindlichkeit in der ehemaligen DDR*, Cologne: ISG – Sozialforschung und Gesellschaftspolitik.

Sarlvik, B. and Crewe, I. (1983) *Decade of Dealignment*, Cambridge: Cambridge University Press.

Saeter, M. (1980) *The Federal Republic, Europe and the World*, Oslo: Universtetsforlaget.

Schäuble, W. (1991) *Der Vertrag*, Stuttgart: Deutsche Verlags-Anstalt.

Scharpf, F. W. (1990) 'Zwischen Baum und Borke. Deutsche Einheit und europäische Einigung bedrohen den Föderalismus', *Die Zeit* (14 September) 14.

Scharrer, H-E. (1990) 'The Internal Market' in Schweitzer, C. and Karsten, D. (eds) *The Federal Republic of Germany and EC Membership Evaluated*, London: Pinter, 148.

Schelsky, H. (1975) *Die Arbeit tun die anderen. Klassenkampf und Priesterherrschaft der Intellektuellen*, Opladen: Westdeutscher Verlag, 2nd edn.

Schelsky, H. (1961) *Der Mensch in der wissenschaftlichen Zivilisation*, Cologne and Opladen: Westdeutscher Verlag.

Scheuch, E. (1991) *Wie deutsch sind die Deutschen? Eine Nation wandelt ihr Gesicht*, Bergisch Gladbach: Gustav Lubbe Verlag.

Schlauch, W. (1990) 'Defence and Security: The SPD and West–West Relations in the 1980's', *Politics and Society in Germany, Austria and Switzerland*, 3 (1), 1–21.

Schlink, B. (1991) 'Deutsche–deutsche Verfassungsentwicklungen in Jahre 1990', *Der Staat*, 30(2), 163–80.

Schmähl, W. (1990) 'Alterssicherung in der DDR und ihre Umgestaltung in Zuge des deutschen Einigungsprozesses', Bremen: *Universität Bremen Arbeitspaper*, 10.

Schmid, J. (1990) *Die CDU: Organisationsstrukturen, Politiken und Funktionsweisen einer Partei im Föderalismus*, Opladen: Leske und Budrich.

Schmidt, U. (1987) *Zentrum oder CDU. Politischer Katholizismus zwischen Tradition und Anpassung*, Opladen: Westdeutscher Verlag.

Schüddekopf, C. (ed.) (1990) *Wir sind das Volk. Flugschriften, Aufrufe und Texte einer deutschen Revolution*, Reinbek: Rowohlt.

Schultz, R. (1987) 'Die Bundestagswahl 1987 – eine Bestätigung des Wandels', *Aus Politik und Zeitgeschichte* (21 March) 3–17.

Schweigler, G. (1973) *Nationalbewusstsein in der BRD und der DDR*, Düsseldorf: Bertelsmann.

Schweitzer, C. C. and Karsten, D. (1990) *Federal Republic of Germany and EC Membership Evaluated*, London: Pinter.

Shively, W. P. (1979) 'The Development of Party Identification among Adults', *American Political Science Review*, 73, 1039–54.

Singer, O. (1992) 'The Politics and Economics of German Unification: from Currency Union to Economic Dichotomy', *German Politics*, 1(1) (April). 78–94.

Smith, G. (1982) 'The German Volkspartei and the Career of the Catch-All Concept', in Döring, H. and Smith, G. (eds), *Party Government and Political Culture in Western Germany*, New York: St Martin's Press and London: Macmillan.

Smith, G. (1986) *Democracy in Western Germany; Parties and Politics in the Federal Republic*, Aldershot: Gower.

Smith, G. (1989) 'The Ambivalence of European Liberalism', in Kirchner, E. (ed.), *Liberal Parties in Western Europe*, Cambridge: Cambridge University Press.

Smith, G. (1991) 'The Resources of a West German Chancellor', *West European Politics*, 14/2, 48–61.

Smith, G., Paterson, W. E. and Merkl, P. (1989) *Developments in West German Politics*, London: Macmillan.

Sodaro, M. J. (1990) *Moscow, Germany and the West from Khrushchev to Gorbachev*, London: Cornell University Press.

Søe, C. (1989) '"Not Without Us!" The FDP's Survival, Position and Influence', in Merkl, P. H. (ed.), *The Federal Republic of Germany at Forty*, Cambridge: Cambridge University Press.

Sontheimer, K. (1983) *Zeitenwende? Die Bundesrepublik Deutschland zwischen alter und alternativer Politik*, Hamburg: Hoffmann und Campe.

Spence, D. (1991) *Enlargement without Accession*, London: Chatham House Publishers.

Sperling, J. (1991) 'A Single European Space and the Prospects for the Atlantic Economy', unpublished paper, March.

Der Spiegel (1990) *Das Profil der Deutschen*, Hamburg: *Spiegel Spezial*.

SRU (1988) *Der Rat von Sachverständigen für Umweltfragen*.

Statistisches Bundesamt (ed.) (1989) *Datenreport. Zahlen und über die Bundesrepublik Deutschland*, Bonn: Bundeszentrale für politische Bildung.

Stoltenberg, G. (1990) 'Managing Change: Challenges and Tasks for the Eurogroup in a Changing Political Environment', *NATO Review*, 38 (4) 15–18.

Sturm, R. (1991) 'Die Zukunft des deutschen Föderalismus', in Leibert, Ulrike and Merkel, Wolfgang (eds), *Die Politik zur deutschen Einheit*, Opladen: Leske, 161–82.

Sturm, R. (1992) 'The Industrial Policies of the German Länder and European Integration', *German Politics*, 1 (3).

Stürmer, M. (1986) 'Die Suche nach der verlorenen Erinnerung', *Das Parlament*, 36.

Szabo, S. (1990) *The Changing Politics of German Security*, London: Pinter.

Teltschik, H. (1991a) 'Neither "Political Dwarf" nor "Superpower": Reflections on Germany's New Role in Europe', *German Comments*, 21, 17–25.

Teltschik, H. (1991b) *329 Tage*, Bonn: Bertelsmann.

Thaysen, U. (1990) *Der Runde Tisch. Oder: Wo blieb das Volk? Der Weg der DDR in die Demokratie*, Opladen: Westdeutscher Verlag.

Thies, J. (1991) 'Germany: Tests of Credibility', *The World Today*, 47 (6) 89–90.

Thies, J. and Wagner, W. (1991) *Das Ende der Teilung*, Bonn: Verlag für Internationale Politik.

Ullmer, R. (1991) 'Beschäftigungsgesellschaften', *Express* (4/1991) 4.

Umweltgutachten (1987) (December 1987), Stuttgart and Mainz: Kohlhammer.

US Information Agency (USA) (1984) *The West German Successor Generation: Their Social and Political Values*, Washington, D.C.: US Information Agency.

Veen, H.-J. (1991) 'Die Westbindung der Deutschen in einer Phase der Neuorientierung', *Europa Archiv*, 46 (2) 31–40.

Vogel, B. (ed.) (1991) *Das Phänomen: Helmut Kohl im Urteil der Presse*, Stuttgart: Deutsche Verlags-Anstalt.

Voigt, D., Voss, W. and Meck, S. (1987) *Sozialstruktur der DDR*, Darmstadt: Wissenschaftliche Buchgesellschaft.

Walter, N. (1989) 'Aussiedler sind keine Kostgänger', *Frankfurter Allgemeine Zeitung* (5 August).

Wattenberg, M. (1990) *The Rise of Candidate-Centred Politics*, Cambridge, Mass.: Harvard University Press.

Weber, H. (1985) *Geschichte der DDR*, Munich: Deutscher Taschenbuch Verlag.

Weber, H. (1986) *DDR. Dokumente zur Geschichte der Deutschen Demokratischen Republik, 1945–1985*, Munich: Deutscher Taschenbuch Verlag.

Wegener, H. (1990) 'The Transformed Alliance', *NATO Review*, 38 (4) 1–8.

Weidenfeld, W. and Krote, K. (1991) *Die Deutschen: Profil einer Nation*, : Klett-Cotta.

Weidenfeld, W. and Zimmermann, H. (eds) (1989) *Deutschland Handbuch – Eine doppelte Bilanz, 1949–1989*, Munich: Hanser.

Weidenfeld, W. (ed.) (1990) *Die Deutschen und die Architektur des Europäischen Hauses*, Cologne: Verlag Wissenschaft und Politik.

Weidner, H. (1989) 'Die Umweltpolitik der konservativ–liberalen Regierung', *Aus Politik und Zeitgeschichte*, B47–48/89 (17 November) 16–28.

Weidner, H. (1989/1990) 'Die Umweltpolitik der konservativ–liberalen Regierung, Scheidewege', *Jahresschrift für skeptisches Denken*, 19, 129–56.

Weisser, U. (1991) 'European Security at Issue: Baltic and Gulf Developments Pose New Challenges', *German Comments*, 22, 39–45.

Weizsäcker, R. von (1991) 'Gulf War Not a Sign of Things to Come: An Interview with President Richard von Weizsäcker', *German Comments*, 22, 6–14.

Wessels, W. and Regelsberger, E. (1988) *The Federal Republic of Germany and the European Community: The Presidency and Beyond*, Bonn: Europa Union Verlag.

Wettig, G. (1991) 'German Unification and European Security', *Aussenpolitik*, 42 (1) 13–19.

Wicke, L. (1990) 'Bausteine einer Umweltsanierungsstrategie für die DDR', *Zeitschrift für angewandte Unweltforschung*, 3, 125–33.

Willis, F. R. (1965) *France, Germany and the New Europe 1945–63*, Oxford: Oxford University Press.

Wilms, G. (1991) 'The Legal Statute of Berlin after the Fall of the Wall and German Reunification', *Zeitschrift für Ausländisches Öffentliches Recht und Völkerrecht*, 51 (2), 470–93.

Winkler, G. (1990) 'Sozialpolitik in der DDR', *Soziale Arbeit*, 3, 99–101.

WSI Mitteilungen, 5 (1991).

ZDWF (Zentrale Dokumentationsstelle der freien Wohlfahrtspflege für Flüchtlinge e.V., Bonn) (1991) *Fluchtursachen bekämpfen – Flüchtlinge schützen, Argument zur gegenwärtigen Asyldiskussion*.

Zelle, C. (1990) *Sozialer Wandel, flexibles Parteiensystem und flexible Wähler*, St Augustin: Konrad Adenauer Stiftung.

Index